AF531794

HISTORY OF MODERN INDIA

(1885 A.D.—1947 A.D.)

[For B.A./M.A., and other Examinations]

By
Hukam Chand

ANMOL PUBLICATIONS PVT. LTD.
NEW DELHI - 110 002 (INDIA)

ANMOL PUBLICATIONS PVT. LTD.

4374/4B, Ansari Road, Daryaganj
New Delhi - 110 002
Ph.: 23261597, 23278000
Visit us at: www.anmolpublications.com

History of Modern India (1885 A.D.—1947 A.D.)

First Published, 2005

PRINTED IN INDIA

Published by J.L. Kumar for Anmol Publications Pvt. Ltd., New Delhi - 110 002 and Printed at Mehra Offset Press, Delhi.

Contents

Preface

History of Modern India (1885 A.D. 1947 A.D.) as a paper is being taught at the graduate and post graduate level in B.A., M.A., Competitive Examinations and other History courses syllabus in almost all the Indian Universities and Institutions. The various courses conducted by institutions at the Central and State level too have been considered in respect of their syllabus, course contents and requirements. Thus the material presented here would be of interest as well as great use to the students of B.A., M.A. and other Competitive Examination's. This book will provide complete knowledge of the aspects of education policy of british and impact on economy, national movement struggle, rise of left parties, Wavell Plan, Mountbatten Plan, Nehru Report, Leaders of Gandhi Era & Indian Acts, Growth of Muslims Separatism and Constitution of Indian Republic etc. have been discussed briefly here.

The major topics dealt in this book are—Education Policy of British and Impact on Economy; National Movement Struggle; Swarajya Party; Rise of Left Parties; Civil Disobedience Movement; Extremist Movement; The Montangue Chemsford Reform; Wavell Plan; Mountbatten Plan; Nehru Report; Leaders of Gandhi Era & Indian Acts; Farmer Movement; Growth of Muslims Separatism; Constitution of Indian Republic.

Hukam Chand

1

Education Policy of British and Impact on Economy

Education is a derivative of the word educatum which means to 'draw out' that which is latent in the child. True education makes us fit to play our part efficiently as enlightned members of the community in all the spheres of life—religious, moral, social, economic, political, national and international. Five periods of the development of education in India.

First Period (1765-1813)

1. It should be noted here that education before the commencement of British rule in India was not considered as the responsibility of the state because during this period the state never considered itself to be a welfare state. The education during this period was purely the concern of the native priestly class. Pathshalas were attached to the temples where the Pandits used to impart education to a fraction of people. Similarly, there were Maktabs attacked to the Mosques where the Maulvis imparted education to the Muslims. Instruction on a mass scale, as we have now, was totally absent in this period and the Western education had not yet been introduced in the country the period under review. There was a complete shortage of the printed books for use in the temples and the mosques. Female education on any Government scheme was not at all known and this fact was clearly pointed out by the Simon Commission Report.

2. When the East India Company acquired territories in various parts of India, it found that both the Hindus and the Muslims were

running their educational institutions linked with their religion. As already pointed out above, they found that the Pandits taught Sanskrit to the Hindus in their Pathshalas and the Maulvis taught to the Muslims in the mosques. Therefore, to begin with, the Company left the Indian system undisturbed and respected the endowments made by the Indian rulers to the cause of education. Hence, the East India Company did not take much interest in the education of their Indian subjects. Partly because of its own difficulties and partly because of its exclusive interest in trade, the Company remained indifferent towards the educational problem. Some irregular and abortive efforts towards their education were, of course, made by Warren Hastings and the Christian Missionaries during this period. Warren Hastings established the Calcutta Madrasa in 1781 and another was started at Benares in 1792. The Calcutta Madras was set up "to qualify the sons of Mohammedan Gentlemen for responsible and lucrative offices in the State." The subjects taught in this Madrasa were Theology, Logic Rhetoric, Grammar, Law, Natural Philosophy, Astronomy, Geometry and Arithmetic. A few years later, as already pointed out above, another educational institution was set up at Benares "for the preservation and cultivation of the Laws, Literature and the religion of the nation, to accomplish the same purpose for the Hindus as the Madrasa for the Mohammedans and especially to supply qualified Hindu Assistants to European Judges." In 1785, Sir William Johns, with the assistance of the Governor-General, established the Bengal Asiatic Society for the encouragement of Historical researches. Similarly after a few years, Charles Grant, one of the Directors of the Company, submitted a memorandum in which he lamented low moral conditions of the people of India. He asked the Company to improve their condition by imparting to them a knowledge of the English language which was to serve as a "key which will open them a world of new ideas." His view was that just as the Muslim rulers had taught Persian to the natives, in the same way Englishmen should teach English to the Indians.

Second Period (1811-1833)

1. Lord Minto and Education. In 1811 Lord Minto regretted the neglect of literature and science in India and suggested improvements in existing colleges in addition to the establishment of new ones. It should however, be noted here that long before the enactment of the Charter Act of 1813 the urgency of educating the natives had been emphasized both in Indian and abroad. Men like Charles Grant and Wilberforce had emphatically impressed, though in vain, upon the Directors at Home the dire need of the spread of education among the Indian subjects. As pointed out above, Lord Minto and his colleagues like. T. Lumseden. G. Hewett and Cole-Brook in Indian were equally eager for the encouragement of education in India. Consequently, a Minute was issued in 1811 embodying many valuable suggestions for the improvement of education in our country. Consequently, the Charter Act of 1813 set apart an annual sum of one lakh of rupees for the spread of education amongst the British inhabitants in India. The clause inserted in the Charter Act of 1813 was that "a sum of not less than one lakh of rupees in each years shall be set apart and applied to the revival and improvement of literature and for the introduction and promotion of knowledge of the sciences in the inhabitants of the British territories in India."

2. Raja Ram Mohan Roy formed an association for founding an institution where the Hindus were to receive instruction in European languages and sciences. The Hindu College was founded in 1817. In 1818 the Bishop of Calcutta opened an institution which was to serve the double purpose of training young Christians as preachers and of imparting a knowledge of the English language to the Hindus and the Muslims. Raja Ram Mohan Roy opposed in vain the establishment of a Sanskrit college at Calcutta, but nobody bothered about this protest.

3. Elphinstone. In his Minute of 1823, Elphinstone urged the establishment of schools for teaching English and European sciences. In a communication to the Commissioners for Indian affairs, Elphinstone wrote thus: "I conceive it is more important to impart a high degree of education to the upper classes than to diffuse a much lower sort of it among the common people. The most important branch of education is that designed to prepare natives for public employment. If English could be at all diffused among person who had the least time for reflection, the progress of knowledge by means of it would be accelerated in a tenfold ratio since every man who made himself acquainted with a science through English would be able to communicate it in his own language to his countrymen." He proposed the establishment of a school at Bombay where English might be taught "classically" and where instructions might also be given in that language on History, Geography and Science. In 1833, he set up a similar school at Poona. In 1834 was started the Elphinstone College at Bombay.

Third Period (1833 1854)

By this time, the demand for the study of English had increased tremendously. English books were being sold by thousands. There was practically no demand for Sanskrit and Arabic books. In order to satisfy the popular demand. English classes were attached to the Calcutta Madrasa and Sanskrit College at Calcutta. The same was done in Agra College which was established in 1811. In spite of that, the Oriental Colleges were not popular. It should however, be pointed out that Mr. Adams, who temporarily was the successor of Lord Hastings, however, appointed a Committee of Public Instruction in 1823 to find out the best way of utilizing the grant granted in 1813 and the money so far accumulate for the spread of education in India. But unfortunately there emerged out a controversy among the members of the Committee on the issue of the type of education to be imparted to the Indians and the medium of instruction necessitated for the purpose. One group of the Committee headed by Dr. Wilson favoured the spread of Oriental Learning while the other led by Macaulay advocated the cause of Western education. It would therefore, be proper to discuss the arguments advanced by each of the two groups in support of their contentions, as has been done in the following lines:

1. *(a)* It was contended by the first group that the clause regarding the revival and promotion of literature in the East India Company's Charter Act of 1813 was meant to apply chiefly to the revival and encouragement of Hindu and Mohammedan literature. *(b)* It was also contended that the public faith being pledged to the

existing system, *i.e.*, the study of Oriental languages, to alter the appropriation of any of the funds which hitherto had been spent in encouraging the study of Sanskrit and Arabic would be a downright spoliation. *(c)* It was also contended that the Oriental classics were the proper subjects for Oriental study. *(d)* Further it was contended that the Sanskrit and Arabic languages being the languages in which the legal and religious ideas of the hundreds and millions of people were expressed were entitled to special encouragement at the hands of the Government.

2. In reply to the arguments advanced by the Orientalists, the Anglicists argued their case to each of the above points, as follows: *(a)* The Act of Parliament contained nothing about the particular languages or sciences which were to be studied, much less the Arabic and Sanskrit languages. *(b)* That the grants made from the public purse for the encouragements of literature differed in no respect from the grants which are made from the same purse for other subjects of real or supposed utility. To quote Macaulay, "We found the sanatorium on a spot which we suppose to be healthy. Do we thereby pledge ourselves to keep a sanatorium there if the result should not answer our expectations?" *(c)* Macaulay argued, "The Government ought to employ its public funds in teaching what is worth knowing. English is better worth knowing than Arabic or Sanskrit for a "a single sheet of a good European library was worth the whole native literature of India and Arabia." *(d)* It was replied by the Anglicists that neither as the language of law nor as the language of religion have Sanskrit and Arabic any peculiar claim to state encouragement.

Lord Macaulay's Minute and Bentinck's Resolution. The controversy between the two groups raged for more than a decade till Lord Macaulay, the President of the Committee of Public Instruction, decided in favour of European literature and sciences to be taught in English. William Bentinck, the then Governor-General of India, agreed with Anglicists and issued on the 7th Of March, 1835 his celebrated Resolution which contained the following points:

(1) "That the great object of the British Government ought to be the promotion of European literature and science amongst the natives of India and that all funds appropriated for the purpose of education would be best employed on English education alone.

(2) That while the colleges of Oriental learning were not to be abolished, the practice of supporting their students during their period of education was to be discounted.

(3) That Government funds were not to be spent on the printing of Oriental works; and

(4) That all the funds at the disposal of the Government would henceforth be spent in imparting to the Indians a knowledge of English literature and science."

Expansion of Education Between 1835-1853

1. In connection with the work of education, it is pertinent to refer to the part played by the Missionaries in the spread of Western Education in this country. The Danish Missionaries opened an institution for the training of the teachers in 1716. Similarly, they opened two charity schools in Madras in 1717. , They also opened English Schools at various other palces in the country. The names of Missionaries like Carey, Marshman and Ward are famous for their work that they started in the field of education at Serampore in 1793. By the year 1820, the Missionary societies were busy in doing a lot of work in the field of education but their primary object was not to educate the people but preach Christianity amongst them because they felt that the spread of English language would pave the way for spread of Christianity in India. The Missionaries also opened a Wilson College in Bombay and the Christian College in Madras. At Agra also the St. Johns College was established by the Missionaries in 1853. Even at Masaulipatam and Nagpur. Missionary Colleges were started, making holding of the Bible Classes in these colleges compulsory. Or. Duff writes, "one great object was to convey as largely as possible the knowledge of our ordinary improved literature and sciences to the

young persons, but another and a more vital object was to convey a thorough knowledge of Christianity with its evidences and doctrines.

2. The years from 1835 to 1853 saw a considerable progress in the field of education. The schools and colleges were opened at various places in the country. Brahmo Samaj started many Vernacular institutions in the country. Dalhousie opened an Engineering College at Roorkee. Bentinck founded a Medical College at Calcutta. Lord Auckland modified Bentinck's Resolution in favour of Vernaculars and granted Rs. 500 a month to the Asiatic Society of Bengal to carry on Biblisthica Indian Series of Sanskrit Arabic and Persian text. In provinces other than Bengal, Bihar and Orissa, the work of education was carried on with a rapid speed. Elphinstone in Bombay, Munro in Madras and Thomson in Agra opened English Schools and Colleges. Thomson also made a new experiment in the field of education. He started Halqa Bandi (Circle) School System, according to which a few villages were grouped into a unit and one English School was started for that unit. The scheme made provision for one middle school in a Tehsil and a high school for a district.

3. Government Resolution of 1884: The cause of Western Education through English was further strengthened by Lord Hardinge who laid down the condition that no one could enter into the Government service unless he possessed the English knowledge. The Resolution provided that for public employment in every case, preference would be given to those who had been educated in Western science and were familiar with English language.

Fourth Period (1854-1904)

1. "Though during the preceding periods, sufficient was done to promote Western Education in this country, yet the progress of education during the last two decades was much below the expectation. Vernacular education was no longer considered the concern of the Government. Private enterprise was not much appreciated No liberal grants were made by the Government to private institutions. Even the expenditure on the English education was quite insignificant. It badly failed to cater to the full educational

needs of the people for lack of funds. In view of all these defects and difficulties, the Government appointed a Parliamentary Committee to enquire into and report on the matter in question which the Government felt had become urgent. It was, therefore, on the report of this Committee that Sir Charles Wood, the then President of the Board of Control, outlined a scheme of education known as 'Wood's Despatch' 1854."

Sir Charles Wood's Despatch to the Court of Directors has been described the Magna Carta of English Education in India. It set forth a scheme of education far wider and more comprehensive then any which had been suggested so far. It enunciated the aim of education as the diffusion of Arts. Science, Philosophy and the Literature of Europe. The Wood's Despatch, after having stressed the importance of education, also emphatically stressed in this Despatch that it was the sacred duty of the British East India Company to "confer upon the natives of India those vast moral and material blessings which flow from the diffusion of useful knowledge."

HISTORY OF EDUCATION IN INDIA 1818 TO 1885

The Hindus and the Muslims had their educational institutions when the English East India Company acquired territories in India. The educational institutions of the Hindus were called pathshalas and the instruction was provided by the Pandits in Sanskrit. The Muslim Maulvis taught Persian and Theology in their mosques. The educational institutions of the Muslims were called maqtabs and madarsas. The educational institutions of the Hindus and Muslims were linked with their religions. The Company on acquiring territories did not interfere in the existing system and these were left undisturbed.

The East India Company made some irregular efforts in the time of Warren Hastings, though the English language was not taught there. He established Calcutta Madarssa in 1781 to qualify the sons of Muslim gentlemen for responsible and lucrative offices in the State. Instructions were given in Theology, Logic, Rhetoric, Grammar law, Natural Philosophy, Astronomy, Geometry and Arithmetic. After some years in 1792 a similar educational institution was started at Banaras to accomplish the same purpose for the Hindus as the Madarsa performed for the Muslims. It was to supply qualified Hindu assistants to European Judges. In 1785 Sir William Johns, with the assistance of Governor-General established the Bengal Asiatic Society for the encouragement of Historical researches.

In 1793, the Charter of the Company was to be renewed and Wilberforce moved a resolution emphasising the necessity of educating the Indians. He suggested the sending of school masters and missionaries to India. His move was opposed in the House of Commons and it was maintained that the Hindus had "as good a system of faith and morals as most people." It would not be proper to give them any kind of learning other than what they possessed. After some years Charles Grant, one of the Directors of the Company, submitted a memorandum lamenting the low moral conditions of the people of India. He was of the opinion that the Company should make arrangements to impart to them knowledge of English Language. In short the real work of education during the viceroyalties of Warren Hastings and Cornwallis was carried on by the Baptist Missionaries like Carey, David Hare Marshman, Ward, Thomas etc., who founded schools for the natives, translated the Bible into 26 Indian languages and thus contributed to the spread of Christianity and western Education in India. Lord Minto in 1811 regretted the neglect of literature and science in India.

Progress from 1813 to 1854. The educational policy of the Company changed in 1813. The Charter Act of 1813 laid down that the Company was to spend at least one lakh of rupees a year on the education of Indians. It was, however, not clarified whether the money was to be spent on Western or Indian education. The amount was allowed to accumulate for more than two decades because the government could not decide how was it to be spent up. It was further not clarified whether education was to be imparted through the English medium or Vernaculars. A controversy started regarding these points. There were two schools of thought. The Orientalists advocated the imparting of native type of education through the Vernaculars. Their leader was H.H. Wilson. The other school, called the Anglicists, advocated the imparting of Western education through English medium. Its leader was Macaulay. The controversy was finally solved in 1835 by Lord William Bentinck. He accepted the viewpoint of the Anglicists.

This decision had some advantages from the viewpoint of the government. Firstly, it could get cheap clerks. Secondly, the spread of Western education would increase the demand for British goods. This decision had some advantages from the viewpoints of the Indians also. Firstly, they could get government jobs. Secondly, it brought the Indians in contact with the Western sciences and literature. It widened their mental horizon. Thirdly, English became the lingua franca of educated Indians and thereby helped in the development of nationalism in the long run.

Government Resolution of 1844. A Government Resolution of 1844 in the time of Lord Hardinge provided that, in case of public employment, preference would be given to those who had been educated in Western science and were familiar with the English language. It created economic interest in the study of English language.

In the meantime, educational institutions for Western education through English medium were being started by private initiative also. Raja Ram Mohan Roy was instrumental in founding Hindu College at Calcutta in 1817. Elphinstone started an institution at Bombay and another at Poona.

The Work of the Missionaries. The missionaries had already started various educational institutions. The Danish missionaries opened an institution for the training of teachers in 1716. They started an institution at Calcutta in 1818 to train young Christians as preachers and to impart knowledge of English to the Hindus and Muslims. Wilson College at Bombay and the Christian College at Madras were started by the missionaries. St. John's College was founded at Agra in 1853. Missionary Colleges were started at Masulipatam and Nagpur also.

Sir Charles Wood, President of the Board of Control, sent his famous Despatch on Education to India in 1854. It is popularly known as Wood's Despatch. It set forth a comprehensive scheme of education for India and it has rightly been called. "The Magna Carta of English Education in India." The following were its important features:

(a) The study of Indian language was to be encouraged. These was arrangement for the teaching of English language, wherever there was demand for it. The English and the Indian languages were to be the media for the diffusion of European knowledge.

(b) It defined the aim of education as the diffusion of Arts, Science, Philosophy and Literature of the West.

(c) It was felt that the time had come for the establishment of Universities in India. These were to be established on the model of London University. These were to be examining bodies only. Each University was to have a Chancellor, a Vice-Chancellor, and a Senate. There were to be professorships for different branches of learning like Law. Calcutta and Bombay were to have the first universities. Another university could be established at Madras. The universities could be set up in such places where there was a sufficient number of students for degree classes.

(d) The number of government schools and colleges was to be increased. More middle schools were to be started. Greater attention was to be paid to elementary education.

(e) The system of scholarships to brilliant candidates was to be introduced.

(f) There were to be institutions for training the teachers.

(g) The system of grants in-aid was to be started to help private initiative in the field of education. The principle of religious neutrality was to be followed in making these grants.

(h) Female education was to be encouraged.

(i) There was to be a Director of Public Instruction in every province. He was to be assisted by Inspectors and Deputy Inspectors.

The universities soon grew up. Universities were established at Calcutta, Madras and Bombay in 1857. Punjab and Agra Universities were set up in 1885 and 1887 respectively.

Wood's Despatch was no doubt a landmark in the history of Education in India. But its admirers have over estimated its importance as it was not free from defects:

1. It laid down no solid scheme to run the schools as contemplated by the scheme.
2. It made the universities mere examining bodies and not the teaching bodies.
3. The native languages did not receive any attention.
4. The private enterprise did not stand bright prospects for the future.
5. The despatch was also incomplete as most of its schemes were not implemented by the government.

The Hunter Commission (1882). Lord Ripon appointed a commission in 1882 to inquire how far effect had been given to the principles of Wood's Despatch of 1854 and to suggest measures to carry further the policy laid down in that. It made the following recommendations:

(a) It advocate the gradual withdrawal of the State from the direct management of the institutions of higher education. A college or a secondary school was to be handed over to the Indians provided there was reasonable prospect that the cause of education would not suffer.

(b) Ordinary and special grants should be made to the colleges.

(c) New regulations should be framed regarding the award of scholarships.

(d) An attempt should be made to prepare a model textbook containing the fundamental principles of natural religions so that it could be taught in all government and non-government colleges.

(e) The principal or one of the professors in each government and aided college was to deliver a series of lectures on the duties of a man as a citizen in each session.

(f) There were to be alternative courses in big colleges.

(g) All elementary schools were to be inspected by the officers of the Education Department.

(h) Primary education was to be given greater attention and a part of provincial revenues was to be reserved for it.

(i) There should be certain general principles regarding college fees and exemptions from them.

(j) Special measures were to be adopted to promote education among the Muslims.

(k) Secondary Schools were to be handed over to private management wherever possible.

(l) Greater attention was to be paid to the physical and mental education of the students.

The Government of India accepted most of the recommendations of this Commission. In short the above recommendations aimed at:

1. Encouragement of Vernacular Education.
2. The increased reliance upon private enterprise; and
3. The Indianization of education by gradual withdraw of governmental control by employment of more Indian teachers and also by subordination of missionary activities in the field of education.

ECONOMIC IMPACT OF BRITISH RULE

The British conquest had a pronounced and profound economic impact on India. There was hardly any aspect of the Indian economy that was no changed for better or for worse during the entire period (1757-1947) of British rule. The main economic impacts of the British rule on India may be mentioned under the following heads:

(A) The economic policies followed by the British East India Company and the British Government led to the rapid transformation of India's economy into a colonial economy whose nature and structure were determined by the needs of the British economy. In this respect the British conquest differed from all previous foreign conquests. The previous conquerors bad overthrown Indian political powers but had made no basic changes in the country's economic structure, they had become gradually a part of the Indian life, political as well as economic. The peasant, the artisan and the trader had continued to lead the same type of existence as before. The basic economic pattern, that of self-sufficient rural economy, had been perpetuated. Change of rulers had merely meant change in the personnel of those who appropriated the peasant's surplus. But the English conquerors were entirely different. They totally disrupted the traditional structure of the Indian economy. Moreover, they never became an integral part of the Indian life.

(B) Commercialisation of Indian agriculture began during the British rule. The commercialisation of Indian agriculture took place not to feed the industries of India because India was far behind in industrial development as compared to Britain, France, Belgium and many other European countries of 18th century. It was primarily to feed the British industries that it was taken up and achieved only in case of those agricultural products which were either needed by the British industries or could fetch cash commercial gain to Britain in the European or American market. For example, several efforts were made to increase the production of cotton in India to provide raw and good quality cotton to the cotton-textile industries of Britain which were growing fast after the industrial revolution (1740-1860) in Britain. India and more than that tea and coffee plantation were encouraged in India because these could get commercial market abroad. Mostly their plantations were controlled by the English. Jute was another product received attention of the English because the jute-made products got a ready market in America and Europe. The Commercialisation of agriculture was beneficial only to British planters, traders and manufacturers and partly Indian traders and money landers who worked as middlemen for them. Most of the Indian people suffered miserably due to the British policy of the commercialisation of the Indian agriculture. It resulted in reduced area under cultivation of food crops. The net result of this change was that India failed to produce even that much food crops which could provide even two square meals a day to its population. The misery was further enchanced because the population of India was increasing every year, fragmentation of land was taking place because of the increasing pressure on land and modern techniques of agricultural production were not introduced in India. It became difficult for them to get even sufficient food. In 1945, Sir Manilal B. Nanavati, formerly Deputy Governor of Reserve Bank of India observed in his presidential address to the sixth conference of the Indian Society of Agricultural Economics at Banaras: "During the last 75 years continuous deterioration in the condition of the masses is taking place. In 1880 India had a surplus of food stuffs to the extent of 5 million tons and today we have a deficit of 10 million tons. The consumption of food was then estimated at 1½ lb. per individual and now it is 1lb. Nearly 320 per cent of the Indian population is estimated to be suffering from chronic malnutrition and under nutrition."

(C) Impoverishment of the peasantry. The peasant was also progressively impoverished under British rule. The following policies and factors contributed to it:

(i) In the very beginning of British rule in Bengal, the policy of Clive and Warren Hastings of extracting the largest possible land revenue had led to such devastation that even Cornwallis complained that one-third of Bengal had been transformed into "a jugle inhabited only by wild beasts."

Nor did improvement occur later. In both the permanently and the Temporarily Settled Zamindari areas, the lot of the peasants remained unenviable. They were left to the mercies of the zamindars who raised rents to unbearable limits, compelled them to pay illegal dues and to perform forced labour or begar, and oppressed them in diverse other ways. The condition of the cultivators in the Ryotwari and Mahalwari areas was no better. Here the Government took the place of the zamindars and revived excessive land revenue which was in the beginning fixed as high as one-third to one-half of the produce. Heavy assessment of land was one of the main causes of the growth of poverty and the deterioration of agriculture in the 19th century.

(ii) Due to wrong economic policies of the British Government the population pressure on Indian agriculture had increased very much. Increased pressure of population on land promoted the small and uneconomic land holdings poor means of irrigation and lack of modernization of agriculture. These all factors contributed to the impoverishment of peasantry.

(iii) The harmful effects of an excessive land-revenue demand were further heightened by the rigid manner of its collection. Land revenue had to be paid promptly on the fixed dates even if the harvest had been below normal or had failed completely. But in bad years the peasant found it difficult to meet the revenue demand even if he had been able to do so in good years.

(iv) The evil of high revenue demand and increasing pressure population on agriculture was made worse by the fact that the peasant got very little economic return for the revenue be used to pay to the landlords and British Government. The British Government adopted indifferent attitude towards the welfare of the peasantry. The British Government spent very little on improving agriculture. It devoted almost its entire income to meeting the needs of the British-Indian administration, making the payments of direct and indirect tribute to England and serving the interest of British trade and industry. Even the maintenance of law and order tended to benefit the merchant and the money-lender rather than the peasant.

(v) Whenever the peasant failed to pay land revenue, the British Government put up his land on sale to collect the arrears of land revenue. But in most cases the peasant himself took this step and sold part of his land to meat in time the government demand. In either case he lost his land. Such situations increased the impoverishment of the peasantry.

(D) The revenue policy of the British-increased pressure of population on agriculture, existence of several intermediaries between the peasants and the British Government, subdivision and fragmentation of land holdings, illiteracy, some wrong traditions and extravagance etc. gave birth to a serious problem of Indian agriculture that is, rural indebtedness. But more than these, the policy of the British Government was directly responsible for it. The demand of the revenue was very high, the collection of the revenue was done in a very rigid manner by the officials and zamindars; the government did nothing to remove the intermediaries who came into existence even where Ryotwari and Mahalwari system existed, by the first half of the 19th century, the government started collecting revenue in cash except in such on lying areas as Assam; all these steps of the government shows that government created such situations which promoted rural indebtedness. Because all these measures, in one way or the other forced the Indian peasants to borrow money from the local money lenders who charged not only heavy interest but also took advantage of ignorance and illiteracy of the peasants and resorted to deceitful measures, such as false accounting, forged signatures, making the debter sign for larger amounts than he had actually borrowed etc.

In pre-British times, the money-lender was subordinated to the village community. He could not behave in a manner totally disliked by the rest of village. For instance, he could not charge usurious rates of interest. Infact, the rates of interest were fixed by usage and public opinion. Moreover, he could not seige the land of the debtor, he could not at most take possession of the debtor's personnel assets and liabilities like jewelleries or part of his standing crops. By introducing transferability of land the British revenue system enabled the money-lender or the rich peasant to take possession of land. Even the benefits of peace and security established by British through their legal system were primarily reaped by money-lender in whose hands the law placed enormous powers; he also used the power of purse to turn the expensive process of litigation in his favour and to make the police serve his purposes. Moreover, the literate and shrewd money-lender could easily take advantage of the ignorane and illiteracy of the peasant to twist complicated processes of law to get favourable judicial decisions. In the zamindari areas the peasants were left to the mercies of the zamindars who raised rents to unberable limits and compelled them to pay illegal dues also. Gradually the cultivators in the Ryatwari and Mahalwari areas sank deeper and deeper into debt and more and more land passed into the hands of the money-lenders, merchants, rich peasants and other moneyed classes.

The Indian peasant had hardly any savings for critical times and whenever crops failed he fell back upon the money lender not only to pay land-revenue but also to feed himself and his family. The presence of intermediaries whose number has gone on multiplying enhanced further the actual demand of revenue many fold. What in fact, happened was that the zamindars, and in case of Mahalwari and Ryatwari systems the government gave right of collecting revenues to certain other individuals who became intermediaries between them and the peasants. These intermediaries in turn, gave this right to somebody else on profitable terms. Thus, by a chain proceess, a large number of rent receiving intermediaries between the peasants and the government sprang up. In some cases, in Bengal there number went up as high as fifty.

As the government wanted to collect the land revenue in cash and by a fixed date, the peasants therefore, were many times forced to sell a part of their land or to sell their produce at cheaper rate to the local money-lender or baniya. The absence of a just marketing system for the peasants and the growing commercialisation of agriculture also helped the money-lender cum-merchant class to exploit the Indian peasantry. The poor peasants had to sell their produce just after the harvest and at whatever price they could get as they had to meet the demand of the government, the zamindar and the money-lender. All these factors not only increased the poverty of the peasants but forced them to beg to loan and, in absence of any proper substitute, mostly from the local money-lender.

(E) Stagnation and Deterioration of Indian Agriculture. As result of over crowding of agriculture, excessive land revenue demand, growth of landlordism, increasing indebtedness, and the growing impoverishment of the cultivators Indian agriculture began to stragnate and even deteriorate resulting in extremely low fields per acre. A brief description of all these factors is given here:

(i) Overcrowding of Indian agriculture and increase in subinfeudation during the British rule led to subdivision and fragmentation of land into small holdings most of which could not maintain their cultiyators. The extreme poverty of the overwhelming majority of peasants left them without any resources with which to improve agriculture by using better seeds and cattle, more manures and fertilizers, and improved techniques of agriculture productions. Nor did the cultivator, rack-rented by both the Government and the landlord have any insentive to do so. After all the land he cultivated was rarely his property and the bulk of the benefit which agricultural improvements would bring was likely to be reaped by the horde of absentee landlords and money-lenders.

(ii) In England and other European countries the rich landlords generally invested capital in land to increase its productivity with a view to share in the increased income. But in India the absentee landlords, both old and new, performed no useful function. They were mere rent receviers who had often no routes in land and who took no personal interest in it beyound collecting rent.

(iii) The British Government could have helped in improving and modernising agriculture. But the Government refused to recognise any such responsibility. A Characteristic of the financial system of British India was that, while the main burden of taxation fell on the shoulders of the peasant, government spent only a very small part of it on him. An example of this neglect of peasant and agriculture was the step motherly treatment meted out to public works and agriculture improvement. While the Government of British India had spent by 1905 over 360 crores of rupees on the railways which were demanded by British business interests, it spent in the same period less than 50 crores of rupees on irrigation which would have benefitted millions Indian cultivators.

(iv) At a time when agriculture all over the world was being modernized and revolutionised Indian agriculture was technologically stagnating, hardly any modern machinery was used. What was worse that even ordinary implements were centuries old for example, in 1915 there were only 930,000 iron ploughs in use while wooden ploughs numbered 31.8 million. The use of inorganic fertilizers was virtually unknown, while a large part of animal manure, *i.e.*, cowdung, night-soil, and cattlebones, was wasted. In 1922-23 only 1.9 per cent of all cropped land was under improved seeds. By 1938-39 this percentage had gone up only to 11 percent. There was hardly any spread of primary education or even literacy in the rural areas. Further more, agricultural education was completely neglected by the British Government. In 1939 there were only six agriculture colleges with 1,306 students.

(F) Ruin of Indian Handicrafts Cottage Industries

(i) There was a sudden and quick collapse of the urban handicrafts was caused largely by competition with the cheaper imported machine-goods from Britain. The British government imposed a policy of one-way free trade on India after 1813 and the invasion of British manufacturers, in particular cotton taxtiles, immediately followed. Indian goods made with primitive techniques could not compete with good produced on a mass scale by powerful steam-operated machines. The ruin of Indian industries, particularly rural artisan industries, proceeded even more rapidly once the railways were built. The railways enabled British manufacturers to reach and uproot the traditional industries in the remotest villages of the country. The cotton weaving and the spinning industries were the worst hit. Silk and woollen textiles industries faired no better and a similar faith overtook the iron, pottery, glass, paper, metal, shipping, oil-pressing, tanning and dyeing industries.

(ii) Apart from the influx of foreign goods, some other factors arising out of British conquest also contributed to the ruin of India industries the oppression practised by the British-East India Company and its servants on the craftsmen of Bengal during the second half of the 18th century, forcing them to sell their goods below the market price and to here their services below the prevailing wage compelled a large number of them to abandon their ancestral professions. In the normal course Indian handicrafts and cottage industries would have benefitted from the encouragement given by the Company to their export.

(iii) The high import duties and other restrictions imposed on the import of Indian goods into Britain and Europe during the 18th and 19th centuries, combined with the development of modern manufacturing industries in Britain, led to the virtual closing of European markets to Indian manufacturers after 1820.

(iv) The British East India Company annexed many Indian states and their territories under its direct control and rule. The gradual disappearance of Indian rulers and their courts who were the main customers of town handicrafts also gave a big blow to these industries. For instance, the production of military weapons depended entirely on the Indian states. The British purchased all their military and other government stores in Britain.

(v) According to most of the Indian historians the British policy of exporting raw materials to England from India also adversely affected and greatly injured Indian handicrafts and cottage industries. Because due to this factors the price of raw materials like cotton and leather raised very much. This increased the cost of handicrafts and reduced their capacity to compete with foreign goods.

(G) The ruin of Indian handicrafts were reflected in the ruin of the towns and cities which were very famous for their manufacturers. Cities which had withstood the ravages of war and plunder failed to survive British conquest. Dacca, Surat, Murshidabad and many other populour and flourishing industrial centres were depopulated and laid waste.

(H) The tragedy was heightened by the fact that the decay of the traditional industries was not accompanied by the growth of modern machine industries as was the case in Britain and Western Europe. Consequently, the ruined handicraftsmen and artisans failed to find alternative employment. The only choice opend to their was to crowd into agriculture. Moreover, the British rule also upset the balance of economic life in the villages. The gradual destruction of rural crafts broke up the union between agriculture and domestic industries in the countryside and thus contributed to the destruction of self-sufficient village economy. On the one hand, millions of peansants, who had supplemented their income by part-time spinning and weaving now had to rely over whelmingly on cultivation; on the other, millions of rural artisans lost their traditionally livelihood and became agricultural labourers or petty tenants holding tiny plots. They added to the general pressure on land.

(I) Infact, India became an agricultural colony of manufacturing Britain which needed it as a source of raw materials for its industries. No where was the change more glaring than in the cotton textile industry. While India had been for centuries the largest exporter of cotton textiles and goods in the world, it was now transformed into an importer of British cotton products and an exporter of raw cotton.

(J) An important development in the second half of the 19th century was the establishment of large scale machine based industries in India. Though it was confined mainly to the plantations and a few consumers goods industries like textiles. There was limited development of mining like coal and iron. The ownership of these industries except the textile was predominantly European and mostly Britain. Infact, the industrial developments of India began only when British had sufficient surplus capital at home which needed investment spheres abroad. Indian could provide a good place for investment to the British capitalists and financiers as labour was available cheap here. That is why, the industrialisation of India was started by the British capitalists, the profits of which were again drawn by the British and delivered to the home country. The Indian capitalists were first shy of entering the field and when they entered they faced heavy odds. Therefore, the industrial progress of India was very slow.

IMPACT AND LEGACY OF BRITISH RULE IN INDIA

In a series of well-written articles contributed to the New York Daily Tribune in 1853 Marx made an excellent analysis of the problems of Asiatic society, especially in India and China, in the larger background of the rise of British capitalism in its frantic search for a colonial policy and a world market. With a rare insight Marx portayed:

(i) an analysis of the pre-colonial Indian situation—social, economic and political.

(ii) assessed the impact of British rule and European capitalism upon it till the middle of the 19th century.

(iii) projected into the future and prophesied the future results of British rule in India.

Regarding the destructive role of Britain in India, Marx referred to Britain's wanton destruction of indigenous society with the comment that England was actuated by the vilest interests, and was stupid in her manner of enforcing it. England's economic role in India was a crude plundering of India's wealth and its parasitic battening on Indian economy. Referring to Britain's regenerative work in India, which had just begun to transpire and whose essence lay in the reversal of those specific characteristics that lay at the root of Asiatic stagnation, Marx noted in 1853 the following signs:

(a) the unprecedented consolidation of the political unity of India, strengthened by the newly-laid telegraph lines;

(b) the development of railway lines ending village isolation and the introduction of steamships linking India so closely to Europe that 'that once fabulous country will thus be actually annexed to the Western World';

(c) economic development of India in the interests of the English millocracy, the railway system being the forerunner of modern industry;

(d) the introduction of private property rights in land—a great desideratum of Asiatic society;

(e) the emergence of a free press and a class of educated Indians imbued with European science and endowed with the requirements for Government.

(f) the rise of modern industry which would dissolve the hereditary divisions of labour.

Marx expected these developments to fulfil Britain's positive and constructive histologic mission in "laying of the material foundations of western society in Asia." Unfortunately, Britain's role in modernizing India has turned out to be different from what he prophesied.

The impact of British rule may be summarised under the following heads:

(A) Political. Political unification of India under one centralised government was perhaps the most significant development under British rule. The inexorable logic of imperialism worked a full circle till the whole of India from the Himalayas to Cape Comorin and from Chittagong to the Khyber Pass passed under British control. If the British Indian provinces were under 'direct' British rule, Indian States came under 'indirect' imperial rule.

Britain also gave to India-what British writers are never weary of emphasising—the Blessings of Peace. She maintained a strong army both for external defenee and maintenance of internal security. Britain also organised a strong police for maintenance of law and order-all at a heavy expense to the Indian taxpayer.

Jawaharlal Nehru made a pertinent observation that the British undoubtedly rescued India from chaos and anarchy—that chaos and anarchy which was partly at least due to the aggressive and ambitious policy of the East India Company and their representatives in India.

Another impact of British rule was the emergence of the spirit of Indian nationalism and the growth of the Indian nationalist movement. If political necessities compelled the imperial rulers to have a single administrative set-up for the whole of India, considerations of military defence and economic exploitation goaded them to develop the means of transport and communications through a network of roads and railways and efficient organisation of the post and telegraph systems. These developments gave India the appearance of unity and fostered the spirit of one-mindedness. The emergence of an English educated middle class intelligentsia and the development of the modern press fostered the modern concepts of nationalism, nationality, political rights etc. which in turn cleared the ground for the formation of an all-India political organisation like the Indian National Congress.

Enlightened imperialists like A.O. Hume, William Wedderburn, George Yule, Alfred Webb, Henry Cotton tried to keep the Indian National Congress as a 'loyal and innocuous' organisation in the beginning and even used its official platform for pro-British and anti-Russian propaganda. The Indian National Congress came of age in the beginning of the 20th century and started questioning the very moral right of Britain to rule India. The demand for Swaraj followed.

The development of Indian nationalism was never to the liking of British rulers of India. They used a thousand and one methods to weaken the movement. The Anglo- Indian bureaucracy which looked upon the Congress as a Hindu organisation worked hard to keep the Muslim community away from political agitation. The introduction of the system of reservation of seats for different communities in the Central Legislative Council, Provincial Legislative Councils and even Local Bodies; the principle of reservation of government jobs on communal basis in the junior civil services, in the police, in the army and other services-were all calculated to hinder the development of a healthy political and social outlook on national issues. The British also regimented the Indian Princes as a Third Force in Indian politics. The policy of 'counterpoises' roped in not only the Indian princes, but also the bigzamindars and even the scheduled castes among the Hindus. Thus British policies struck at the very root of the solidarity of Indian nationalism. Before Britain quit India in 1947, it partitioned India into two independent states of India and Pakistan and left the Indian princely states a potential source for mischief. The fear of Balkanization started Indian in the face. Thus the India National Congress goal of a strong undivided free India was shattered, mainly due to the machivellian policies of imperial Britain. The British who had always claimed credit for reating a strong unified India left behind a divided and weak India.

Britain also claimed to have introduced in India a parliamentary system of government with the larger ideal of a democratic setup for the country. British writers are never weary of reiterating the existence of oriental despotism from the earliest times down to the Mughal times, particulary emphasising that no other system of government had been known in the country. Britain, it is claimed, inherited the autocratic system of government, but decided to introduce a liberal scheme of administration. The origin of democratic political ideals is traced since the governor-generalship of William Bentinck. A beginning towards the introduction of a representative system was made by the Indian Councils Acts of 1861, 1892 and 1909. It is also claimed that a conscious direction to British policy in India towards self-government was given by the Government of India Act, 1919 and extended by the Government of India Act, 1935 throught the introduction of dyarchy and provincial autonomy.

(B) Law and Administration. Perhaps the most abiding impact of British rule has been in the field of law and administration. The British rulers introduced the Rule of Law in their territories. Even the meanest subject enjoyed personal liberty. For example, the principle of habeas corpus provided that no person could be arrested or kept in prison without a written order from the local executive-cum-judicial authority, even if the Viceroy desired otherwise. Even Government servants, for acts done by them in their official capacity, could be sued in the law courts. A natural corollary to the principle of rule of law was the principle of Equality, before the Law. This certainly was a novel feature in a caste-ridden society. Further, the British rulers carried out a Codification of Law. The Code of Civil Procedure (1859), the Penal Code (1860) and the Code of Criminal Procedure (1861) laid down in clear, precise and exact language the law applicable to all citizens, high and low irrespective of the caste, creed or religious professions of the parties involved. The British also set up a gradation of courts, civil and criminal, for the trial of petty to heinous crimes with the right to appeal to High Courts and even an appeal to a Committee of the Privy Council in civil suits.

The legal system introduced by the British was not without its shortcomings. It was complicated and beyond the comprehension of the common man. It was very expensive and the rich had the opportunity to wear out the poor and the uneducated. Falsehood, chicanery and deceit paid high dividend. The inordinate delay in the decision of cases was another negative feature of the system. The lawyer class had vested interest in prolonging cases and pleading for clients who could afford to engage them. Even the government of the free India has not been able to remove these deficiencies from the legal system. Perhaps, the worst aspect of the legal system in British times was the special procedure laid down for trial of Europeans in criminal cases.

The organisation of an Indian Civil Service which worked according to set rules and with machine-like efficiency and impartiality was another striking feature of the administration in contrast to the personal rule of the monarch or his governors as the case might have been in pre-British times. The LC.S. officers worked as Collectors, Magistrates and Judges and maintained a high standard of impartiality and integrity unmindful of the likes or dislikes of the Governor General or even the Prime Minister of England. Prof. RB. Misra writes "Among the contributions of British rule in India the creation of the Indian Civil Service is one of the most remarkable.

The much-praised I.C.S. was not without its drawbacks. In spit of repeated resolutions of the British parliament and announcements by the British monarchs about recruitment to the I.C.S. on the basis of competitive examination irrespective, of racial considerations, the I.C.S. remained a close preserve of Europeans. Various subterfuges-like holding the examination in London alone, keeping low the maximum age limit for enterance, drawing the syllabus to suit English boys interview evaluation, riding tests-were used to keep the Indians out of these services.

Further, the much-praised virtue of efficiency became a vice because it was, as Rabindranath Tagore put it, 'uhtouched by hand' *i.e.* they became insensitive to the feelings of the people and to the new currents of thought and never bothered to gain the goodwill an co-operation of the people whom they despised. Worst still, the I.C.S. developed a cult of its indispensability for India and unconsciously developed the sense of identifying India with their own interests. As Jawaharlal Nehru has put it, "They ran India, they wore India and anything that was harmful to their interests must of necessity be injurious to India". Indian nationalists rightly resented the fabulous salary and liberal allowances and still lavish pensionary benefits paid to the I.C.S. and interpreted these as a big channel in the drain of wealth from India. Oababhai Naoroji described the I.C.S. as 'leeches' which sucked Indian blood.

(C) Education, Oriental Studies and Indian Renaissance. Intellectually 18th century India presented the picture of a stagnant society. The traditional system of education had greatly suffered during the political instability of the period. The new Renaissance spirit of scientific enquiry, scepticism, humanism and aggressive materialism which was rapidly transforming the West had not reached India. The political confusion of the 18th century which European intervention further accentuated delayed the infiltration of progressive ideas into India.

The Christian missionaries of Serampore—Carey, Ward & Marshman—with the Cross in their hands were the first to open schools for Indian Children. Their educational endeavours were just a means for their higher aim of proselytization. Compulsion of administrative organisation, commercial penetration and need for cheaper clerks to man the lower rungs of the administration goaded the British government to provide in the Charter Act of 1813 a clause requiring the East India Company to annually set apart a sum of one lakh of rupees on the improvement of education in India. Some progressive Indians like Ram Mohun Roy urged the government to spend this fund on instructing Indians in mathematics, natural philosohy, chemistry, anatomy and other useful sciences. The Company's authorities dillydallied for two decades before a final decision was taken by the Committee of Public Instruction in 1835 under Lord Macaulay's chairmanship and adopted by William Bentinck's government to spend the allocated amount for "English education alone".

Some painstaking British scholars devote themselves to the study of Sanskrit, philology, Indian culture and Indian history. Sir William Jones indentified Chandragtipta Maurya with Sandrokottus of Greek historians and this proved a landmark in Indian chronology, James Prinsep and Henry Masser deciphered the Brahmi script translated the Asokan incriptions and many texts of Buddhist literature. This opened a new chapter in the history of ancient India.

English writers take credit for England having heralded the Indian Renaissance. Percival Griffiths writes, "Whatever else of good or evil Britain may have achieved in India, she may justly claim to have brought about the great Indian Renaissance". It is hard to believe that modern political thought and scientific advances of the 18th and 19th centuries would not have reached India but for the British imperial rule in India. From times immemorial India had followed an open-door policy and even during the age of primitive means of transport and communications had maintained effective trade and cultural links both with the East and the West. Thus the wind of new ideas from the West would have reached India even without British rule.

The British over-emphasis on education through the English medium and faith in the 'infiltration theory' limited the spread of education to an elite class and neglect of the education of the masses, thus creating a gulf between the English-educated and the masses. The Government turned its face even against the spread of higher education towards the last quarter of the 19th century when it found its spread working against imperial interests.

The British pattern of liberal education and educational policies contained some inner contradictions. The emergence of modern political consciousness, political organisations and political agitations were as much a result of British educational policies as a reaction to imperial policies. It was a section of the English educated intelligentsia which exposed the true nature of imperial rule and provided leadership to modern political movements. Taken in this light the Macaulayan scheme of education proved beneficent to it.

(D) Social and Cultural Impact. Western impact has been all pervading in the fields of Indian social life, has greatly influenced art, architecture, painting, literature, poetry, drama, novels and even Indian religious and philosophy. The pace-setters in these fields have been English public servants and men of letters and the carriers were largely the English-educated class who dominated the few professions of journalists, teachers, layers, doctors etc. It was this Indian intelligentsia who spearheaded most of the social and political organisations in the country.

Change is a continuous process and India certainly would have witnessed social changes with or without British contact. Even after the British have quieted India, world currents in social outlook, dress, food habits, movies styles and even fashions and hair styles are penetrating deep into Indian life just as Indian models in some spheres are influencing world models.

The British rulers built town-halls after the Renaissance palazi style, railway stations in the Gothic cathedral style, government buildings and secretariat offices in the western style with an admixture of traditional Mughal models. The Western educated class copied these models in their private buildings and personal residences. In the field of painting Ravi Varma, Abanindranath, Gogonendranath, Jamini Ray and Amrita Sher Gil were greatly influenced by the Western style. In the field of literature Rabindranath Tagore, Aurobindo Ghosh, Sarojini Naidu, Mulk Raj Anand, R.K. Narayan—to mention only a few names-were influenced by the English pattern.

English words and idioms have penetrated into vernacular languages. Words like station, railway, cinema, hospital, vote, election, restaurant, hotel, union etc. are understood even by the illiterate living in remote villages of India. Similarly, phrases like Government's responsibility, right to work, right to food, shelter and social security, right to organise the workers, right to equality before the law, right to freedom of speech, debate, movement etc. etc. have become common-place idioms in Indian life.

(E) Economic Impact. Since the main motivation behind British intrusion and subsequent domination of India was commercial and economic, the British impact in the economic sphere has been the most deleterious and devastating. Britain used the most sophisticated methods to exploit India's vast and rich economic potential. If even after two centuries of the most close contanct and complete control of Indian economy by the British-technologically the most advanced nation in the world-India in 1947 presented the picture of an economically underdeveloped nation with hunger, poverty, low national income, the responsibility must lie squarely on the shoulders of the British-imperial rulers.

Indian agriculture received the maximum care under the East India Company primarily because the main source of state income was land revenue. The Company tried various experiments to maximize the land revenue by resort to the method of 'open auction to the highest bidder.' The system of farming of land revenue did not work. Cornwallis introduced the Permanent Settlement of Land Revenue in

Bengal, Bihar and Orissa in 1793. Subsequent administrators introduced the Ryotwari system in Bombay Presidency and most parts of the Madras Presidency, the Mahalwari system (a variation of the Zamindari system) in V.P. and with some further variations in the Punjab. The Zamindari system encouraged absentee landlordism and created a host of intermediaries between the state and the cultivator-all working to the misery of the cultivator. Even in the Ryotwari tracts, the excessive land revenue demand-periodically revised upwards-brought in the money-lender as an important factors in rural India. Rural indebtedness, backward methods of cultivation, inadequate irrigation facilities resulted in pauperization of the rural masses.

Indian industry suffered the maximum at the hands of the British intruder. The superiority and extensive sales of Indian handicrafts in Europe and even in the British markets was anathematic to the interests of the commercial East India Company. The Whig government of the early 18th century imposed heavy duties on Indian textile imports in Britain. However, after the Napoleonic wars, the "Indian markets were increasingly thrown open to British industrial products. The same British government which had earlier excluded Indian cotton goods from English markets by high protective legislation, now permitted British machine-made goods to be poured into India duty free or at nominal duties. This policy of one way free trade which ruined Indian handicrafts was the price India had to pay for the loss of her freedom. Even a British writer, H.H. Wilson has conceded that Britain "employed the arm of political injustice to keep down and ultimately strangle a competitor with whom he could not have contended on equal terms." Karal Marx, writing in 1853 commented. "It was the British intruder who broke up the Indian handloom and destroyed the spinning wheel. England began with depriving the Indian cottons from the European market; it then introduced twist into Hindustan and in the end inundated the very mother country of cotton with cottons".

Could Indian handicraft industry stand the challenge possed by rising capitalism and industrial Revolution? The capitalist mode of production and bourgeoisie commerce had destroyed handicraft industries in European countries too. While in Europe the desructive process had been accompanied by a corresponding growth of new forces of industrial production, the peculiar unhappy situation in the Indian economic scene was that the loss of the old word was without the emergence of a new world.

Britain's interest lay in converting and preserving India as an 'agricultural farm' of industrialised Britain. Thus, the British rulers deliberately carried out the policy of 'ruralization' and 'peasantization' of Indian economy. Whatever few Indian industries developed under the situation created by World War I and the economic depression of 1930's suffered from another disability that these were mostly controlled by British finance and capital. True, textile, cement, jute, paper, sugar, pig iron industries started in India, but the country lagged behind in the development of iron and steel, heavy engineering and metallurgical industries.

The 'gestation theory' popularized by modern Anglo-American scholars does not hold good even after a casual scrutiny of facts and figures. England's role in India was imperial, the Englishmen's mission in India was economic exploitation, the Whiteman's Burden was the burden of wealth that the whiteman carried out of India.

Undoubtedly, British rule has left behind indelible marks, for good or for bad, on almost every aspect of Indian life. European ways of thinking and European patterns have taken firm roots among urbanities who control the strings of India's destiny. The rich legacy of difficulties, particularly in the economic field, are an ever present reminder of the exploitative character of European imperialism in India.

Free India cannot at one stroke write off the deep influences of two centuries of British imperial rule in India. The British rulers created a new structure of colonial institutions, a colonial economy, a colonial society and even a colonial ideology. The institutions of landlordism, politically-loaded casteism, comunalism, regionalism etc. etc, which were encouraged by imperial rulers to perpetuate their rule are evils defying easy eradication. Further, 'distorted modernisation' has created new problems.

□

2

National Movement Struggle

For nine years after the Surat split the Congress was dominated by the moderates. The British Government took advantage of the dissensions in the ranks of the Congress to widen the gulf between the parties and to drive a wedge between the Hindus and Muslims. The Moreley Minto Reforms were meant to rally the moderates and to conpolise the fast flowing currluts of Indian nationalism. They also marked a decisive stage in the British policy of using Indians against Indians. By conceding separate electorates to the Muslims these reforms strongly entrenched communalism and hit the national movement below the belt. Another sympathetic justure to the moderates was the reversal of the Partition of Bengal, a royal boon announced as the Durbar held at Delhi on the occasion of the visit of their majesties King George V and Queen Mary.

It was not long before the people saw through the imperialistic game. they found the Reforms of 1909, quite unsatisfactory in their actual working. They had asked for bread and were given only stones. They found that the enlarged Legislative Councils only veiled autocracy behind an artificial majority. The substance of power was retained by the irresponsible executive while the farm was conceded to the legislature. They realised the danger inherent in the separate electorates granted to the Muslims.

The Muslim League continued its separate existence from the Congress for a long time. In 1916 the Conferences of the Congress and the Muslim League were held at Simultaneously at Lucknow and a pact known as Lucknow Pact was arrieved at between the two. A joint plan with regard to constitution reforms was prepared and the Congress accepted the demand of the Muslims for separate electorate and increase in number of seats to them. This unity could not continue for a long time because the demands of the Muslims went on increasing day by day.

Rowlatt Act and Jallianwala Bagh Tragedy. The Indians extended their whole hearted support to the British in the First World War (1914-18). The Indians had to suffer on account of the increase in prices low salaries, lack of goods, spread of Plague and influenza etc., during the period of war. The freedom had also been restricted by the Indian Defence Rules. Inspite of this the British did not care for their sacrifice and co-operation and published Montague Chelmsford Report in 1918 and declared that this was to be the basis of future reforms. The Indians were greatly disappointed. In the same year the Government Passed Rowlatt Act which provided for the speedy trial of offences without any right of appeal. It also provided that the search of a place and the arrest of a suspected person could be confined for a period of one year in the first instane and to there years in all.

Inspite of the warning of Sir Teg Bahadur Sapru many innocent persons were arrsted under Defence of India rules. Hartals were observed in the whole of the country. There were wide spread revolts in Pubjab where Sat Pal and Dr. Kichbi were arrested. On April 12, 1919 General Dyer declared that no meetings or gathering of people were to be held. Inspite of this declaration a meeting was organised at about 4.30 P.M. on April, 13, 1919 at Jallianwala Bagh. The Government made no attempt to check the holding of the meeting but when the meeting was taking place in which about 10,000 persons were present Gen. Dyer reached there with troops. He closed all the gates except one of the Jallianwala Bagh and ordered the troops to fire. For ten consecutive minutes he kept up a merciless fusillade—in all 1650 rounds on that seeting mass of huminity caught like rats in trap vainly rushing or the few narrow exists for lying flat on the ground to escape the rain of bullets. While giving evidence before the Hunter Enquiry Committee, Lala Girdhari Lal said that there must have been 10,000 dead bodies in the garden. General Dyer contended that he wanted to teach them a lesson so that they might not laught at him. He would have fired and fired longer he said if he had a required ammunition. He had only fired 16,000 rounds because his ammunition had run out." The happening in the Punjab distressed Rabindra Nath Tagore so much so that he gave up the title of "Knighthood" which had been bestowed upon him by the Government of India.

MAHATMA GANDHI AND THE NON-CO-OPERATION MOVEMENT

Mahatma Gandhi entered the scene of Indian Politics in the year 1915. After the death of Lokmanya Tilak on 31st July 1920 the power of the Congress came into the hands of Mahatma Gandhi. Thus by 1920 his popularity and influence had considerably increased in Indian politics. In 1920, Gandhi ji started Non-Co-operation Movement. Hitherto Gandhi ji also believed in the justice of the British and he had extended his whole hearted suppot to the British in the First World War. But his faith was shaken on account of Jallianwala Bagh tragedy, Martial Law in Punjab and the Report of Hunter Enquiry Committee. On the otherhand, the Muslims of India had started a Khilafat Movement on account of terms of treaty made by the Allied nations with Turkey with a view to strengthen the unity of Hindu. Muslims Gandhi ji also extended his support and Co-operation to the Khilafat Movement.

Gandhi ji started the Non-Co-operation Movement and adopted the following programme:

1. Surrender of titles and honourary offices and resignation from the nominated posts in local bodies.

2. Refusal to attend Government duties, Durbars and other official and non-official functions.

3. Withdrawl of children from Government Schools and Colleges and establishment of national schools and colleges in every province.

4. Refusal on the part of military, clerical and labouring classes to offer themselves as recruits for service in Mesopotamia.

5. Boycott of British Courts by lawyers and litegants and establishment of private attribution courts for the settlement of private disputes.

6. Withdrawl by candidates from election to the reformed councils and refusal on the part of voters to vote.

7. Boycott of foreign goods.

Gandhi ji believed that if people extended their whole hearted co-opertion and remained non-violent, they could get Swaraj within a year. The Hindus and Muslims both took active part in the Movement. Foreign goods were burnt in different parts of the country and the student left their colleges. Gandhi ji gave up the title of 'Kaisare Hind.' Hartals were observed in protst of the Prince of Wales visit to India. The Government tried to supress the movement mercilessly. The Satyagrahis were mercilessly heaten and all the leaders were arrested. As many as 25,000 persons were sent to Jails. In 1921 Gandhi ji gave seven days notice to the Governor General to release the non-violent agitators.

Chauri Chaura Incident. In this incident, a mob of 3000 persons killed 21 policemen and one inspector and burnt the police post at Chauri Chaura. Gandhiji who stood for complete non-violence was shocked by this incident and ordered that the movement he suspended. The other Congress leader severely critisised Gandhiji for suspending the movement suddenly. Gandhiji was arrsted and sentenced to six years imprisonment. But on account of illhealth he was relased in February 1924. According to Subash Chandra Bose ; "To sound the order of retreat just when public enthusiam was reaching the boiling point was nothing short of a national calamity." According to C.R. Dass : "The Mahatma opens a compaign in a brilliant fashion, he works it up with skill, he moves from success to success till he reaches the zenith of his compaign but after that he loses his nerve and begins to fatter." According to Polak. "The Muslims wilted under the blow and it was never again possible to restore the confidence and fraternity that had united the two communities during this brief period of alliance."

The Swarajist Party. After the suspension of Non-Co-operation Movement, the Country had no programme for the time being. Chitrayan Das, Moti Lal Nehru and C. Kelkar formed the Swarajist Party with in the Congress and decided to enter the Legislative Assemblies in order to oppose the policies of the Government. Dr. Aneari and D. Raja Gopalachari were the staunch supporters of Gandhiji. They were against the entering of the Legislative Assemblies.

But the resolution was accepted in the special session of Congress held in Delhi. Consequently elections were fought and the Congress gained majority in several provinces in the elections of 1934. However, they could not achieve much by their opposition to the Government Policies. Lord Reading the contemporary Governor-General in India offered a proposal for a Round Table conference in order to draft the constitution of India. But his proposal was rejected. The Swarajism Party declined after the death of Chitranjan Das in 1925.

Simon Commission. In 1927, the British Government appointed a Royal Commission headed by Sir John Simon to submit a report on the constitutional development in India after the enactment of the Government of India Act 1919. All parties boycotted the meetings of the Simon Commission because all its members were Britishers and no a single Indian was taken on the Commission. Where even the Commission went it was welcomed with black falgs and the slogans 'Go back Simon'. Commission submitted its report in 1930 on the basis of which the Government of India Act, 1935 was passed.

Nehru Report. Lord Buckinhead, Secretary of State for India asked the Indian leaders to draft a constitution of India which was acceptable to all. A Committee was formed under the Chairmanship of Pt. Moti Lal Nehru and the report it perpared was called Nehru Report. The Committee had drafted a constitution which demanded Dominion Status for India. The report was considered by the Congress in its annual session of 1928 held at Calcutta. Pt. Jawahar Lal Nehru and Subhash Chandra Bose were in favour of complete Swaraj. However, some leaders were satisfied by Dominion Status for the time being. Efforts of Mahatma Gandhi brought about a compromise between the two groups and the Congress passed a resolution that if the said constitution was not accepted by December 1929 the Congress would not be bound to accept it and would start the non-violent Civil Disobedience Movement.

CIVIL DISOBEDIENCE MOVEMENT OF 1932 AND THE DANDI MARCH

On 31st October 1929 Lord Irwin the Contemporary Governor-General Lord Irwin declared that the object of the British Government was to grant Dominion Status to India but no definite date could be fixed. Hence the Congress passed the resolution of complete independence in 1929 at Lahore session under the Presidentship of Jawahar Lal Nehru 26th January 1930 was declared as Independence Day. The programme of Civil Disobedience Movement was also fixed. Gandhiji wrote a letter to Lord Irwin informing him regarding his decision to break the law regarding salt along with his colleagues in the Sabarmati Ashram. On March 12, 1930 he started his famous Dandi March. It was a signal for the start of Civil Disobedience Movement all over the country. The Government arrested a large number of Congress workers and many persons were even shot dead.

Gandhi Irwin Pact. The First Round Table conference was held in London on November 12, 1930, but the Congress refused to take part in it. The Government released the Congress leaders on 16th February 1931. Gandhi Irwin Pact was made 31st March 1931. With the efforts of Tej Bahadur Sapru and Jayakar. All the Congress workers were released and peaceful picketing of liquer shops was allowed. On his part Gandhiji agreed to participate in the Second Round Table conference and to stop the boycott movement. It was at this time that Bhagat Singh collegues were hanged to death. This sent a ware of resentment all over the country.

Poona Pact. The experience of the Second Round Table conference clearly showed Gandhiji that the ways of the British Government were quite different. He decided to restart the Civil

Disobedience Movement. But he and almost all the members of the Congress Committee and other leaders were arrested and sent to jails. The Indian National Congress was declared as an illegal institution. About lakh persons were imprisoned. The British Prime Minister Macdonald announced the Communal Award which provided separate electorate for scheduled castes. But Congress refused to accept this decision. Gandhiji who was in prison under took a fast unto death as a protest against the provision of a separate electorate for the Scheduled Caste Hindus. But a timely compromise made by Dr. B.R. Ambedkar, the leader of the Depressed classes saved the situation from growing worse. The out come was the Poona Pact by which the number of seats reserved for the Depressed classes was nearly doubled. These seats were to be filled up by a joint electrorate out of the panel of names selected by the Depressed classes. This arrangement hit hard the Caste Hindus although it maintained the intigrity of the Hindu Community Gandhiji broke his fast and nationalist India heaved a sigh of relief.

Decline of Civil Disobedience Movement. The severe measures adopted by Lord Willingdon made the continuance of civil disobedience difficult and by the middle of 1934 the movement subsided for a time. Mean while Parliament passed the Government of India Act 1935 providing for an all India Federation. The scheme of federation never materialised owing to the opposition of the Congress and the Indian princes. But provincial Autonomy came into operation from April 1937. On the assurance of the Provincial Governors that they would not ordinarily interfere with the work of the ministers, the Congress decided to work the provincial part of the new constitution. In the elections that took place in 1937 the Congress swept the polls in the general constituencies. Congress ministeries were found in seven out of eleven provinces and coalition ministeries were formed in Sind and Assam. It was only in Bengal and the Punjab that the League predominated. The Congress ministeries did some commendable work relating to primary education, prohibition of liquirs and the improvement of the villages and the pesants. But the Congress ministeries lasted only for 20 months. The Second War broke out in 1939 on account of the War policy the British Government and on the question of giving support and co-operation to the British Government during war, the Congress Ministeries resigned.

Rift between the Congress and the League. The phenomenal success of the Congress in the elections of 1937 alarmed Mr. Jinnah. He expected that Congress League coalition ministeries would be formed in all the provinces. But the Congress refused to form coalitions unless the Leagues ceased to function as a separate group. To this proposal of the Congress the League refused to agree. Mr. Jinnah openly declared "Muslim can expect neither justice nor fair play under Congerss Government." The majority of muslims 'accepted this view and began to rally round the League. Mr. Jinnah acquired a new personal authority and became the undisputed leader of his community. He began to complain against the unfair treatment of the muslims in the Congress provinces and to circulate stories of as trocities never substantiated, against the Congress Governments. Even European officials have testified to the justice and efficiency of the Conrgess Governments. But Mr. Jinnah was determinated to give a bad name to the Congress and went on with his fulminations.

Split in Congress. About this time there was a split in the Congress Camp. The Rightists led by Rajaji and Vallabha Bhai Patil were devoled followers of Gandhiji. They counselled patience and were not as yet prepared to organise the forces of national life for the overthrow of British imperialism. The leftists were led by Subhash Chandra Bose. He stood for a bold policy and thought that the time was rise for an all out National resistence against foreign rule. The two groups came to grips on the occasion of the election of the Congress President for the Tripura Session of 1939. Subhash Chanrda sought re-election for President ship but was opposed by the Rightists who at Gandhiji instance set up Dr. Pallabhi Sitaramayya as a rival candidate. Bose won the but was forced out by the Right wingers who prevented him from securing a favourable working committee. Subhash Chandra then formed a new group knwon as the Forward Bloc. It was very tragic that Bose who had succeeded in winning the confidence of his country men failed to win the confidence of India's greatest man.

Resignation of Congress Ministeries. The Congress ministeries did good work in the Provinces but were not destinued to function long. When the Second World War broke out in 1939 and England dectaired War against Nazi Germany India was dragged into be ill-gerency even with out the formality of consulting the wishes of the Congress with great chagrin the working Committee of the Congress protested against this attitude and asked the British Government to declare clearly its War aims in regard to democracy in so far as India was concerned. A few days after the Congress demanded that "India be declared an independent nation and present application should be given to this status to the largest possible extent." The British Government was neither explicit in the declaration of its war aims nor agreeable to the demand of the Congress. The Muslim League was very Jabiland and Mr. Jinnah heaved a sigh of relief and asked the Muslims of the country to observe a 'day of deliverance.' The resignation of the Congress Ministeries was perhaps a serious tactical blunder. Through out the War the Congress wat out of power and the British Government had no alternative but to woo the Muslim League Mr. Jinnah took full advantage of the situation.

India and the Second World War. The rapid success of Germany and the fall of France in the Summer of 1940 caused per turbations in India. Gandhiji issued appeals to the people to remain quiet declaring, "we do not seek our independence out of Britain's ruin". The Congress thought out of office offered to co-operate with the war efforts of the allies if a provisional national Government was set up at least at the centre. But the British Government would not yield. The viceroy Lord Lintithgow in a statement published on 8th August 1940 made it clear that the British Government could not contemplate the transfer of their present responsibilities for the peace and welfare of India to any system of Government whose authority was desired by large and powerful elements in Indian national life."

Jinnah's Two Nation Theory. The Capital which the British Government was making of the Communal disharmony encouraged Mr. Jinnah. He began to ignore all other Muslim organisation like the Jamait-ul-ulemas and Ahrar and demanded that the Muslim League should be recognised as the only authoritative organisation of the Musalmans in India. He declared that in India democracy based on majority rule would not be workable. The cap the climax he declared at the Lahore Session of the Muslium League that the Muslims were not in minority but a separate nation and that they must have their separate home land with a separate state *i.e.*, Pakistan. The two nation theory thus propounded dashed to the grounds all hopes of Hindu Muslims unity. Psychosis among the Musalmans and they were led to believe that in an independent India the Muslims would be in the minority and so would lose the preference which they now enjoyed under the British rule. Hence the "Partition of India is the only solution" declared Mr. Jinnah. To Mahatma Gandhi "on the otherhand the communal question was not an unbridgeable gulf" between the Congress and the Muslim League.

MENANCE IN JAPANESE INVASION

Mean while the international situation had become extremely serious. Japan had declared war against England and had joined resounding victories. The Japanese had captured Singapore and Rangoon and were about to knock at the eastern defences of India. A United War front against the Japanese menance was urgently needed. But it was a difficult task in view of the communal discard and Indian distrust of British sincerity. This distrust was recently intensified by Mr. Churchills's declaration that the Atlantic Charter was not applicable to India. Realising this serious situation the British Government sent Sir Stafford Cripps to India, to resolve the Indian dead lock and rally all the force of India's life against the Japanese menance.

The Cripps Mission. The Cripps mission arrived at Delhi in March 1942. Sir Stafford Cripps opend negotiations with the representatives of various Indian parties and put forward his proposals in a Draft Declaration. It provided that India was to have Dominion status and a constitution making body after the end of the War. In the meantime, the British Government was to retain control of the Defence of India as part of their World War effort with the co-opeation of the Indian peoples Cripps virtually repeated the August offer of 1940. His proposals were rejected by every single party or group and Mahatma Gandhi characterised the pledge about the future settlement of the constitution as "a post dated cheque on a bank that was obviously failing."

THE AUGUST MOVEMENT 1942

Quit India Resolution August 1942. The failure of Cripps mission produced a feeling of frustration in the minds of the Indian people at a time when they were alarmed and exited at the rapid approach of the Japenese army at their gates. The Congress leaders felt that only the people's War' could avert the Japanese menance and in order to mobilise the full resources of the people a complete transfer of power to Indian hands was necessary. Accordingly the working committee of the Congress met at Wardha in July 1942 and published a resolution asking the British Government to withdraw from India. This "Quit India" resolution was endorsed by the All India Congress Committee which met at Bombay on 8th August1942. It also declared that should the British Government refuse to withdraw a mass struggle on an All India scale would be started under Gandhiji's leadership.

Spontaneous Revolt all over India. Gandhiji and all the top Congress leaders were arrested. All Congress Committees were banned. The sudden removal of all the prominent leaders produced a terrible explosion of popular feelings. They were mass repulses and disorders in almost every part of the country and these took a very serious turn at Midnapur and other eastern districts of the United Provinces. The repressive measures spread a wave of violence through out the country. On account of the lack of guidance of the leaders, the people adopted violent means for the attainment of independence. Except the Communist Party and the muslim League almost all the parties of the country took active part in the movement. Shri Jai Prakash Narayan, Dr. Ram Monohar Lohia and Shrimati Aruns Asaf Ali made a significant contribution in the movement of 1942. Considerable government property was destroyed by the people. Crowds gathered in cities and rural areas and attacked what seemed to them symbols of British power such as police stations, post offices, railways etc. The unarmed and leaderless mobs faced police and military firing on not less than 538 occasions. The Government put down the disturbances with the exceptional ferocity Gandhiji at the age of 73 undertook a fast for three weeks as a protest against Government atrocities. There was great anxiety felt all over the country.

Netaji Subash Chandra Bose and the I.N.A. Besides internal disturbances the British Government had to face a serious external danger while the August Movement was dying out, the battle of Indian freedom was going on in a different quaiter and under different leadership. Subash Chandra Bose a most gallant fighter for India's freedom disappeared from his Calçutta house where he was interned and made his way to Germany (1941). Thence he went to Japan and finally reached Singapore. At the time of Japanese conquest of Malaya a large number of Indian soldiers in the British army had fallen into the hands of the Japanese. They were released and Subash Chandra Bose who was now called Netaji organised them into Indian National Army or Azad Hind Fauj. He also set up the Azad Hind Government at Singapore in 1943. Netaji's army marhced up the frontiers of India and even penetrated into the Indian territory. Eventually the army was compelled to Surrender to the British for want of provisions. Netaji's during move gave a very bad headache to the British Government and is more significant than is usually realised. The case with which Indian soldier whose loyalty till now was unquestioned transferred their allegiance to a national leader, must have convinced thoughtful Britishers that the Indian army was no longer dependable part of British imperialism.

RAJAJI FORMULA, WAVELL PLAN AND SIMLA CONFERENCE

The Muslim League had demanded the formation of Pakistan in the Lahore Session in 1940. But when the Congress started the Quit India Movement in 1942 Mohammad Ali Jinnah declared that this movement aimed not only to drive away the Britishers out of the country but also to usurp the rights of the Muslims that they could live in independence only after the division of India. In order to solve the problem C. Raja Gopalachari made a plan which is known as Rajaji Formula. In the summer of 1945 the Contemporary viceroy Lord Willingdon Wavell went to London to have consultations with the members of British Cabinet. After his return, he organised Simla Conference in order to sovle the constitutional tangle of India. Both the Congress and the Muslim League took part in the Simla Conference but the conference could not succeed on account of the attitude of the Muslim League. The proposals of the plan offered by the Governor-General are known as Wavell Plan.

THE LAST PHASE OF THE STRUGGLE

The Advent of the Labour Party. In August 1945 Mr. Churchill the arch imperialist fell from power and the Labour Government headed by Mr. Atlee took office. It was an important factor which expedited the solution of Indian constitutional dead lock. Mr. Atlee took a realistic view of events in India and realised that the demand for national independence had become irresistible. The trial of some of the officers of the Azad Hind Fauj produced a bitter feeling of resentment all over the country. These happeanings convinced Mr. Atlee of necessity of taking early action and he announced the depatch of the Cabinet Mission to discuss with Indian leaders as to the best way in which political power could be eventually transferred to Indian hands.

The Cabinet Mission. The Cabinet mission was composed of Lord Pethic Lawrence, Secretary for State, Sir Stafford Cripps, President of the Board of Trade and Mr. A.V. Alexander, First Lord of the Admirality. The Mission held a series of conference with the Congress and the Muslim League delegates but failed to fined common ground between the two irreconcilable parties. As the leaders of the two parties agrred to differ the Cabinet Mission issued a statement on the 6th May 1946 lying down the basic lines of the future political set up of India. The Union, that is the federal Centre should have cxclusive control of foreign affairs, defence and communications. Provinces were to have complete autonomy and were to exercise all powers except those vested in the centre. The Provinces of British India were to form three groups:

(a) Groups A comprising the Hindu majority provinces of Madras Bombay C.P. U.P. Bihar and Orissa.

(b) Group B comprising the Muslim-majority prvinces of the Punjab the North West Frontier Province, Baluchistan and Sind.

(c) Group C consisting of Bengal and Assam.

Each group was to settle its own constitution, the representatives of all of them together with the representatives of such Indian states as would join the Union were meet in a constituent Assembly to draft a constitution for the Union. Any province could withdraw from any of the groups after the first general election under the new constitution.

For the administration of India during the period of constitution making the Mission emphasised the immediate need of an interim Government backed by the major political parties. The constitutional plan of the Cabinet Mission thus consisted of the elections were

(a) Federation

(b) Provincial Autonomy

(c) Grouping of States

(d) Constituent Assembly

(e) Interim Government.

held in September 1945. Inspite of many obstacles a large number of Congress Candidates were elected unopposed in provincial and Central Assemblies. In April 1946 Congres formed Ministries in all the provinces having Hindu majority and North Western Frontier Province. The Muslim League formed ministry in Bengal and Sindh. In Punjab a joint ministry of the Congress, Akalis and the Unionist was formed. It was-now obvious that the Congress was the largest party in the country of it had scored one crore and ninety lakhs votes. On 15th March 1946, the British Prime Minister Lord Atlee made a significant declaration in the House of Commons India's right.

Interim Government and the Direct Action. The proposal of the Cabinet Delegation was an honest attempt at balancing Hindu and Muslim intersts. The delegation definitely rejected the Muslim claim for a separate constituent Assembly and a separate state. But it tacitly conceded the two nation theory of the League by grouping the provinces on communal lines. The Muslim League accepted the proposals' of the Mission for it found that the foundation of Pakistan was inherent in them. The Congress rejected the proposals for an interim government but agreed to participate in the constituent Assembly. The Muslim League pressed the Viceroy to form an interim government without the Congress members. But Lord Wavell refused to accede to this demand. At this the Muslim League became furious and reversed its decision to accept the Cabinet Mission Plan and threatened Direct Action.

Matters came to a crisis when the results of elections for the Constituent Assembly were announced. The reuturn of the overwhelming majority of the Congress member alarmed Mr. Jinnah. He called it brute majority of the Congress. He threw his constitutional methods to the winds and mated the Muslims to 'direct action' to secure their rights. The direct action was directed not against the British Government which enslaved the Indians but against the possible Hindu domination. The Muslims observed August 16 as the 'Direct Action Day.' The Muslim League Government under the Primiership of H. Suhrawardy played havoc with the civic life of the habitants of Calcutta. The League gangsterism started with stabbings of brutal murders of which the Hindus were the victims. But soon the Hindus began to retaliate with effect. The orgy of murder and arson continued for four days resulting in the loss of 5000 lives and 15,000 injured. It was a most shameful chapter in the annals of India. Neither the League ministry nor the English Gvernor and English Viceroy took any steps to check the lawlessness.

Riot in Bihar and Noakhali. The Killing in Calcutta was followed by similar happenings in Noakhali and Tipperah (East Bengal) where the Muslims formed an overwhelming majority of population. Violence begot violence. The Hindus of Bihar were swept off their feet by the account of attrocities committed on their Keith and Kin in Calcutta. They broke into terrible riots in several places in which the Muslims were the Principle sufferes.

Interim Government. Lord Wavell formed the Interim Government with Pandit Jawhar Lal Nehru as Vice President (2nd September). At first the League refused to join it but was entually persuaded by the Viceroy to do so. Lord Wavell, in pact wanted to use the Muslim Members as a Counter poise to the Congress influence. Five League members entered into the interim Government and began to play the part of the "King's party' destroying all team spirit by their disruptive technique. The absence of co-operation made the interim Government "bi-partism rather than a real coalition." Worse still, the League refused to join the Constitutent Assembly and went to declare that it was not a properly constituted body and that its decisions were invalid and ultravires.

Atlees Announcement 1947. On 20th February 1947, Mr. Atlee declared that exisiting state of tension and uncertainty in India "is fraught with danger and could not be indefinitely prolonged." Hence he made the momentous announcement that it was the definite intention of this Majesty's Government to "effect the transfer of power to responsible Indian hands" by a date not later than June 1948. This declaration was followed by a series of League fomented riots all over the Punjab. They were attended with a degree of ferocitty and cruelty which pen shrinks from recording. Against the organised might of the Muslim police backed by the Muslim frenzied Muslim masses the Sikhs and the Hindus had no chance. Some Six million Hindu and Sikh refugees streamed out of the West Punjab leaving a tale of misery and slaughter unequalled in the history of the human race.

DIVISION OF INDIA AND THE ATTAINMENT OF INDEPENDENCE

Mount Batten Plan. In March 1947 Lord Mount Batten the last Viceroy of India succeeded Lord Wavell. He came here Commissioned to accelerate the pace of India's march to freedom.

In his broadcast of 3rd June 1947, he out lined the procedure to be followed for the transference of power into Indian hands. It was decided to partition India into two nations—Indian and Pakistan. Both the Congress and the Muslim League accepted the plan of partition. The British Parliament soon passed the India Independence Act according to which the Dominions of India and Pakistan became independent with effect from the mid night of 15th August, 1947. There were communal riots after the independence in Pakistan as well as in India. The Constituent Assembly completed the work of drafting the constitution of India on 26th January, 1949. The new constitution of India came into force from 26th January 1950. India became a Sovereign Democratic Republic standing for justice, equality, liberty and fraternity. Dr. Rajendra Prasad was elected the President of the Indian Republic while Mr. Jinnah became the first Governor General of Pakistan.

India is free again but she lost the unity which had ever been the charished ideal of her great poets, philosophers and statesmen. It was a heavy price which she had to pay for her internal dissensions.

CAUSES OF THE RISE OF NATIONALISM IN INDIA

The national feeling began to grow in India during the second half of the nineteenth century. It was not the result of a single factor. It was the product of a number of factors operating during the period extending over several decades.

The history of Indian nationalism suggests three well marked phases according to Dr. Raghuwansi. They are as:

(a) The first is the period of ascendancy of liberalism lasting till the stormy regime of Lord Nathaniel Curzon. This period witnessed the growth of nationalist agitation on constitutional lines.

Political agitation during this period lacked vigour and effectness and was exclusively an upper middle class agitation. The spirit of nationalism was especially marked in Bengal, Bombay and Madras.

(b) In this phase nationalism acquired a more dynamic and threatening character. There was reaction against westernisation, which was intensified by economic factors. The Swadeshi and Boycott movements following the partition of Bengal in 1905, produced a tremendous on vulsion of patriotic spirit. Revolutionary methods also came into play.

(c) In the final phase, the Gandhian epoch (1920-1947) Indias nationalism acquired greater vitality and adaptability. The World War I turned the scales against liberalism for ever and prepared the ground for the bloodless victories of Gandhism. In 1920-22 was launched the non-co-operation movement for the redress of Punjab and Khilafat wrongs. Simon Commission came in 1927. Civil Disobedience Movement in 1930-34 advanced the cause of freedom through the three Round Table conferences.

The most important factors which contributed to the growth of national feeling were the following:

(a) **Contact with the West.** The establishment of British rule brought the Indians in intimate contact with the West. Nineteenth century in Europe was the century of nationalism and the educated Indians imbibed these ideas. Italy and Germany achieved national freedom in the second half of the ninteenth century. This gave encouragement to the educated Indians to achieve freedom and become a free nation.

(b) **Improved Means of Communication.** The means of communication also began to improve about the middle of the nineteenth century. Grand Trunk Road was completed and railways were introduced in the time of Lord Dalhousie. The improved means of communication enabled people of the different parts of the country to come in intimate contact with one another. It created a feeling of oneness among them. The Indian leaders could easily move to different parts of the country, come in contact with one another and address the people.

(c) **Spread of the English Language.** India is a vast country and its people speak different languages. Hence it was difficult for the people of different parts of the country to understand one another. The British rule in India led to the introduction of the English language. Many people began to study this langauge in different parts of the country. English language enabled the educated persons of different provinces to understand one another. It became the lingua franca of the educated class in India and enable the educated people of different parts to communicate their thoughts with one another. It made them feel that they were one.

(d) **Conquest of India by the British.** The Indians had not enjoyed long periods of political unity before the coming of the British. Even when it was achieved under rulers like Ala-ud-Din it was shortlived. The British conquered the whole of India and kept it under control for a long time. It enabled people to think in terms of the unity of the country. British Imperialism made the people of the whole of India feel that they were one. Submission to one foreign authority helped in the development of the feeling of nationalism among the Indians.

(e) **Contribution of Scholars and Reformers.** Many scholars carried out researches into the history and culture of ancient India. Some of them were Max Muller, Monier, Williams, Colebrooke, Ranade, R.G. Bhandarkar. Their writings revealed the greatness achieved by the Indians in the past. It created among the people of India feeling of pride in the past and a faith in the future.

The religious and social reformers like Raja Ram Mohan Roy, Devendra Nath Tagore, Ishwar Chandra Vidyasagar, Swami Dayanand, Ramakrishna Paramhansa, Vivekanand presented a glorious picture of India's past and appealed to the people to revive those good old days. Col. Olcott was of the opinion that Swami dayanand exercised "great nationalising influene upon his followers". Swami Vivekanand also inspired self-confidence among the Indians. the Queen of his adoration was Mother India. Mrs. Annie Besant also helped the cause of India in nationalism by her writings.

(f) **Discontent of the Indians.** Before the outbreak of the Mutiny in 1857, there were many Englishmen who worked for the good of India. There was a lot of bloodshed on both sides during the Mutiny. The Europeans wreaked vengeance afterwards. The policy of repression created discontent in the country. The Europeans began to behave arrogantly towards the Indians. The Indians had to make way for the Europeans even in the railway compartments. The latter were tried by European judges and were either let off free or were given very mild punishments. The Europeans believd that the life of European was worth the lives of many Indians. They further believed that the Indians understood only fear and nothing else Such an attitude of the Euroepeans made the Indians discontented.

(g) **Contribution of Indian Press.** The Indian Press, English as well as Vernacular, aroused national consciousness among the people of India. Newspapers like ' The Indian Mirror'. Bombay Samachar'. ' The Amrit Bazar Patrika, ' The Hindu Patriot', 'The Bengalee', ' The Kesari', ' The Hindu', had strong nationalist tone and diffused ideas of nationalism among the people.

Many literary figures also contributed to the growth of nationalism. The writings of Din Bandhu Mitra, R.C. Dutt, Hem Chandra Banerjee, Bankim Chandra Chatterjee and Rabindra Nath Tagore also made people national minded.

(h) **Anti-Indian Policy of Lord Lytton.** Lord Lytton followed an anti-Indian policy. He held the famous Delhi Durbar in

1877 when several parts of India were in the grip of a terrible famine. It was even remakred. "Nero was fidding while Rome was burning." The unjust Second Afghan War was costing the Inidan treasury good deal. The Indian Press bitterly criticised this policy and Lord Lytton passed the Vernacular Press Act in 1878 to stop this criticism. It placed restrictions on the Vernacular Press, and not on the newspapers published in English. The Indian Arms Act was passed in 1878. The Indians had to get licence to keep arms but no such licence was needed for the Europeans. This Act made invidious distinction between the Indians and the Europeans. It imposed a badge of racial inferiority on the Indians. All these measures were resented by the people of India and contributed to the rise of national movement.

(i) **Ilbert Bill Controversy.** Lord Ripon tried to remove some of the grievances of the Indians but, before he could do that, the famous Ilbert Bill controversy started. This Bill aimed at giving authority to the Indian Judges to try the Europens even in non-presidency towns. The Anglo Indians and the European raised great hue and cry against this. A compromise was at last made. It was agreed that a European could claim trial by a jury consisting of at least half the Europeans and Americans, if his case was before an Indian judge. The Indians had already formed national organisations of provincial character in some provinces. Now they felt the need of having an all-India national organisation. Such an assoication called Indian National Congress was founded by A.O. Hume, a retired British civilian officer, in 1885.

(j) **Indian Press and Literature.** The Indian press (Hindi and English) gave a fillip to national consciousness. There was the Anglo-Indian press also which was anti-nationalist. The Indian press was critical of government measures. It advocated racial equality and wanted the government of the country to be managed by the Indians themselves.

The shortage of national platform was supplied by the Press. It awakened the educated classes and inclucated in them patriotic sentiments and national consciousness. In this context, popular literature was developed in the Indian languages, especially in Bengali. Bankim Chandra's "Anand Math" is the Bible of modern Bengali patriotism. 'Bande Mataram' song first appeared in this book.

(k) **Bad Economic Condition.** The economic condition of the Indians was very bad. The English education was becoming widespread and many educated Indians were unemployed. The Indians felt that the British were exploiting their country and that was the cuase of the poverty of India. According to Blunt, the Finance Minister of India looked more to the interests of Great Britian that to those of India. The free trade policy of the Government of India stood in the way of the development of the country. Bad economic condition caused discontent with the British rule and helped in the development of national feeling.

(l) **Durbars and Improvement of Communications.** In 1877, an imperial Durbar was held. It gave national leaders and workers the idea of holding all-India conferences and also of organising national institutions on an all-India basis. The Indian leaders had not so far visualised and realised the need and importance of the Indian leaders from all corners of the country collecting together. Thus the holding of Durbars turned out to be truly a blessing in disguise.

RISE OF MUSLIMS CONTRIBUTION

The British were alarmed to see the wide spreading influence of the congress and therefore, tried to create rift between the Hindus and the Muslims. They created a section of Muslims who regarded the congress as an institution of the Hindus and demanded the founding of a separate institution for Muslims. Being influenced by Mr. Beak, the Principal of the Mohammadan Anglo Oriental College, Aligarh, Sir Sayed Ahmed Khan founded Annual Muslims Education

Conference in 1886, and Mohammadan Defence Association in 1893. Apparently these institutions aimed to protect the interest of the Muslims but in fact their real aim was to check the Muslims from joining the congress. In the course of time, the Muslims sent a deputation to meet the contempory Viceroy Lord Minto in order to have separte electoarte for the Muslims.

It is unfortunate that the Muslims as a community were in different to the congress movement. Some Muslims leaders it is true, attended the congress and a few of them were elected Presidents but as a class they held aloof. Several factors were at work which determined their attitude towards the Congress and a separatist term to their politics:

Decline the Position of the Muslims. The Muslims were heavily depressed by the consolidation of the British rule in Northern India. It was a great blow to their pride and self respect to find themselves Ousted from all positions of power and authority. The last vestige of their influence in administration was gone when Vernacular was substituted for Persian as the Court language. The ardent spirits among them broaded over the past in sullen resentment. They hated British rule and western culture and were in term evoled upon with suspicion by the Government. Hence they supported Wahabi Revivalism which was definility anti-British and took a prominent part and the great uppeanal of 1857, in the hope of restoring the fallen fortunes of their community.

Indifference to English Education. Muslims orthodox had turned its back on English education as un-Islamic. Hence the Muslims failed to share in the intellectual renaissance brought about by western thought and science and conveyed through the English language. As a consequence all avenues of preferment thrown open by English education were closed to them. The Hindus our the other hand forged a head and by their progressive trends began to outstrip the Muslims in every walk of life. This heightened their sense of frustation and the Muslims began to think that the Hindus had stolen a march upon them.

Work of Sir Sayed Ahmed Khan. The man who did most the raise the Muslims Community from the slough despair and depression was Sir Sayed Ahmed Khan. His father held an office of rank in the Mughal Court and he joined the service of the company as a judical officer in the subordinate capacity. He clearly realised that if the Muslims were to retcive their lost positon they must have English education and win the support of the British Government. So he set to himself to wool the British and to persuade his co-religiourists to reconsider their attitude towards English Education. In 1875 he founded the Muhammadan Anglo Oriental College at Aligarh. This was his greatest service to his community. His college not only promoted higher education among the Muslims but fastered a spirit of solidarity by giving them a common ideology.

Aligarh Movement. The Principal of the M.A.O. College gave to the institution a distinctly communal tern and a missionary spirit. Hence forth the Aligarhman became the symbol of Muslim solidarity and the spear head of the Muslim movement everywhere in India. Sir Sayed kept aloof from the Congress and did his best to wean away his fellow-Muslims from the National Movement. He did so not from any unpatriotic motive. He felft that the Congress demand for representative government would injure the interest of the muslims who in India formed a small minority. In 1883 he declared in the Governor Generals Council that the "System of election, pure and simple can not safely be adopted. The larger commonity would totally overside the interest of the smaller community". Sir Sayaed thought that the intersts of the community would be better served by co-operation with the British Government than by opposition to it. Hence he courted the support of the British authorities as rival organisation to the Congress. All these proved short lived but they indicated the lines along which the awakening of the Muslims was to develop. The fear of majority rule first expressed by Sir Sayad Ahmed Khan was echoed half century later by Mr. M.A. Jinnah who became about what he called the brute majority of the Congress.

The Muslim League. The communal bent given to the Muslim politics by Sir Sayed and Principal Beek was sedulously nursed by the

British authorities. The technique of British rule in India was to incourage the fissiparous tendencies arising from religion and provincialism. The British Government wanted to utilise Muslim Communalism as a Counter poise to the growing Indian Nationalism which was largely the product of Hindu nationalism. Hence in 1906 some of the high British officials engineered a Muslim deputation to the Viceroy, Lord Minto, to promote the cause of Muslim separalism. It made a strong claim for communal representation with which the Viceroy expressed complete sympathy. The members of the deputation were entertained by the Viceroy at a garden party at Simla and he wrote about the day as 'very eventful day and an eopoch in Indian history." A high official sent a congratulatory message to the Veceroy saying "that a very very big thing has happened ... it is nothing less than the pulling back of sixty two millions of people from joining the ranks of the seditions opposition.

CONTRIBUTION MADE BY DADA BHAI NAUROJI

Dada Bhai Nauroji affectionately known as the Grand Old man of India served India for 61 long years. He was permanently settled in English and was elected a member of the House of Commons. For some time, he was the Prime Minister of Baroda. He founded the British Indian Society in England to carry on propaganda in favour of India.

He was elected the President of the Congress thrice viz in 1886, 1893 and 1906. He took the opportunity to exhort the British "not to drive this force (the educated Indians) into opposition instead of drawing it to your own side." He hoped that "our faith in the instinctive love of justice and fair play of the United Kingdom is not misplaced."

He was elected the President of the Congress in 1906 as the moderates felt that he was the only person who was not likely to be opposed by the Extremists. At that time there was a lot excitement in the country. The anti partition agitation was going on in Bengal. Swadeshi and Boycott were in the air. Even in 1906 Dada Bhai Nauroji had not given up his faith in the justice of the Englishmen.

However, it cannot be denied that the credit of demanding Swaraj from the Congress platform for the first time goes to Dada Bhai Nauroji. Swaraj was the key note of his presidential address at the Calcutta Session. To quote him, "we do not ask for favours, we want ony justice. Instead of going into any further divisions or details of our rights as British citizens the whole matter can be comprised in one word—self government or Swaraj like that of the United Kingdom or colonies." It was under his Presidentship in 1906 that four resolutions on self-government, boycott movement. Swadeshi and national education were passed by the Congress.

Dadabhai Nauroji was the first Indian politician to draw the attention of the people to the drain of India's wealt to Great Britain as a result of the British rule in India. He gave his views in the famous book entitled, "Poverty and the British rule in India". Dadabhai Nauroji wrote this to J.D. Sunderland in 1905. "The lot of India is a very sad one. Her condition is that of a master and slave; but it is worse ; it is that of a plundered nation in the hands of constant plunders with the plunder carried away clean out of the land."

The name of Dadabhai Nauroji comes first in the list of Indian patriarchs who beginning his connection with the Congress from its very out set, continued to serve it till the evening of his life. Dada Bhai lived and labored and has left behind him not only the noble example of a dedicated life but also in flesh and blood his grand daughters who are maintaining the noble traditions created by him. According to C.Y. Chintamani. "For 61 long years in England and India by day and by night in circusmtances favourable and adverce in the face of discouragement which would have broke the heart of a smaller man, Dadabhai Nauroji served the Motherland with undeviating purpose, with complete selflessness and with vitality of faith which put to shame most young man. Withall, he was the greatest of souls and the most charitable in judgement and never made a personal enemy. In respect equally of the highest personal character and the greatest public services. Dadabhai Nauroji was of the leftist ideal his countrymen could set before themselves respectively to follow at a distance." Again, "The public life of India had been adorned by a galaxy of brilliant intellects and selfless patriots, but there has been in our time none comparable with Dadabhai Nauroji". According to Gokhle, "If ever there is the divine in man, it is in Dadabhai Nauroji."

CONTRIBUTION OF A.O. HUME

The Congress was founded by A.O. Hume, a retired British civilian officer, in 1885. It is said that the first idea of Hume was to have a body to discuss social matters of the country. He changed his original idea at the suggestion of Lord Dufferin. The idea in founding the Congress was to have an organisation which was to perform the same functions which Her Majesty's Opposition performed in England. Lord Dufferin wanted that this body should meet every year and point out to the government its shortcomings. The Congress was to act as a safety value for popular discontent. It was to provide a peaceful and constitutional channel for the expression of Indian unrest so that it might not drift towards terrorism. The aim of Hume was not to save British Empire from disruption. His object was to provide the Indians with an organisation which would make them fit for liberty and self-government in the long run.

The first period of the development of Indian National Congress extends from 1885 to 1905. It was the period of moderate nationalism. The Congress was not a revolutionary body during this period. Its leaders declared loyalty to the British Government several times. Its leaders during this period believed that the British Government would do justice and redress their grievances. They spurned the idea of agitation and unconstitutional means. They carried on their work by debates, propaganda petitions and deputations. They adhered to the policy of appeals. Their methods have been described as political mendicancy.

The attitude of the Government towards the Congress was friendly in the beginning. Lord Dufferin gave a party to the delegates of the second session of the Congress. The Governor of Madras entertained the third session of the Congress. The attitude of the Government changed after a short time. Lord Dufferin condemned the Congress in 1888 and called it "microscopic minority" of educated

Indians. A circular of 1890 forbade Government employees from attending the mettings of the Congress. The Congress was gradually adopting a policy of criticism.

The first session of the Congress was held at Bombay under the Presidentship of W.C. Bannerji, a leading barrister of Calcutta. The most important delegates were Pherozshah Metha, Dadabhai Nauroji, Dinshaw Wacha and K.T. Tilang. It was attended by people from different parts of the country.

The second session was held in Calcutta in 1886 and its members were entertained at a garden party by Lord Dufferin. The third session was held at Madras in 1887 and the members were entertained by the Governor of Madras.

The friendly attitude of the government changed after this because the Congress leaders started a strong propaganda among the masses. Hume, in a pamphlet, appealed to the prosperous people of England not to forget the starving Indians. He made arrangements for carrying on propaganda through the Press in England. He was able even to enlist the support of a few members of the British Parliament.

The Congress of 1888 was held at Allahabad and the site for the holding of the Congress session was purchased by the Maharajadhiraj of Darbhanga. The Congress session of 1889 was held at Bombay and was attended by Charles Bradlaugh, a Member of Parliament. The Congress wanted the government to introduce further reforms. It was partly due to the agitation carried on by the Congress that the Indian Councils Act of 1892 was passed.

Dadabhai Nauroji, a member of the House of Commons, was the President of the Lahore session of the Congress in 1893. He was heartily welcomed by the people on his way from Bombay to Madras. He brought a message of co-operation and encouragement from the Irish Members of Parliament. The Congress session of 1894 held at Madras was presided over by Alfred Webb, an Irish Member of Parliament. Surendra Nath Bannerjee presided over the Poona session of the Congress in 1895. Gopal Krishna Gokhale presided over the

Barnaras session of the Congress held in 1905. The session of 1906 held at Calcutta was presided over by Dadabhai Nauroji and he unfurled the Swarajya flag.

GOPAL KRISHNA GOKHLE AND HIS POLITICAL THOUGHTS

Gopal Krishna Gokhle was born at Kolahpur in 1866. He possessed remarkable qualities of head and heart and rose rapidly in life. He became a graduate at 18, a professor at 20 a member of the Bombay Legislative Council at 22 and President of the Indian National Congress at 39. He had an enormous capacity for hard work. His knowledge was vast, varied and exact. He was a master of direct expression and lucid exposition.

He started his life as a teacher, as a follower of Justice Ranade, Dr. Zacharias rightly points out that never had a Guru a more apt pupil than Ranade in Gokhle. He imbibed the spirit of the master and never wavered from the path of moderation and sweet reasonableness as laid down by Ranade. He joined the Deccan Education Society and very soon he became the principal of the Fergusson College. He became the editor of the Quarterly Journal of the Poona Sarvajanik Sabha in 1887. Later on be became the Honrary Secretary of the Decrran Sabha. In 1897, he went to England to give evidence before the Welby Commission on Indian expenditure. He attacked salt tax as levied in India on account of the suffering which was caused to the poor people. He criticised the policy of the Government in excluding the Indians from the higher jobs in the country. He condemned the partition of Bengal and bitterly observed thus :

"Then all I can say goodbye to all hope of co-operating in any way which bureaucracy in the interest of the people." In 1905 he again went to England to do propoganda on behalf of India. He went to South Africa and helped Mahatma Gandhi in his work and no wonder it was on his suggestion that Mahatma Gandhi decided to come to India to start his public life in his country. In 1905, Gokhle founded the Servants of India Society for the purpose of training public workers pledged to work for the Motherland on a pittance and subject to rules of rigid discipline as well as loyalty to the Empire. In the preamble to the constitutions of the Society Gokhle wrote thus : A sufficient number of our countrymen must now come forward to devote themselves to the cause in the spirit in which religious work is undertaken. Love of the country must fill the heart that, all else shall appear as of little moment by its side."

Gokhle had always a soft corner in his heart for the "starving, strunken, shrivelled up ryot toiting and moiling from dawn to dark to earn his scanty meal, patient, resigned, forbearing beyond measure entirely voice less in the Parliament of his rulers and meekly prepared to bear what ever burdens God and man mignt be pleased to impose upon his back."

His Place in History. While the Extremists in India dubbed him as a "Fanit hearted Moderate" who was prepared to be a willing tool in the hands of the British Government, the reactionaries described him as a "seditionist in disguise". As a matter of fact, he was neither a revolutionary nor a reactionary. He hated both the extremes. He was a constructive statesman who understood and fought for the rights and liberties of the people of India. While he emphasised on the Government the necessity of understanding the point of view of the Indians, he requested the latter to move cautiously. It has rightly been pointed out that Gokhle interpreted popular aspirations to the Viceroy and the Government's difficulties to the Congress." The people disparaged his moderation and the Government deprecated his extremism. His role was that of a unifier and reconciler. His view was that while both Britain and India stood lose mutual jealousies and hatred, a lot could be gained by goodwill and healthy cooperation.

Gokhle attached great importance to the maintenance of law and order and was ready to grant the Government of India extra-ordinary powers to cope with the situation. Although the Indian Press Act, 1910 was a drastic step on the part of the Government of India and was condemned by the public opinion in the country.

If he asked the people of India to move slowly, he impressed upon the Government the necessity of following the progressive polity towards India. No wonder he moved Morley to grant immediately an instalment of reforms with a view to winning over a part of the people on the side of Government. The part played by Gokhle in the passage of Minto Morley Reforms is well known. He referred to the reforms at the Madras Session of the Indian National Congress as "a large and glorious concession" by the Government to the people of India. He held the view that the people were never interested in disorder and chaos. If they were driven to that path, there was always some cause of discontent. The wise course to adopt was no one of repression, but to analyse the situation and to remove the sources of trouble. "There is only one way in which the wings of disaffection can be clipped and that is by the Government pursuing a policy of steady and courageous conciliation." According to Hoyland, "He was a great master of the possible, a constructive Statesman of the first rank, a bringer together of East and West in the common service of the needy : above all an idealist, a farseer, a prophet of new era of inter-racial goodwill and cooperation." According to Tilak, "Gokhle was the diamond of India, the jewel of Maharashtra and the prince of workers". According to Mahatma Gandhi. "Sir Pherozeshah had seemed to me like the Himalayas unscalable, Lokmanya like the ocean one could not easily launch forth on the sea. But Gokhle was as the Ganges--it invited one to its bosom. In the sphere of politics that Gokhle occupied in my heart during his life time and occupies even now has been and is unique." According to Lala Lajpat Rai, "Gokhle was the noblest and the best of Congress workers and his patriotism was of the highest and noblest type.

LOKMANYA BAL GANGADHAR TILAK AND HIS CONTRIBUTION

Bal Gangadhar was born on 23rd July 1856 and he died in August 1920. He was born in a Brahmin family in Maharashtra. He was a staunch Hindu and was well versed in the Hindu scriptures, He took his law degree in 1879 and in collaboration with Agarkar started a school for giving cheap education to the people. The Poona New English School founded by them made wonderful progress with in a short time. He started 'Kesri' and the 'Maratha' in conjunction with other workers. He was also associated with the foundation of the Deccan Educational Society and the Fergussen College.

He started anti cow killing societies, akharas, lathi clubs with the objects of creating among the people of Maharashtra a mainly spirit so that they might be able to sacrifice themselves for the freedom of the country. He organised the Ganpati Festival and in doing so his purpose was to infuse among youngmen both religious and patriotic fervour. They were to learn to work together with courage, enthusiasm and discipline. The Ganpati Festival became more and more popular every year and it brought millions of Maharashtrians together on the same platform. Tilak also started the Shivaji Movement in 1895. His object was to inspire the youth of India to follow the example of Shivaji and release India from the political bondage of the foreigners. On the occasion of Shivaji Festival, there were lectures, fighting with lathis, processions, Kathas and singing parties About Afzalkhans murder by Sivaji Tilak observed thus, "With benevolent intention's Shivaji murdered Afzalkhan for the good of others. If thieves enter out house and we have not sufficient strength in our wrists to drive them out, we should without hesitation shut them up and burn the malive".

In 1897, Tilak arrested for sedition and sentenced to 18 months rigorous imprisonment by Judge Strachey. The Jury which tried him consisted of six Europeans and three Indians and all the Europeans found him guilty while all the Indians found him not guilty. In 1908 he was tried for sedition and sentenced to six years imprisonment. He was tried by a jury consisting of seven Europeans and two Indians. All the Europeans found him guilty and all the Indians found him not-guilty. Tilak had to spend six years of imiprisonment in Mandelay Jail in Burma from 1908-1914.

Tilak brought a suit against Sir Velentine Chirol for libel and personally went to England to conduct that case. The Government of India and the British bureaucracy whole, beartedly helped Chirol and no wonder suit was lost in 1919.

When the First World War started in 1914, he asked the people of India to help the British Government to the best of their ability.

When he did so he expected a reciprocal gesture from the British Government. Instead of any reciprocal gesture on the part of the Government, the authorities in India put all kinds of obstacles in the Home Rule Movement started by him. The workers were not allowed to hold their public meetings. The result was that Tilak began to criticise the Government openly. His definite stand was that unless the people of India were assured of Home Rule, they must not help the British Government in War.

National Language. Tilak was the first Congress Leader to suggest that Hindi written in Devenagri Script should be the national language of India. At a conference of the Nagri Pracharini Sabha held in December 1915 be declared that Devanagri should not only be the common script of the Aryan languages but also of the Script of the national language. Tilak was a research scholar of international fame. He managed to produce works on the antiquity of the Vedas. "The orient and the Arctic Home of the Vedas". Likewise his 'Gita' Rahasya which was written during his long imprisonment in Mandlay Jail is a monumental work and is rightly considered as his greatest contribution to philosophical thought. He demolished the old theory that a liberated soul had no obligation towards his fellow beings.

Philosophy of Defiance. He laught the philosophy of difiances to the people of India. He was born in an age which can be described as dark. The powerful impact of foreign rule had reduced the people to a state of utter helplessness. The failure of the Indian mutiny had broken the will of the people to resist the British Raj. It is true that the Indian National Congress was founded in 1885 but the British Government did not take it seriously. It was regarded as something harmless and mildly liberal. It passed resolutions of loyalty to the crown and prayed for the safety and prosperity of the British Empire. The moderates pointed out the defects in the system of British administration in India but they were always afraid of challenging the British authority. The result was that their eloquent and fiery speches left the British rulers cold. They knew that their fire did not burn and their flourishing swords had no edge to them.

Tilak believed that the policy of the Congress must be changed. The Congress must learn to defy authority. It must be ready to sacrifice for the sake of winning freedom for the country. He did not want the people to be violent for the realisation of India's freedom but if India could not be free by peaceful means, there was no harm in using violence as well. He advocated the programme of Swadeshi and boycoll of foreign goods. He did not want the Congress to fight for small gains. He wanted to fight for the ideal of independence of the country. He started the National Party to change the programme of the Congress. The moderates had their way up to 1914 but they could not stand against him. He carried the day. He converted the Congress from the admirers of the British Government into rebels against the British Empire. It has rightly been pointed out that Mahatma Gandhi and Pt. Jawahar Lal were able to rear the grand edifice of Swaraj on the foundation of Lokmanya Tilak. There was fire in the speeches of Tilak. He was fearless in what he said. He did not care for the consequences. He was regarded as the most dangerous man by the British Government. He has been called the father of Indian unrest. The Governor of Bombay wrote thus to the Secretary of State for India in 1908 : "He (Tilak) is one of the chief conspirator peshaps the chief conspirator against the existence of the British Government in India, all the weak points of which he has made a careful study. His Ganpati Festivals, Shivaji celebrations Paisa Fund and National Schools were all instituted for one purpose, the overthrow of British Rule." He forestalled, Gandhi in the movements that the Mahatma launched after Tilak's death, no rent campaign, boycott of Government service, prohibitions, Swadeshi were all preached and practised by him. "He talked of complete independence as back as 1897. Swaraj is my birth right and I shall take it was his new slogan which infused life in the youngmen of India. His was the life divine and his countrymen elevated him not only to the position of Lokmanya but adored him as Tilak Bhagwan. In the encircling gloom, he appeared with a torch in his hand." He was regarded as great as Shivaji. During the disturbances in Bombay in 1908 a medal was struck having the effigy of Shivaji on one side and that of Tilak on the other. The names of Shivaji and Tilak were frequently coupled together and the latter came to be known as the man who is to expel the British from India. According to Swami Sharidha Nand. "Maharaj Tilak occupies an exalted position among the pioneers of political work who were the first to preach the doctrine of political unity. What other hero has suffered so much in the service of the motherland as this illustrious person has done.

Comparison of Tilak and Gokhle. Dr. Pattabhi Sita Ramayya the famous author of the "History of the Indian National Congress" has attempted a comparison of Tilak and Gokhle in these words : "Tilak and Gokhle were both patriots of the first order. Both had made heavy sacrifices in life. But their temperaments were widely different from each other. Gokhle was a moderate and Tilak was an extremist. Gokhle's aim was to improve the existing constitution Tilak was to reconstruct it. Gokhle had necessarily to fight it Gokhle stood for cooperation wherever possible and opposition wherever necessary. Tilak was inclined towards a policy of obstruction, Gokhle's primary concern was with the administration and its improvement, Tilak's supreme concern was the nation and its up building, Gokhle's ideal was love and sacrifice, Tilak's was service and suffering, Gokhle's method sought to win the foreigner, Tilak's to replace him."

CONTRIBUTION RAJA GOPALACHERI

Lord Mountbetten was succeeded by C. Rajagopalachari as the first and last Indian Government-General of India. The most important event of his time was the police action in Hyderabad.

Police Action in Hyderabad. Encouraged by the Nizam, the Razakars under the leadership of an Orthodox Muslim named Oasim Rizvi had created terror in Hyderabad. The Government of India was therefore, compelled to take police action against Hyderabad. On December 23, 1947 and within five days Qasim Rizvi and his Junta were defeated and Hyderabad became a part of the Indian Union.

Trial of Nathu Ram Godse. Another event during the Governor-Generalship of C. Rajagopalachari Nathu Ram Vinayak Godse and

Apte were sentenced to death and some other accused were banished from the country on account of the murder of Mahatma Gandhi.

Merger of the Indian States in the Indian Union. The gradual merger of the native states also continued during this period Matsaya Union and Rajasthan were joined to constitute the province of Rajasthan. Likewise Kolahpur, Sirohi and Baroda were included in Bombay and Sandur was included in the Province of Madras. Tehri and Garhwal, Banaras and Rampur were included it the province of Uttar Pradesh. The Indian Government took up the administration of Bhopal into their hands. Tripura and Manipur were also merged with the Indian Union and were placed under chief Commissioners.

The problem of the merger of Junagarh presented some difficulty. The state of Junagarh (in Kathiawar) was ruled by a Muslim ruler although the Hindus were in majority in that state. The nawab of the state wanted to merge his state with Pakistan. The people of Junagarh protested against the decision of the Nawab of Junagarh. There disturbances in the state. The Nawab fled away to Pakistan and the Dewan requested the Government of India for help to establish peace in Junagarh. Indian Military was sent there to establish peace. Thereafter, a refrendum was hold to know the opinion of the people as to whether they wanted to merge with India or Pakistan. About 99% of the people voted in favour of their merger with India thus Junagarh also became a part of the Indian Union.

Attempts to Improve Finances of India. The financial condition of the country was very critical at this time. The Government of India sent a delegation to London to make an agreement with the British Government. A three year agreement was made. The British military property was estimated at 133 crores and this sum was paid off. The expenditure of the Indian Government had considerably gone up and new means of income were not tackled. It created a situation financial crisis. The Government was compelled to increase paper currency. It had adverse repercussions. The prices of the commodities went up high and the sufferings of the common man increased. A conference of economists, representatives of employees of the banks and the representatives of the Government was held at

New Delhi. It was decided to reduce the expenditure of the Government as much as possible. The Development Plans of the centre and the states should be checked and the unnecessary ones should be dropped or postponed. Death duty or estate duty was imposed.

Labour Welfare. In order to improve the conditions of the labourers Factory Act was passed. Labour Welfare Officers were to be appointed in the establishments where more than 500 worker worked. Minimum Wages Act, Employees State Insurance Act etc. were also passed. The policy of nationalisation was announced in order to encourage the trade and commerce in India and to improve the industrial condition of India. In order to encourage the cottage industries Central Emporium was organised and Industrial Finance Corporation and state organisations were established.

Relations between India and Pakistan. The relations between India and Pakistan had further deteriorated and the problem of kashmir had made the situation all the more serious. The commission sent by the United Nations failed to create friendship and good will between the two nations. The War in Kashmir was stopped on the mid night of January, 1949. The portion of Kashmir which was under the occupation of the army of Pakistan remained under his occupation while the area under the occupations of Indian army remained under the occupations of India. Both the nations slowly and gradually with drew their armies. After the cease fire treaty, a conference of the representatives of the two countries was held and an agreement regarding the evacuce property of the refugees was made.

The constitution of India came into force from January 26, 1950 and from that day India became a Sovereign Democratic Republic. Consequently C. Rajagopalachari had to resign from his post and in his place Dr. Rajendra Prasad was elected as the First President of Indian Republic.

CONTRIBUTION OF DR. RAJENDRA PRASAD

Dr. Rajendra Prasad was elected as the first President of the Republic of the India. He remained on this post from 1950 to 1962.

He was true follower of Mahatma Gandhi and won the good will of all by his nobility and simplicity. He was lovingly called Ajat Shatru *i.e.*, a person who has no enemy. Pt. Jawahar Lal Nehru was the Prime Minister of India during his presidentship.

Progress of India. India made a lot of progress during his presidentship. In order to improve the social and economic conditions of India Five Year Plans were launched in India. The two Five Year Plans were completed and the Third Five Year Plan was started. Under the impact of these economic plans India made great progress in the fields of agriculture and industry. But the shortage of foreign exchange created many serious problems for the Government of India. Inspite of all the difficulties India made a remarkable progress in different fields. New dams, factories, Research institutes, universities, Medical and engineering colleges, etc. were opened. The railways were reorganised.

Policy of Non Allignment. Indian's policy of non-allignment evolved under the able guidence of Pt. Jawahar Lal Nehru. In the Pacific Relations Conference which was held on October 3, 1950 India declared that she will always follow the policy of non allignment, India vigorously followed this policy of non-allignment and joined neither the Anglo American bloc nor the Communits bloc. This policy aimed not only to avoid joining either of the blocs but also to maintain friendly relations with all states. Sometimes Indias policy of non-allignment led to misunderstanding and often this policy put India in very acokward position. However, India continued to follow this policy by and by her role began to be appreciated. This policy enhanced the prestige of India in the eyes of the world.

Other Events. India Pakistan goodwill conference and India Afghanistan Peace Treaty are other important events of his time. India entered into commercial and cultural relations with many prominent countries of the world. U.S.S.R., U.S.A., Canada, Britain and West Germany actively participated in the development of the industries in our country. Bhilai, Durgapur and Rourkela steel plants set up by Russia, U.K. and West Germany respectively are the fine examples of India's friendship with these countries and their participation in India's economic devlopment India gave the proof of her non-alligned policy in respect of Korea, Tibet etc. India sent a medical mission to Korea on the request of the United Nations. She also played a prominent part in solving the Korean problem. When China attacked Tibet and entered Lhasa in November 1950, the Government of India protested against this and gave shelter to Dalai Lama and thousands of Tibetan refugees. In June 1953 Pt. Nehru went to England to participate in the coronation celeberation of Queen Elizabeth. Pt. Nehru also visited America, U.S.S.R., China, Japan, Germany and other countries in order to develop amicable and better friendly relations with these countries and clarified the foreign policy of India.

CONTRIBUTION OF DR. S. RADHA KRISHNAN

Dr. S Radha Krishnan was elected as the Second President of the Indian Republic in May 1962. He had been the Vice President of India from 1950 to 1962. He was an eminent educationist philosopher and teacher. Pt Jawahar Lal continued to be the Prime Minister of India. Hence the same foreign policy continued and no significant change was made in it.

The War with China. Inspite of India's best efforts to maintain friendly relations with China, the latter continued to extend her frontiers at the cost of India. The Government of India sent many protests but with no effect and ultimately China attacked India on 20th October 1962. There was a remarkable awakening among the citizens of India who forgot their mutual dissenssions and differences in this hour of emergency. However, India was not prepared to face the attack of China and Indian armies were defeatd on all fronts. But for the help received from the friendly countries India would have been in a very precarious position. The help of the friendly countries particularly of America and Britain enabled India to make a stand and China finally made a unilateral declaration of cease fire.

Death of Pt. Jawahar Lal Nehru. Pt Jawahar Lal Nehru died in 1964 and was succeeded by Shri Lal Bahadur Shastri as the Prime

Minister of India. The main event of the Prime Ministership of Lal Bahadur Shastri was the attack of Pakistan.

Pakistan Invasion 1965. Pakistan attacked India all of a sudden in 1965 and achieved some successes in the early stage of the War. But ultimately the Indian armies not only repulsed the Pakistani attack but were also able to occupy a good bit of Pakistani territory. On account of the good officers of Soviet Union, a cease fire was arranged Tashkent. Declarion was made where in both the countries agreed to live in peace. Despite the said agreement, the relations between the two countries have not improved and tension still continues.

Devaluation of Indian Rupee. The financial condition of India was very critical at this time. The devaluation of Indian rupee had to be made in order to give stability to Indian currency and to bring it at part with international standard. The strikes lockouts layoffs further created difficulties. The prices of essential commodities soard. There was a severe famine in Bihar on account of the failure of rains. the conditions created all round discontent among the people. Third General elections were held in the country at this time. The economic discontant had its repurcussions on the election results. The Congress suffered heavily.

CONTRIBUTION OF DR. ZAKER HUSAIN (1967-69)

In the Third General Election, the majority of the Congress was greatly reduced. This led to a serious contests for the office of Presidency of India. The main contestants for the post were Dr. Zaker Husain the Congress nominee and Chief Justice V. Subha Rao who resigned his chief justiceship of India to fight the election Subha Rao had the support of all the other parties. Zaker Husain was, however elected as the Third President of the Indian Republic. Mrs. Indra Gandhi the daughter of late Pt. Jawahar Lal Nehru was appointed the Prime Minister of India after the death of Lal Bahadur Shastri. The country was passing through difficult times. On account of the failure of the rains severe famine prevailed in Bihar, Rajasthan and some other parts of the country. Relief was provided to the people of the famine stricken areas. A good deal of money was spent by the centre as well as the states to improve the lot of the people. The Government took a lesson from the famine and gave top priority to agriculture. The efforts of Government hial fruits and in the next agricultural season *i.e.*, 1967-68 there was a bumber crop.

It is now agreed that India has now made a headway in the field of agriculture and industry. Now she is self-sufficient in the matter of food grains'. The non-congress Governments which were formed in several states could not continue for a long time. In as mady as five states Presidents rule had to be declared. Legislative Assemblies were dissolved and mid-term elections were ordered. Dr. Zaker Husain died in May, 1969 without completing his five year term of Presidentship.

GROWTH OF NATIONAL MOVEMENT IN INDIA FROM 1918 TO 1928

The Indians had given whole hearted support to the British Govenrment during the First World War. They had helped in war effort with men and money. They had to suffer due to high prices, low wages, shortage of supplies, plague and influenza, the Liberty of the people had been curtailed under the Defence of India Rules. In return for all this, the British Government Announced Montague-Chelmsford Report in 1918 which was to form the basis of the forth coming reforms. It greatly disappointed the Indians, Mrs. Annie Besant declared that the scheme was "ungenerous for England to offere and unworthy for India to accept."

When such were the general feelings of the people the Government of India passed the infamous Rowlatt Act in 1918. The Act provided for the speedy trial of offences without any right of appeal. A special court consisting of three Judges of a High Court was to be set up and it could meet at any place in camera. It was authorised to admit evidence which, was otherwise not admissible under the Indian Evidence Act. Unanimity was required for passing death sentence but ordinary decisions could be taken by the majority vote of the judges. The Provincial Government could ask a person to furnish security or notify his residence or reside in a particular area or to report himself to the police. The Act provided for search of a place and the arrest of a suspected person without warrant.

The Congress under the leadership of Mahatma Gandhi decided to start Satyagraha. He declared 30th March, 1919, the day of hartal all over India. The date was later on charged to 6th of April. The hartal was observed at many places on both days. There were clashes between the people and the police at Delhi. Mahatma Gandhi decided to see the situation himself but was arrested at Palwal railway station and sent back to Bombay.

There was trouble in the Punjab. Hartal was observed on 30th of March and 6th of April at many places. The Government of the Punjab passed orders for the deportation of Dr. Satya Pal and Dr. Kitchlew to Dharamsala on 9th of April. This led to a hartal in the city. Many unarmed people marched to the residence of the Deputy Commissioner to demand their release. They were checked on the way and fired at by the police. The infuriated mob started arson and assault on the Europeans. The troops were called out and the mob dispersed.

General Dyer issued a proclamation that no meetings were to be held but no steps were taken to bring it to the notice of the general public. An announcement was made by the the leaders of the public that a meeting would be held on 13th of April, the Baisakhi Day, at 4.30 p.m. in the Jallianwala Bagh. General Dyer and the authorities took no action to stop the meeting at the right time and it was attended by people numbering between 6,000 and 10,000. The garden was practically closed on all sides except one entrance. General Dyer came through the entrance with armoured cars and troops. One thousand, six hundred and fifty rounds were fired, as a result of which 379 people were killed and 2000 were wounded. Miss Sherwood, a lady doctor, was assaulted in a street but was saved by some people. Even then all the people passing through that street were made to crawl on the ground. The conveyances of the Indians were requisitioned for the use of the Europeans. Water and electric supply were cut off. Flogging was common. The administration of

Martial Law was even more rigid at Lahore. Private conveyances were taken for the use of the Europeans. Shopkeepers were made to open shops. Severe penalties were prescribed for the defecing and removal of Martial Law notice. Stern steps were taken at Gujranwala, Kasur and Sheikhupura.

Mahatma Gandhi called off the Satyagraha because there were clashes between the people and the Police at Delhi and a few other places. Later on he had to admit that he made a Himalayan miscalculation.

NON-CO-OPERATION MOVEMENT

The next important step in the development of the National Movement was the starting of Non-Co-operation Movement by the Congress under the leadership of Mahatma Gandhi. It was a revolutionary step because the Congress for the first time decided to follow a policy of direct action. Several factors were responsible for this change. Firstly, Mahatma Gandhi had lost faith in the good sense of the English due to Jallianwala Bagh tragedy, Martial Law in the Punjab and the Report of the Hunter Committee. He felt that the old methods must be given up. Secondly, the Liberals had withdrawn from the Congress over the question of the acceptance of the Reforms of 1919 and the Extremists were in control of the Congress.

Thirdly, the Indian Muslims resented the harsh terms imposed by the treaty of seves on Turkey. They were further irritated by the fact that the British Government was doing nothing for the preservation of the office of the Khalifa. They started Khilafat Movement to agitate for the preservation of the religious office of the Khalifat. Mahatma Gandhi thought that Hindu-Muslim unity could be achieved by taking up the cause of Khilafat.

A special session of the Congress was held at Calcutta in September 1920 under the Presidentship of Lala Lajpat Rai. The Non-Co-operation Resolution moved by Mahatma Gandhi was carried by a majority of 1885 against 1873. It clearly started the programme of non-co-operation. Titles were to be surrendered. Non-co-operators were to resign from honourary offices and nominated posts. They were not to attend Government functions and were to windraw their children gradually from schools and colleges. Law courts were to be boycotted and private arbitrations courts were to be set up. They were neither to contest the election nor to vote. Swadeshi cloth was to be used.

Non-Co-operation Movement became widespread. Many Hindus and Muslims joined it. Foreign goods were burnt. Many students left schools and colleges, and national institution like Kashi Vidyapith and Jamia Millia were started. About 20,000 Charkhas were manufactured. Many surrendered their titles. Hartals were observed in Bombay and Calcutta when Prince of Wales visited these places in 1921.

Non-Co-operators were mercilessly beaten and their meetings were dispersed with force. All Congress leaders except Gandhi were imprisoned. He was not arrested because the Government feared trouble from his arrest. About 25,000 persons were not behind the bars. Mahatma Gandhi now decided to sart mass Civil Disobedience Movement and gave seven days' notice to the Governor-General. It could be postponed only if all non-violent non co-operators were released and the Government announced the absolute non-interference with all non-violent activities. Before the notice period of seven days expired, the Chauri Chaura tragedy occurred. The mob of about 3,300 persons killed 21 policemen and the inspector, some of whom were burnt alive in a police station. It was too much for the non-violent Mahatma Gandhi to tolerate and he gave orders for the suspension of Non-Co-operation Movement. Mahatma Gandhi was bitterly criticised for this. The Government finding his popularity waning, prosecuted and sentenced him to imprisonment for six years.

Mahatma Gandhi was bitterly criticised by Pt. Moti Lal Nehru, Lala Lajpat Rai, Subhash Chander Bose and C.K. Das for suspending Non-Co-operation Movement. It was, however, justified later on by Pt. Jawahar Lal Nehru on grounds of practical politics. Chauri Chaura incident was not a solitary one. There was no discipline among Congress volunteers. Cases of violence were on the increase. All leaders of the Congress except Mahatma Gandhi were imprisoned.

The Non-Co-operation Movement failed in its objects, Firstly, it failed to secure the redress of Punjab wrongs, Secondly, the object of saving of the office of the Khalifa was not achieved. The Turks themselves exiled the Khalifa and abolished the Khilafat in 1922. Thirdly, the sudden suspension of the movement adversely affected Hindu-Muslim relations.

The movement proved useful in one way. The Congress from constitutional body became a revolutionary organisation. In the words of Coupland, "He (Gandhi) had done what Tilak had failed to do. He had converted the national movement into a revolutionary movement. He had taught it to pursue the goal of India's freedom, not by constitutional pressure on the Government, still less by discussion and agreement, but by force, non the less force because it was meant to be non-violent. And he had not only made the national movement revolutionary, he had also made it popular. It had hitherto been confined to the urban intelligentsia; it had made no apeal to the countryfolk. Gandhi's personality had deeply slirred the country side."

The Swarajist Party

The Swarajist Party became a powerful section in the Congress after 1923. The suspension of Non-Co-operation Movement by Mahatma Gandhi had created a gap and it was filled by the Swarajist Party. Its leaders were C.R. Das, Moti Lal Nehru, N.C. Kelkar etc.

The object of the Swarajists and the Congress was the same, that is, the establishment of Swaraj of Dominion Status within the British Empire, but their methods were different. The Congress believed in a policy of constructive programme. The Swarajists stood for the negative policy of obstruction. They advocated a policy of "unifom, continuous and consistent obstruction". They were to non-co-operate wth the bureaucratic machinery of the Government. They decided to enter the legislatures with the idea of obstructing their work.

The Swarajists did well in the election of 1923. They got a clear majority in the Central Provinces. They were the largest party in Bengal Legislative Assembly and C.R. Dass was able to win a few other members and command a majority. They captured 45 seats out of 145 in the Central Legislative Assembly. The Swarajist Party refused to form the Ministry and the Government had to take over the Government in its own hands. In Bengal, it rejected the salaries of two ministers and forced them to resign. In the Central Legislative Assembly, it rejected the budgets for 1924-25, 1925-26 and 1926-27. Its members refused to attend functions arranged by the Government and Governor-General. The Swarajists very frequently walked out of legislature and Sir Tej Bahadur Sapru called this party "patriotism in locomotion".

This party began to grow weak in 1925 due to two reasons. Firstly,it was felt that the negative policy of their party would lead nowhere. Secondly, C.R. Dass died in 1925 and this also weakened the party.

Simon Commission (1927)

The British Government appointed Simon Commission in 1927 to report about the constitutional progress in India since the inauguration of the Reforms of 1919. All its members were Englishmens and it was boycotted by all the parties in India. Hartals were observed and it was welcomed with black flags. Its members were asked by the people everywhere to go back. Still it completed its work and submitted its report in 1930 which was made the basis for the Government of India Act of 1935 by Sir Samuel Hoare, Secretary of state for India.

Nehru Report

The All Parties Conference met at Calcutta in 1928 and appointed a committee under the chairmanship of Pt. Moti Lal Nehru to draft a constitution for India. It recommended that India should be a secular State. There was to be joint electorates for the minorities in accordance with population, with the right to contest additional seats. It recommended Dominion Status for India. The report was rejected by Jinnah.

STAGES THROUGH WHICH THE FREEDOM MOVEMENT PASSED FROM 1928 TO 1947

The development of the Congress during this period may conveniently be divided into several periods.

(1) Civil Disobedience Movement and Gandhi-Irwin Pact. The Congress at its Calcutta session in 1928 wanted to pass a resolution declaring complete independence as its goal. Mahatama Gandhi intervened and a resolution was passed declaring Dominion Status as the goal. Mahatma Gandhi gave an assurance that he would himself lead the movement for independence, if the British Government did not confer Dominion Status by the end of 1929. Lord Irwin declared in October 1929 that Dominion Status was the goal of the British Government in India but no time limit was set. A session of the Congress was held at Lahore in December 1929 under the Presidentship of Pt. Jawahar Lal Nehru and a resolution was passed declaring complete independence as the goal of the Congress. 26th of January, 1930, was declared as Independence Day.

It was decided to launch Civil Disobedience Movement. It started with Mahatma Gandhi's famous march to Dandi Beach to violate Salt Laws. Thousands of Congress volunteers were sent behind the bars. The Government used every kind of repression but the movement could not be crushed. The Congress boycotted the First Round Table Conference held in 1930.

Gandhi-Irwin pact was made at last in 1931 due to the intervention of Jayakar and Sir Tej Bahadue Sapru. Its terms were the following:

(a) Civil Disobedience prisoners, not guilty of violence, were to be released.

(b) Fines, which had not been realised, were to be remitted. The fines already realised were not to be refunded.

(c) The safeguards to be embodied in the new constitutional set-up were to be in the interest of India.

(d) Immovable property confiscated by the Government was to be returned. Where it had been sold, the transaction was to be considered final.

(e) Mahatma Gandhi was not to press for a public enquiry into the allegations against the conduct of the police in India.

(f) The boycott of non-Indian goods was to be discontinued if it was exclusively against the British goods with a view to exerting pressure for political ends.

(g) The Government of India was to withdraw the ordinances promulgated in connection with the Civil Disobedience Movement.

(h) The Congress was to withdraw Civil Disobedience Movement.

(i) The Congress agreed to partcipate in the deliberations of the Second Round Table Confecence.

(j) Where the posts rendered vacant by resignations had been permanently filled, the Government was not bound to reinstate their former employees. Other cases of resignations were to be considered on their merits. The Local Governments were to follow a liberal policy in such cases.

(k) The right of manufacturing salt was to be conceded to the people living in salt areas.

It has been said in defence of the Pact that the Congress saved the people from a lot of suffering and repression. On the other hand, it has been condemned on the ground that Mahatma Gandhi was not able to save the lives of Sardar Bhgat Singh and his comrades.

Mahatma Gandhi attended the Second Round Table Conference as the sole representative of the Congress but it yielded no results due to the attitude of Jinnah. It could not arrive at any agreed formula regarding the representation of different Communities. Mahatma Gandhi expressed his intention of starting civil disobedience and was arrested immediately on reaching India under the orders of Lord willingdon.

(2) Communal Award (1932). Ramsay Macdonald, Prime Minister, gave his famous communal Award in August 1932. It gave separate representation to the Scheduled Castes. Mahatma Gandhi protested against this and observed fast unto death. The leaders of Caste Hindus and of Scheduled Castes met at Poona and made Poona Pact to save the life of Mahatma Gandhi. It was decided not to give separate representation to the Scheduled Castes. They were to be given some seats out of general seats. They were also to have the right of contesting general seats. The Poona pact was accepted by the British Government and necessary modifications were made in the Communal Award.

The Government of Great Britain published a White Paper in 1933 containing constitutional proposals to be embodied in the Act. The elections to the Central Legislative Assembly were held in 1934 and the Congress secured a large number off seats.

(3) Congress and Government of India Act of 1935. The British Parliament passed the Government of India Act of 1935. The elections were held and the Congress was able to get majority in six out of the 11 provinces. Only the provincial part of the Act was put into practice. The Governors were given special powers and special responsibilities. The Congress asked the Governors to give an assurance that they would not interfere in the day-to-day affairs of the ministers. They declined to give such an assurance and the Congress refused to form the ministries. At last the Governors Under instructions from the Governor-General gave an assurance that they would not interfere in the day-to-day affairs of the ministers and the Congress formed ministries in July 1937. The Second World War started in September 1939. The Congress asked the British Government to declare whether the War Aims of the Allies would apply to India or not. The British Government refused to make such a declaration and the Congress ministries resigned in November 1939.

(4) Rejection of the August offer. In August 1940, Lord Linlithgow made an offer to expand the Executive Council of the Viceroy. The object was to secure the co-operation of the Indians in the war effort. The Congress rejected the August offer.

(5) Congress and the Cripps Proposals. The British Cabinet sent Sir Stafford Cripps in March 1942 with certain proposals. The Indians were to have the right of making their constitutions after the war. All the departments, except Defence, were to be at once transferred to Indian hands. The Congress was prepared to accept the long-term scheme and not the interim scheme. Moreover the Congress did not like the attitude of "take it or leave it" because it left no scope for negotiations.

(6) Quit India Resolution (August 1942). All India Congress Committee passed Quit India Resolution on 8th of August 1942. The government arrested Mahatma Gandhi and all the members of the Congress Working Committee. The Congress organisation was banned and the police took possession of its offices. The people reacted violently and revolted. There was collapse of the machinery of the Government at several places. Jinnah was taken by surprise by the Quit India Movement and declared that the object of the movement was not only to turn out the British but also to subjugate the Muslims. He asked the Muslims to keep aloof.

(7) League's Rejection of C.R. Formula And wavell proposals. Rajagopalachari made some proposals to the Muslim League to solve the problem and these are popularly known as Rajagopalachari C.R. Formula. The Muslims were to be given the substance of what they wanted. Still it was rejected by Jinnah. Lord Wavell made some proposals at the Simla Conference in 1945 to solve the constitutional problem in India, but the conference failed due to the attitude of Jinnah.

(8) From Cabinet Mission Plan to Partition and Independence. The Labour Government sent cabinet Mission to India in 1946 with certain proposals which are popularly know as Cabinet Mission Plan. It could not bring about a compromise between the Congress and the Muslim League. Then it announced its own proposals on 16th of May 1946. These were a compromise between the Muslim League demand for Pakistan and the Congress demand for a united India. The scheme was rejected by the Congress and accepted by the League. Then the Congress accepted it and the Muslim League rejected it. The Muslim League observed 16th of August as the Direct Action Day.

Pandit Jawahar Lal Nehru formed interim Government on September 2, 1946. There were riots in Noakhali and Bihar. The Muslim League joined Interim Government with the idea of wrecking it. There was confusion in the country. The British Prime Minister Attlee declared that the British would leave India by June 1948. Lord Mountbatten was sent as Governor-General in March 1947 and he declared that the country would be divided as soon as possible. His June 3rd Plan was accepted by all the parties. The British Parliament passed Indian Independence Act in July 1947 creating the Dominions of India and Pakistan. India became independent on 15th of August 1947.

BIRTH OF THE CONGRESS

Perceiving the increasing intensity of the Indian feelings A.D. Hume a retired civilian wanted to divert them into a constitutional channel. He feared that unless a safe out let was found the discontent of the people would fester beneath the surface and will eventually lead to dangerous consequences. In a letter addressed to the graduates of Calcutta University, he exhorted them to found an organisation, for the moral, material and political progress and their motherland. He enlisted official support for his proposal Lord Dufferin encouraged the formation of some responsible organisation. He was convinced that India needed a political organisation "which would perform the function which Her Majesty's opposition did in England." According to Mr. Hume's plan was taken up by some prominent Indians and the Indian National Congress was ushered into existence in December 1885. It met at Bombay under the Presidency of Mr. W.C. Banerjee a prominent Bengalee barrister and was attended by only seventy two delegates. The pancity of attendence was due to the fact that

Surendra Nath and other prominent leaders could not attend the Congress because of the Simultaneous Session of the Indian National Conference in Calcutta. As the two organisations had the same objects in view, the separate existence of the Indian national conference was no longer necessary and so it merged itself into the National Congress. It was arranged that the Congress should meet every year during the Christmas weak in some important town by turns.

Objects of the Congress. The first session of the Indian National Congress was attended by prominent persons like Pherozshah Mehta. Dadabhai Naoroji, K.T. Talang, Dinshaw Wacha etc., while delivering the Presidential address W.C. Banerjee the President of the first session of the Indian National Congress laid down the following as the object of the Congress:

(a) The eradication by direct friendly personal inter course of all possible race, creed or provincial prejudices amongst all the lovers of the country and the fuller development and consolidation of those sentiments of national unity that took their origin in our beloved Ripon's eve. memorable reign.

(b) The authoritative record of the matured opinions of the educated classes in India on some of the most important and pressing social questions of the day.

(c) The promotion of personal intimacy and friendship amongst all the most earnest workers in our Country's cause in the various parts of the empire.

(d) The determination of the methods by which during the next twelve months it is desirable for the native politicians to labour in public interest."

The Congress was an All India Institution and had the support and Co-operation of the Hindu's Muslims, Parsees, Sikhs, Christian Anglo-Indians and Europeans. W.C. Banerjee the first President of the Indian National Congress was an Indian Christian. Its next President was Dadabhai Naoroji who was a Parsee.

FIRST PHASE OF THE INDIAN NATIONAL CONGRESS 1885-1905

During this period the Congress though a national body mainly represented the educated middle class intelligensia, men of legal, medical, engineering and literary professions. Its deligates were mostly drawn from the cities who had hardly any contact with the masses.

The organisation had been launched with the blessings of Lord Dufferin. The Congress took pride the British connection and looked upon the British Government not as an ananlgomist but as an ally. In 1886 Dadabhai Naoroji Presiding over the Calcutta Session dwelt at length on the "blessing of British rule" and his remarks were cheerd by the audience. Mr. Hume moved resolution of three times three cheers for the most Gracious Majesty the Queen Empress and a further resolution for long life of the Queen. Shri Anand Mohan Bose as Congress President declared in 1898 : "The educated classes are the friends and not the foes of England her natural and necessary allies in the great work that lies before her."

There was implicit faith in British sense of justice and fair play. The Congress Leaders belived that all they had to do was to prepare their case and present and plead it before the English Government and Nation and their grievances would be redressed and justice done. With a view to educating the English people about the real needs of India in 1890 a decision was taken to hold a session of the India National Congress in London in 1892 but owing to the British elections of 1891 the proposal was postponed and afterwards never revived S.N. Banerjee explained that the object of the Congress was, "not the supression of British rule in India, but the broadening of its basis, the liberalising of its spirit, the enabling of its character and placing it on the unchangeable foundation of a Nation's affections."

In the first phase of its life the Indian National Congress simply demanded a few concessions and not liberties for the Nation. True, Lokmanya Tilak used the word Swaraj or self government towards the last decade of the nineteenth century but it did not become popular. It was not a revolutionary body and its leaders declared loyalty to the British Government several times. They were against the idea of agitation and unconstitutional means and preferred to carryout their work by debates, propoganda, petititions and deputations. In 1890 a deputation of the Indian National Congress went to England and demanded representation of 50 per cent elected candidates in the Legislative Assemblies slowly and gradually more and more youths joined Congress. There was an increase in self confidence among the Indians and after 1905, the ultimation of the Congress became the attainment of independence. The achievements of the period were decried by the Progressive otherwise called the Extremist leaders of the early twentieth century. The policy of the moderate leaders or the 'Old Guards' was criticised as 'political mendicancy. In all fairness it must be said that men like Dadabhai Nauroji, Sir Pherozeshah Mehta, Sir Den Shah Wacha, Gopal Krishna Gokhla, Surendra Nath Banerjee etc., were the most progressive elements in Indian Society and true patriots. They earnestly withed the betterment of Indian Society and worked to lessen the harshness of British rule. They did a lot of spade work. Dr. Pattebhai Sitarammaya sums up the achievements of the early leaders then : "we can not blame them for the attitude they adopted as pioneers of Indian political reform any more than we can blame the brick and mortar that is buried six feet deep in the foundation and plenth of a modern edifice. They have made possible the superstructure, storey by storey by colonial self government, Home Rule with in the Empire Swaraj and the top of all complete independence."

Second Phase (1905-1916)

The early years of the 20th century witnessed the emergence of a new and younger party within the Congress which decried the ideology and methods of the old leaders and advocated the adoption of Swaraj as the goal of the Congress to be achieved by more selfreliant and independent methods. The new group came to tbe knwon as the Extremist Party in contrast to the older one which began to styles as the Moderate Party.

Causes for the Birth of Extremist

(a) The process of rejnvenations started from within India. The various socio-religious reform movements rekiaded love for India's philosophy thought and history. A new sense of pride was felt in India's past culture and achievements. It was increasingly realised that many of India ills were due to the demoralising effects of foreign rule and consequent poverty of the people.

(b) The younger element wth in the Congress were dissatisfied with the progress of the past two decades and were disgusted with the cold and reactionary attitude of the Government. They criticised the old methods of peaceful and constitutional agitation which they described as 'political mendicancy' and wanted to adopt European revolutionary methods to meet European Imperialism. On his return from England in India 1905 Lala Lajpat Rai told his country men that the British democracy was too busy with its own affairs to do any thing for India, that the British Press was not likely to champion their aspirations and that it was very difficult to get a hearing in England. He exhorted the people that if they really cared for their country, "they would have to strike a blow for freedom themselves and they should be prepared to give unmistakable proof of their earnestness."

(c) The terrible famines of 1896-97 and 1899-1901 followed by bubonic plague took a very heavy toll of life. The Government relief machinery was inadequate, slow moving and badly organised. Tilak was arrested when he criticised the callous and ineffective government machinery. Riots broke out in the Deccan and the Government tried to stifle public opinion and suppress lawlessness. The events revealed to Indians their plight of uttar helplessness. The people attributed the phenomenon of ever-recurring famiens to the anti-national economic policy followed by the Government.

(d) The Imperialist policies of Lord Curzon provided the immediate occasion for the brith of Extremism with in the Congress. The storm which had been brewing for sometime actually burst out in acts of violence and terrorism. He refused to recognise that India was a Nation characterised their activities as the 'letting off of gas.'

He insulted the Indian intelligantsia and talked very low of Indian character. The Calcutta Corporation Act, the Official Secrets Act, the Indian Univrsities Act and above all the Partition of Bengal created sesentment and provoked violence. Curzon became the most hated person in India and with him the British Imperialism as the worst enemy of India.

(e) Events out side India exercised a powerful influence on the younger generation. The humiliating treatement meted out to Indians in British Colonies, especially in South Africa created anti-British feeling. Nationalist movements in Egypt, Persia, Turkey and Russia gave Indians new hopes and new aspirations. Indian Nationalists gained more confidence and drew inspiration from Abyssinias repulsion of the Indian army (1896) and Japan's thumping victory over Russia (1905).

Objectives and Methods of Extremist Group

The extemist group was organised under the leadership of the Trio-Lal, Bal and Pal (Lala Lajpat Rai, Bal Gangadhar Tilak and Bipain Chandra Pal) Tilak gave the slogan of the new group when he said, "The objective of Swaraj or self-Government was to be achieved even if it meant a clash with the authorities and involved sacrifices. The view point of the moderate group was explained by Gokhle when he said, "we are not beggars and our policy is not menticancy."

The new leadership sought to create in the people a passionate love for liberty accompanied by a spirit of sacrifice and a readiness to suffer for the cause of the country. They strove to root out from the peoples minds the omnipotence of the ruler and instead give them self-reliance and confidence in their own strength B.C. Pal explained: "untrained in the crookes ways of civilised diplomacy they had believed what their rulers have said, either of themselves or of their subjects as gospel truth. They had been told that people of India were unfit to manage their own affairs and they believed it be true. They had been told that people were weak and the government was strong. They had been told India stood on a lower plane of humanity and England's mission was to civilise the Semibarbarous natives. They commenced to make what are called counter-passes in hypnotism and at once woke the people to a sense of their own strenth and an appreciation of their own culture."

The Extremist advocated boycott of Foreign Goods, Swadeshi and National Education. The Swadeshi movement was designed to encourage house industry and provide the people with more opportunities for work and employement. Soon it was discovered that economic boycott might prove a powerful weapon against economic exploitations by the foreigners. It was believed the newly rising Indian manufacturing class would liberally provide funds for the Congress and thus strengthen it. Lala Lajpat Rai summed up : "we desire to turn our faces away from Government House and turn then to huts of the people.

A National Scheme of Education was to replaces the boycott of Government Controlled Universities and Colleges. The extremists encouraged Co-operative Organisations, Voluntary Associations were set up for rural sanitation, preventive police duties, regulation of fairs and pilgirm gatherings for providing relief during famines and national calamities. Arbitration Committees were set up to decided civil and non-cognizable disputes.

HISTORY OF INDIAN NATIONAL CONGRESS

The history of the Congress which is synonymous of the history of the national movement may be devided into the three periods:

(1) Reformative stage

(2) Militant Nationalism

(3) Ghandhian Era

(1) Reformative Stage. The Indian National congress was founded in the year 1885. Prominent pesons of all religions and castes had joined the Congress. It was a national organisation. In the beginning, the Congress aimed to increase the number of Indian members in Central and Provincial Legislative Assemblies through constitutional mean. When Lokmanaya Tilak came to the political secene independence became the goal of the Congress. The Britishers were successful in establishing an organisation of the Muslims against the Congress. In 1888 Sir Sayed Ahmed Khan founded an institution named Anglo Muslim Defence Association. The leaders of the Congress believed in the policy of appeals and petitions. The early Congress "with all its professions of loyality studied moderation and appealing way, begging tone, did in those days a great amount of spade work in national awakening political education and in uniting Indians and in creating in them the consciousness of a common Indian nationality." The attitude of the Government changed because the Congress was slowly and gradually adopting a policy of criticism of the Government.

(2) Militant Nationalism. On the one hand the Congress was drifting away from its loyalty towards the Government had started criticising the policies of the Government on the other hand extreme leaders like Lokmanaya Tilka, B.C. Pal. Aurobndo Ghose and Lala Lajpat Rai etc., had joined the Congress. Slowly and gradually extreme and revolutionary nationalism was developing. Some of the main causes of the rise of extremism were:

(a) ***Bad Economic Condition.*** On account of the continuation of the foreign rule there was a constant drain on the economic resources of the country. The economic condition of the people was constantly deteriorating. The leaders felt that only the freedom of the country could solve economic condition of the people.

(b) ***Famine and Plague.*** Famine and Plague in Presidency further increased the discontent among the people. About 20 million people were affected by the famine. During this period of famine the Government celebrated the Jubilee of Queen Victoria.

(c) ***Dissatisfaction with the Indian Councils Act of 1892.*** The new Act of 1892 did not satisfy even the moderates. It did not give anything substantial to the Indians. The people now increasingly felt that the policy of appeals and prayers had yielded nothing.

(d) ***Revival of Hinduism.*** Swami Vivekananand and Aurobindo Ghose declared that independence is the goal of life and Hinduism alone will fulfil this aspiration of ours." The Theosophical Society also made signafican contribution in the revival of Hinduism.

(e) ***Ill-treatment of the Indians Abroad.*** The Indians who went aborad were very badly treated. The treatement meted out in South Africa was very bad. Restrictions were imposed on the free movement of the Indians and they felt that the main cause of their humiliation was their slavery.

(f) ***Reactionary Regime of Lord Curzon.*** The anti-Indian Policy of Lord Curzon was also greatly responsible for the rise of the extremists. Many reactionary Acts were passed during the regime of Lord Curzon. These mesures further increased the discontent among the people and they began to think seriously of some means and ways to oppose the policy of the Government.

(g) ***Partition of Bengal.*** Yet another cause for the rise of extremists was the partition of Bengal. The reactionary measures of Lord Curzon had already irritated the people. The partition of Bengal in 1905 added fuel to fire. The people of Bengal felt they have been 'humiliated, insulted and traiked.' The partition of Bengal was considered as a subtle attack on the growing solidarity of Bengal Nationalism. Lala Lajpat Rai and B.G. Tilak were the prominent leaders who were leading the extremists. 16th October 1905 was declared as a day of protest throughout the Country. The tying of Rakhis, hortals and observance of fasts and boycott of foreign goods were some of the important measurs observed by the extremists. The position of the extremists in the Congress was quite strong by the year 1905.

Differences between the Policies and Methods of Moderates and Extremists. The following were the differences between the policies and methods of the moderates and the extremists:

(a) The moderates were in favour of extending support to the British Government whereas the extremists were totally against it and were in favour of the boycott movement.

(b) The moderates wanted to bring a change in the existing Constitution whereas the extremists were in favour of rebuilding it.

(c) The extremist wanted to drive away the British India by any means, whereas the moderates wanted to bring about a change on the heart of the British in their favour.

The Surat Session of the Congress. In the Surat Session of the Congress in 1907 there was an open drift between the two groups and the moderates were able to secure the majority and the other group became separate from the Congress and did not stop its movement. Tilak made a where wind tour of the country and advocated the people to join the boycott movement. The extremist were regarded as a great danger to their existence by the British. The leaders of the extremist group were arrested and imprisoned.

Since Tilak was in Mandalay Jail (Rangoon) from 1908 to 1914 the progress of the extremists was not satisfactory. After his release the position began to change. However, Tilak was not in haste and wanted to have a compromise with the moderates. Gokhle was also making efforts for the compromise. But the compromise talks broke off on account of the insistence of a Pherozeshah Mahta. Pherozeshah Mehta selected Sir Styendra Sinha, a former member of the Viceroy's Executive Council for the Presidenthsip of 1915. Congress but Satyendra Sinha died before the Session.

The Home Rule Movement. In 1915 Mrs. Annie Besant announced her decision to established a Home Rule League on the model of Irish Home Rule Movement. The Home Rule Legue was to be an auxiliary to the Indian National Congress. In 1916 Mrs. Annie Besant set up a Home Rule League at Madras. Tilak orgaised his own Home Rule League at Poona. Both the Leagues worked the Unison and aimed at the achievement of self-government. The League's objectives was to educate the people and to provide the Congress demand for self-government with the support and strength of a nation united in knowledge of itself and its single aim. Indian asked this before the war, India asks for it during the war, India will ask for it after the war but not as reward but as a right does she ask for it. The Home rule movement reached its zenith in 1917. But the Government took stern measures against the movement and Mrs. Besant was made prisoner. A movement was started for her release and Tilak threatened to start passive resistence. But in the meantime, the Secretary of State for India made an annoncement in 1917 promising responsible Government to the people of India by stages. Slowly and gradually the Home Rule movement died out. Mrs. Besant was elected the President of Congress in 1917. Mr. Montagu visited India the same year and held talks with the representatives of the people. His report was published in 1918 and the Govt. of India Act was passed in 1919.

3. The Third Phase or the Gandhian Era (1919-1947). During this period the object of the Congress was the attainment of Swaraj by all legitimate means with in the Empire if possible and without it if necessary. In 1930 came the unequivocal declaration of Purna Swaraj or complete independence was the goal of the Congress. The period was dominated by the personality of Mohan Dass Karam Chand Gandhi who introduced new ideas into Indian politics. Gandhiji depricated the policy of violence and underground plots but preached open and active resistence to injustice. He advocated the adoption of the policy of Satyagreha *i.e.*, non-violent non-co-operation towards a government which did not look to the interests of the governed and was high handed and oppressive. The Congress movement gradually became a mass movement. The Congress organisation was considerably strengthened and its constitution made more democratic. Gandhiji used to explain his programme for strengthening India by pointing to the five fingers of his hand, exhorting the people to practise five virtues—spinning, removal of untrouchability, sobriety (non-consumption of alchohal or opium), Hindu Muslim unity and equality for women.

The Great World War (1914-18) gave a big shock to Imperialism by advocating the principle of self-determination. During the war the

Congress gave ample demonstration of loyalty. Mahatma Gandhi showed great enthusiasm and urged the Gujrati peasants to join the army. The events of the year 1919 greatly disillusioned Gandhiji and from a co-operator he became non-co-operator. The passing of the Rowaltt Acts (giving the executive extensive powers to arrest and detain persons without trial), the Jallianwalla Bagh tragedy and the Khilafat wrongs gave a new turn to Indian Politics.

Non-Co-operation Movement of 1920

In 1920 the Congress accepted the policy of non-co-operation towards the unjust Government. The policy involved renunciation of Government titles, boycott of legislatures, law courts, educational institutions foreign goods and finally non-payment of taxes. On the constructive side people urged to develop the sprit of discipline and self sacrifice to set up national educational institutions, decide their disputes by mutual arbitration, take to hand weaving and use of Swadeshi goods. Gandhiji toured the whole country to whip up enthusiasm of the people. In 1921 about 30,000 persons courter arrest. Much against the wishes and instructions of Gandhiji, the movement led to a serious mob violence and Chauri Chaura in U.P. where a police station was burnt and a number of police officials killed. Gandhi ji atonce suspended the non-co-operation movement and declared that Swaraj stank in his nostrills and that without adequate discipline and restraint on the part of the people the movement had proved to be a Himalayan blunder Gandhiji advised constructive work to the people.

Swaraj Party. Dissatisfied with Gandhiji's policies C.R. Dass and Moti Lal Nehru founded the Swaraj Party advocated the programme of Council entry. They hoped to wreck the functioning of Legislative Councils by a policy of uniform continuous and consistent obstruction. In the election of 1923 the Swarajists secured an absolute majority in Bengal, and the Central Provinces and by their tactics made impossible for the ministers to function.

❐

3

Swarajya Party

When C.R. Das and the other Bengal leaders were in Alipore Central Jail, they evolved a new programme of non-cooperation with the Government through Legislatures. Their idea was to enter the Legislatures in Large numbers and "carry on a policy of uniform continuous and consistent opposition to the Government." While presiding over the Bengal Provincial Conference of Congress workers at Chittagong in May 1922. Mrs. C.R. Das expressed the sentiments of her husband and pleaded for a change in the tactics and approach of the Congress. Her view was that the policy of carrying non-co-operations into the Legislative Councils was 'worth a trial".

Motilal Nahru also shared the view of C.R. Das. He was released from Jail by the British Government in June 1922. A meeting of the All-India Congress Committee was held at Lucknow but there was no unanimity with regard to the future programme of the Congress. However, this committee set up the Civil Disobedience Enquiry Committee under the Chairmanship of Hakim Ajmal Khan. Those who were against Council-entry urged that the proposal involves a distinct violation of the principle of non-cooperation and a clear departure from the policy of the Congress. It will mean an admission of the failure of non-cooperation because even the particular form of non-cooperation in the Councils was discussed and rejected by the Congress in the special session held at Calcutta. Although there was a strong section in favour of entering the Councils, they were against total obstruction and would rather follow a policy of responsive cooperation. A campaign of entry into Councils would mean a diversion of the public attention and energy from the constructive programme and would have the effect of relegating it to the cold shode of neglect. It is absolutely impossible to secure a majority in the Councils sufficient to create deadlocks in the manner contemplated. As a large number of non-cooperators, including the most eminent leaders, are disqualified from the membership of the Councils by reasons of sentences of imprisonment for over six months passed against them, it will be inconsistent with self-respect and dignity for other non-cooperators to think of entering into the Councils. As Mahatma Gandhi pointed out in the Calcutta session of the Congress in 1920, it was not a goot and honest policy to enter into an institution in order to wreck it. Moreover, indiscriminate obstruction will be a manifest violation of the oath of allegiance which every member has to take before accepting his seat in the Council. Mahatma Gandhi was opposed to Council-entry on grounds which still hold good. The chances are remote for obtaining such a majority at the elections as it is one of the essential conditions of the success of the scheme. Even if there be such a majority, the Government will not be brought to its knees through the Councils' deadlock as the government had many weapons like veto in its possession.

Similar arguments were put forward by the groups favouring Council entry. They contended that political tactics are never immutable. They must change with the change of circumstances. While defending the suspension of the non-cooperation movement, Mahatma Gandhi had observed, "Consistency is a desirable quality, but it becomes a 'hobgoblin' when it refuses to see facts". He adopted Satyagraha in March 1919, abandoned it after the disturbances in April and pleaded for cooperation at the Amritsar Congress. After another three months, he began a march back from non-cooperation. Six months later, non-cooperation became the accepted creed of the Congress. After a year's working, it was extended by the All-India Congress Commitee to include Civil Disobedience. Though the two movements were radically different in character, the change was effected without any authorisation for the Congress. The Ahmedabad Congress approved of this change and laid down that "Civil Disobedience is the only civilised and effective substitute for armed rebellion.' The country was asked to suspend all other activities and concentrate on Civil Disobedience. Then at Bardoli, the Working Committee, under the advice of Mahatma Gandhi, asked the country to suspend all aggressive activities and concentrate on the constructive programme. As the nationalists were out of the way it was a walk-over for the Moderates and they took full advantage of the opportunity to fill up the Councils. Mahatma Gandhi hoped that the Moderates would resign as an overwhelming majority abstained from the polls. In spite of a resolution to that effect in the Nagpur Congress and numerous meetings and even special conferences, the Moderates clung to their seats. The object of keeping the Council Chambers empty was virtually defeated by the entry of the very persons who ought not to have been there. We made the cooperation of others easy. It will be suicidal to repeat the same story. Assuming that the Councils cannot do any good, it cannot be denied that they can and are doing immense harm. If we do not contest, we shall be out again for three years, in course of which many repressive measures affecting the daily life of the people will be enacted with the help of the so-called representatives of the people. Under these circumstances, it is a question for consideration how far the hold of the Congress over the masses can remain unaffected. The policy of abstention seems to have lost its charm and it is not at all unlikely that a greater percentage of voters will poll at the coming election thus rendering nugatory the success of the non-cooperation. A non-cooperator who secures his election to the Council with a definite mandate from his constituency to obstruct the proceedings at every step, does not act improperly if he enters the Council with the avowed object of paralysing it after giving an undertaking in the form, "I will faithfully discharge the duty upon which I am about to enter." He can faithfully discharge his duty only by acting strictly in accordance with the mandate. The proposed into the Councils involves a change in the programme and should therefore obtain the sanction of the Congress, but it is not inconsistent with the principles of non-cooperation. As a matter of fact, it was not included in the original programme of non-cooperation and was not considered as an essential feature of it at the beginning. An opportunity now presents itself to vindicate our national self-respect. We can carry the fight into the camp of the government and tell them plainly that so long as our men are in jails and other wrongs are not redressed, we refuse to cooperate with you. This would be the only dignified reply to terrorism and repression of the government. The evidence adduced before us strongly supports the belief that we shall be in a very substantial majority in all the Provinces if the Congress and the Khilafat daclare in favour of entering into the Councils. There can be no greater paralysis of the system than the government by veto. But even if the constructive programme be pushed in right earnest, a substantial success would take a long time to come and in the meantime "the nation will have gone completely under." Realising this, the Ahmedabad Congress advised a resort to Civil Disobedience. That as failed and the country is not now prepared to embark upon general mass Civil Disobedience. There is a stalemate. We must therefore have something else as nearly approaching Civil Disobedience as possible.

The Report of the Enquiry Committee was published in October 1922 and it was followed by an acrimonious discussion all over India between the orthodox section of the Congress and those who favoured entry into the Councils. The whole question was discussed at length in the meeting of the All-India Congress Committee held in Calcutta on Novemeber 20-24, 1922. "At the end of five days' analysis, criticism, invective and diatribe, the Committee resolved that the country was not prepared for mass disobedience." It authorised the Provincial Congress Committees to sanction limited Civil Disobedience.

The Annual Session of the Congress was held at Gaya on December 26, 1922 under the Presidentship of C.R. Das in a tense atmosphere. In his Presidential address. C.R. Das made a vigorous plea for Council-entry. He declared, "These Councils must be either mended or ended. Hitherto we have been boycotting the Councils from outside. We have succeeded in doing much—the prestige of the Councils is diminished and the country knows that the people who adorn those chambers are not the true representatives of the people. It should be the duty of the Congress to boycott the Councils more effectively rom within. Reformed Councils are really a mask which the bureaucracy has put on. I conceive it to be our clear duty to tear this mask from off their face. The very idea of boycott implies, to my mind, something more than mere withdrawl. The boycott of foreign goods means that such steps must be taken that there may be no foreign goods in our market. The boycott of Reformed Councils, to my mind, means that such steps must be taken that these Councils may not be there to impede the progress of Swaraj. The only successful boycott of these Councils is either to mend them in a manner suitable to the attainment of the Swaraj or to end them completely. C.R. Das emphasised the two-fold aspects of the non-cooperation movement. One was destructive and the other constructive, complementing each other and always going hand in hand. He asked, "Judged by this principle, what is wrong about the desire either to convert the Councils into institutions which may lead us to Swaraj, or to destroy them altogether?

The question was hotly debated both in the Subjects Committee and in the open session of the Congress Rajagopalachari moved the resolution against Council-entry to which there were several amendments in the Subjects Committee. There were two different sections amongst the supporters of Council-entry. Both of them agreed to contest the elections. However, while one held that the elected members should refuse to take the seats, the other wished to leave the question open to be decided by the next Congress. The first view was sponsored by Srinivasa Aiyangar and the second by Motilal Nehru. His view was that the best way of proceeding forward was to enter the Councils solidly and using that weapon to brak the citadel of bureaucracy. Srinivasa Aiyangar's motion of contesting elections but not entering Councils was first put to vote and was lost 107 voted for and 139 against it. Rajagopalachari's motion that all voters shall abstain from standing as candidates for the Councils and from voting for any such candidate was pressed to a division and was carried by 203 votes against 87. In the open session of the Congress the resolution of Srinivasa Aiyangar was defeated by 1740 votes against 894 votes and Rajagopalachari's motion was carried by a large majority. The Congress also passed resolutions maintaining the boycott of government and government-aided and affiliated educational institutions as well as the boycott of law Courts by lawyers and litigants.

The success of the no-entry supporters seemed to be complete and there was a great jubilation in the Congress camp. However, it was short-lived. The reason was that the Swarajya Party would not take the defeat lying down and was determined to carry on the fight.

The Congress concluded its session at Gaya on December 31, 1922 and the All-India Congress Committee met on January 1, 1923. However, before the business started, C.R. Das announced his resignation as Congress President and made a statement in explanation or justification of his action. He contended that the proceedings of the Congress convinced him. It was therefore his duty to resign the Presidentship. However, he declared, "I am not leving the Congress in the conviction that I shall be able to convert the minority in to majority at no distant date."

Those who were in favour of Council-entry issued a manifesto forming and constituting themselves into a party within the Congress, called the Congress Khilafat Swaraj Party. It accepted the creed of the Congress, namely, the attainment of Swaraj by all legitimate and peaceful means and also the principles of non-violent non-cooperations. C.R. Das was elected the leader and Motilal Nehru, with three others, were elected as Secretaries. The manifesto announcing the formation of the Party was assented to by more than hundred persons including, among others, Hakim Ajmal Khan, V.J. Patel, N.C. Kelkar, Satyamurti and M.R. Jayakar.

There was obviously a split in the Congress. The differences between the two groups were further widened by intemperate and irresponsible utterances of the Press. "Mutual recrimination became the order of the day and motives concorted in editorial conclaves were gratuitosly fathered upon the leaders." The bitterness filtered down to all sections of the people. The result was that very little was done to carry into effect the constructive programme of the Congress. Some of them aimed at mass Civil Disobedience through constructive programme, while others preferred the Khaddar and national education programme.

The leaders of the Swaraj Party showed great activity in organising their Party. They conducted a vigorous propaganda all over the country—Motilal Nehru in upper India, Patel in Bombay and C.R. Das in Bengal, C.P. and South India.

In March 1923, the first Conference of the Swarajist Party was held at Allahabad at the residence of Motilal Nehru and the future programme of the party was decided. It was declared that the immediate objective of the party was to attain dominion status. The keynote of their programme was obstructionism. The members of the Swarajist party were to contest elections of the issue of the redress of the wrongs done by the British bureaucracy, to oppose every measure of the government and to throw ot all legislative enactments proposed by the british Government. The view of the Swarajists was that the seats in the legislature must be captured so that they did not fall into the hands of undesirable persons who were tools in the hands of the bureaucracy in the country.

The Conference was followed by another series of propaganda tours by the leaders. C.R. Das stormed the citadel of orthodoxy in Madras and his success had its reprecussions in other parts of the country.

Early in February 1923, Maulana Abul Kalam Azad made an attempt to bring about a compromise between the two sections of the Congress. After repeated failures, he succeeded in making them agree to a truce till April 30, 1923. The Council propaganda was to be suspended on both sides during the period. The compromise did not satisfy the Extremists in both the sections and at the end of the period, each section accused the other for violating the terms of the compromise.

Although the Working Committee of the Congress consisted entriely of no-changers, the All-India Congress Committee passed a resolution in May 1923 in Bombay that no propaganda be carried on amongst the voters relating to the boycott of Councils. The result of the resolution was that six prominent members of the Congress Working Committee, including Rajendra Prasad and Rajagopalachari, tendered their resignation. They represented a fairly large body of non-partisan Congressmen who were seriously perturbed by the rivalry between the two sections within the Congress and tried to remove it by some sort of a compromise. This party was able to assert itself at the meeting of the All-India Congress Committee at Nagpur where it was decided to suspend the operation of the Congress resolution boycotting the Councils and hold a special session of the Congress to discuss the issue.

The Special session of the Congress was held at Delhi on September 15, 1923 under the Presidentship of Maulana Abul Kalam Asad. Maulana Azad himself advocated the policy of Council-entry. All the parties looked towards him for support. Although Muhammad Ali was himself a non-cooperator, he realised the growing strength of the Swarajist Party led by C.R. Das and Motilal Nehru and felt that the only statesman-like policy was to allow the Swarajists to wreck the Councils without any hindrance from the Congress. It was a great diplomatic manoeuvre on his part to announce in the Congress that he had received a wireless message from Yeravada where Gandhiji was confined in Jail, in favour of lifting the ban of Council-entry. This had a great effect upon the minds of the audience. Both the groups were doing their best to win over more and more supporters but the chances seemed to be in favour of the Swarajists. However, the following compromise resolution was adopted : "While reaffirming its adherence to the principle of non-cooperation this Congress declares that such Congressmen as have no religious or other conscientious objections against entering the legislatures are at liberty to stand as candidates and to exercise the right of voting at the forthcoming elections, and this Congress therefore suspends all propaganda against entering Councils. The Congress at the same time called upon all Congressmen to double their efforts to carry out the constructive programme of their great leader, Mahatma Gandhi, and by united endeavour to achieve Swaraj at the earlist possible moment." This resolution was re-affirmed at the regular annual session of the Congress held at Co-canada in December 1923. It was declared that 'non-cooperation could be effected as much from inside the Councils as from ourside."

When Mahatma Gandhi was released in February 1924, Motilal Nehru went to see him at Juhu to secure his "passive cooperation at least if not his active sympathy." The view of Mahatma Gandhi was that Council-entry was inconsistent with his programme of non-cooperation. However, he gave full liberty to the members of the Swarajist Party to pursue their programme in the Councils unfettered by any obstructed from the "No-Changers." Later on, Mahatma Gandhi agreed to a compromise with C.R. Das and Motilal Nehru. The Swarajist Party was to continue its work in the Councils and other Congressmen were to work outside the Councils.

Work of Swarajist Party

As regards the Swarajist Party, it fought the elections of 1923. It refused to come to any understanding with the Liberal Federation. the attitude of the Liberals was considered to be unpatriotic as the latter refused to criticise or condemn the bureaucracy for their acts of omission and commission. The Swarajist Party won a majority in the Legislative Council of the Central provinces. It was the dominant party in Bengal. It also won good support in U.P. and Bombay. However, the Swarajist Party was at it best in the Central Asssembly under the leadership of Motilal Nehru. By wining over the support of Nationalist Party and a few other members, the Swarajist Party was able to command a working majority and thus was able to accomplish a lot. On February 18, 1924, the Swarajist Party was able to get a resolution passsed by which the Government was requested to establish full responsible Government in India. A demand was also made that a Round Table Conference consisting of the representatives of India should be called at an early date to frame a Constitution for India. Motilal Nehru was requested to become a member of this Committee but he refused. Some of the demands in the budget of 1924-25 were rejected by the Central Assembly as a result of the efforts of the Swarajist Party. The Assembly also refused to allow the Government to introduce the entire Finance Bill. A resolution was passd with the help of the Swarajist demanding the release of certain political prisoners. The Swarajist resorted to the technique of frequent walk-outs as a mark of protest against the policy of the Government.

They boycotted all receptions, parties or functions organised by the Government. What was done in the Central Assembly was also done in those Provincial Legislatures where the Swarajist had some influence.

Surendranath Banerjee wrote, "If these obstructionist tactics inside the Councils are a prelude to revolutionary methods outside, by inflaming the minds of the masses, they are intelligible and perhaps logical; otherwise they are futile and meaningless. They will not wreck the Government, but may deprive it of its popular element, and a return to the old bureaucratic system be the outcomce of persistene in this policy. The obstructionists may temporarily pose as heroes who have defied an autocratic government, but they will leave behind them for the countrymen the bitter harvest of their sinister activities.

In spite of all the opposition by the Swarajist Party, the work of the Government continued as usual. This forced the Swarajist Party to reconsider its original policy of "undiluted opposition." This was particulary so after the death of C.R. Das in June 1925. In the Central Provinces, Shri S.B. Tamble, the Swarajist President of the Legislative Council, was appointed a member of the Executive Council of the Governor and he accepted that office. His action was approved that office. His action was approved of by N.C. Kelkar and other prominent members of the Swarajist Party of Maharashtra. Kelkar did not approve of the rigidity of the attitude of the Swarajist Party and he advocated "a policy of revolt from hidebound obstruction."

V.J. Patel was elected the Speaker of the Central Assembly and he accepted the same. Although Motilal Nehru had rejected previously the offer to be a member of the Muddiman Committee, he agreed to be a member of the Skeen Committee, which was set up by the Government to report on the early Indianisation of the Army. Lala Lajpat Rai entered the Central Assembly as a Swarajist and agreed to becomethe Deputy Leader of the Swarajist Party.

Differences Among Swarajists

Differences arose among the members of the Swarajist Party. The Executive Committee of the Party met at Nagpur in November

1925 and condemned the action of Tambe as "a flagrant breach of discipline" and called it as "treachery to the Party." Motilal Nehru stuck to his party programme of "Coopeation, non-cooperation, construction, destruction, as occasion and national intersts demanded." He threatened to take action against Kelkar and M.R. Jayakar, but they pointed out that Motilal Nehru had himself set the example by agreeing to be a member of the Skeen Committee. Kelkar raised the slogans of "Back to Amritsar" and "Back to the Lokmanya." There was open criticism of the other. However, on December 4, 1925, the members of the party agreed not to criticise one another in public. At the Kanpur session of the Congress, the following resolution was adopted : "No member of the Swarajist Party in the Council of State, in the Legislative Assembly, or in any of the Provincial Councils shall thereafter, attend any meeting of any of the said Legilslature or any of their Committees, except or the purpose of preventing his seat from being declared vacant and of throwing out the provincial budget or other measures involving fresh taxation." Pandit Madan Mohan Malaviya moved the following amendment to this resolution : "That the work in the Legislatures shall be so carred on as to utilise them to the best possible advantage for the early establishment of full responsible government, cooperation being resorted to when it may be necessary to advance the national cause and obstruction when that may be necessary for the advancement of the same cause." This amendment was seconded by M.R. Jayakar. However, the amendment was rejcted. The result was that Jayakar, Kelkar and Dr M.S. Moonje resigned from their Legislatures.

Efforts at Compromise Fail

Efforts were made to bring about a compromise among the erstwhile members of the Swarajist Party. With that object in view a meeting was held at Sabarmati in April 1926 and it was attended, among others, by Jayakar, Kelkar, Lala Lajpat Rai, Dr. Moonje and M.S. Aney. With great difficulty, an agreement was arrived at, but the same did not last long. Voices were raised by many Congressmen who contended that "the position of the Congress had been compromised even more at Sabarmati than at Kanpur." Serious differences arose between Motilal Nehru and the other members of the Swarajist Party. Motial Nehru maintained that office was to be accepted by the members of the Swarajist Party only if the Governor-General and the Governor agreed not to interfere with the work of the Ministers and the Ministers were given complete control of the services in the Transferred Departments. Differences also arose between Motilal Nehru and Lala Lajpat Rai about the work in the Central Assembly. The result was Lala Lajpat Rai resigned from the Congress party in the Central Assembly.

At the annual session of the Indian National Congress, the following resolution was adopted : "The work in the country shall be directed to the education of the people in their political rights and training them to acquire the necessary strength and power of resistence to win those rights by carrying out the constructive programme of the Congress with special reference to popularising the spinning wheel and khaddar, promoting intercommunal unity, removal of untouchability, ameliorating the condition of the suppressed classes, and removal of the drink and drug evil, and shall include the capture of local bodies.

The Swarajist members of the Legislative Assembly and the Council of State shall vote for the rejection of the Finance Bill and then immediately walk out. The Swarajist members of such Provincial Councils as may be in session at the time shall also leave their seats and all members of such Councils as are not in session at the time not attend further meetings of the said Councils and shall likewise report themselves to the special committee. No member of the Swarajist Party in the Council of State, in the Legislative Assembly, or in any of the Provincial Councils shall thereafter attend any meeting of any of the Legislatures or any of their committees, except for the purpose of preventing his seat from being declared vacant and of throwing out the provincial budget or other measures involving fresh taxation. But the special committee will allow the Swarajist members of any legislature to attent the legislature when such attendance is in its opinion essential for some special emergency.

Swarajist Party Disappears from Scene

General elections were held under the Government of India Act, 1919 in Novemeber 1926. The Swarajist Party was able to improve its position, but the members of the Nationalist Party lost heavily. However, as other parties came into the field, the position of the Swarajist Party was not strong anywhere and consequently, it became difficult for it to follow successfully the police of "Continuous, constant and uniform obstruction." Motilal Nehru was left alone. There was a general feeling among the Congressmen that the policy of "consistent and persistent" obstruction was not doing any good to the country. At its annual session held at Gauhati, the Congress decided that Congressmen would "refuse to accept ministerships or other offices in the gift of the Government and oppose the formation of a Ministry by other parties, until, in the opinion of the Congress or the All-India Congress Committee, a satisfactory response is made by the Government to the National Demand." They would throw out all proposed legislative enactments by which the bureaucracy sought to consolidate its powers. However, Congressmen would move resolutions and support measures and bills which were necessary for advancing the economic, agricultural, industrial and commercial interests of India and for the protection of the freedom of person, speech, association and of the press and the consequent displacement of bureaucracy.

The view of Dr. Tara Chand is that the resignation of the Swarajist from the Central Assembly brought the experiment of utilizing the legislatures to expedite the establishment of self-government at an early date to an end. They had realised from the very beginning that they could not offer continuous and unmitigated non-cooperation from within as they were not in a majority. However the tactics followed by them were not devoid of results. The most important result was to convince the Government of India that the transfer of power on the Dominion model was not an issue which could be brushed aside as impracticable and unattainable within any conceivable time. Malacolm Hailey, the Home Member, admitted that the question had been raised and Dominion Status had been made a live issue. All future plans of reforms henceforward had to accept Dominion Status as the major premise of the problem. Another valuable result was that it brought home to the rulers the realisation of the great parliamentary ability of the nationalist leaders and their organisational capacity for electioneering and offering opposition in Parliament. The success of the Swarajists to consolidate the forces of opposition revealed the basic weakness of the Government of India act 1919 which had created an irresponsible executive which was confronted with a legislature in permanent opposition. It was neither the presidential system of the United States nor the parliamentary system of Great Britain. It was clear that the illogical Indian system could only lead to deadlocks and eventually to a breakdown. The necessity of changes in it was evident. The difficulty of working the existing system is clear from the correspondence between the Viceroy and the Secretary of State for India. One of the early difficulties arose when there was a difference of opinion between the Viceroy and the Secretary of State on the question of effecting economy in military expenditure and Indianizing the military services.

SIMON COMMISSION REPORT (1930)

The Report of the Simon Commission was published in May 1930. First of all the Report considered as to what should be the ultimate constitutional framework of India and what should be the place of the provinces in that framework. The Report declared that the framework could not be of a unitary type. That must be federal, not merely in response to the growth of provincial loyalties but primarily because it must embrace all India.

The Report recommended that dyarchy should be abolished in the provinces and the whole field of provincial administration should be entrusted to ministers responsible to their Legislatures. "Each province should as far as possible, be the mistress in her own house." It was pointed out that the retention of reserved subjects implied the continuance of control over that part of the provincial administration by the Central Government and the Secretary of State for India and that was not a desirable thing. The Governor was to be allowed to select those Ministers who commanded a majority in the Legislature.

He was not to appoint a ministry on the advice of the Prime Minister or the Chief Minister. In all legislation and administration, ministers were to be free from interference by the Governor except for such stated vital reasons as the maintenance of the safety of the province or the protection of the minorities. The Report recommended that the question of making Sind and Orissa as separate provinces should be given further expert examination. However, it should be decided for.[Thwith to separate Burma from India. The North-Western Fronteir Province was considered to be ripe for the first step in constitutional advancement.

The Report made certain recommendations which aimed at preparing the case for an All-India Federation. The Central Legislature was to be refashioned on the federal principal. The members of the Federal Assembly were to be representatives not of sections of the people of India at large but of the provinces. They were to be elected by the Provincial Councils. The elections and nominations to the Council of State were also to be on a provincial basis. The distribution of seats amongst the various provinces for the Federal Assembly was to be roughly on population basis.

So far as the Central Executive was concerned, there was a note of "gradualness" in the Report. No substantial change was recommended. There was to be no responsible Government at the centre. There was to be no dyarchy even at the centre. It was pointed out that there was the need of keeping the centre strong and stable "while the provincial Councils were learning by experience to bear the full weight of new and heavy responsibility." The reason given for this was not the immediate need of the political situation in India, but the ultimate needs of the Federation. It was started that the provinces must fined themselves before the nature of their participation in a federal government could be determined.

An All-India Federation was to be set up in the distant future. The idea that "the Federation of Greater India can be artificially hastened or that when it comes, it will spring into being at a bound," was rejected. For the present only one new step was recommended. In order to "foster the sense of need for further developments and bring more nearly within the range of realisation other steps which are as yet too distant and too dim to be entered upon and described", a Council for Greater India should be set up, representing both British India and the Indian States. That Council should have authority to discuss in a consultative capacity all matters of common concern which were to be drawn up in the form of a list and given as Schedule.

The Government of India Act 1919 had provided for setting up a Commission after every 10 years for enquiring into the working of the reforms and the naming of the recommendations for the future. The new constitution should be so elastically framed as to enable it to develop by itself. The Provincial Legislatures should have power to modify their own composition and procedure and self-government should grow not by making laws but by usages and conventions. The impressive unanimity of the commissioners who from their known party antecedents must clearly have sacrificed all but their deepest convictions to attain it, ought to have commended their sagacious and temperately worded conclusions to men of goodwill." However, the Report was condemned by the Indians. The British Government itself had also partly forestalled it and ultimately side-tracked it, although some of its recommendations were ultimately embodied in the Government of India Act 1935.

The Indian point of view was that the recommendations of the Simon Commission were the most unsatisfactory. While the Indian demand was for complete independence or at least Dominion Status, what was actually recommended by the Commission was hopelessly inadequate. There was no recommendation for a responsible government at the Centre. Too many restrictions and limitations were put on what was given in the provincial sphere and no wonder, such recommendations were not welcomed in the country.

Dr. Tara Chand writes thus about the Simon Commission Report, "It deliberately omitted any mention of Dominion Status even as the distant goal of India's political progress. It recommended no transfer of power retaining all authority in the hands of irresponsible Central Government. In the provinces dyarchy was to be abolished, but the autonomy was hedged by the grant of special powers to the Government of India over financial matters. The Commission instead of rejecting the vicious principle of separte electorates against which it had given cogent arguments perpetuated it, offering an additional sop to communal intransigence."

Even the Viceroy was not satisfied with the recommendations and he wrote to the Secretary of State for India on June 20, 1930 : "The fundamental omission of all his Report, as I read it, is his very obvious and deliberate refusal to take the bandage off his eyes and admit the existence of the Dominion Status claim in terms."

Round Table Conferences (1930-31)

After the publication of the Simon Commission Report and its condemnation by the people of India, the British Government called the first Round Table Conference in London. The conference met in November 1930. As the Congress leaders were in jail, the government appointed safe men belonging to other parties, communities and interests to represent India. Representatives from the Indian states were also invited to participate in the deliberations and included men like Sir Mirza Ismail, Sir Akbar Hydari and the Maharja of Bikaner. There were lengthy discussions on the question of the future from the Government of India. The form of the new Government of India was to be an all-India Feberation in which the British India provinces and the Indian states were to join. Subject to special reservations and safeguards as might be considered necessary for the transitional period, the Federal Government was made responsible to the Federal Legislature. Provinces were to be given autonomy in their own affairs. At the end of the first Round Table Conference, Prime Minister Ramsay MacDonald made the following important statement : "The view of this Majesty's Government is that responsibility for the Government of India should be placed upon legislatures, Central and Provincial, with such provisions as may be considered necessary to guarantee, during the period of transition, the observance of certain obligations and to meet other special circumstances, and also with such guarantees as are required by minorities to protect their political liberties and rights. In such statutory safeguards as may be made for meeting the needs of the transitional period, it will be a primary concern of His Majesty's Government to see that the reserved powers are so framed and exercised as not to prejudice the advance of India through the new Constitution to full responsibility for her own government. Pledge after pledge had been given to India that British Raj was there not for perpetual domination. Why did we put in your hands textbooks from which we draw political inspiration ? If we meant that the people of India should forever be silent and negative subordinated to our rule, have our Queens and Kings given you pledges ? Why has our Parliament given you pledges ? Finally, I hope and trust, and I pray that by our labours together India will come to possess the only thing which she now lacks, to give her the status of a Dominion amongst the British Commonwealth of Nations—what she now lacks for that—the responsibilities and the cares, the burdens and difficulties, but the pride and the honour of responsible self-government."

As it was not considered advisable to proceed with the work of the final form of the future constitution of India in the absence of the representatives of the Indian National Congress, it was decided to call a Second Round Table Conference and in the meanwhile, efforts were to be made to bring about a reconciliation between the Congress and the government. The efforts of Sir Tej Bahadur Sapru and M.R. Jayakar were crowned with success and the famous Gandhi-Irwin Pact was signed in March 1931. The government released all the political prisoners. Mahatma Gandhi withdrew the civil disobedience movement. Mahatma Gandhi left for London to attend the Second Round Table Conference as the sole representative of the Congress. In spite of the magnetic personality of Mahatma Gandhi and his devotion to the work in hand, the communal tangle could not be solved. Mahatma Gandhi gave a carte blanche to Mr M.A. Jinnah but all efforts for a settlement failed on account of the uncompromising attitude of Mr. Jinnah and the part played by Sir Samuel Hoare, the then Secretary of State for India, in persuading Mr. Jinnah not to come to any settlement with Mahatma Gandhi by offering him better terms.

It is true that as a result of the economic crisis in the world and especially in England, the Labour Government of Ramsay MacDonald had been replaced by a National Government, but Ramsay MacDonald managed to follow his previous policy with regard to India at the Second Round Table Conference. Many problems were considered, but the members could not come to any definite conclusion. As regards the question of communal represention, Ramsay MacDonald made it clear that if the various communities in India did not come to any definite settlement, the British Government would be forced to give its own award regarding the same.

HOME RULE MOVEMENTS

The Irish people raised the demand for Home Rule and in September 1914, the Irish Home Rule Act received the royal assent. The grant of Home Rule to Ireland made Home Rule a respectable phrase. Mrs. Annie Basant explains why she chose the slogan of Home Rule : "I used the words Home Rule instead of self-government. The first is shorter: self-government is four syllables and Home Rule only two. For a popular cry a short name is better than a long one. Moreover, it was a more explicit phrase because self-government might mean independence, and so, to show that you did not mean a break between Great Britain and India, it was necessary to add, "within the Empire and so you have a great mouthful 'self-government within the Empire on colonial lines.' I prefer to call it Home Rule. The advantage is that it is a cry for freedom without separation." This term was borrowed from Ireland as it "reconciled freedom with no separation." To quote him, "In India too, the term Home Rule serves the useful purpose. For while it excludes the policy of separation... it elevates to the proper pedestal the policy of India being governed for Indians and by Indians." The ideal of Home Rule was adopted in India because it "briefly and beautifully expressed the subject matter or the claim for self-government within the Empire." The term was familiar to the Englishmen and saved them from all the imaginary terrors which the word Swarajya created in their minds.

Annie Besant

Mrs. Annie Besant was in the England in 1914. During her stay there, she tried to form an Indian party in the Parliament. However, she was no successful but she availed of the opportunity to arouse sympathy for the cause of India by her public addresses. She conducted propoganda in England in favour of granting self-government to India. She set up a Home Rule League and addressed a crowded meeting in the Queen's Hall, London.

In September 1915, she made a speech at Bombay in which she pleaded for Home Rule or self-government for India. To quote her, "I mean by self-government that the country shall have a government by councils, elected by all the people, elected with power of the purse, and the government is responsible to the House. Then I mean that there should be an elected element in the Imperial Council and that the Government there—the holders of portfolios shall be responsible to the elected House with the power of the purse in the hands of the representatives of the people. I mean that in the provinces, provincial parliaments also shall be wholly elected with the Ministry responsible to the Parliament, and that the Governor shall act as the King acts in England, his power being limited."

On 25 September 1915, she made a formal annoncement about the Home Rule League in New India : "After conversation in India and correspondence with England, which have been going on for many months and the beginning of which goes back to discussions held last year with some English politicians and sympathisers with India, it has been decided to start a Home Rule league, with 'Home Rule for India' as its only object, as a auxiliary to the National Congress here and its British Committee in England, the special function of the Committee being to educate the English democracy in relation to India, and to take up the work which Charles Bradlaugh began and which was prematurely struck out of his hands by death." Mrs. Annie Besant moved a resolution embodying her ideas in the Bombay Congress session in 1915 but the same was ruled out by Congress President on the ground that it contravened Article 1 of the Congress constitution.

The Moderates did not like the idea of the Home Rule League on the ground that "such an organisation would serve to overlap and perhaps weaken the Congress." The Moderates did nothing to give effect to the resolution of the Bombay Congress. No Home Rule Draft Scheme was prepared before 1 September 1916. Mrs. Annie Besant felt that she was absolved of the undertaking. She decided to organise the Home Rule League on a regular basis. It was formally inaugarated on 15 September 1916 with its headquarters in Madras.

Two hundred branches of the Home Rule League were set up all over India. Through the Home Rule page in New India, Mrs. Annie Besant advised the Branches about the work to be done. The members were to set up classes to lecture on political subjects. They were to establish libraries where the public could read literature on politics. Pamphlets on political issues were to be prepared and circulated. The League members were required to undertake social work in their areas, participate in municipal activities and organise public meetings and lectures to keep the objectives of the Home Rule before the public. About 26 pamphlets were issued in English and some in local language. They criticised the machinery of the government of India and a demand was made for self-government. Mrs Annie Besant herself made a whirlwind tour all over the country and delivered lecutres at Calcutta, Lucknow, Allahabad and other small and big cities. She criticised the foreign policy of the government, the expenditure on Home Charges, the methods of recruitment by government, the neglect of industries and education, land-revenue policy, etc.

Tilak

Tilak who had come back from Burma after six years of imprisonment, also decided to set up Home Rule League. The question was first mooted by J. Baptista in his Presidential Address at the Poona Conference held on 8 May. After welcoming the re-entry of Tilak into active politics after six years, he suggested that the World War offered a suitable opportunity to the Indians to demand Home Rule while helping the government in its war-efforts. Tilak concentrated his attention upon this along with the question of re-entry of the

Extremists into the Congress. As Tilak was as yet outside the Congress, he could give effect to his ideas without any interference from any quarter. On 28 April 1916 the Indian Home Rule League was set up with its headquarters at Poona. The object of this Legaue was to "attain Home Rule or self-government within the British Empire by all constitutional means and to educate and organise public opinion in the country towards the attainment of the same."

In the middle of 1916, Tilak went on an extensive tour for doing propaganda in favour of Home Rule. He explained Home Rule as a form of government within the British Empire in which the rule of the bureaucracy will be replaced by an administration responsible to the people. He appealed mainly to the masses while giving simple illustrations. He made it clear that he had no quarrel with the Emperor. To quote one of his talks, "Who rules India? Does the Emperor come and do it? It is carried on through servants like Viceroy, Governor, Collector... If it be said that the present Governor or Collector is not wanted and another should be brought, would that constitute sedition? Does the Emperor lose anything whether the administration is carried on by the civil servants or by our Belvi Sahib? The rule still remains, the Emperor still remains." He posed the questions: 'Why do we ask for Swarajya ? Are we fit for it? and answered : "We want only this one thing today. When this one is got, the remaining things come into our possession themselves... Why are we not fit (for Swarajya)? Have we no nose, no eyes, no ears, no intellect? Can we not write, have we not read books, can we not ride a horse? You bring from England a new man of 21 years as Collector. Has has any experience at all? He at once becomes the superior of a Mamladtdar of 60 years' experience who gets Rs. 150 to 400 a year and has to stand before the young man." For one generation, for two generations or three generations? It there any end to this? Or must we, just like this, work under you like slaves till the end?

In his speeches, Tilak declared emphatically that Home Rule was the only cure for India's political ills and grievances, that liberty was the birth-right of every man and the aspiration to get one's liberty was the essence of a human nature. A small minority outside

India could not be allowed to rule arbitrarily. In one of his speeches. Tilak observed, "Those who are ruling over you do not belong to your religion. race or even country...We do not want the Secretary of State who has been created a son-in-law... Basic Changes must be brought about so as to promote the well-being of the people... The question of Swarajya is in whose hands should be the administration carried on in our India?... The Swarajaya agitation is now carried on in the belief that this administration if carried on by some one else, or some other visible form would be more beneficial to the people than when carried on by those by whose hands it is now carried. To entrust to the people the responsibility of administrating their own affairs is the best principle in politics... There is no question about this. The same principle prevails in the country of those that are governing here in this land of ours. When these people go back to their country they have to uphold that principle...We want rights. We want a certain sort of arrangement giving happiness. We will get it. Our children will get it.

In one of his speeches, he declared that the man who had to live in England and manage the affairs of the whole Empire got Rs. 5,000, while the person who carried on the administration of India here got Rs. 20,000 per month and that was due to the fact that he was paid at the cost of India. Tilak stated ironically : "This is India, Go and eat." Continuing, he stated, "For the sort of injustice that is taking place in India, there is no other remedy than that the power should pass into the people's hands and rest in the hands of the people...We must decide upon the arrangement as regards what is to be done in our homes, what is to be done in our villages, what is to be done in our Presidency and what is to be done in our country... There are no means of salvation for us unless we have (self-rule) in our possession.

While winding up the first Annual Conference of the League held at Nasik on 17-18 May 1917, Tilak emphasized the role of the League and its difference from the Congress. According to him, the Congress was merely a deliberative body whose only or main function was to pass pious resolutions. On the other hand, the Home Rule

League was pledged to work zealously throughout the year for the sole object of achieving Home Rule. He did not thank those who wished the League a long life, but would prefer that the League be dissolved in two years after the grant of Home Rule to India.

In March 1917, the Government of India issued a circular letter to the local governments laying down the policy to be followed with regard to the Home Rule movement. In cases where the law was violated, prosecutions were to be launched without any hesitation. Students were to be prohibited from attending meetings where Home Rule was likely to be discussed. "It is scarcely necessary to state that neither the reforms recommended by the government of India nor any reforms which His Majesty's Government are likely to approve, can bear resemblance to the extravegant demands for the grant of early Home Rule to India which the agitators present to their deluded audiences. It is evident, therefore, that wider the hopes that are excited by the Home Rule organisation, the greater will be the disappointment and the more violent the protest when the actual reforms that may be aproved by His Majesty's Government come in due course to be promulgated." "In these circumstances, it is most important that the several Local Governments should take steps to check these extravagant expectations which have been engendered by the Home Rule agitators. It seemed desirable that the Local Governments should, through their experienced officers, point out to all Indians who are likely to listen to reason that any thought of early Home Rule should be put entirely out of mind. They should warn all men of light and leading and all those who have hereditary influene over the people at large to dissociate themselves from the Home Rule campaign as it is at present being conducted."

Government Attitude. The Government decided to curb the activities of the Home Rule Leaguers who were in the forefront of the agitation. The existing statutes were tightened. There was already the Ingress to India Oridnance of September 1914 to prevent the entry of undersirable alines into India. The Defence of India Act of March 1915 suprerseded the oridnary criminal law of the country and action under it could be taken against the agitators. The provisions of the Indian Press Act. 1910 were strictly enforced to stop the propoganda of the Home Rule Leaguers. Circulars were issued by which the students of the schools and colleges were forbidden from taking part in the Home Rule movement. In July 1916, Tilak was prosecuted for delivering seditious speeches and was ordered to furnish a personal bond of Rs. 20,000 "with sureties of Rs. 10,000/- each to be of good behaviour for a period of one year." Similar action was taken against Annie Besant. She was ordered to furnish security for her press and The Commonweal and New India. In all she deposited Rs. 20,000 and the whole amount was forfeited by the Government. The Government also took action against Annie Besant and her two associates, B.P. Wadia and G.S. Arundale. It is stated that the Governor of Madras called Annie Besant for an interview and told her that she was to be interned. Her reply was : "There is just one thing I should like to say to Your Excellency and that is that I believe you are striking the deadliest blow against the British Empire in India." Mrs. Besant had been expecting action of this nature for some time. "Unless the Government can muzzle the whole Indian Press as well as Reuter," she wrote, "the news of my internment will run round the world and proclaim how England, fighting for liberty in Europe and posing as its champion is more false to liberty in India than she is even in Ireland, is in India an autocracy, naked and unashamed, under which neither liberty of person and speech nor possession of property is safe." In the same issue of the paper, Mrs. Besant published a singed article in which she discussed how to carry on the Home Rule propaganda if the League was declared to be an unlawful association. There was a lot of indignation all over the country against the internment of Annie Besant. Protest meetings were held every where and the repression by the police was condemned. Mr. M.A. Jinnah joined the Home Rule League immediately after the internment of Annie Besant and her associates. A joint meeting of the All-India Congress Committee and the Council of the Muslim League was held on 28 July 1917. The work done by the Home Rule League was praised and the attitude of the Government was condemned.

Tilak did not suspend or relax the Home Rule agitation. He knew that it was the agitation which had forced the government to meet the demands of the people of India halfway and it was therefore necessary to carry on the agitation in order to obtain substantial concessions from the government. The Home Rule movement became more and more popular and tended to become a mass movement.

The activities of Tilak after the statement of Montagu in August 1917 were described in an official report as follows : "The capture of the Congress organisation by Mrs Besant and Tilak is complete. The Moderate party in the Congress is extinguished. The Congress is completely identified with Home Rule." After his arrival in India, Montagu had an interview with Tilak on 27 November 1917 and he tried in vain to secure the support of Tilak for his Reform proposals. He wrote in his Diary that Tilak "is at the moment probably the most powerful leader in India and he has it in his power, if he chooses, to help materially in the war effort.

There is no doubt that the Home Rule agitation practically ousted the Moderates from the political field. Neither Pherozeshah Mehta nor Gokhale could have possibly prevented his re-entry into the Congress even if they were alive. Even the utmost efforts of the Moderate leaders could not prevent the election of Tilak's nominee. Mrs Annie Besant, as President for the Congress session in December 1917.

The Congress session held in Calcutta in 1917 with Mrs Annie Besant as the President was a great triumph for the Home Rule movement. There was a record gathering with nearly 5,000 delegates and an equal number of visitors, including 400 ladies. The general view was that it was "the Congress of Mrs. Besant and Mr. Tilak—of Mrs. Besant more than of Mr. Tilak." With her usual eloquence, Mrs. Besant made a vigorous plea in her presidential address for the immediate introduction of a Bill in the British Parliament for the establishment of self-government in India, preferably in 1923 and not later than 1928.

"India demands Home Rule for two reasons : one essential and vital, the other less important but weighty. First because freedom is the birthright of every nation; secondly because her most important interests are now made subservient to the interests of the British Empire without her consent, and her resources are not utilised for her greatest needs. It is enough only to mention the money spent on her Army, not for local defence but for Imperial purposes, as compared with that spent on primary education.

"It is not a question whether the rule is good or bad. German efficiency in Germany is far greater than English efficiency in England; the Germans were better fed, had more amusements and leisure, less crushing poverty than the English. But would any Englishmen therefore desire to see Germans occupying all the highest positions in England? Why not? Because the righteous self-respect and dignity of the free man revolt against foreign domination, however superior. As Mr. Asquith said at the beginning of the War, such a condition was 'inconceivable and would be intolerable'. Why then is it the one conceivable system here in India?... Thank God that India's eyes are opening; that myriads of her people realise that they are men, with a man's right to manage his own affairs. India is no longer on her knees for boons; she is on her feet for rights. It is because I have taught this that the English in India misunderstand me, and call me seditious; it is because I have taught this that I am President of this Congrss today.

At this time, an incident took place which gave an impetus to the Home Rule movement. The Delhi War Conference was held in April 1918 and prominent national leaders from all parts of India were invited to attend it. However, the name of Tilak was missing. When this fact was brought to the notice of the authorities, the Governor of Bombay included the name of Tilak among the provincial leaders who were called in for consultation. While supporting the resolution on recruiting Indians in the army, Tilak stated that the enthusiasm of the people of India would be better roused if the appeal was coupled with a promise of Home Rule. This was not liked by the Governor and he asked Tilak to sit down. The repely to Tilak was that if he could not express his views freely, he had no option but to walk out and as he left the meeting many others like Mahatma Gandhi. B.G. Horniman Kelkar and a number of others followed him.

This incident annoyed the members of the Bombay Home Rule League. They resented the public insult to the members of the Indian Home Rule League. On 16 June 1918, a huge demonstration was held at Shantaram's Chawl. The day was Home Rule Day and was celebrated with a demonstration of volunteers flying flags throughout the city and collecting funds in aid of the Home Rule League. The principl market centres remained closed. In the evening, a meeting was held which was presided over the Mahatma Gandhi. A resolution was passed disapproving the methods and measures of the Government for the utilisation of the manpower and resources of India. In his speech, Mahatma Gandhi condemned the behaviour of the Governor. Mr. Jinnah expressed his doubt about the genuineness of the promises of the Government. The members also decided not to attend any meeting presided over by Lord Willingdon, Governor of Bombay, so long as he did not publicly withdraw his objectionable words.

The agitation for Home rule also continued in the press. In one of his editorials, N.C. Kelkar, editor of Mahratta, stated that India was determined not to take rest or allow England to take rest so long as she was not granted Home Rule. India would not and could not accept any "half-way house" to her ambition. Her people would not rest content with the crumbs thrown to them. To quote, "She refuses to regard her present position of milchcow to the British Empire as dignfied. There is no glory in being a bondman, though attached to the retinue of the most illustrious master in the world... The clash of arms is much better for mankind than an emasculating peace. Erring but responsible manhood is preferable to a life-long though secure tutelage. The rugged national life, the uneven social surface in pre-British times, was certainly preferable to the dead level and the dull uniformity, established by the steamroller of British rule in which first class eminence is impossible and all aspiring poppies are always in danger of being cut down."

A Home Rule for India League was established in London with headquarters at 1, Robert Street, Adelphi. It worked in cooperation with the British Committee of the Indian National Congress, the Britain and India Association and United India Society. The representatives of these bodies appointed a Consultation Committee for the purpose of taking concerted action in the advocacy of the Indian demand for home rule. Mrs. Annie Besant sent a message to the British labourers in England : "We are demanding Home Rule as our birth right... Help us to become a free Commonwealth under the British Crown and we will bring our manpower to secure the world peace. Our People have died in your war for freedom."

The result of the activities of the Home Rule Leagues was that eminent Americans and Englishmen wrote and spoke for self-government in India. A committee of members of Parliament was formed in London for the purpose of pressing forward the claims of India for self-government. In 1918, the Labour Party Conference at Nottingham unanimously passed a resolution in favour of Home Rule for India.

In order to counteract the agitation of the reactionary elements in England against the grant of responsible government to India, the Home rule League of Mrs. Besant had sent a deputation to England. The Home rule League of Tilak had also grown by leaps and bounds. At the Annual Conference of the Home Rule League, a resolution was passed urging the necessity of sending immediately a strong deputation of representative and influential men to England. Accordingly, Mr. Joseph Baptista left for England in July 1917 and carried on a campaign of lectures throughout the country. Tilak collected money for sending a Home Rule League deputation to England and one consisting of the Hon'ble Mr. Narasimha Aiyar and four others sailed in two batches on 10 March and 18 March 1918. They safely reached Gibraltar but were forced to disembark there and returned to India under the orders of the British War Cabinet.

In the meantime, Tilak decided to lead in person a deputation to England. Although the Government of India was as anxious to send him as he was to go, the War Cabinet informed the Government of India that they would not like the "energies of the civil population" which "should be concentrated on work essential to the prosecution of the war, to be distracted by violent inflammatory propaganda." The contention of the Government of India was that Tilak was "more dangerous" in India than he was likely to be in England. Ultimately, the Government of India prevailed upon Tilak to agree to the condition that he would not indulge in "political agitation". In September 1918. Tilak left for England and the first thing he did there was to seek the withdrawl of the ban imposed on him. His contention was that when a member of the Justice Party of Madras who suffered from a similar impediment had got it cancelled, there should be no discrimination in his case. The result was that the restrictions imposed on him were removed.

In order to carry on Home Rule campaign in the United States, Lala Lajpat Rai, with two others N.S. Hardikar and K.D. Shastri, was sent of the United States. They opend a branch of the Home Rule League at San Francisco which had been the centre of activities of the Ghadr Party for many years. On 20 May 1919, Harkdisar sent a report to Tilak informing him of the work done in America on behalf of the Home Rule League : "From the 9 February to the 6 May, a period of 86 days, I travelled through 20 states of the Union. I gave 83 popular addresses and arranged 25 different conferenes. The conferences were held in ten states and 25 large cities and were the result of 24 extensive tours. I sold 4,000 copies of 'Self-Determination for India' and 1,500 copies of 'Get Together on India'. In all the cities I was received at principal colleges and by the chief newspaper proprietors. Going from one place to another to speak. I could only arrange conferences at 25 places and had to refuse nine invitations.

Lala Lajpat Rai also sent a report in which he said, "Dr. Hardikar has returned from his tour which was very successful from every point of view. He brought new members, established new branches and secured also some funds. We have been issuing occasional bulletins to the United States Press giving them a summary of what we put in the English Press." He also sent a leaflet by Norman Thomas entitled, "Rebellion in India". Thomas was one of the speakers at an Irish Revolutionary meeting in New York at which the Indian question was also discussed.

The Government of India was receiving the reports that Lajpat Rai's wide publicity campaign in the United States was producing tremendous effect. The Bombay Government and the members of the Executive Council of the Viceroy were perturbed over what they called the "slandering" anti-British propaganda which the Indians and their friends were carrying on in the American Press. They had the reports examined by a senior officer who suggested counter-propaganda by the Government of India in the United States and the same was done. However, that was not much of a success as compared with the Home Rule campaign.

In the work of propaganda in Great Britain and the United States, the Congress was nowhere in the campaign which was carried on in the name of the Home Rule League and under the direction of Tilak. He was the torch-burner and the torch-bearer.

THE SURAT SPLIT

From 1905 to 1907 A.D., the struggle between various trends with the national movement was fought out also at the annual sessions of the Indian National Congress, culminating in the Surat Split of December 1907 A.D.

The agitation against the partition of Bengal made a deep impact on the Indian National Congress. All sections of the Congress united in opposing the partition. At its Banaras session of 1905 A.D., Gopal Krishna Gokhale, the President of the Indian National Congress, soundly condemned the Partition of Bengal as well as the reactionary regime of Lord Curzon. The Indian National Congress also supported the Swadeshi and Boyacott movement of Bengal.

There was much public debate and disagreement between the moderate and the militant nationalists. While latter wanted to extend the mass movement in Bengal as well as in the rest of the country, the moderates wanted to confine the movement to Bengal and even there to limit it to Swadeshi and Boycott. They did not like to include the programme of National Education and goal to achieve the Self-Government. There was a tussle between the two groups at Calcutta session for the presidentship of the Indian National Congress for that year (1906). In the end, Dadabhai Naoroji, respected by all nationalists as a great patriot, was chosen as a compromise. Dadabhai Naoroji electrified the nationalist ranks by openly declaring in his presidential address that the goal of the Indian National movement was 'self-Government or Swaraj' like that of the United Kingdom or the Colonies. But the differences diving the two groups of the nationalist movement could not be kept in check for long. They were not able to see that their oulook and methods, which had served a real purpose in the past, were no longer adequate. They had failed to advance to the new stage of the national movement. The militant nationalists, on the hand, were not willing to be held back. Different interpretations were given of all four major resolutions throughout 1907.

The moderates did not approve of all that happened at Calcutta session in 1906 and tried to undo the same at the next session of the Congress. Ferozeshah Mehta managed to shift the venue of the next session from Nagpur to Surat. Both groups came prepared for a confrontation, there were uproarious scenes on the opening as rumours spread that all for Calcutta resolutions would be dropped. The name of Dr. Rash Behari Ghose (he was very moderate) was proposed for the Presidentship. When Surendranath Banerjee got up to second the proposal, attempts were made to shout him down and pandemonium prevalied in the Pandal. The meeting had to be adjourned on the next day, Dr. Rash Bihari Ghose was elected the President, but when he got up to deliver his Presidential address, Bal Gangadhar Tilak ascended the plaform, stood in front of the President and demanded that he be allowed to address the audience. He refused to submit to the ruling of the chair that he could not be allowed to address at that stage. While this tussle was going on, the rank and file of the Extremists created trouble and there were clashes. All efforts to persuade Tilak failed. He stood with folded hands and refused to got to his seat unless he was bodily removed. Some persons from Nagpur and Poona rushed to the platform with lathis in their hands. Chairs were thrown at the dais and sticks were freely used. The session had to be suspended. As such the combined session could not be held and both the groups parted. Now the Moderates framed their own constitution and closed their doors to any of the Extermists. On the other hand, the Extremists intensified their activities and Tilak took the banner of patriotic nationalism to every nook and corner of the country. He said,—"We are the masters of our fortune and can govern them if we only make up our minds to do so, Swaraj is not far off from us. It will come to us, the moment we learn to stand on our own legs. Swaraj is my birth right and I will have it."

But, the long run, the split did not prove useful to either party. The moderate lost touch with the younger generation of nationalists. The British Government played the game of 'Divide and Rule' and tried to win over moderate nationalist opinion so that the militant nationalists could be isolated and suppressed. To placate the modern nationalists it announced constitutional concessions through the Indian Councils Act of 1909 which is known as the Morley-Minto Reforms of 1909. In 1911, the Government also announced the cancellation of the partition of Bengal. Western and eastern Bengals were to be reunited while a new province consisting of Bihar and Orissa was to be created. At the same time the seat of the Central Government was shifted from Calcutta to Delhi. On the other hand, repressive measures were undertaken against the extremist leaders, Tilak was imprisoned in a Burmese jail for six years. Restricitions were imposed on many newspaper. After nine years the two groups came together again in 1916 because this alliance was necessary to frustrate the divide and rule policy of the British Government.

CIRCUMSTANCES RESPONSIBLE FOR THE PARTITION OF INDIA IN 1947

Following were the Causes leading to the partition of India in 1947 :—

(a) The partition of our country in 1947 was the most painful event for us. The situation responsible for the partition did not arise suddenly in 1947. Many factors played a role in leading to this situation. Most important factor responsible was the 'Divide and Rule' policy of the British Government. The situation was encouraged by the birth and growth of the Muslim League. The idea of the creation of Pakistan was first initiated by Dr. Iqbal in 1931. The failure of the League in the election of 1937 is not co-opting the

League by the Congress in the Ministry etc., were other factors. The role of the Muslim and Hindu communal parties, the wish of Hindu and Muslim leaders to acquire power hurriedly also led to the situation responsible for partition. In 1946 when the Interim Government was formed under the leadership of Nehru, at first Muslim League joined it but later it boycotted the Constituent Assembly and was responsible for inviting communal riots in many parts of the country.

(b) In the atmosphere of communal riots the British Government reached the conclusion that it was not proper to keep India further under its control and delay in the matter might lad to the deterioration of the situation. British Prime Minister, Atlee declared on 20th February, 1947 that Britain would quit India by June 1948. Muslim league started emphasizing its demand for Pakistan all the more. Communal riots married the jubilation over the approaching independence. In 1946 there were communal riots in Bengal, Bihar, Bombay, and many other parts of the country in which thousands of Hindus and Muslims had to lose their lives. Gandhiji and other leaders made an unsuccessful attempt to put down the fire of communalism. British Government adopted an indifferent attitude of indifference towards these communal riots.

(c) Acceptance of the Mountbatten Plan by major political parties. All the major political parties gave their acceptance to this plan before the 30th June. Muslim League immediately accepted the plan happily even though it was truncated to deliberate over the plan. Congress session was held in Delhi on the 14th and 15th June, 1947. To prevent the large scale blood shed resulting from communal riots, the India leaders accepted the plan of the partition of India. But they did not accept the "Two-Nation Theory". Congress and other— Nationalist leaders turned down the demand of the League for 1/3 of India on the basis of population. In the N.W.F.P. and Sylhet district of Assam where the influence of the League was doubtful it was agreed to hold a plebiscite. In other words, the Indian leaders accepted the partition of the country but its basis was not religion (Hinduism and Islam).

(d) Lord Mountbatten and his plan. To make the task of transfer of power easy British Government appointed Lord Mountbatten as the Viceroy of India in place of Lord Wavell. He reached India on March 22, 1947 and immediately started negotiations with the various leaders of India from which he derived the conclusion that only solution to Indian political tangle was the partition of the country and creation of Pakistan. Taking stock of the whole situation as well as the attitude of the two main political parties he went to London on 18th May, 1947.

(e) Partition. The task of determining the boundaries of both India and Pakistan began immediately. On the other hand communal riots started in the country immediately after the proposal of partition. They mostly happened in Punjab. Within a few months a total of 5 lakh people fell victim to communal violence. Lakhs of people were rendered homeless. Amidst this genocide the country was declared Independence on 15th August, 1947. The contry was partitioned and the British transferred power to the Independent Nations of India and Pakistan. In Pakistan were included the areas of West Punjab, East Bengal, Sind and N.W.F.P. Indians overthrew the British rule after a struggle of about 90 years. Unfortunately the victory of this glorious struggle was tarnished by those hated events which took place immediately before and after the attainment of Independence in various parts of the country. Pandit Jawaharlal Nehru became the first Prime Minister of independent India and Sardar Vallabbhai Patel became the Deputy Prime Minister and the Home Minister. At the time of Independence, the British Government had given freedom to about 562 Native States to join either of the two countries or remain independent but with great diplomacy. Sardar Patel succeded in including majority of the Native States in the Indian Union. Only Junagarh, Hyderabad and Kashmir showed some hesitation in joining the Indian Unions.

❒

4

Rise of Left Paties

The terms Left and Right were first used as political terms in France during the French Revolution to distinguish the pro-Revolutionaries (the Left) from the anti-Revolutionaries (the Right). The terms acquired a wider connotation after the Industrial Revolution and the rise of Socialist and Communist thought.

Circumstances Favouring Growth of Left Ideologies in India. Leftism in India grew out of the special politico-economic circumstances prevailing in India towards the end of the First World War and was inextricably intertwined with the mainstream of the nationalist movement. These circumstances were:

(1) The romantic appeal of the revolutionary ideas of Marx coupled with the reflected glory of the new regime in the U.S.S.R. fired the imagination of the Indian intellectuals, political leaders, the terrorists and even the workers and made them conscious of a new ideology loaded with a socio-economic content.

(2) Gandhiji's slogan Swaraj and Swadeshi and his attempt to carry the message to every nook and corner of India gave a new orientation to the political movement. Even the workers and peasants were drawn into the mainstream of national life. The new development provided a fertile ground for inauguration of an organised and ideologically inspired socialist movement.

(3) A volatile section of the new generation of educated middle class with the spectre of unemployment starting them in the face had lost faith in the 19th century liberalism and all

that it stood for and was attracted towards individualistic terrorism or the new revolutionary socialist ideology.

(4) A section of the radicals felt unhappy with the 'weak and watery reformism' of Gandhi, labelled him as the leader of the 'forces of reaction' and saw his cult of non-violence as an obstructive element in the development of a real revolutionary mass struggle against British imperialism and its indigenous allies. These radicals also questioned the exclusive emphasis on Swaraj without a socio-economic dimension.

(5) The First World War brought in its train crippling financial burdens, rising prices of necessities of life, famine conditions and manipulative profiteering—all exposing the evils of imperialist-capitalist domination.

The Left Movements

Left movements in India developed into two main streams:

(1) Communism which functioned as a branch of the International Communist Movement and was by and large controlled by the Comintern and

(2) The Congress Socialist Party which functioned as left wing of the Indian National Congress and drew inspiration from the philosophy of Democratic Socialism. Both these movements drew support from the anti-imperialist sentiments prevalent in India.

The Communist Party. Towards the end of 1920, M.N. Roy and other Indian emigres at Taskhent announced the formation of the Communist Party of India. In India on 1 September 1924, Satyabhakta in a press note released immediately after the conclusion of Kanpur Conspiracy trial announced that he had formed the C.P.I. with himself as the Secretary.

The history of the Communist movement can be divided into five distinct phases:

First Phase. After receving thorough training at Moscow at the Communist University for Toilers of the East and assured of adequate financial support from Moscow, the first band of Communist revolutionaries Crossed into India only to find themselves accused of organising a conspiracy against the King Emperor. The movement picked up somewhat only after the Communist Party of Great Britain took upon itself to supervise and energise the movement in India. One of its emissaries, Philip Spratt arrived in India in December 1926 and organised a number of unions, edited newpapers and launched some youth and front organisations. Four Workers' and Peasants' parties were organised in Bengal, Bombay, the Panjab and the U.P.

The Communist movement during this period attracted notice by its being involved in conspiracy trials thrice, viz. the Peshawar Conspiracy Trial (1922-23), the Kanpur Conspiracy Trial (1924) and the Meerut Conspiracy Trail (1929-33). The Meerut Trial which continued for over three and a half years and ended with the conviction of 27 persons (half of them being nationalists or trade unionists) made martyrs of the Communists. The anti-British stance of the Communists gained for them sympathy of the nationalists. The Congress Working Committee set up a Central Defence Committee, sanctioned a sun of Rs. 1,500 and the defence case was pleaded by eminent nationalists like J.L. Nehru, K.N. Katju and F.H. Ansari. Gandhiji visited the prissoners in the jail in 1929 and expressed sympathy for the Communist leaders. In that atmosphere of unreserved sympathy for the Communists, the Congress members of the Central Legislative Assembly successfully opposed the enactment of the Public Safety Bill (1928)—a bill directed against Communists in India. The long drawn-out trial also provided a handy opportunity to the Communist leaders to make politically-loaded propaganda speeches that received wide coverage in the nationalist press.

In July 1934 the CPI was declared an illegal organisation.

Second Phase. At a time when the nationalist movement under Gandhiji's leadership made giant strides forward in arousing the masses against imperialist stranglehold, the CPI suffered from both organisational and ideological articulation. Receiving its cue from the decisions of the Communist International of 1928, the CPI attacked both the right wing and the left wing in the Indian National Congress. It were the times when the Congress had boycotted the Simon Commission (1928), adopted the resolution on Purna Swaraj (Dec. 1929), and launched the Civil Disobedience Movement (1930-31, 1932-34). The CPI sought to steal the thunder from the Congress popularity by attempting to project the triangular character of the contest (the people's struggle not only against foreign imperialism but also against Indian, exploiters). It attacked the petty-bourgeois-nationalist leadership of Gandhiji and charged him with acting as the tool of imperialism and thereby betraying the revolutionary struggle of the masses. It even denounced the Congress Left wing as a counter-revolutionary force and 'a dangerous obstacle to the victory of Indian nationalism.'

Third Phase. Taking policy directions from the deliberations of the Seventh Congress of the Communist International (Moscow, 1935) R.P., Dutt and Ben Bradley published their thesis entitled The Anti-Imperialist People's Front in India in March 1936. Dutt Bradley labelled the Indian National Congress as merely the united front of the Indian people in the nationalist struggle. They advised the Communists to join the Indian National Congress, utilise its solid party organisation, strengthen the left-wing within the Congress (C.S.P.) and oust the reactionary right-wing elements. The Communists, the CSP and the Trade Unionists planned to organise a Front Populaire on the basis of a common minimum programme. The Communist leadership failed to take advantage of the favourable circumstances or broaden the social base of their movement and the popular front never came into existence. All the same, profiting from the tide of rising mass upsurge and quickneing all-round political activity in the latter half of the 1930's, the Communists emerged from their political quarantine and found again a place among the radical elements in Indian politics.

Fourth Phase. When the Second World War broke out the Indian Communists, under advice from the Comintern leaders, continued their United Front Policy against all types of Imperialism (includingg Fascism and Nazism). Rather, the Communists scored a point over the Indian National Congress with the latter's initial vacillation and pro-British attitude of leaders like Gandhiji.

The Indian Communists, however, found themselves in a very false position when in June 1941 Hitler attacked the Soviet Union, the Fatherland of Socialism. The Communists in India staged a right about turn and relabelled the war as a 'people's war' and announced full support for the Allied-Russian war effort. The Government of India rewarded the CPI by declaring it a legal organisation in 1942. The Communists extended all possible support and even acted as British "spies" in suppressing the popular revolt of 1942.

Fifth Phase. During the period the CPI's posture was pro-Muslim; it sought to further widen Congress-League alienation and encourage all separatist elements and work for the division of India into a number oif sovereign states. Its strategy was to tighten control over at least one such state and to make it as a base for the liberation of the rest of India. Unfortunately, however, the Muslim League spurned the idea of an alliance with the Communists.

In 1942 the CPI adopted a resolution declaring India to be a multi-national state and identifying as many as 16 Indian "nations". In 1946 they put forward before the Cabinet Mission a plan for division of India into 17 separate sovereign states on the model of the Balkans or the U.S.S.R. By 1947 the Communist movement in India had lost whatever place it had in Indian politics and the CPI was in complete disarray. When national emancipation from British imperialism was the dominant instinct of the people, the CPI's extra-natonal loyalties and exclusive dependence on European models made it a suspect organisation. In fact the Communists' concept of Proletarian Internationalism could not be reconciled with India's national aspirations. Further, Marxism's basic articles of faith in 'class antagonism' and 'violence' are alien to Indian tradition. However, Marxist-Leninist philosophy, shorn of its extra-national loyalties, has some relevance to independent India. The yawning gap between the rich and the poor and the under-developed condition of Indian economy are favourable climatic conditions in which Marxist Socialism can take root in India and serve as the beacon-light for the down-trodden masses.

The Congress Socialist Party. The Congress Left wing emerged as a 'rationalist revolt' against the mysticism of Gandhism on the one hand and dogmatism of Communism on the other. Their ideological inspiration came from Marxism and Democratic Socialism and they stood for anti-imperialism, nationalism and socialism. Subhash Chandra Bose explained that the Congress Leftists were not only anti-imperialists but they also desired reconstruction of national life on a socialist basis. For the achievement of their goal they had to fight on two fronts:

(a) Light foriegn imperialism and its Indian allies.

(b) Fight the milk-water nationalists (the Rightists) who were prepared for a deal with Imperialism. In other words, they stood for complete independence and Socialism; they wanted Swaraj not for the classes but for the masses.

The disillusionment with Gandhian ideology and technique of nationalists struggle when Gandhi suddenly announced the with-drawal of the Non-Cooperation Movement in 1922, when the nation stood on the verge of a popular revolt. Gandhi played a similar card when he suspended the Civil Disobedience Movement in 1931 and called it off in 1934 and advised Congressmen to resort to individual satyagraha. The left-wing came to the conclusion that dogmatic adherence to the theory of Non-Violence 'was unsustainable' and based on 'slippery foundations.'

The Congress Socialist Party was not a rival political organisation to the Congress but was launched "to work within the Congress, to strengthen it, to mould and shape its policies. All the same, the Right-wing of the Congress labelled Congress Socialists as 'internationalists' and thus undependenable for the struggle for national liberation. The Communist branded the Congress Socialists as Social Fascists and 'fake socialists'. The Congress Socialists hit back by describing the Indian Communists as 'satellites of the U.S.S.R.', as 'social-chauvinists' and charged them 'with betraying socialism and distorting Marxism dialectics'.

The CSP condemned the Government of India Act 1935 as an anti-people united front of imperialism and the forces of national reaction and was critical of the Congress Party's acceptance of office in the provinces in 1937. It was because of the Socialist pressure that the Congress Election Manifesto of 1936 contained a programme for the removal of the socio-economic grievances of the people. The CSP disagreed with the Congress offer of conditional help for British war effort as it maintained that the war was a conflict between the partners of imperialism for repartition of the world.

The CSP was not in favour of negotiated settlement for the transfer of power but advocated the need for a revolutionary struggle to destroy edifices of imperialism, feudalism and communalism in India.

The Congrees Socialists described the Muslim League 'in league with Britain' and Jinnah as traitor to his country and tool of the imperialist. They hoped for Hindu-Muslim unity not on the basis of temporary pacts or agreements but 'by laying emphasis on the economic issues which equally affected the Hindu and Muslim masses of the country".

The CSP described the Partition of India as an act of surrender by the Congress leadership and admitted its own failure and that of the wider revolutionary movement in working out an alternative and positive policy.

Minor Leftist Parties

The Communist movement in India served as a nursery for the growth of many minor leftist parties during 1939-40. Most of these leftist parties centred round personalities and became near-defunct after the central figure disappeared.

The Forward Bloc. After losing the leadership contest with Gandhi, Subhash Chandra Bose formed the Forward Bloc in March 1939. The Bloc accepted the creed, policy and programme of the Congress but was not bound to have confidence in the Congress Hingh Command. It sought to rally all anti-imperialist radical and progressive groups under one banner.

Bose opposed the Congress attitude of co-operation with the British war effort and went abroad to seek military help for the liquidation of imperialism in India. In 1947 the All India Forward Bloc described the transfer of power as a bogus transfer and alleged that the frightened bourgeois had entered into partinership with British imperialism to defeat the mass struggle.

Revolutionary Socialist Party. The terrorists of the early 20th century provided the nucleus for the organisation of this party which was lauched in 1940. It stood for violent overthrow of British imperialism and establishment of Socialism in India. Ideologically the R.S.P. was closer to C.S.P. than the Communist party. The R.S.P. refused to support the allied war effort even after the U.S.S.R. had joined the Allies. The party described the transfer of Power and Partition as a "back-door deal between the treacherous bourgeois leadrship of the Congress and Imperialism".

Other Minor Parties. The Bolshevik Party of India was established in 1939 by N. Dutt Mazumdar, the Revolutionary Communist Party was launched by Saumyendranath Tagore in 1942 and the Bolshevik-Leninist Party was announced in 1941 by a group of Trotskyite revolutionaries like Indra Sen and Ajit Roy.

M.N. Roy, the pioneer of the Communist movement in India organised the Radical Democratic Party in 1940 after his complete disillusionment with Marxism. He veered round to the view that the Indian Revolution could not be brought about by the proleariat alone but only udner the leadership of a multi-class party.

THE HOME RULE LEAGUES

On 28th July the First World War Broke out between Great Britain, France, Italy, Russia, Japan and United States of America on one side and Germany, Austria-Hungary and Turkey on the other. In India the years of war marked the maturing of nationalism. More of the moderate nationalists adopted an actively pro-British attitude mainly in the mistaken belief that grateful British Government would repay India's support with gratitude and enable it to take a long step forward on the road to Swarajya. In 1915 two prominent leaders of the moderate group Dadabhai Naoroji and Gopal Krishna Gokhale died. After the death of Dadabhai Naoroji and Gopal Krishna Gokhale the leadership of the Congress came into the hands of the extremists led by Tilak and Annie Besant. They saw clearly that the British Government was not likely to give any real concessions unless popular pressure was brought to bear upon it.

In 1916 Mrs. Annie Besant announced her decision to establish a Home Rule League on the model of Irish Home Rule Movement. The Home Rule league was to be an auxiliary to the Indian National Congress. In 1916 Mrs. Annie Besant set up a Home Rule League at Madras. Tilak organised his own Home Rule League at poona. Both the Leagues worked the Unison and aimed at the achievement of self-government. The Leagues objective was to educate the people and to provide the Congress demand for self-government with support and strength of a nation united in knowledge of itself and its single aim. Mrs. Annie Besant said, "I am Indian tomotoms waking up all the sleepers so that they may wake and work for their motherland." It was durig this agitation that Tilak gave the populr slogan : "Home Rule is my birth-right, and I will have it."

Tilak went on a whirlwind tour of the country in 1916 and appealed to the people to unite under the banner of the Home Rule League. His target was not the British Empire or the Emperor of India but the bureaucracy in India. In his public speeches, he declared emphatically that Home Rule was the only cure for India's political ills and grievances. He said that a small minority from outside India could not be allowed to rule the country arbitrarily.

Annie Besant also toured the country and created a lot of enthusiasm among the people for the national cause. Her articles in the commonweal and New India were very popular. C.Y. Chintamani says; "Annie Besant stirred the country by the spoken as well as the written word, as scarcely as any one else could do." Annie Besant's work was particularly among the women of India who showed "uncalculating herosim, endurance and the selfless sacrifice of the feminine nature."

The British Government could not be expected to keep quiet in the face of a stir created by the Home Rule League and their leaders and it decided to curb the activities of those leaders who were in the forefront of the movement. Mrs. Annie Besant was detained and Tilak was ordered to fill a personal bond of twenty thousand rupees and provide two securites of ten thosand rupees each. Lokmanya Tilak appealed to the Bombay Court against these ordered and they were cancelled. New India had to deposit a security of Rs. 2000 in 1916 and it was confiscated and a fresh security of ten thousand rupees had to be deposited. In 1917, the government prohibited students of schools and colleges from attending Home Rule meetings. Tilak's entry into Pubjab and Delhi was banned. Dr. Besant, Arundale, and Wadia were interned. Pandit J.L. Nehru while commenting on these arrests said that, "the atmosphere became electric and most of the youngmen felt exhilarated and expected big things in the future." This made the Home Rule Movement more popular. All the Provincial committees of the Congress elected Mrs. Besant as the next President of 1917 session. The movement could not go beyond because soon Mahatma Gandhi took the reins of the Congress in his own hands and after 1919 started the Gandhian era in Indian politics.

The Ghadar Party

The Ghadar Party. This party was founded in 1913 by the Indians residing in America and Canada. Majorty of the members of the party were Sikh Jawans and peasants, while the majority of its leaders were educated Muslims or Hinuds. It had branches in several countries. Apart from America and Canada, this organised its branches in Maxico, Japan, Philippines, Malaya, Singapore, Thailand; Indo-China etc. After the First World War this party started sending its workers, supporters and weapons to the Indian revolutionaries. Hardayal who was the organiser of the party in U.S.A., published a journal, 'Ghadar', in various language—Millions of dollars were collected and contributed to pay for their (Ghadarities) expenses. Several people gave their life-long savings and sold their valuable belongings like ornaments, property and lands. The Ghadarities sent messages to Indian services and soldiers at many places urging them to break in revolt at an appropriate time. This party planned to launch a violent struggle from Punjab on 21st February 1915. Unfortunately, the British authorities came to know of these plans and took immediate action. The rebellions regiments were disbanded and their leaders were either imprisoned or hanged. But those who love freedom are never afraid of all these things. Inspired by the Ghadar Party, 700 men of the 5th Light Infantry at Singapore revolted under the leadership of Jamadar Chisti Khan and Subedar Dundey Khan. But they also failed. It is said that 37 members of these revolutionaries were publically executed while 41 were sentenced to life imprisonment. Prominent workers of this party were Barkatullah, Raja Mahendra Pratap, Jatin Mukerjee (popularly known as Cama 'Bagha Jatin'), Ras Behari Bose, Lala Hardayal, Madam Cama etc. were some of the prominent Indians who carried on revolutionary activities and anti-British propaganda in different countries. They dreamt of a free India. No doubt their dream could not become true in their life time but they inspired their brothers and sisters so greatly that the activities of revolutionaries continued even after them.

The Lucknow Pact

Lucknow session of the Indian Congress or the Lucknow Pact. In the beginning of 1916 A.D. most of the nationalists realized that disunity in their ranks was injuring their cause and that they must put a united front before the government. The growing feeling in the country and the urge for national unity produced two historic developments at the Lucknow session of the Indian National Congress in 1916 A.D. Firstly the two wings of the Congress were reunited. Mrs. Annie Besant made sincere efforts to unite the moderates and the extremists. The death of Gopal Krishan Gokhale and Ferozshah Mehta in 1915 A.D. cleared the hurdle in the way of unification of the two wings and the constitution of the Congress was so amended in 1915 that the Extremists could get entry into it. Thereforee, in 1916 A.D. the two wings joined hands with each other at the Lucknow session of the Indian National Congress. The Lucknow Congress was the first united Congress since 1907 A.D.

Secondly at Lucknow, the Indian National Congress and the All India Muslim League sank their old differences and put up common political demands before the government while the War and the two Home Rule Leagues were creating a new sentiment in the country and changing the character of the Congress, the Muslim League had also been undergoing gradual changes. The War period witnessed further developments in that direction. Consequently, in 1914 the Government suppressed the Alhilal of Abul Kalam Azad and the Comrade of Maulana Mohammed Ali. It also interned the Ali brothers—Maulana Mohammed Ali and Shaukat Ali, Hasrat Mohani, and Abdul Kalam Azad. The League reflected, at least partially, the politically militancy began to outgrow the limited political outlook of the Aligarh school of thought and moved nearer to the politics of the Congress.

The unity between the Congress and the League was brought about signing of the Congress—League Pact, known popularly as the Lucknow Pact. An important role in bringing the two together was played by Lokmanya Tilak. The two organisations passed the same resolutions at their sessions, but forward a joint scheme of political reforms based on separate electorates and demanded that the British Government should make a declaration that it would confer self-government on India at an early date. The Lucknow Pact marked an important step forward in Hindu-Muslim unity. Unfortunately, it was based on the notion of bringing together the educated Hindus and Muslims as separate entities. The Lucknow Pact, therefore, left the way open to the future resurgence of communalism in Indian politics. But the immediate effect of the developments at Lucknow was tremendous.

The unity between the two wings of the Congress and the pact between the Congress and the League had its desired effect at that time. The British government felt that some sort of constitutional reforms were necessary in India after the War. Therefore, in 1917, the then Secretary of State Mr. Montague declared that the aim of the British policy in India was the gradual development of self-governing institutions with a view to the progressive realisation of Responsible Government in India as an integral part of the British empire." It, ultimately resulted in the passing of the Act of 1919 and establishment of 'Dyarchy' in the provinces.

THE SWADESHI AND BOYCOTT MOVEMENT

The Bengali leaders felt that mere demonstrations, public meetings, and resolutions were not likely to have much effect of the rulers. More positive action that would reveal the intensity of popular feelings and exhibit them at their best was needed. The answer was Swadeshi and Boycott. Swadeshi literally, meaning of one's own country,' aimed at the promotion of indigenous industries and strengthen the nation. It was also an effective method of developing patriotism. The promotion of Swadeshi was accompanied by the advocacy of Boycott. People were asked to boycott foreign goods. It was realised that by organising the boycott of foreign goods which were mainly British, sale of these goods would suffer. This would hurt Britain's economic interests and the British Government would be forced to bow before the Indian demands.

In fact, the Swadeshi and Boycott were powerful instruments directed against the British rule. They attacked the foreign rule where it hurt most. About Swadeshi, Lajpat Rai said, "I regard it as the salvation of my country. The Swadeshi movement ought to make us self-respecting, self-reliant, self-supporting and last, not least, mantly. The Swadeshi movement ought to teach us how to organise our capital, our resources, our labour, our energies and our talents, for the greatst good of all Indians, irrespective of creed, colour or caste. In my opinion, Swadeshi ought to be the common religion of the United India." On the Boycott movement, he said, "The meaning of the boycott is this.... The primary thing is prestige of the government and the boycott strikes at the root of that prestige. The illusory thing they call prestige is more powerful and potent them authority itself and we propose to do this by boycott. We desire to turn away our faces from the Government House to turn them to the huts of the people."

Programme. This movement started first of all in Bengal, mass meetings were held all over Bengal where Swadeshi or use of

Indian goods and boycott of British goods were proclaimed and pledged. In many places public burnings of foreign cloth were organised and shops selling foreign cloth were picketed. The Swadeshi movement was an immense success.

The Swadeshi movement gave a great deal of encouragement to Indian industries. Many textile mills, soap and match factories, handloom weaving concerns, national banks, and insurance companies were opened. Acharya P.C. Ray organised his famous Bengal Chemical Swadeshi Stores. Even the great poet Rabindranath Tagore helped to open a Swadeshi store.

The Swadeshi movement had several consequences in the realm of culture. There was a flowering of nationalist poetry, prose and jounalism. The patriotic songs written at the time by poets like Rabindranath Tagore. Rajani Kant Sen, and Mukunda Das are sung in Bengal to this day. Another constructive activity undertaken at the time was that of National Education. National education institutions were literary, technical or physical education was imparted were opened by nationalists who regarded the existing system of education as derationalising and, in any case, inadequate. On 15 August 1906, a National Council of Education was set up.

Effects. The effects of the Swadeshi and Boycott movements wer*e* very signficant. They can be described under the following heads:

(a) **Encouragement of Native Industries.** Many cloth mills, soap and matchbox factories, cottage factories, national banks and insurance companies were opened. Acharya Prafula Chandra Rai opened his famous Bengal Chemical Swadeshi Stores, famous Guru Rabindranath Tagore contributed towards opening of Swadeshi Bhandar. Thus native industries got encouragement and partially the problem of unemployment was solved.

(b) **Effect on Literature.** Because of this movement articles were published in the native newspapers for the propagation of Swadeshi. National poetry, prose, songs and poems were composed. The lanes and roads of Calcutta were full with cries of Bande Mataram and National Anthem.

(c) **Use of Indigenous Products Increased.** The main programme of this movement was the propagation of native goods. Consequently, people got a feeling of using native things, this led to encouragement of cottage industries in the country. Their production increased and demand of foriegn goods suffered a set back.

(d) **Spread of National Education.** To carry on the propogation of national education, the National Council of Education was founded on the 15th August, 1906 and a national college was founded in Calcutta. These were very great creative works.

(e) **Role of Muslims.** Many Muslim leaders played an important role in this movement: for example, famous leader Liyaqat Ali Khan and professional Gazainan played very active role in this movement. Many other middle and upper class Muslims, However, remained neutral, or led by the Nawab Salimullah of Dacca even supported partition of the plea that East Bengal would have a Muslim Majority.

(f) **Role of the Students.** The students boycotted government schools and colleges. They played an important role in propagation of native and boycott of foreign products. They refused to bow before governmental repression.

(g) **Role of Women.** The women participated in the processions and picketing. Their co-operation was always forth coming hereafter.

(h) **The effect on British Government.** This movement just shook the British Government. The Government did not remain a silent spectator to these happenings. It let loose a reign of repression in Bengal. Meetings of the agitators were broken, political leaders were put to confiement without trial, the students were debarred from appearing in the examinations and government services, shouting of Bande Mataram was banned newspapers were suppressed, the Muslims were encouraged to oppose the Hindus, the picketeers were lathicharged and all sorts of threatening and intimidation were given to the symphathisers of the movement. However, the movement died out by the first decade of the 20h century and the partiton could not be anulled before 1911.

(i) **All-India Nature of the National Movement.** In this Swadeshi and Boycott Movement all the sects, men and women, old and young, from Bengal to Bombay and from Madras to Delhi and Punjab took part.

FEATURES OF INDIAN CONSTITUTION OF 1950 A.D.

The representative charter of the Constituent Assembly has Sometimes been challenged, but, if we go into the method by which it was elected we can easily come to the conclusion that nothing would have been more representative of the Indian people under the circumstances. The Constituent Assembly was elected by indirect election by members of the Lower Houses only of the Provincial Legislatures and each Provinces and each India State or group of States was allowed seats in proportion to its respective population roughly in the ratio of one to a million. The seats in each Province were distributed among the three main categories, Muslim, Sikhs and General, on the basis of population. Members of each community in the Provincial Legislative Assembly elected their own representatives by the method proportional representation with a single transferable vote. While these principles applied to the British Provinces, the method of selection in the case of representatives of the Indian States was to be determined by consolation with the Princely Rulers. The total numbers of members so elected from the British Provinces was 292 and from the Indian States 93 but when the Muslim League decided to withdraw its members from the Constituent Assembly of India, and the Assembly reassembled on 31 October 1947 the total membership was reduced to 299.

The Constituent Assembly of India took up its responsibility in great earnestness and carried it out in a spirit of great idealism and with a sense of dedication to the best interests of the country. It appointed a large number of committee, such as the Union Constitution Committee, the Union Powers Committee, and the Committee on Fundamental Rights, and discussed the reports of these committees most thoroughly. On 29 August 1947 the Constituent Assembly appointed a Drafting Committee under the Chaimanship of Dr. Ambedkar, one of the leading intellectuals of the country so far as understanding of the constitution was concerned, and this committee came out with a Draft Constitution of India in February 1948. Enough time was provided to all sections of the India people to study the Draft Constitution and express their views on it fully and frankly. The second reading of the clauses was completed 17 October 1949, and the third reading on 26 November, 1949 when the Constitution received the signatures of the President of the Assemby and was declared as passed. While certain provisions of the Constitution—those relating of citizenship, elections, provisional Parliament, etc.—were given immediate effect to, the rest of the Constitution effect to, the rest of the constitution came into force on 26 January 1950, a day reminiscent of India's declaration of complete independence as its ultimate goal twenty years ago.

The Preamble to the Indian Constitution. A preamble is a declaration of objectives, a sort of preface, with which a constitution begins. It is an introduction, not the body of the Constitution. It tells us what the makers of the Constitution want or what are the objectives of the Constitution.

The Preamble to the Indian Constitution sets out the ideals that the State should follow. These ideals are democracy, socialism secularism and national Sovereignty, and the provision of justice, equality and liberty. The Preamble says "We, the people of India, having solemnly resolved to constitute India into a Sovereign Society Secular Democratic Republic and to secure to all its citizens :"

"Justice : social, economic and political, Liberty of though, expression, belief, faith and worship equality of status and off opportunity; and to promote them all.

Fraternity assuring the dignity of the individual and unity and integrity of the 'Nation'.

In our Constituent Assembly this twenty sixth day of November, 1949, we do hereby adopt, enact and give to ourselves this Constitution."

The preamble is not a part of the legal section of the Constitution. No one can go to a court and say that the Preamble has not been enforced by the government. Still, it is very important. Because, it shows the way the government ought to run.

Features of the Indian Constitution

(1) Lengthy and Written Constitution. One of the distinctive features of the Constitution is its length. It is the most lengthy and detailed constitutional document any country has so far adopted. The original Constitution contained as many as 395 Articles and 8 Schedules, to which additions have been made by the subsequent amendments. The very fact that the Constitution is an amalgam of accumulated wisdom from all directions has made it necessary for the Constitution makers to ensure that no element of uncertainly was left in it. The task of reconciling the concept of Fundamental Rights, taken from the American model, with the Parliamentary system of Government, taken from England, was not an easy one by itself and the details had to be spelt out clearly. The makers of the Constitution were trying to impress upon the future Government of the country that the Constitution was not only a legal document but an instrument of social change. Again, in order to see that the Constitution did not break down during a situation of crisis, created by external aggression, internal turmoil or financial break down, they had to add laborious provisions relating to the Emergency of one kind or the other. The fact that the Constitution was based in good measures on the Act of 1935, which itself was a lengthy document, was also responsible for making the Constitution lengthy.

(2) Founder of Sovereign, Secular, Socialist, Domocratic Republic. Our Constitution came into force with affect from 26th January 1950. From this very day our country became a Sovereign, Democratic Republic. These ideals have been clearly mentioned in the preamble to our Constitution. Though India became a secular state since its independence and adopted the ideal to became a socialist pattern of society from the day she adopted its constitution, even then the Constitution was further made more clear by the addition of the words. 'Socialist and Secular', in the preamble by the forty-second amendment of the constitution in 1976. The meaning and significance of these words are as:

(i) ***Secular.*** Constitution of India declares that India is a secular state. It means that there is no state religion of India. The citizens are free to follow and practice the religion of their own choice. All the religions are equal in the eyes of state.

(ii) ***Socialist.*** India has been declared a socialist state by the 42nd amendment in 1976. According to this the government will do every possible work for the social and economic progress and welfare of the country. There is freedom from all forms of exploitation—social, political and economic . Every citizen will be provided with equal oppoturnities to progress in life. The ideal of equality reveals incomplete if it is restricted only to political sphere. It must extend to social and economic life too.

(iii) ***Sovereign.*** Sovereign means absolute independence, a government which is not controlled by any other power. When India was under British rule, it could not be called Sovereign country. But now India is absolutely free in deciding its internal and external policies.

(iv) ***Democratic.*** India has been declared democratic. The word denotes that—we have chosen Democracy as our way of life and we will govern ourselves through democratic institutions. Our constitution has given full and final powers to decide by whom they should be governed. Here every citizen enjoys political rights and the country is governed by the elected representatives of the people.

(v) ***Republic.*** The preamble declares India to be a Republic. It means that the Head of the state is not a monarch but a president indirectly elected by the people.

(3) Parliamentary Government. The Indian Constitution establishes a parliamentary Government in India. We do not have the Presidential form of government like America. The Parliament is supreme in our country. The Prime-Minister and the Cabinet are responsible to the Parliament. The President is a nominal head.

(4) Federal Government. Our Constitution has opted for a Federal structure. This means that the government is divided between two levels—the Centre and the state. Our written Constitution has clearly distributed Powers between the Centre and the States like America. Different States are not combined in our country but for the convencience of the administration our country is divided into States. That is why India is a union of States. The Centre is definitely stronger than the States, even though there is a Federal government in our country. The Constitution also establishes the system of independent and impartial judiciary.

(5) Independent Judiciary. The Constitution of India also establishes the system of independent and impartial judiciary. This is to ensure that judiciary is not influenced by the executive government when it takes its decision. This also ensures that the judiciary plays an important rule in case of conflict between the centre and the State governments.

(6) Fundamental Rights. Our constitution has provided several fundemental rights of the all round development of citizens.

(7) Direct Principles of State. Our Constitution has also provided a few directive principles of State Policy for the Union and the State Government. These principles guide the government to work for the welfare of the citizens. The government should follow these moral precepts.

(8) Unitary Features of our Constitution. In ordinary circumstances our country has a federal form of government but in an emergency the centre takes away some of the functions of the state. During an emergency, we have a unitary form of government in our country. In ordinary times also the government follows some features of the unitary form of government. In India there is a single citizenship and a uniform judicial system. The Central Government is the final authority to make laws on the subjects in the concurrent list. Moreover residury powers are given to the centre.

(9) Secular State. Every citizen has the right to profess any religion according to the Indian Constitution. The state cannot declare any religion as a state religion. All the religions are equal in the eyes of the government. No discrimination is ever made against any citizen because of religion.

(10) Universal Adult Franchise. The Constitution of India establishes the system of universal Adult Franchise. Under this system, every Indian citizen above the age of twenty one has a right to vote and participate in choosing the government.

(11) Emergency provisions. The Indian Constitution has also laid down some emergency provisions to cope with difficult times and situations of danger when government could not be run as in ordinary times. In case of national emergency fundamental rights can be restricted.

(12) Fundamental Duties. The Original constitution of India made no description of duties. However through 42nd amendment 10 fundamental duties have also been included in it.

(13) Safeguards for Oppressed and Deprived Classes. The Indian constitutions has several provisions which seek to proteet the interest of those people, who have been traditionally oppressed and deprived. Specially the scheduled castes and scheduled tribes.

CHANGE ATTITUDE OF BRITISH TOWARDS INDIA AFTER 1945

With the end of the Second World War in Europe in April 1945, India's struggle for freedom entered a new phase. The Revolt of 1942 and the INA had revealed the herosim and determination of the

Indian people with the release of the national leaders from jail, the people began to look forward to another, perhaps the final, struggle for freedom.

The new struggle took the form of a massive movement against the trial of the soldiers and officers of the INA. The government decided to put on trial in the Red Fort at Delhi Generals Shah Nawaz, Gurdial Singh Dhillon, and Prem Sehgal of the INA, who had earlier been officers in the British Indian Army. They were accused of having broken their oath of loyalty to the British Crown. On the other hand, the people welcomed them as national heroes. Huge popular demonstrations demanding their release were held all over the country. The entire country now seethed with excitement and confidence that this time the struggle would be won. They would not let these heroes be punished. Bt the British Government was this time in no position to ignore Indian opinion. Even though the Court Martial held the INA prisoners guilty the Government felt it expedient to set them free.

Following are the factors which changed attitude of the British Government:

(a) **Weakness of Britain.** Some historians are of the opinion the decision of the Labour Party to give independence to India soon was inspired by the fact that due to the disastrous consequences of the First and Second World Wars Britain had become very weak. Her military power had weakened. She herself had become financially depended on America.

(b) **New Labour Government.** After the World War II Labour government was formed in Britain. The new government was against colonialism and it had promised to give independence to India, so it sent the Cabinet Mission immediately to negotiate with the Indian leaders about the transfer of power.

(c) **Changed Balance of Power of the World.** According to some historians Britain changed her attitude after World War II because of this great war, she lost her financial and military power. She no longer remained the supreme power in the world. America and Russia emerged as the two great powers and these two supported Indians independence. In short, Britain had to change her attitude due to the presence of world powers.

(d) **Rebellions Feeling in the Indian Army.** The most powerful basis of every government is army and now in Indian army feeling of Nationalism had been aroused and it had demonstrated its patriotism on many occasions. At the call of Netaji in 1943 many Indian ratings of the Navy revolted against the British Government in Bombay. The increasing discontent against the British in the army forced the British government to change its attitude towards the Indian people.

(e) **Strong current of Indian Nationalism.** During the World War II there was a rapid spread of Nationalism among the Indians. On the one hand government is shaken by the military activities of Subhash Chandra Bose and on the other hand Gandhi gave the slogan of "Do or Die" during the Quit India Movement of 1942. Though Azad Hind Fauz got defeatd and Quit India Movement of 1942 was suppressed by the British Government through repression and terror yet the Government knew that the reign of terror could not continue in the fully awakened India for a long time particularly where nationalism and patriotism spread even amongst Army and Navy. We should remember these words of the Prime Minister of Britain, Lord Atlee, that Britain was conceding Indian Independence because Indian Army was not loyal to Britain and she (Britain) cannot afford to keep foreign armies in India to keep her under control.

(f) **Increasing Discontent Amongst the Farmers and Workers.** More than 70% of the Indian population are peasants and labourers. Gradually awakening took place even amongst them. In many parts of the country peasants carried on movements to lessen the tax burden and getting facilities of loan. At the call of the Nationalist leaders they stopped giving rent. Strikes began in the plantations, mills and factories.

(g) **Revolt and Discontent in the Native States.** The British used to consider the Native States as their supporters for quite sometime. But in 1945-47 the people of Hyderabad, Kashmir, Travancore, started the activities like strikes, demonstrations and destruction at the instance of Nationalist leaders. These activities led the British to realise that discontent against them was rapidly increasing even amongst the Native States.

(h) **Rule out India was no Longer Lucrative.** After the war the financial condition of India deteriorated greatly. Because of the adequate development of industries in India and the rise of nationalist feelings British imports declined greatly. Government could not impose more taxes. The Government thought that they could preserve their financial interests to some extent by giving independence to India and win over her sysmpathy and goodwill.

(i) **Fear of Communism.** Communism was spreading rapidly in the neighbouring country, China. It had also spready gradually in India. Because of the political fallings of the Congress, people could have turned towards Communism and for this matter also she took early steps to give Independence to India.

(j) **Asiatic Nationalism.** After the Word War II national movements spread rapidly in Asia. Negotiations were going on amongst leaders of many Asian countries for mutual cooperation. This renaissance and new spirit of Asia also led the British Government to thnik that it was impossible to continue the colonial system now.

(K) **Congress-League Agreement.** Congress and League came to an agreement with regard to creation of Pakistan. British no longer had this excuse that she could not give independence to India till the communal question was not settled.

❑

5

Civil Disobedience Movemet

There was no other alternative so Gandhiji launched the Civl Disobedience Movement. Unfortunately, at this time, the tragedy of Chauri Chaura occurred which changed the course of Indian history. Chauri Chaura is a police station, 15 miles from Gorakhpur in U.P. As a result of vigorous picketing, there was hardly any customer of foreign cloth or liquor in the local bazaar. On Febraury 1, 1922, a zealous police officer beat some volunteers who were engaged in peaceful picketing. The result was that all the volunteers of the neighbouring villages, numbering about 500, accompanied by a large crowd, went to the police station and asked for an explanation of the conduct of the police officer. Some neutrals pacified them and the whole party moved on. After they had proceeded some distance, there was a hue and cry in the rear. It was alleged that the police roughly handled some of the stragglers in the rear. The result was that the mob returned and began to throw brickbats. The armed police fired on the mob and dead bodis of two persons were found near the police station. It is possible that some wounded persons may have been removed by the mob. After some time, the firing stopped, probably because the police had exhausted their ammunition. On their approach, the policemen went inside and bolted the door. The mob set fire to the building. Some of the policemen perished and those who were driven out by the heat and smoke were thrown back into the fire after being besmirched with kerosene.

No official inquiry was held into the happenings. However, the President of the District Congress Committee made the following statement: "The scene presented a most horrible and gruesome appearance. Two buildings were still burning. The roofs of almost all the buildings had been burnt down. Some boxes and trunks belonging evidently to the members of the police force were found lying open without their contents. Twenty-two corpses, more or less burnt and disfigured, were lying there, seven having been almost completely burnt.....Besides these burnt corpses, there were two corpses, apparently of men of the mob, which were not burnt, one of them clothed in khaddar which had a gunshot wound. There was a very large number of brickbats and kanker, evidently used in attacking the police found in the compound. The last had a gunshot wound in the thigh and the chowkidars had brickbat wounds on their heads and bodies. It is said that all the police force stationed there, including the armed guard which had been sent there a day before, as some trouble was apprehended, had been murdered except two who were out on duty elsewhere, and one constable who managed to escape."

After the incident at the police station, many persons were arrested. More than 200 persons were put up for trial. In the course of the sessions trial in 1923, 170 person were convicted and sentenced to death. The others were sentenced to long terms of rigorous imprisonment. All of them filed appeals in the Allahabad High Court. In their judgement delivered on April 30, 1923, the two English judges confirmed the sentences of death passed on 19 persons who were considered to be the ring leaders and had taken a prominent part in the attack on the police. Three accused were found guilty of rioting only and were sentenced to two years' rigorous imprisonment.

The incident of Chauri Chaura was too much for Mahatma Gandhi who stood for complete non-violence. On February 11 and 12 1922, an extraordinary session of the Congress was called in Bardoli and it adopted a resolution expressing indignation at the violence used at Chauri Chaura and called for the suspension of the civil disobedience campaign throughout India. The resolution was in these words : "In view of the repeated warnings every time that mass civil disobedience has been imminent, some popular violent outburst has taken place indicating that the atmosphere in the country is not non-violent enough for mass civil disobedience, the latest instance being the tragic and terrible events at Chauri Chaura, near Gorakhpur, the Working Committee of the Congress resolves that mass civil disobedience contemplated at Bardoli and elsewhere be suspended, and instructs the local Congress Committees forthwith to adivse the cultivators to pay the land revenue and other taxes due to the government whose payment might have been suspended in anticipation of mass civil disobedience and instructs them to suspend every other preparatory activity of an offensive nature.

"The suspension of mass civil disobedience shall be continued till the atmosphere is non-violent as to ensure the non-repetition of atrocities such as at Gorakhpur or hooliganism such as at Bombay and Madras.

There was no positive response on behalf of the government in spite of the suspension of the civil disobedience movement. The government had its own view in the matter. The Viceroy had tried to create a wedge between Gandhiji and Maulana Mohammed Ali by using a speech of the Mualana referring to his desire to cooperate with the Amir of Afghanistan in case he invaded India. If trouble comes between him and Gandhi it means the collapse of the bridge over the gulf between Hindu and Mohammadan. If Mohammed Ali does what Gandhi desires and that no doubt will be to make the declaration (for apologizing)—Mohammed Ali will be lowered in the public esteem." Another move of the Government was to come to a clash with Gandhiji and arrest him. That being an important matter, Sir William Vincent, the Home Member, had recorded a minute on October 10, 1921 in which he discussed the pros and cons of the arrest of Gandhiji. The reasons given by the Home Member in favour of the prosecution of Gandhiji were:

(a) the serious effect which our inaction in face of his seditious speeches is having on the administration and upon all officers of government from Gazetted rank down wards,

(b) our inaction in preventing many who are against non-cooperation from coming into the open and driving many into the Gandhi camp,

(c) the impression created among Mohammandans that they alone were prosecuted and the Hindus were treated with greater consideration,

(d) Gandhiji may at any time force the government to prosecute him when the Prince of Wales was in India and that might be troublesome,

(e) a prosecution seems inevitable sooner or later and if we have to take such a step, the present is not an unsuitable time at the beginning of cold weather to initiate suh a prosecution and deal with any disorder,

(f) the real danger of delay is that no government in the position of the Government of India can allow such open sedition or attacks on the risk of reaching a time when the poison has gone so deep that prosecution is really impossible.

The reasons given by him against the prosecution of Mahatma Gandhi were:

(a) Gandhi is pledged to secure Swaraj by the end of December 1921 and his failure to do so may lead him to give up the movement and will certainly and naturally discredit him.

(b) He is losing a number of educated supporters who are opposed to his present activities, Muhammadans are angry because their leaders have been prosecuted; the Hindus are irritated because the Khilafat question is being made much of; the cloth movement is not likely to be a success in Madras on account of the Moplah rising.

(c) The danger of imprisoning Gandhiji at this time would increase his influence very greatly. He is now not only regarded as a great national hero, but by the ignorant as semi-devine. He certainly wants to be made a martyr in order to sucure support for his movement, thus consolidating it at a time when many of his schemes have failed.

(d) The result of prosecution would be a great increase in unrest and probably disorber just on the eve of the visit of the Prince of Wales.

(e) If we do not prosecute Gandhiji at this stage, we must expect hartals and abstensions from ceremonies in connection with the visit of the Prine of Wales. If on the other hand we prosecute him, we shall certainly encourage open demonstrations against His Royal Highness and may be faced with such wide disorder as to make it necessary to postpone the visit.

(f) The question of modification of the Trukish peace terms in favour of Turkey may be considered so that the Muhammadans may leave Gandhiji's movement. On the whole, the view of the Home Members was that the arrest and prosecution of Gandhiji should be postponed.

However, when the visit of the Prince of Wales to India was over and the civil disobedience campaign was suspended by Gandhiji in Febraury 1922, the Government of India decided to take action against him and Mahatma Gandhi was arrested on March 13, 1922. He was tried at Ahmedabad in the court of Mr C.M. Broomfield Mahatma Gandhi pleaded guilty to the charges levelled against him.

According to Gandhiji

"The greatest misfortune is that Englishmen and their Indian associates in the administration of the country do not know that they are engaged in the crime I have attempted to describe. I am satisfied that many English and Indian officials honestly believe that they are administering one of the best systems devised in the world and that India is making steady though slow progress. They do not know that a subtle but effective system of terrorism and an organised display of force on the one hand and the deprivation of all powers of retaliation or self-defence on the other have emasculated the people and inducted in them the habit that has added to the ignorance and the self-deception of the administrators. Section 124-A under which

I am happily charged, is perhaps the prince among the political sections of the Indian Penal Code designed to suppress the liberty of the citizen. Affection cannot be manufactured or regulated by law. If one has no affection for a person or thing, one should be free to give the fullest expression to his disaffection so long as he does not contemplate, promote or incite violence.

"In fact Gandhiji believe that I have rendered a service to India and England by showing in non-cooperation the way out of the unnatural state in which both are living. In my humble opinion non-cooperation with evil is as much a duty as is cooperation with good. But in the past, non-cooperation has been deliberately expressed in violence to the evil-doer. I am endeavouring to show to my countrymen that violent non-cooperation only multiplies evil, and that as evil can only be sustained by violence, withdrawal of support of evil requires complete abstention from violence. Non-violence implies voluntry submission to the penalty for non-cooperation with evil. The only course open to you, the Judge and the assessors, is either to resign your posts and thus dissociate yourselves from evil if you feel that the law you are called upon to administer is an evil and that in reality I am innocent, or to inflict on me the severest penalty if you believe that the system and the law you are assisting to administer are good for the people of this country and that my activity is, therefore, injurious to the public weal."

Mahatma Gandhi was convicted and sentenced to six years' imprisonment as in the case of Tilak on a similar charge. However, he was released in February 1924 on grounds of health.

Before the departure of Gandhiji from the court at Ahmedabad, there were huge crowds to bid him good-bye. Their eyes were full of tears. Mrs Sarojini Naidu describes the scene in these words : "The pent-up emotion of the people burst in a storm of sorrow as a long, slow procession moved towards him in a mournful pilgrimage of farewell, clinging to the hands that had toiled so incessantly, bowing over the feet that had journeyed so continuously in the service of his country. In the midst of all this poignant scene of many-voiced and myriad-hearted grief, he stood untroubled, in his transcendent simplicity, the embodied symbol of the Indian nation—its living sacrifice and sacrament in one."

Commenting on the conviction of Gandhiji, Dwijendra Nath Tagore wrote : "The present government appears to me to be bound hand and foot by the evil precedence of the high handed British rulers of the past and the short sighted ill-advisers of the present times, so that it is incapable of doing towards the people of India anyting that is wise, good, just and humane. On the contrary, it is always ready to do anything that is unwise evil, unjust and inhuman at the bidding of a handful of mercantile adventures and those favourable priests of Jehovah whose god is the merciless God of Joshua and his gang rather than the Heavenly Father of Jesus Chist, so far as it can do with impunity."

Criticism of the Mahatma's Action in Suspending the Movement

The action of Mahatma Gandhi in suspending the Movement was severely criticised from many quarters. According to Dr. Pattabhi Sitaramayya, "Long letters were written from behind the bars by Pt. Motilal Nehru and Lala Lajpat Rai. They took Gandhi to task for punishing the whole country for the sins of a place." According to Subhash Chandra Bose C.R. Das was "beside himself with sorrow". To quote Bose. "To sound the order of retreat just when public enthusiasm was reaching the boiling point was nothing short of a national calamity." According to Jawaharlal Nehru, "We in prison learnt to our amazement and consternation that Gandhi had stopped the agreessive aspect of our struggle, that he had suspended civil disobedience." He asked : "Why should a town at the foot of the Himalayas be penalised if a viliage at Cape Comorin failed to observe non-violence ? Isolate Chauri-Chaura and if need be, Gorakhpur, but go on with civil disobedience, individual and mass."

According to C.R. Das, "The Mahatma opens a campaign in a brilliant fashion, he works it up with skill, he moves from success till he reaches the zenith of his campaign but after that he loses his nerve and begins to falter." According to Polak, "The Muslims wilted under the blow and it was never again possible to restore the confidence and fraternity that had united the two communities during this brief period of alliance."

The Muslims felt that their own grievances, including the Khilafat question, had been pushed into the background and they had been utilized merely to further the Hindu aim of Swaraj for India. At that time in the Punjab there was prevalent a common joke that Swaraj meant Swah (ashes) for the Muslims and Raj for the Hindus. This kind of feeling among the Muslims was shared by their leadedrs who, however, realised the necessity of concealing it in order to maintain at least a semblance of much-desired communal unity.

However, Pt. Jawaharlal Nehru justified the action of Mahatma Gandhi later on, on ground of practical politics. The incident of Chauri Chaura was not a solitary one. It was only the last straw. There was practically no discipline among the volunteers. There were frequent cases of violence. As practically all the leaders of the Congress were in jails with the exception of Mahatma Gandhi, it was not possible to lead the movement on the right lines. Towards the end of 1921, there had occurred the Moplah rising in Malabar with the object of establishing a Khilafat State. However it took a communal turn and the Moplahs slaughtered not only a few British officials but far more Hindu neighbours. If the movement had not been stopped by Mahatma Gandhi, there was every possibility of more violence in the country and that would have given the government a chance to crush the same with a lot of curelty.

Shortcomings of the Movement

As regards the shortcomings and achievements of the Non-Cooperation Movement, the movement apparently failed to achieve its object of securing the redress of Khilafat and Punjab wrongs. The Swaraj was not attained in one year as promised by Mahatma Gandhi. According to Subhas Chandra Bose, "The promise of Swaraj withn one year was not only unwise but childish." The Congress ought not to have identified itself with the Khilafat Movement. According to Polak, the Khilafat Movement "rested on a wrong foundation. While Indian Muslims were reviving the romantic, old world tradition of an

Islamic theocracy, the Turks in whose interest they believed they were acting, were tossing it aside as medieval lumber." Under Kamal Pasha, Trukey became a secular State and the institution of the Khilafat was abolished in 1922 and the Khalifa himself was exiled. The sudden suspension of the movement increased Hindu-Muslim tension. There started "a series of communal riots which raged, with brief intervals, for many years and surpassed in bitterness the records of the past."

Achievements of the Movement

However, there is a lot to be said in favour of the achievements of the Non-Cooperation Movement. According to Subhas Chandra Bose, "The year 1921 undoubtedly gave the country a highly organised party organisation. Before that the Congress was a constitutional party and mainly a talking body. The Mahatma not only gave it a constitution and a nation-wide basis, but what is more important converted it into a revolutionary organization. Uniform slogans were repeated everywhere and uniform policy and ideology gained currency from one end of India to the other. The English language lost its importance and the Congress adopted Hindi as the lingua franca for the whole country. Khadi became the official uniform for all Congressmen." According to Coupland. "He (Gandhi) had done what Tilak had failed to do. He had converted the national movement into a revolutionary movement. He had taught it to pursue that goal of India's freedom by constitutional pressure on the government, still less by discussion and agreement, but by force, none the less force becaues it was meant to be non-violent. And he had not only made the national movement revolutionary, he had also made it popular. It had hitherto been confined to the urban intelligentsia; it had made no appeal to the country folk. Gandhi's personality had deeply stirred the countryside."

Again, "We found the whole countryside afire with enthusiasm and full of a strange excitement. Enormous gatherings would take palce at the briefest notice by word of mouth. One village would communicate with another, and the second with the third and so on, and presently the whole village would empty out and all over the fields there would be men and women and chidlren on the march to the meeting place....Their faces were full of excitement and their eyes glistened and seemed to expect strange happenings which would, as if by a miracle, put an end to their long misery." According to A.R. Desai, "With the seciton of workers and peasants participating in it, the nationalist movement which was restricted to the upper and middle-classes till 1917, got a mass basis for the first time." The Non-Cooperation Movement added to the self-reliance of the people. They were no more afraid of the strength of British Government. The prisons lost their terror and became places of pilgrimage for the liberation of the country. Swadeshi became popular. Khadi became the uniform of the Indian patriots. The Congress became a mass movement.

The progressive participation of the capitalist class in the non-cooperation movement was symbolized by the active cooperation of Seth Jamna Lal Bajaj and others. In a speech delivered by him at the Nagpur Session of the Congress in 1920, he stated that he considered it to be the proudest occasion in his life when a person like him had been allowd the proud privilege to "worship at the highest altar of motherland". While exhorting the members of his class who appeared to him to have remained rather "listless towards national Yajna", he said that they too had certain grave responsibilities towards their country and they should realise them at the time of the national crisis. They should look upon the organisation of the non- cooperation movement as the only available and most helpful instrument to put pressure on the alien regime.

Those who participated in the non-cooperation movement came from every stratum of Indian society. There were princes like the Maharaja of Nabha. There were the peasants who were stricken with poverty and oppressed and exploited by the zamindars. There were the members of the merchantile classes and discontented industrlists. There were shopkeepers and traders. There were exploited and overworking artisans and labourers. There were unemployed white-collar clerks and babus. There were lawyers and writers with nationalists back-ground and patriotic college and university students.

Inspired by the ideal "let there be no distinction between rich and poor, high and low, they are all bed-fellows in adversity", every class appeared to be feeling that without mutual surrender there was no hope for their country. All these became more or less united on the political platform of the Congress to attain their common object.

Maulana Abul Kalam Azad, Maulavi Kifayat Ullah, Azad Subhani and others played upon politically and socially obscurantist plans of issuing Fatwa declaring it impermissible for the Muslims to become the members of the government councils, to plead as Vakil before the British courts, to read in government schools and to keep honorary posts and titles. It was emphatically declared in the Fatwa that to serve in the police and the army was a great sin because they had to fire upon their brethren. The distribution of the Fatwa in public, its sticking in running train carriages and distribution to the passengers along with sermonising the Indian sepoys going on leave or travelling by train, undoubtedly played an important part in inciting the people against the government.

By his agitation, Gandhiji created a new situation in the country. He gained a hold on the population greater than that of any former nationalist leader. He organised successfully a widespread resistance to British authority unparalleled since 1857-58. Under Congress leadership he set up a national powerful movement directed towards conflict rather than cooperation with the British Government and enjoying a large following among the town population throughout the country. The people lost all fear of imprisonment. British rule rested on the tacit consent of the bulk of the population but Gandhiji had sown that among the illiterate classes, such consent was no longer assured.

C.R. Das observed thus in the Gaya session of the Indian National Congress held in 1922 : "It is assumed that a movement must either succeed or fail, whereas the truth is that human movements—I am speaking of genuine movements—neither altogether succeed nor altogether fail. Every geneuine movement proceeds from an ideal and the ideal is always higher than the achievement... Was the Non-cooperation Movement in India a success ? Yes, a mighty success when we think of the disire for Swaraj which it has succeeded in awakening throughout the length and breadth of this vast country. It is a great success when we think of the practical result of such awakening, in the money which the nation contributed, in the enrolment of the members of the Indian National Congress and in the boycott of foreign cloth. I go further and say that the practical achievement also consists of the loss of prestige suffered by educational institutions and the courts of law and the reformed Councils throughout the country... Yet it must be admitted that from another point of view, when we assess the measure of our success in the spirit of arthemtic, we are sure to face with 'the petty done' and the 'undone vast'...I say to our critics : I admit we have failed in many directions, but will you also not admit our success where we have succeeded ?"

Dr. R.C. Majumdar says that the most outstanding feature of the non-cooperation movement was the wilingness and ability of the people in general to endure hardships and punishments inflicted by the Government. It is true that the movement collapsed but the memory of its greatness survived and was destined to inspire the nation to launch a more arduous campaign. The movement served as a baptism of fire which initiated the people to a new faith and new hope and inspired them with a new confidence in their power to fight for freedom. As a result of this movement, the Congress movement for the first time became a really mass movement. The national awakening not only penetrated to the people at large but also made them active participants in the struggle for freedom. Moreover, the Indian National Congress was truned into a genuine revolutionary organisation. It was no longer a deliberative assembly but an organised fighting party pledged to revolution.

Table Conference (1931)

Mahatma Gandhi attended the second Round Table Conference as the sole representative of the Congress. The Conference lasted upto December 1, 1931. The subjects discussed were the future constitutional structure for India and the representation of minorities. Mahatma Gandhi demanded control over defence forces and foreign affairs. His view was that "If these were granted, he would not himself aspire to complete independence." It was brought to his notice that his stand was a deviation from the Lahore Resolution of 1929. But the view of Mahatma Gandhi was that Dominion Status would ultimately lead to complete independence. There was a complete deadlock on the question of representation of minorities. M.A. Jinnah, H.H. the Agha Khan, Zaffarullah Khan and B.R. Ambedkar were not willing to come to a settlement with Mahatma Gandhi. On October 8, 1931, Mahatma Gandhi declared : "It is with deep sorrow and deeper humiliation, that I have to announce utter failure on my part to secure an agreed solution of the communal question through informal conversation among and with the representatives of different groups." Before the Plenary Sessions of the Conference held on December 1, 1931 Prime Minister Ramsay MacDonald declared that the British Government held the view that "responsibility for the Government of India should be placed upon the Legislatures, Central and Provincial, with such provisions as may be necessary to guarantee during the period of transition, the observance of certain obligations and to meet other special circumstances and also with such guarantees as are required by the minorities to protect their politial rights." The British Government was prepared "to recognise the principle of responsibility of the Executive to the Legislature, if both were constituted on an All-India Federal basis." The Prime Minister expressed the view that the "N.W.F. Province should be constituted a Governor's Province of the same status as other Governor's Provinces and that Sind should be constituted a separate Prvoince if satisfactory means of financing it could be found." The Prime Minister also declared that as the Indian leaders had failed to agree, the British Government will decide "as wisely and justly as possible, what checks and balances the constitution is to contain to protect the minorities from unrestricted and tyranncial use of the democratic principle expressing itself solely through the majority power." It is pointed out that the statement was the outcome of a secret alliance between the British Government and the representatives of the Muslim League. It is stated that when the speech of the Prime Minister was over, Mahatma Gandhi declarded that they had "come to the parting of ways" and their ways would hereafter "take different directions."

GANDHIJI'S RETURN AND AFTER

Mahatma Gandhi came back to India on December 28, 1931. On December 29, he sent a telegram to the Viceroy in which he expressed his great concern over the happenings in the country. He particularly referred to the uncalled for shootings and arrests.

Lord Willingdon and his Government believed that Lord Irwin had committed an error in negotiating with the Congress and singing a truce and they had no intention of repeating the same. The Viceroy was "perfectly clear as I have always been that Gandhi is a sort of Jekyll and Hyde and while he may possibly have his saint-like side, on the other he is the most Machiavellian bargaining little political humbug I have ever come across." When Gandhiji asked for an interview with the Viceroy, he was asked first to repudiate his colleagues and to agree not to discuss Bengal, the U.P. and the North-West Fronteir Province where also a number of stern ordinances had been imposed and Abdul Ghaffar Khan had been arrested. These terms could not be acceptable to Gandhiji. When the Working Committee decided on a resumption of Civil Disobedience, Gandhiji, Patel and other leading Congressmen were arrested. On January 4, 1932, the Government of India issued four ordinances, viz., The Emergency Powers Ordinance, Unlawful Instigation Ordinance, Unlawful Association Ordinance and Prevention of Molestation and Boycott Ordinance. Within a short time, the number of ordinances reached thirteen. The scope of these ordianances was very comprehensive and they covered "almost every activity of Indian life". Even Sir Samuel Hoare, Secretary of State for India, was made to admit that those Ordinances were "very drastic and severe". The view of Winston Churchill was that the Ordinances were more drastic than any that were required "since the Mutiny".

By January 10, 1932, all the leading Congressmen were behind the prison bars. Not only the Congress was declared illegal, but even those organisations which were in any way connected with it or were sympathetic towards it, were declared illegal. Youth leagues, students' associations national schools and institutions, Congress hospitals, Swadeshi concerns and libraries were all declared illegal. The action taken by the government in 1932 created a veritable reign of terror. There was no rule of law and there was no administration by civilised methods of the modern age. The British rulers in India sank to the level of the barbarous tyrants of the Medieval Age. The only parallel in modern Europe is to be found in the atrocities committed by Hitler and his associates in Germany.

The India League sent a delegation consisting of a majority of Englishmen to India in 1932 in order to see with their own eyes as to what was happening in the country. That delegation of the India League submitted a Report and Bertrand Russell wrote a preface to that Report in which the following passage occurs : "There has been no lack of interest in the misdeeds of the Nazis in Germany; they have been fully reported in the Press and have been commented on with self-rigteous indignation. Few people in England realise that misdeeds quite so serious are being perpetrated by the British in India."

It is stated in the Report of the Delegation of the India League that in 1932 the Ordinances and Acts passed deprived Indian people of the rights of personal freedom and safeguards which most British people believe.

POONA PACT (1932)

When on the publication of the Communal Award, it was found that the British Government was determined to give separate communal representation to the depressed classes, Mahatma Gandhi wrote to the British Prime Minister requesting him not to do so. The result was that Mahatma Gandhi went on fast unto death and his condition began to deteriorate. This put the Indian leaders in great difficulty. There were hectic negotiations and ultimately the Poona Pact was signed in September 1932 and accepted by the British Government. The poona Pact reserved certain seats for depressed classes out of the general seats in the provincial legislatures as follows. Madras 30, Bombay with Sind 15, Punjab 8, Bihar and Orissa 18, C.P. 20, Assam 7, Bengal 30 and U.P. 20. The total of the reserved seats for the depressed classes was 148.

The Communal Award was in keeping with the British policy of "devide and rule". If the Muslims were to vote only for the Muslims and the Muslim Legislators had to look to the Muslim voters alone, there could be no friendly relations between the Muslims and the Hindus and with the passage of time, the two communities were bound to be away from each other. The final outcome could only be separation and that was what actually happened in 1947. It was this Communal Award which enabled Mr. Jinnah to appeal to the Muslim voters in the name of Islam and Pakistan. It can be pointed out the so-called Muslim interests could be safeguarded by reserving a certain number of seats for them but without separate Muslim electorates. In that case, the Muslims would have been returned to the legislatures to protect the Muslim interests but they would have been elected by voters who were not only Muslims but also Hindus, Christains, Sikhs, and others. In this manner the evil of communalism would have been avoided. But that could happen only if the British Government and its officials were anxious to maintain the unity of India. The sad fact was that they were not at all interested whether such decision would ultimately affect the unity of the country irrevocably or not.

Lord Zetland criticized the Communal Award in these words : "It is one thing to concede separate communal electorates for the purpose of giving minorities reasonable representation in the various legislatures; it is an entirely different thing to employ the system for the purpose of conferring upon a majority community in any particular province a permanent majority in the legislature unalterable by any appeal to the electorate. Such a course has never hitherto been adopted. It was considered and rejected by the Statutory Commission, who declard that a claim submitted to them which in Bengal and Punjab would give to the Muslim community a fixed and unalterable majority in the general constituency seats, was one which they could not entertain; it would be unfair, they wrote, that the Mohammedans should retain the very considerable weightage they now enjoy in the six provinces and that there should at the same time be imposed, in the face of Hindu and Sikh opposition, definite majoirty in the Punjab and Bengal unalterable by an appeal to the electorate."

In his Presidential Address to the Congress Nationalist Party Conference held at Calcutta in August 1934, Pandit Madan Mohan Malaviya remarked : "At present, we are living under one government, of course a foriegn government, but what shall we get by means of this communal electorate ? Not a Government by the people, for the people and of the people, but a Government of one community over another. In the Punjab, it will be a Government by Muslims of Hindus, and in the United Provinces it will be a Government by Hindus of Mulims. It will not be democracy. It will be a special kind of despotic Government. It will be tyranny of one community over another and it is this despotism which the Communal Award seeks to instal."

Dr. Tara Chand writes that no greater disservice could have been done to Indian's aspiration for independence than the decision of MacDonald on the Communal problem. It gave the recognition of the Government to the following minorties : Muhammadans, Depressed Classes, Backward Classes, Indian Charistians. Anglo-Indians, Europeans, Commercial and Industrial Classes, Landholders, Labour, Universities and Sikhs. A fixed number of seats were allocated to each minority and special separate electorates were assigned to each. The scheme encouraged not the Muslims but the other groups also to consider themselves as national units with their particular interests separate from the interests of the general body of Indians. Nothing could be a more efficacious method of fractionalising the country and preventing the growth of the consciousness of nationality. The vicious principle of separate communal electorates was given the widest extension possible so as to make the working of responsible Government almost impossible. The plan took it for granted that the programmes and parties in India at the Centre and in the provinces would be determined not by economic, political and social considerations but on the basis of religious and communal interests. From the foundations upwards, the entire structure—constituencies, elections, ministries—was organised on communal lines. The British prejudice against the Hindus was cleverly concealed and the bias in favour of the Muslims was covered under a show of fairness. At the same time, the imperial interests were safeguarded both against a possible Muslim volte face as well as the actual antagonism of the Hindus.

THE UNITY CONFERENCE (1932)

An attempt was made at this time to settle the differences between the Hindus and Muslim and Pandit Madan Mohan Malaviya and Maulana Shaukat Ali took the initiative in this matter. On October 7, 1932, the President of the All-Parties Muslim Conference decalared that "it was highly inopportune to reopen the question of separate versus joint electorate and that the Muslim Community was not prepared to give up this safeguard." However, he expressed his willingness "to consider definite proposals comprehending all the vital issues involved, if initiated by the majority community." This gave some hope to Pandit Malaviya and he requested the All-Parties Muslims Conference to appoint a Committee to negotiate with the representatives of the Hindus and Sikhs. The Committee was set up and consequently on November 3, 1932 the Unity Conference met at Allahabad.

The representatives of the Hindus, Sikhs, Muslims and Indian Christians took part in it. They were able to agree upon many points. However, there were differences on the question of Muslim representation in the Cenral Legislature and the Bengal Legislature. The Muslims demanded that they be given at least 51% of the total seats in Bengal but that was not possible unless the Europeans were willing to surrender some of the seats allottted to them under the Communal Award. As regards the Central Legislature, the British Government declared that the Muslims would get 33-1/3% of the British India seats in the Central Legislature. As the British Government had awarded to the Muslims more than what was being offered to them at the Unity Conference at Allahabad, the Unity Conference had little chance of success. On November 20, 1932, the representatives of the various Muslim organisations, including the Muslim League, met in Delhi and declared that the proposed basis of agreement devised at Allahabad was "injurious to Muslim interests, impracticable and unacceptable." It was also declared that "since the majority community were obstinately and irrevocably opposed to granting us safegurards and protection, which, as a minority, we are entitled to, and since no further advance towards responsible self-Government for India was possible except on the basis of the Award, it was advisable, even with its obvious defects from the Muslim point of view, to accept it." It is true that a few meetings of the Unity Conference were held even in December 1932, but they failed to result in any unity.

THIRD ROUND TABLE CONFERENCE

The Third Round Table Conference was called by the British Government rather reluctantly as it was of the opinion that the rest of the work could be done in India. The result was that the session of the Third Round Table Conference lasted from November 17, 1932 to December 24, 1932. The Labour Party did not participate in its deliberations and the Indian National Congress was unrepresented. The delegates to the Conference merely discussed the Reports of the various committees appointed by the Second Round Table Conference and decided a few more points.

THE WHITE PAPER (1933)

When the whole scheme regarding the future constitution of India was thrashed out, the British Government issued in March 1933 a small document known as the White Paper. It gave in detail the working basis of the new Indian Constitution with dyarchy at the Centre and responsible Government in the provinces. As was to be expected, the White Paper was condemned by the Indian public opinion, but the British Government went on with its programme.

In April 1933, a Joint Select Committee was appointed to examine and report on the Government proposals as contained in the White Paper. The Committee consisted of 16 members each from the House of Commons and House of Lords and its Chairman was Lord Linlithgow.

THE GANDHI-IRWIN PACT (MARCH 1931)

As regards the terms of the Pact, both the Congress and the Government were required to do certain things. The Government of India was to make concessions and the Congress was to withdraw the Civil Disobedience movement. It was agreed that the Government would take steps for the participation of the representatives of the Congress in the future discussions that were to take place on the scheme of Constitutional Reforms. The Civil Disobedience movement was to be effectively discontinued and reciprocal action was to be taken by the Government. The Congress was to discontinue the organised defiance of the provisions of any law, the movement for non-payment of land revenue and of other legal dues, the publication of news sheets in support of the Civil Disobedience Movement and attempts to influence civil and military servants or village officials against the Government or to persuade them to resign their posts. The boycott of non-Indian goods was to be discontinued if it was exclusively against British goods. Mahatma Gandhi agreed not to press for a public enquiry into the allegations against the conduct of police in India. The Government was to withdraw the ordinances promulgated in connection with the Civil Disobedience movement. The notifications declaring associations unlawful under the Criminal Law Amendment Act of 1908 were to be withdrawn in so far as those notifications were issued in connection with the Civil Disobedience movement. Pending prosecutions were to be withdrawn if those were filed in connection with the Civil Disobedience Movement and related to offences which did not involve violance other than technical violence or incitement to such violence. Where the Local Government had moved any High Court or had initiated proceedings against certain lawyers in connection with the Civil Disobedience movement, applications were to be made by the Government for their withdrawal. Prosecutions against soldiers and policemen involving disobedience of orders were not to come within the scope of these provisions. Fines which had not been realised were to be remitted. Where an order for the forfeiture of security had been made but the security had not been realised, the fine was to be remitted. Fines which had been realised and securities fortfeited under any law, were not to be returned. Additional police imposed in connection with the Civil Disobedience movement at the expense of the inhabitants of a particular area was to be withdrawn at the discretion of the Local Government. The Local Government was not to refund any money, not in excess of the actual costs, that had been realised, but it was to remit any sum that had not been realised. Movable property which had been seized in connection with the Civil Disobedience movement was to be retruned, if the same was still in the possession of the Government. Movable property forfeited or attached in connection with realisation of land revenue or other dues, was to be returned. Where the movable property had been sold by the Government, no compensation was to be paid and the sale proceeds were not to be returned. Immovable property taken into possession by the Government under Ordinance IX of 1930 was to be returned in accordance with the provisions of that Ordinance. Land and other immovable property in possession of the Government which had been forfeited or attached in connection with the realisation of land revenue or other dues was to be returned. Where immovable property was sold to a third party, the transaction was to be regarded as final. Where the posts rendered vacant by resignations had been permanently filled up, the Government was not bound to reinstate their former employees. Other cases of resignations were to be considered on merits. However, the Local Governments were to follow a liberal policy in the matter of re-employment of Government servants and village officials who applied for reinstatement. However, the Government was to allow the collection or manufacture of salt free of duty to persons residing within a specified distance from the seashore. It was specifically provided that if the Congress failed to give full effect to the obligations of the settlement, the Government was to be at liberty to take such action as might be considered necessary for the protection of the public and individuals and the due observance of law and order.

The Gandhi-Irwin Pact had a mixed reception. The people of India welcomed it as a great victory for the Congress. It was pointed out that the Congress had saved the people from a lot of suffering on account of the repression which was in store for them. Pt. Jawaharlal Nehru tells us that at the time of negotiations between the Government and the Congress, all sorts of people came to Delhi and those who were formerly affraid of coming nearer to the Congress were brought nearer to it and they tried to make amends for their past behaviour. Even the communalists tried to come to an understanding with the Congress. Mahatma Gandhi described the Pact as a victory for both the sides. He felt that the enthusiasm of the people was waning and the campaign might not last long. He was also worried on account of the attitude of the Muslim Legaue and hence he was willing to come to a compromise with the Government. Likewise, Lord Irwin felt that it was desirable to come to a compromise with the Congress. The Civil Disobedience movement had undermined respect for law and order. There were riots and assassinations of officials and policemen. These things were demoralising the Government. Lord Irwin also realised that influence and not power, would better serve the interests of England in India. England at that time was involved in the world wide economic depression and the Viceroy would not like make the situation worse by allowing the Civil Disobedience Movement to continue. Under the circumstances, it was realised that "prudence was the better part of valour" and hence the Pact was signed.

According to Ram Gopal "The Gandhi-Irwin Pact was an inconvenient document, not to the Congress but to the bureaucracy which was now pinned down to a certain defined behaviour in dealing with the men (Congressmen) who were in the past disposed of arbitrarily. The bureaucracy would have to put up with peaceful picketing which it never tolerated under any conditions and in regard to which it even ignored the law. It would have to prepare lists of dues collected illegally by officers, often with its connivance. It would have to behave as a party to the Pact, which would mean climbing down from the position of arrogance and inaccessible superiority. The bureaucracy would not submit to this humiliation, and most of its members continued behaving in the old fashion hallowed by a long tradition of British rule.

Sir Penderal Moon points out that Lord Irwin and the British Government were acting on the premises that British rule in India would come to an end in the not distant future. In accordance with the declaration of 1917, India was being steadily advanced toward self-government. It was for this reason that Lord Irwin and the British Government were justified in going to great lengths to win the confidence and cooperation of the Congress even when it was in open revolt against them. Many Englishmen in India recognised the wisdom of the decision of Lord Irwin to come to terms with Gandhi, but the majority were critical. The Muslims denounced the betrayal of the loyal to the disloyal. In general, the Indians welcomed the prospect of a compromise. The majority of the Congress workers were tried of the struggle and the public at large was sick of it. Gandhi sensed the widespread desire for a settlement and he approached the talks in a conciliatory manner. Gandhi was convinced of the sincerity of Lord Irwin who himself was impressed by the personality of Gandhi To quote him, "I came to have no doubt whatever that, if Mr Gandhi gave me his word on any point, that word was absolutely secure, and that I could trust it implicitly. On the other hand, I found what had always been my impression being confirmed, namely, that though intentionally he was completely sincere, yet in some matters he was the victim of unconscious self-deception. The tendeny to this showed itself in the importance he attached to different matters and the weight that he seemed prepared to give to different kinds of evidence."

Sir Penderel Moon writes. "The settlement was an armistice, not a final peace; an opportunity to give cooperation a trial, not a resolve to enter into a permanent partnership. Congress was embarking on cooperation deliberately, but only provisionally; and though Gandhi at this time genuinely hoped to make the provisional truce a lasting peace, the younger elements in the Congress leadership did not share this hope." Again, "It is permissible to regard the Civil Disobedience movement of 1930 and the Gandhi-Irwin Pact as the peak of Gandhi's political achievement. During the rest of his life there were to be some glorious episodes, but politically it is an almost unrelieved record of misjudgement and failure. Civil Disobedience in 1930 also failed in its avowed objects—neither Independence nor the Eleven Points were secured. But as an example of disciplined mass pressure it was a most remarkable success. Coincident with it, and surely partly caused by it, the British Government at the beginning of 1931 set India on the last lap of the road to Independence, from which there could be no turning back."

Dr. R.C. Majumdar writes that the Pact caused a great disappointment to many, particularly to Subahs Bose and his followers who openly expressed their dissatisfaction. However, a large section regarded the Pact as a great victory for Gandhi and the Congress. The view of R.C. Majumdar is that in one respect, the Pact was a valuable gain in a long view of things. For the first time in the history of British India, the British Government condescended to treat the Indian National Congress on footing of equality as a political opponent and entered on a prolonged negotiation with its accredited agent to settle the terms of peace. The very fact that the Viceroy and Gandhi put their respective signatures on a "treaty of peace" put the Indian National Congress on a high pedestal and increased its prestige and stature. This was no small gain and British statesman like Churchill fully realised that they had yielded ground and the British prestige suffered a setback. The very fact that Gandhi ascended the staircase of the Viceregal Lodge, day after day, to carry on diplomatic negotiations on behalf of the Congress, made it patent to all that henceforth the British authority in India must take due cognizance of the great national organisation which was fighting for India's freedom.

However, the critics of the Pact contend that Mahatma Gandhi "unwittingly sold India." Men like Winston Churchill felt that the Viceroy had sold Great Britain to Mahatma Gandhi. It is stated that Jawaharlal Nehru was shocked to read the reservations and safeguards agreed upon by Mahatma Gandhi as they allowed the British Government to continue their control over Indian affairs. The view of Subhas Chandra Bose was that the Pact was a great disappointment to the politically minded sections of the people and the youth organisations in the country. The Pact was also condemned on the ground that Mahatma Gandhi was not able to save the lives of Sardar Bhagat Singh and his comrades. As a matter of fact, when Mahatma Gandhi went to attend the Karachi session of the Congress soon after signing the agreement, there were Black Flag demonstrations and shouts of "Down with Gahdhi" and "Gandhi truce has sent Bhagat Singh to the gallows."

Dr. S. Gopal writes that it appeared to most members of the Working Committee and above all to Jawaharlal, that Gandhi had been outwitted and in return for some empty phrases which recognized the indispensability of Congress in any Indian settlement, had yielded on every crucial issue and ignored the longterm objectives. Gandhi threatened to retire if his settlement was repudiated and demanded personal loyalty even if not approval. Jawaharlal was in tears and more aware than ever that the loss of his father was more than a personal one. Never had Motilal's clear-sightedness and ruthlesseness in negotiation been more needed. The view of Jawaharlal was that the settlement was a self-inflicted defeat. He would not have agreed with the claim of Lord Irwin that he had built a breakwater against the great agrarian forces which were being harnessed by Jawaharlal by ensuring the loyalty of the older politicians on the side of "conservatism". Gandhi had not broken, but only ignored, the logic of the struggle for freedom. That could end only with the attainment of independence. The result was that there was no peace but a truce. The temporary phase was bound to pass soon and the nation required the leadership of the man who had called a depressed people to life and action.

The spirit in which the Gandhi-Irwin Pact was signed did not last long. In spite of protests from all quarters the Government carried out the execution of Sardar Bhagat Singh, Sukh Dev and Raj Guru on March 23, 1931 in connection with the Lahore Conspiracy Case. On April 18, 1931, Lord Irwin was succeeded by Lord Willingdon. The new Viceroy had no intention to abide by the terms of the Pact. In the United Provinces, the armed police and the magistracy terrorised and harassed the people. The Congress Flag was burnt. Women were insluted. The holding of public meetings was prohibited and those who violated the law were prosecuted. The confiscated property of the peasants was restored with great difficulty in Gujarat. Congressmen were imprisoned without trial in Bengal. Legal practitioners were required to give undertakings. Prisoners were not released in Bombay. Many students were resticated from schools. There were similar violations of the Pact in Madras and Delhi. Mahatma Gandhi brought those violations to the notice of the Home Secretary to the Government of India and asked for an inquiry, but there was no response. Mahatma Gandhi asked for certain clarifications and those were given because the British Government wanted Mahatma Gandhi to attend the forthcoming second Round Table Conference.

❐

6

Extremist Movement

The terrorist movement started in India towards the end of 19th century and the beginning of 20th century. It was one of the phases of militant nationalism although it was quite different from the extremism of Tilak. The terrorist wanted to end the British rule by violent means. They started creating among the Indians hatred for the British through newspapers, pamphlets and posters etc.

Maharashtra was the first centre of the terrorist. Shyamji Krishore Verma and Vinayak Damodar Savarkar were the prominent revolutionary leaders. In 1899, Rand the Plague commissioner of Poona was murdered in Maharashtra. Shyamji Krishore Verma who was connected with the murder of Rand managed to escape to London where he remained or six years. He esablished Indian Home society and started a monthly journal named the "Indian Sociologist". Later on he had to leave London also. Vinayak Damodar Savarkar also reached London and became the leader of the revolutionary group at the London House. In 1902, he despatched a parcel of 20 Browring automatic pistals with ammuition to Bombay concealed in a box forming the luggage of one Chaturbhuj Amin, a cook at the Indian House. These pistols were sent for the members of Abhinav Bharat Society which was working under the leadership of his brother Ganesh Savarkar. But before the pistols could reach Bombay, Ganesh Savarkar was arrested and sentenced to transportation for life. The members of the Abhinav Bharat Society decided to murder Mr. Jackson, the District Magistrate of Nasik who had passed the sentence of transportation for life. Mr. Jackson was actually shot on 21st December, 1909 and three Bahmery were executed on the charge of murder.

The terrorist of Punjab made attempts to murder Governor-General Lord Hardinge. In the Delhi conspiracy case Amir Chand, Awadh Behari, Balmakand, Basant Kumar and Vishwas were sentenced to death. The return of Sikhs from Canada further strengthened the Terrorist Movement in Punjab. The partition of Bengal by Lord Curzon and the swedeshi movement also contributed to this development. In Bengal Barendra Kumar Ghose the younger brother of Sir Aurobindo Ghose and Bhupendra Nath Dutta brother of Swami Viveka Nand were the promient leaders of the Terrorist Movement, B.K. Ghose started newspapers entitled "Yugantar" and 'Sandhya' to propogate the revolutionary movement.

Revolutionary Programme. A pragramme was chalked out and it consisted of six items:

1. To spread hatred against the Britishers.

2. Fear of unemployment and starvation was to be removed.

3. The Government was to be kept busy by means of Handematrain Processions, swadeshi conferences, and boycott meetings.

4. Youngmen to be recruited and trained in the use of weapons.

5. To manufacture fire arms and purchases them from foreign countries.

6. Money was to be raised by means of raids and dacoities. Their belief was that the rule of the English was established through sheer brute force and therefore, it was right to use brute force against them. An appeal was made to the young man of Bengal in there words : "will the Bengali worshipper of Shakti strin from the shedding of blood ? The number of Englishmen in this country is not above one lakh and half and what is the number of English Officials in each district ? If you are firm in your resolution, you can in a single day bring British rule to an end. Lay your life but first take a life. The worship of the Godders will not be consummated if you sacrifice your lives at the shrine of Independence without shedding blood,

with the help of his Collegues, B.K. Ghose organised secret institutions in Italy and Russia to strengthen the Terrorist Movement.

On April 30, 1908 Mrs. and Mr. Kennedy were murdered. Khudi Ram Bose was arrested and sentenced to death. He became mastry and hero. His photograghs had an immense sale and by and by the young people took wearing of dhotis with Khudi Ram Bose's name woven in the borders of the garment. On December 23, 1907 Mr. Allen the former Magistrate of Dacco was shot dead. About 40 persons including Aurobindo Ghose were arrested. Narain Gosain was made a Government approved but he was shot dead by the terrorists. Among the rest of the accused who were sentenced to death and the remaining ones were awarded long sentences.

The Terrorist Movement spread in other parts of the country also. In Madras the movement spread rapidly and the Government property was destroyed. Pondicherry was a great centre of Terrorist Movement. Prominent leaders like Sardar Bhagat Singh, Yatendra Nath Das and Chandra Shekhar Azad sacrificed their lives for the sake of the country. The Government tried to suppress the movement with all powr and force at their command. The terrorists who escaped the oppression of the Government later on joined the Azad Hind Army of Subhash Chandra Bose, The officers of the terrorists were also in the foreign countries. Shyamji Krishna Verma, Madam Cama and S.R. Rana worked from Paris. In England Madanlal Dhingra protested against the inhuman punishment inflested on the terrorists in India. He shot on 1st July 1909 Sir William Curzon Wyllie the political A.D.C. at India office in Lodnon. He and Vinayak Savarkar were arrested and sentenced to transportation for life.

The Government of India was very much disturbed and alarmed by the rise of terrorism but they allied the moderats, the Muslims and the Zamindars through diplomacy and incrilessly and ruthlessly suppressed the terrorists. Lala Lajpat Rai, Sardar Ajit Singh and Lok-Manya Tilak were arrested and sent to Burma. In 1908 Criminal Law Amendment Act was passed which empowered the Government to declare any Association or Society as illegal. On the one hand, the Government was ruthlessly suppressing the movement and on the other hand the revolutionaries could not get whole hearted support and cooperation of the people who preferred Non-cooperation Movement of Mahatma Gandhi. Thus the terrorist-movement could not became wide spread.

FACTORS RESPONSIBLE FOR THE RISE OF EXTREMISM

There was a gradual rise of Extremism and terrorism in Indian politics between 1892 and 1905. This was due to many factors:

1. Dissatisfaction with the Indian Councils Act of 1892. Indian Councils Act of 1892 failed to satisfy the aspirations of the Indians. It did not give anything substantial to the Indians and even the Moderates were not pleased with it. Many people felt that the policy of appeals and prayers had yielded nothing and the Government regarded this policy as a sign of weakness.

2. Bad Economic Condition. The economic condition of the people was becoming bad. There was a constant drain on the economic resources of the country due to foreign rule. Dadabhai Naoroji, R.C. Dutt and other proved by their writings that the policy of the Government was impoverishing the people. It cared only for the interests of the British manufacturers. Many educated Indians were unemployed and it was felt that only the freedom of the country would solve the econmic difficulties of the people.

3. Ill-Treatment of the Indians Abroad. The Indians were not well-treated in other countries. The treatment meted out to them in South Africa was very bad. Restrictions were imposed on their free movement without any reason. They could not walk on footpaths or travel in first class railway compartments. They could not travel without passes or go out after 9.00 p.m. The Indians felt that the cause of such humiliations abroad was their slavery and India must become free to end this. In England too they were despised as slaves.

4. Famine and Plague. Famine caused great discontent amongst the people. Between 1876 and 1900 eighteen famines broke out in the country. The famine of 1897 affected about twenty million people.

While the people were starving, the Government celebrated the Jubilee of Queen Victoria. The Indians felt that this money should have been spent to give relief to the starving people. The Jubilee celebrations at such a time were considered an act of callousness on the part of the Government.

The outbreak of plague added further to the discontent of the people. The Government adopted some measures to check this fatal disease, but these were adopted without regard to the sentiments of the people. Mr. Rand, the Plague Commissioner of Poona, and his men freely entered even places of worship and apartments of women. Infectious houses were demolished without making alternative arrangements for the staying of their occupants. The result was that Mr. Rand with one of his juniors was shot dead while returning from Bombay after the Jubilee celebrations.

5. Defeats of Italy and Russia. Italy attacked Abyssinia but the Italian forces were defeated at Adowa in 1896. There was war between Japan and Russia in 1904-05 in which the Russians were very badly defeated. These defeats of Italy and Russia broke the spell of the invincibility of European arms. It gave hope to the Indians that they could become free. There was a feeling that England was declining. In the field of commerce. Germany and the U.S.A. were supposed to have gained the upper hand.

6. Reactionary Regime of Curzon. The reactionary regime of Curzon also embittered the Indians. They were not given good jobs. He declared that Englishmen alone by birth and training were fit to rule India, and not the Indians. God had selected Englishmen to rule over Indian and to give them freedom was going against the will of God. He passed many reactionary Acts. The Calcutta Corporation Act of 1899 reduced the number of elected members of Calcutta Corporation from 75 to 50. This reduction of 25 members was only in case of elected members. Thus the elected members lost majority in the Calcutta Corporation and non-elected members came to have majority. The Indian Universities Act of 1904 increased Government control over the Universities. These were left with practically no autonomy. The Official Secrets Act of 1904 increased the powers of the Government. The Official Secrets Acts of 1889 and 1898 related to the disclosure of only military secrets. The Official Secrets Act of 1904 covered also the official secrets relating to information about civil affairs.

7. Partition of Bengal. The partition of Begal by Lord Curzon in 1904 was resented the most by Indians. The idea of Lord Curzon probably was to create a Muslim majority province, though he declared that Bengal was too big a province and the partition of Bengal had been done to increase administrative efficiency. The Indians felt that it had been done to weaken the sodarity of Bengal because it was a politically advanced province. There was vigorous agitation for its repeal.

7. Influence of Revolutionary Doctrines of the West. Extremism also drew its inspiration from the revolutionary doctrines of the west. The struggles for Independence waged by America, France, Italy and Germany had revealed to the Indians that freedom could be achieved not by constitutional agitations but by revolutionary methods. The Indian leaders also remarked that "History does not record any instance when an empire might have been conceded by the rulers to the ruled. You will have to fight for your right."

9. Leadership of Bal, Pal and Lal. The leadersp of Bal, Pal and Lal gave a great impetus to extremism. Bal Ganga Dhar Tilak was the first to call upon the nation. It was he who preached the ideas of Boycott. Swadeshi, non-cooperation etc. He said, "You must realise that you are a great factor in the power with which the administration in India is conducted. You are yourself the useful lubricants which enable the gigantic machinery to run smoothly. Though down-trodden and neglected, you must be conscious of your power of making the administration impossible if you but choose to make it so. It is you who manage the railroad and the telegraph, it is you who make settlements and Collect revenues. If you withdraw yourself the entire machinery will collapse." Thus Tilak taught he people the principle of non-co-operation.

B.C. Pal and Lala Lajpat Rai also worked for the spread of extremist ideas. He also published a series of articles in which he strongly criticised the policies of the British Government. Tilak even said, "Swarajya is my birth right and I shall have it."

METHODS OF EXTREMISTS AND MODERATES

Extremism had become a strong force by 1905 and it continued to be so far about a decade. The methods of extremists were boycott of forign goods, use of Swadeshi goods and national education. Boycott was directed not only against foreign goods but also against Government services, honours and titles.

The most important leader of the Extremists was B.G. Tilak. The extremists differed from the Moderates in the following respects:

(a) The Moderates wanted to work with the existing bureaucracy ; the Extremists were out to obstruct it.

(b) The Moderates wanted to co-operate with the Government, wherever possible; the Extremists stood for opposing it at every step.

(c) The Moderates wanted to improve the existing constitution; the Extremists wanted to reconstruct it.

(d) The Moderates tried to win over the British; the Extremists wanted to turn them out by all means.

There occurred a split between the Modertes and the Extremists in 1907 at the Surat session. The Extremists, however, failed to capture the Congress.

Government Measures Against Extremists. The Government took a serious view of the rise of Extremism in the country and did its best to suppress it. The Extremists were arrested and imprisoned. Secions 124 A and 153-A were added to the Indian Penal Code to deal with the situation. The Government was authorised to ban political organisations suspected of subversive tendencies and to conduct summary trails of political offenders. The right to hold public meetings was curtailed.

Founding of Muslim League. Another development took place in the meantime. The All-India Muslim League was founded in 1906 by H.H. Aga Khan. It was an association of loyalist Muslims and was ment to act as a counterpoise to the Indian National Congress. A deputation of the Muslims underthe leadership of H.H. Agha Khan waited on the Governor-General, Lord Minto, and requested him for separate communal representation for the Muslims in the forthcoming reforms. Lord Minto agreed to concede their viewpoint. The Government of India Act of 1909, popularly knwon as Minto-Morely Reforms, gave separate electorates to the Muslims.

Co-operation between the Congress and the Government (1909-16). The Extremists felt dissatisfied with the Minto-Morley Reforms of 1909 but the Moderates wanted to give a trial to these. There was co-operation between the Congress and the Government between 1909 and 1916 due to several factors. Firstly, the Moderates were incharge of the Congress. Secondly, Lord Harding followed a sympathetic policy towards the Congress. Thirdly, the Partition of Bengal was cancelled in 1911. Fourthly, the most important leader of the Exteremists. B.G. Tilak, was in Prison from 1908 to 1914. The Congress helped the Government a lot during the First World War.

The Moderats found the Reforms of 1909 unsatisfactory after some time. Then the Moderate and the Extremists began to draw closer. A change came in the attitude of educated Muslims due to three factors. Firstly, the Turco-Italian War of 1911 annoyed them. Britain had helped Turkey in the past but now she did not do so. Secondly, they lost faith in the promises of the Government due to the cancellation of the Partition of Bengal. Thirdly, the Balkan Wars of 1912 were regarded by them as a Christian conspiracy to turn Turkey out of Europe. Under the circumstances, the Muslims under the lead of progressive youngmen began to draw closer to the Congress.

The Congress also began to feel that War was drawing on but the British Government was not prepared to declare that self-goverment for the Indians was its aim. July 1916. The Congress and the Muslim League at their Lucknow Session formulated a joint scheme of reforms which is popularly known as Lucknow Pact. This scheme was never put into practice.

Home Rule Movement. The Indian began to feel by 1916 that the British Government was not going to make a declaration of granting home rule to the Indians. Hence Mrs. Annie Besant and B.G. Tilak started Home Rule Movement in 1916. It was not a revolutionary movement. She wanted to awaken the people of India to demand their rights. She declared that Home Rule was the birth right of the Indians. They were not to have it as a reward for their war services to the British. The movement reached its climax in 1917. The Government took strong action. Mrs. Annie Basant was interned, Tilak threatend to start passive resistance. Then came the August Declaration of the Secretary of State for Indian in 1917 promising Self-Government by gradual stages. Then the Home Rule movement gradually came to an end.

Terrorist Movement. While the Indian National Movement was progressing by stages, some persons turned terrorists to achieve independence. Terrorism may be called the militant phase of Indian Nationalism. The terrorists believed that it would not be possible to end foreign rule without the use of force. They were exasperated by the reactionary and repressive policy of the Government. They believed in violent action to demoralise the British administration in India and its Indian collaborators. They smuggled arms and manufactured them for using these against the British. Funds were collected even by dacoities. The earliest storm centre of terrorist movement was Maharashtra. Shyamji Krishan Verma, V.D. Savarkar and Ganesh Savarkar were its important leaders. The revolutionary movement became strong in Bengal after its partition in 1905. Its leaders were B.K. Ghose and B.N. Dutt Pondicherry was another centre. There were revolutionaries in Punjab also and some of them were associated with the attempt on the life of Lord Hardinge in 1912.

The revolutionary movement greatly weakned after 1916 due to several factors. Firstly, the movement was confined to a small circle of youngmen; it did not have the backing of the general public. Secondly, the terrorist movement had no central organisation to direct its activities. Thirdly, the emergence of Mahatma Gandhi as a leader of the National Movement greatly weakened revolutionary movement. The Gandhian method of non-co-operation, civil disobedience and non-violence appealed more to the people than the methods of the terrorists.

CONSTITUTIONAL DEVELOPMENT IN INDIA FROM 1939 TO 1946

Second World War started in 1939 and the Congress asked the British Government to declare whether the Allied War Aims would apply to India or not. The British Government did not make a commitment and the Congres objected to the declaration of war by the Governor-General on behalf of India without consulting the leaders of the Indian political parties. The Congress ministries resigned. Then the Governor either formed minority ministries or took over the administration under Section 93 of the Government of India Act 1935.

August Offer (1940)

Lord Linlithgow, the Viceory and Governor-General of India, madc an offer to the Indians in August, 1940. It is popularly known as August Offer. It was the in form of a statement by the Viceroy on behalf of the British Government. The following were its main points:

(a) The position of the minorities should be safeguarded in any future constitutional change. The British Government would not be a party to the transfer of power to a government whose authority would be denied by a large and powerful element of India's national life. It meant that the Muslim League was to have its way in the matter of the country.

(b) The framing of the new constitution would be primarily the responsibility of the Indians.

(c) The Executive Council of the Governor-General should be at once expanded and an Advisory War Council should be set up.

(d) The constitution-making body would be set up after the war.

(e) The government hoped that in the meantime the parties and the communities would cooperate in war effort.

(f) The statement also promised a full-fledged responsible government in India on the Dominion status model after the termination of the war then in progress.

The August Offer was rejected by the Congress. The August Offer was unsatisfactory and disappointing. The only innovation made by it was the creation of a War Advisory Council and this could hardly evoke any enthusiam among the Indians. It was also regarded mischievous as it gave a clear assurance to the Leaue that no future constitution, interim or final, should be adopted by the British Government without their approval and consent.

Cripps Proposals (1942)

Japan joined the war against the Allies in 1941. Her victorious armies captured the countries of South-East Asia. They occupied Burma and threateued India. In March 1942, the British Government sent Sir Stafford Cripps, the leader of the House of Commons, with certain proposals which are popularly known as Cripps Plan. Its important clauses were the following:

(a) There would be provision for the participation of Indian States in the constitution-making body.

(b) If any province did not like to accept the new constitution, it could retain its present position. It could lagter on join, if it so decided.

(c) The members of the constitution-making body were to be elected by an electoral college consisting of the entire membership of the Provincial Legislative Assemblies. The strength of the constitution-making body was to be about

1/10 of the membership of the electoral college. In the constitution-making body, the ratio of the member of the Indian States to the members of the British India was to be proportionate to their populations.

(d) There would be provision in the new constitution for the protection of racial and religious minorities.

(e) A constitution-making body would be set up immediately after the war.

(f) The British Government proposed that India would be offered full Dominion Status after the war with the right of secession from the Commonwealth.

(g) His Majesty's Government would retain control of Defence during the critical period of the war.

Cripps Proposals an Improvement on August Offer

Cripps proposals were an advance on the August Offer in following respects:

(a) The Indian Union could leave the Commonwealth if the Constituent Assembly so decided.

(b) The framing of a new constitution was to be entirely in Indian hands. Its acceptance was subject to the fulfilment of British obligations. If the Indians could not become free as a single unit they could become free as two or more units. The disagreement among the Indians would not be a ground for the British Government to perpetuate their rule.

(c) August Offer suggested only the expansion of the Executive Council of the Viceroy. Cripps Proposals invited the participation of the Indians in all matters. Only defence was to be in British hands during the period of war.

(d) The August Offer had asked Indians to discuss the principles and the method of framing a new constitution. Cripps

Proposals offered a plan for adopting a constitution-making body if the Indians could not agree upon any other plan.

Criticism of the Proposals

Cripps proposals were criticised by all the parties from their individual points of view. The Congress criticised these on three grounds. Firstly, Cripps at first said that all departments except Defence would be immediately transferred to Indian hands and the Governor-General would act as a constitutional head in those matters. He withdrew the statement at a later date. The Congress accused him of backing away form the offer.

The Hindu Mahasabha opposed the proposals because of the clause of non-accession of provinces and the communal basis of elections. The Sikhs were opposed to the clause relating to the non-accession of the provinces. The scheme was opposed by the Muslim League because the proposals held out the prospects of a single union of India also. Thus the proposals were rejected by all the parties. The scheme failed because it was to be accepted or rejected as a whole.

The Congress passed the Quit India Resolution after this. The government threw Congress leaders and many Congress workers into prisons. There was a lot of repression.

Wavell Plan (1945)

The British Government in 1945 offered new proposals to India. The offer was made through Lord Wavell, the Viceroy and Governor-General of India. The proposals, popularly known as Wavell Plan, proposed the following changes:

(a) All the members of Governor-Gerneral's Executive Council, except the Governor-General and Commander-in-Chief, were to be Indians.

(b) The Executive Council was to contain an equal number of Caste Hindus and Muslims.

(c) Governor-General's Executive Council should be enlarged pending the preparation of a new constitution.

(d) External Affairs Department also was to be transferred to Indian hands.

(e) Section 93 would be withdrawn and responsible governments would be set up in the provinces.

The members of Congress Working Committee were released. A conference of the leaders of different political parties was held at Simla to discuss the propsoals. The Congress accepted the proposals. The Muslim League was not prepared to accept a Congress Nationalist Muslim for the Viceroy's Executive Council because it claimed to be the sole representative of the Muslims. The negotiations thus broke down.

Cabinet Mission Plan (1946)

The Labour Government came into power as a result of the general elections held in Britain in 1945 and C.R. Attlee became the Prime Minister. He sent a mission of three Cabient members to India to sovle the constitutional tangle. It came to be called Cabinet Mission. Its members were Lord Pethick-Lawrence (Secretary of State for India), Sir Stafford Cripps (President of the Board of Trade) and A.V. Alexander (First Lord of Admiralty). It met the leaders of different parties in India but the Indian leaders could not agree among themselves. Then it offered its own plan which is known as Cabinet Mission Plan. The following were its important proposals:

(a) The Union should have an executive and a legislature having representatives from British India and the Indian States. All major communal isues in the legislature should be decided by the representative of the members present and voting as well as a majority of the representatives of each of the two major communities in the legislature.

(b) All subjects other than Union subjects and all residuary powers should vest in the provices.

(c) There could be a Union of India consisting of British India and the Indian States to deal with the Foriegn Affairs,

Defence and Communications. It should have the necessary power to raise finances for these subjects.

(d) The provinces should be free to form groups with executives and legislatures, and each group could determine the provincial Subjects to be taken in common.

(e) The constitutions of the Union and the Groups were to contain provision whereby a province could change its position after every ten years.

(f) The members of the Constituent Assembly were to be elected by the Legislative Assemblies of the provinces on the basis of one representative for one million population. The Sikh and Muslim legislators were to elect the quota of their communities on population basis. The representatives from the provision were to divide themselves into three sections. Section C was to consist of the representatives of Bengal and Assam, Section B of Punjab, Singh and North-Wset Frontier Provinces, while Section A was to consist of the rest of the India. The provinces in each group were to decide whether they should set up their group or not.

(g) The paramountcy over the Indian States was to come to an end.

Merits

(a) Communal issues were to be settled by the majority of the total membership and the majority of the members of each of the two major communities.

(b) The proposals provided for an Indian Union.

(c) The Constituent Assembly was to be constituted on the democratic principle of population strength. The principle of weightage was given up.

(d) All the members of the Constituent Assembly were to be Indians.

(e) There was to be no interference with the work of the Constituent Assembly either by the British Government or by its officials in India.

Demerits

(a) It was not clear whether grouping of provinces was compulsory or not. The Congress was of the opinion that it was not compulsory but the Muslim League took the view that it was compulsory. The Cabinet Mission later on declared that it was compulsory.

(b) The constitutions of the groups were to be framed before that of the Union. It was nothing short of putting the cart before the horse.

(c) There was the provision for safeguarding the rights of Muslim minority but not of other minorities.

FACTORS RESPONSIBLE FOR THE GROWTH OF MILITARY NATIONALISM

Gradually, over the years, the tend of militant nationalism had been growing in the country. It found expression in the nationalist movement against the partition of Bengal in 1905 A.D. before, this, this trend was supported by leaders like Raj Narain Bose, Ashwani Kumar Dutt, Vishnu Shahstri, Paplankar, etc. During the last years of the nineteenth century, due to the unresponsive policy followed by the British government in India, extremism began to grow rapidly inside the Indian National Congress party. The three Bal, Pal and Lal were the most prominent leaders of the extremist faction. This outlook became very popular for some time (1905 to 1919), following factors or causes contribited in its rapid growth:

(a) **Failure of the Moderates.** The initial and earliest leaders of the Congress Surendra Nath Bannerjee, Gopal Krishna Gokhale, Dadabhai Naoroji, Ferozeshah Mehta etc. were liberal or moderate leaders. They believed that British Government could be persuaded to agree to the fact that the demands of the Indians were genuine. They wanted to accomplish all this within the constitutional limits. Therefore they asked the British Government to introduce reforms for the welfare of the Indians through meetings, passing resolutions, sending petitions etc. The failure of the British Government to accept any of the important demands of the nationalists produced disillusionment among the politically conscious people with the principles and methods of the dominant moderate leadership. There was a strong demand for more vigorous political action and methods than those of meeting, petitions, memorials, and speeches in the legislative councils.

(b) Recognition of the True Nature of British Rule. The politics of the moderate nationalists were founded on the belief that British rule could be reformed from within. But the spread of knowledge regarding political and economic questions gradually undermined this belief. The political agitation of the moderates was itself responsible for this to a large extent. The nationalist writers and agitators blamed British rule for the poverty of the people. Politically conscious Indians were convinced that the purpose of British rule was to exploit India economically, that it, to enrich England at the cost of India. They realised that India could make little progress in the economic fields unless British imperialism was replaced by a government controlled and run by the Indian people.

(c) Repressive Political Policy of the Government. The political events of the years 1892 to 1905 also disappointed the nationalists and made them think of more radical politics. The Indian Councils Act of 1892, was a complete disappointment. On the other hand, even the existing politial rights of the people were attacked. In 1898, a law was passed making it an offence to exit" feelings of disaffection towards the foriegn government. In 1899, the number of Indian members in the Caclutta Corporation was reduced. In 1904, the Indian Official Secrets Act was passed restricting the freedom of the press. In the same year, Lokmanya Tilak and other newspaper editors were sentenced to long terms of imprisonment for arousing the people against the foreign government. Thus, the people found that, instead of giving them wider political rights, the rulers were taking away even their few existing rights.

(d) **The policy of the British Government Towards Famines and Plague.** In 1896-1900 severe famines struck the country. Their effect spread in an area of 70,000 sq. miles and took a toll of over 90 lakhs of lives. More than two crores of people were effected by these famines. The relief work done by the government was highly dissatisfactory and the government machinery moved very slowly. Along with that Plague also spread in an epidemic form and in the western part of Bombay Presidency thousands of people died. The steps taken by the Bombay government to cope with the epidemic were so half hearted and inadequate that the people felt greatly enarged and a wave of disstisfaction spred against the English government.

(e) **The Reactionary Policy Followed by Lord Curzon.** Lord Curzon's seven years rule in India has been called in Indian history as that of mission, omission, and commission. This ruthless messenger of British imperialism transpled under foot all the ambitition and aspirations of an awakened India. His frontier policy and his action of sending a military delegation to Tibet were severely criticised. The offical Secret Act of 1904, the Calcutta Corporation Act and the Indian Universities Act were all opposed to the spirit and call of the times and therefore he was greatly criticised every where in India. In addition to this he declared that the Indians were unfit to hold higher posts under the government and that the educated class of the country was dishonest and not trustworthy. This false unjust and unjustifiable accusation of the Indian character by Lord Curzon was greatly opposed by the Indians.

(f) **Backward Social and Cultural Politics of the British Government.** Even socially and culturally, the British rule was no longer progressive. Primary and technical education was not making any progress. At the same time, the officials were becoming suspicious of higher education and were even trying to discourage its spread in the country. The Indian Universities Act of 1904 was seen by the nationalists as an attempt to bring Indian universities under tighter official control and to check the growth of higher education. Thus an increasing number of Indians were getting convinced that self-government was essential for the sake of the social and cultural progress of the country and political enslavement meant stunting the growth of the Indians.

(g) The religious and social reform leaders like Raja Ram Mohan Roy, Swami Dayanand, Mrs. Annie Besant, Bal Gangadhar Tilak, Bipin Chandra Pal, inculted the feeling of self-respect and self-confidence amongst the people. They denied the propoganda of the British that the Indians never had the capacity to run administration of their country. They preached the message of self-respect and asked the nationalists to rely on the character and capabilities of the Indians. They taught the Indians that the remedy to their miserable condition lay in their own hands and that they should therefore become fearless and strong. Swami Vivekananda thought not a political leader, again and again drove home this message. He delcared "If there is a sin in the world it is weakness; avoid all weaknes, weakness is sin, weakness is death.

(h) **Growth of Education and Unemployment.** By the close of the 19th century, the number of educated Indians had increased perceptively. Large numbers of them worked in the administration on extremely low salaries, while many other increasingly faced unemployment. Their economic plight made them look critically at the nature of British rule.

Even more important was the ideological aspect of the spread of education. The larger the number of educated Indians, the larger was sthe area of influence of western ideas of democracy, nationalism and radicalism. The educated Indians became the best propagators and followers of militant nationalism both because they were low-paid or unemployed and because they were educated in modern thought and politics and European and world history.

(i) **International Influences.** Events outside exercised a powerful influence on the young generation. The humiliating treatment meted out to Indians in British colonies, especially in South Africa, created anti-British feelings. Further, nationalist movements in Egypt, Persia, Turkey and Russia gave Indians new hopes and new aspirations. The rise of modern Japan after 1868 showed that a backward Asian country could develop itself without Western control. In a matter of a few decades, the Japanese leaders made their country a first rate industrial and military power, introduced universal primary education, and evolved an efficient, modern administration. The defeat of the Italian army by the Ethiopans in 1896 and of Russia by Japan in 1905 exploded the myth of Euroean superiority.

(j) **Rise of Bal, Pal, Lal and Ghosh.** Though leaders like Raj Narain Bose and Ashwani Kumar Dutt of Bengal and Vishnu Shastri Piplankar of Maharashtra were supporting the extremist outlook even before, yet this feeling and the extremist nationalism became very strong because of the rise of Bal (Bal Gangadhar Tilak), Pal (Bipin Chandra Pal) Lal (Lala, Lajpat Rai), and Arvindo Ghosh. They declared as their aim the attainment of Swarajya and told the people very plainly that freedom requires sacrifice. Alongside a well trained group was ready to give leadership to the countrymen. The influence of extremism increased also because of the movement against partition of Bengal.

MAHATMA GANDHI WAS AN POLITICAL IDEALIST

Mohan Das Karam Chand Gandhi was born on 2nd October, 1889 at Porbandar (Kathiawar) in Gujarat. His mother was an influential religious lady. Infact, he was more under the influence of his mother than that of his father. Since in his school days he had shown certain traits of character which helped him to make experiment with truth and grow in moral strucutre much above the common man. He was hardly of thirteen years when he was married to Kasturba. After studying law in England he had gone to South Africa to start his legal practice. In South Africa. Gandhi protested against the discriminating treatment meted out to Indians. Indian labourers who had gone to settle in South Africa, and the merchants who followed, were denied the right to vote. They had to register and pay a toll-tax. Imbued with a high sense of justice, he was revolted by the injustice, discrimination and degradation to which Indians had to submit in South Africa Colonies. In African countries, Indians could not reside except in prescribed locations which were insanitary and congested. In some of the South African colonies, the Asians, as also the Africans, could not stay out of doors after 9 p.m. not could they use public footpaths. In the struggle against the discriminatroy and racialist policy of the government of South Africa, Gandhi perfected his philosophy of action. In South Africa, he experimented with truth and developed a technique to fight for just rights through 'Satyagraha'. His Satyagraha is based on the twin pillars of truth (Satya) and non-violence (Ahimsa). In keeping with 'Satyagraha Movement' Gandhiji was prepared to go to jail and suffer al kinds of torments.

Gandhiji returned to India in 1915 at the age of 46. In those days the First World War was going on. He like some other nationalist leaders decided to support the British Government in war campaign in the hope of attaining self-government after the war. Gandhi later said : In all these efforts at service, I was actuated by the belief that it was possible by such services to gain a status of full equality for my countrymen." Gandhi showed great enthusiasm and urged the Gujarati peasants to join the army and 'think imperially', if they aimed to win Swaraj. Gandhi's loyalties earned him the epithet of 'Recruiting

Sergeant of the Government' and a model for his services in the Great War. Gandhi started taking keen interest in the Indian national movement. First of all, he discussed the national movement with leaders of the national and than toured the country, to learn the exact condition. He was greatly distressed to see poverty, illiteracy, unemployment backwardness in the country and soon started participating with great enthusiasm in the freedom struggle and serving his country. In 1916 he founded the Sabarmati Ashram at Ahmedabad, which was called Satyagraha Ashram and where his friends and followers were to learn the ideals of truth and non-violence. In 1917 Gandhiji started the First Civil Disobedience Movement against the atrocities committed agaisnt the Champaran (Bihar) peasants." The peasantry in the district was excessively oppressed by the European planters. They we compelled to grow indigo on atleast 3/20 of their land and to sell it at prices fixed by the planters. When he started investigating the condition of these farmers through Euroepan masters he was ordered by the Champaran Distict Magistrate to leave the district. Gandhiji disobeyed this order. The government was thus compelled not only to take back this order but also formed a committee to look into the condition of farmers. Gandhi was also a member of this committee. This was Gandhiji's first great victory in India. Gandhiji supported the hartal of Mill workers at Ahmedabad and gave the man increase of 35% in their wages.

In 1919 Gandhi participated actively in the anti Rowlatt Act agitation. In February 1919, he founded the Satyagraha Sabha whose members took a pledge to disobey the Act and thus to court arrest and imprisonment. Here was a new method of struggle *i.e.* the Satyagraha. This new method of struggle immediately raised the national movement to a new, higher level. Nationalist could now act in place of giving only verbal expression to their dissatisfaction and anger. It was, moreover, to rely increasingly on the political support of the common men. Gandhi aksed the nationalist workers to go to the villages. That is where India lives, he said. He launched his first Styagraha movement (in India) when the government refused to annual the Rowlatt Act. March 30, 1919 was celebrated as Satyagraha

Day all over India. On that day, the people observed Hartal, took out peaceful processions and held public meetings. Gandhijji increasingly turned the face of national movement towards the common and the symbl of this transformation was to be khadi, or hand spun and handwoven cloth, which soon became the uniform of nationalists. A movement of protest spread throughout the country. The government resorted to brutal measures to put drown the agitation and there were lathi charges and firings at a number of places. Let us now known-some of the main political ideas of Gandhiji.

His Main Political Ideas. Gandhiji was one of the greatest men of the modern age. Because of his great achievements and sacrifices, historians have named the cars between 1920 and 1948 as the Gandhi age. He placed before the people the political ideas which mere inspired by Ahimsa, truth, love and justice:

(a) **Truth.** Gandhiji gave the same importance to truth as to Ahimsa. Accoridng to him truth and Ahimsa are two sides of the same coin. He considered the person who loved truth to be an ideal Satyagrahi. He was of the opinion that truth and fact be accepted.

(b) **Justice and Love.** Justice and Love also had a place in his political views. He spent a large part of his life fighting injustice. He raised his voice against the injustice in Bihar, Gujarat and other parts of India and in some countries of the world. He hated evil, not the evil doer.

(c) **Ahimsa or Non-Violence.** The basic principle of Gandhiji's ideas was Ahimsa. In Gandhiji's eyes non-violence was not a weapon of the weak and the cowardly. Only the strong and the brave could practice it. In a famous article in his weekly journal, Young India, he wrote in 1920 that "Non-violence is the law of our species, as violence is the law of the brute, "but that "where there is only a choice between cowardice and violence. I would advice violence...I would rather have India resort to arms in order to defend her honour, than that she should, in a cowardly manner, become or remain a helpless withness to her own dishonour."

(d) Supporter of Hindu-Muslim Unity. Gandhiji considered Hindus and Muslims to be one and loved all classes from the core of his heart. He went on hunger strike till death many times to establish Hindu-Muslim unity.

(e) Purity and Fearlessness. Gandhiji believed in good character, simplicity, purity and natural laws. He considered it a sin to look at evils, listen to it or speak it. He never gave it to injustice and impurity.

(f) A Supporter of Social Equality. Gandhiji did a lot for the welfare of untouchables. He advocated cottage industries charkha, Khadi and rural improvement. He was a great supporter of making village the centre of ideal lfie.

(g) Ideal Rule. Gandhiji's ideal government was like Ram Rajya. He considered an ideal State to be one where people had very large power and where the state and government had little powers. He proposed a curtailment in the army and police. In short, Gandhiji's political views comprised Ahimsa, Truth, Justice, Love and equality.

(h) The Means and End Should be Pure. Mahatma Gandhi was of the opinion that to achieve any noble aim, it was necessary that the means to achieve it shoud be pure. He considered the highest ambition to be improper unless it was achieved by pure means.

CONTRIBUTION OF GOKHALE TO EXTREMIST MOVEMENT

Gopal Krishan Gokhale was born at Kolhapur in a Maharashtrian family in 1866. He possessed remarkable qualities of head and heart. His academic career was brilliant and he became a professor at the age of 20. He became a member of the Bombay Legislative Council at the age of 22. He became Congress President at the early age of 39. He was hard working and his style of writing and speech was forceful. Gokhale was a true follower of Ranade. He joined the Deccan Education Society and soon became its active member. He became the principal of Fergusson College and with a true missionary spirit worked on a nominal salary of 70 rupees per month for about 20 years. Thus we find that he was an eminent educationist and did much for the intellectual uplift of the people.

Gopal Krishan Gokhale had a soft corner in his heart for the poor and wanted to improve their condition. He attacked Salt Tax very bitterly because its incidence mostly fell on the poor people. He founded the Servants of India Society and its aim was to train workers for the service of the people. He wrote in the preamble to the constitution of the society : "A sufficient number of our countrymen must now come forward to devote themselves to the cause in the spirit in which religious work is undertaken. Public life must be spiritualised. Love of the country must so fill the heart that all else shall appear as of little movement by its side".

Different opinions have been expressed about Gokhale's political views. The Extremists called him 'a faint-hearted Moderate', who was prepared to be a tool of the British Government. The reactionaries regarded him a 'seditionist' in disguise. The fact is that he was neither a revolutionary nor a reactionary. He was opposed to extremes. He fought for the rights and the liberties of the people but at the same time he did not ignore or belittle the difficulties of the Government. He tried to impress on the Government that it shouted understand the viewpoint of the Indians, but at the same time he asked the Indians to be cautious and not to got to the extremes. It is said of him that interpreted popular aspirations to the Viceroy and the Government and the Extremists. He believed that the Government as well as the people stood to lose by mutual jealousy and hatred. He did not like that people should resort to violence to achieve political objects. That is why he was prepared to support the Government on the question of enactment of India Press Act of 1910 which sought to stop incitement to violence through the Press. He also tried to impress Lord Minto that reforms should be introduced to win over a part of the people at least. Hoyland has rightly said about Gokhale. "He was a great master of the possible, a constructive statesmen of the first rank, a bringer together of East and West in the common service of the needy; above all an idealist, a foreseer, a prophet of new era of inter-racial goodwill and co-operation. He knew how to play on the national lyre without offending the official ear." Lord Morley once remarked that Gokhale had a plitician's head and a sense of executive responsibility.

The two salient characteristics of Gokhale's politics were his emphasis upon reform before independence and his use of negotiation in place of force. A critic has commented that his methods and those of the Ranadee school were correct for the reform programmes, after independence. but not for Swaraj movements. Nevertheless his vigorous speaking campaigns in England and elsewhere undoubtedly did much to sow the seeds of criticism of British Imperial policy among the British themselves. Even his Brahman rival, Tilak, with whom he had a bitter dispute, paid Gokhale deep homage at the time of his death, "This diamond of India. This Jewel of Maharashtra, this prince of wokers is taking eternal rest on the funeral ground. Look at him and try to emulate him.... Like a triumphant hero he is passing after having made his name immortal."

CONTRIBUTION OF DADABHAI NAOROJI

Dadabhai Naoroji is the first important national leader of modern India. He served this country for 61 years. He had already served India for 40 years when Indian National Congress was formed in 1885. He actively served for 21 years after its foundation. He was elected the first President of the Indian National Congress in 1886. He was elected member of the House of Commons after this from an English constituency. Even in that capacity, he served India loyally and did much to bring the question of the rights of the Indians before the British Parliament and the public of England. He was elected Congress President a second time in 1893. He was elected President a third time in 1906 to keep together the Moderates and the Extremists in the ranks of the Congress. Many Indians had been exasperated by the anti-national regime of Lord Curzon. The Partition of Bengal had acted as the last bitter pill administered to them. Many Congressmen began to turn Extremists. It was felt in 1906 that the Moderats and the Extremists in the Congress would part ways. The Moderates proposed the name of Dadabhai Naoroji for Congress Presidentship because he was the only man whom the Extremists would not have opposed. This shows that he was held in the highest esteem by all sections of the Congress. The strategy of the Moderates proved successful and he was accetped president by the Extremists also. He was popularly known as the Grand Old Man of India. He was the first Indian who demanded Swaraj for the country. He wanted that India should have self-government like Canada or Australia.

Dadabhai was the first Indian to draw the attention of the people to the great economic exploitation of the country. His contention was that India's wealth was being constantly drained to great Britain. He was of the opinion that the imperceptible economic exploitation of India was worse than the plundering raids of invaders like Mahmud of Ghazni, Amir Timur and Nadir Shah. They had plundered the country in the past and taken away a good deal of wealth. But India had not become poor in spite of that. She was able to recover during intervals of peace. The invasions did not permanently impoverish India. Moreover, their plundering incursions did not extend to every nook and corner of India. The case was different with the British rule in India. The wealth was drained, not intermittently, but constantly from this country in the form of salaries of British officers and the sale of British goods. This drain was constant and extended to every part of the country.

Naoroji did not believe in the use of force to achieve the object of Swaraj. He believed in the justice and good sense of the British. They would realise that the Indians should be given self government.

Thus we find that Dadabhai Naoroji devoted himself heart and soul, to the cause of India. Dadabhai had complete faith in the goodness of the British. One of the British officials once asked him, "If we give you news that the British are leaving India with their bag and baggage, how would you feel". Dadabhai replied, "I would certainly welcome this news, but before you reach Aden we shall have to wire you to come back".

Towards the end of his life his faith in the British goodness was also shattered.

CONTRIBUTION OF A.O. HUME

Allan Octavian Hume was a member of the Indian Civil Service and served India in various capacities. As a District Officer he promoted "the cause of popular education, police reform, liquor traffic, the vernacular press, the juvenile reformatories and other domestic reforms." He fought in the Mutiny of 1857 in the distirct of Etawah and saved the British rule there. However upon the restoration of peace in the country he wished the British Government to follow a policy of enlightenment towards the Indians and not one of revenge. The Government on the other hand reprimanded him and warned him not to encourage the people to send their children to school or contribute to their maintenance. But Hume replied mildly, "I cannot but found hopes of indulgence in the intense interest I feel in the subject and the ceaseless attention that I have paid it." Even if the Indian remained politically dependent, Hume argued, they ought to be allowed "to enrich an Empire." At the district level the police and judicial function were combined and Mr. Hume advocated a complete separation of the two duties. All this revenue is the wage of sin. It may in the works of the old adage, be truly said that "ill gotten wealth never thrives." And for every additional rupee that the abkari yields two at least are lost to the public by crime and sepnt by the Government in suppressing it. I at this moment see no hopes of reform; yet I have no doubt whatsoever that if I be spared, I shall live to see effected, in a more Christian like system, one of the greatest consting blots on our Government of India.

Service. A vernacular paper named "The People's Friend" was brought out in 1859 by the end endavours of Mr. Hume. Four years later he pressed for the establishment of a Juvenile Reformatory where the boys were to be separated from the adult criminals and given a chance of reform by discipline, instruction and training is useful things. While he was the Commissioner of Customs be made efforts for the gradual abolition of the vast customs barrier 25,000 miles long which upto his time had kept protected the salt monopoly of the Government of India.

In rural reforms Mr. Hume, though an urban Englishman, took keen interest. His scheme of 1879 for agricultural reform could not be a success. On the question of litigation, he thought that the Civil Courts in the rural districts were directly responsible for the bondage of the cultivators to the money-lenders. He suggested that rural debt cases should be disposed of summarily and finally on the spot by some selected Indians of known probity and intelligence who were to be sent as judges from village to village to settle every case of debt. In their mobile courts they were of associate any one of those inabitants—peferably the village elders who were involved in the case. These moving judges were to be free from any fixed codes or procedure, and of course to hear both the parties on the village platform. In such an open hearing before the neighbours, no villager in personal capacity would seem to tell an untruth because as Mr. Hume cogently argued, everybody knew everybody else's affairs.

Allan Octavian Hume was the Secretary to the Government of India from 1873 to 1879. But he was removed from office because he was too honest and too independent. He refused Lord Lytton's offer of a Lieutenant-Governorship because, as he sacreastically said, he was not equal to the task of feasting that it involved. Lord Salisbury refused to accept a proposal later on to appoint Mr. Hume as the Home Member. He retired from the I.C.S. in 1882.

National Movement. Love for people of India made Hume a completely different Englishman—but more Indian than Indian could be. On retirement he decided to dedicate his life to the service of the Indian masses. He addressed a circular to the graduates of the Calcutta University, requesting them to organise themselves in an organisation for the moral, social and political regeneration of India. He declared that if he could get fifty men, good and true, motivated by the spirit of selfess service, the organisation could be an easy thing. he secured the goodwill of the Governor-General who was in need of some "responsible organisation" through which the needs and grievances of the public could be crystallized and through which the Government could ascertain popular wishes and prejudices. Mr. Hume went to England and succeeded in enlisting the sympathy and support of responsible person for his scheme. On his return in 1883 to India he along with Sir Surendra Nath Banerjee issued an appeal for an Indian National Conference. Thus with his endeavour the first session of the Indian National Conference took shape. The Indian National Congress took its organisational pattern at Bombay in December 1885. It is for his untiring efforts for the purpose that Mr. Allan Octavian Hume is called the Father of Indian National Congress. He was the first General Secretary of the Congress, but continued in the office upto 1907. Throughout his later life he defended the National Congress against its critics. Some critics argue that the Indian National Congress was the result of a conspiracy between Mr. Hume and the Government of India for the sake of the British Empire in India. It is a great mistake to accept this thesis— more so of an ingratitude to that great man who was responsible for setting up a national institution for the Indians—an institution which was destined to bring independence to India.

CONTRIBUTION OF LOKMANYA BAL GANGA DHAR TILAK

Bal Gangadhar Tilak was born in a Brahman family of Maharashtra and was well-versed in Hindu scriptures. He got his degree in law in 1879. He founded in Poona New England School and it made rapid progress. Then he started the 'Kesari' a daily newspaper. He was associated with the foundation of the Deccan Education Society and the Fergusson College.

Tilak wanted to develop courage and spirit of sacrifice among the people. He organised Ganapati Festival to develop religious and patriotic fervour among the people. He started Shivaji Movement in 1895. The idea was to encourage Indian youngmen to follow the example of Shivaji and to secure independence for India. On the occasion of the celebrations of this Festival, there were lectures, fencing exercises with sticks etc. He was sentenced to eighteen months' rigorous imprisonment in 1897 on a charge of sedition. He was tried again for sedition in 1908, sentenced to six years' imprisonment and sent to Mandalay. First World War started in 1914 and he advocated co-operation and support in the war effort. He hoped that the British Government would appreciate the services of the Indians and give self-government to the Indians. There was, however, no gesture of goodwill from the Government even after two years.

The gretest contribution of Tilak to the struggle for independence was that he taught the philosophy of defance to the people. He was born at a time when foreign rule had demoralised the people. The failure of the Mutiny had broken the will of the people to resist the Government. The Indian National Congress was formed in 1885 but it was only a resolution-passing body at that time. Its resolutions professed loyalty to the Government. It requesterd for reforms but was not prepared to challenge the Government. Tilak, however, advocated that the Congress must change its policy. It must learn to defy the Government. Freedom would not come without sacrifices. He did not want people to resort to violence for the realisation of India's freedom but, if India could not be free by peaceful means, there was justifications for violence. He believed that end justifies the means. He advocated the programme of Swadeshi and boycott of foreign goods. The Moderates were in power from 1908 to 1914 and the main reason for this was that Tilak was in prison. He again gained ascendancy after being released from prison in 1914. He converted the Congress from the admirers of the British Government into rebels against the British Empire. He was a great orator and a good writer.

Tilak is sometimes compared to Gokhale. Both wanted to achieve independence for India but the means advocated by them were widely different. Dr. Pattabhi Sitaramayya, in his book "History of Indian National Congress", has attempted a comparison of Tilak and Gokhale in these words, "Tilak and Gokhale were both patriots of the first order. Both had made heavy sacrifices in life. But their temperaments were widely different from each other. Gokhale was a Moderate and Tilak was an Extremist if we may use the language in vogue at that time, Gokhale's aim was to improve the existing constitution, Tilak's was to reconstruct it". The same writer further adds. "Gokhale stood for co-operation wherever possible and opposition wherever necessary. Tilak inclined towards a policy of obstruction. Gokhale's primary concern was with the administration and its improvement : Tilak's supreme concern was the nation and its upbuilding. Gokhale's ideal was love and sacrifice. Tilak's was service and suffering. Gokhale's method sought to win the foreigner, Tilak's to replace him. Gokhale depended upon other's help : Tilak upon self-help. Gokhale looked to the classes and the intelligenisia; Tilak to the masses and the millions. Gokhale's arena was the Council Chamber : Tilak's forum was the village mandap. Gokhale's objective was self-government for which the people had to fit themselves by answering the tests prescribed by the English : Tilak's object was Swaraj which is the birth-right to every Indian and which he shall without let or hindrance have from the foreigner. Gokhale was on level with his age ; Tilak was in advance of his times."

Tilak Versus Gokhale. Tilak and Gokhale are often remembered together. Gandhiji' first impression of the two, as he records is that "the Lokmanya (is) like an Ocean—and one could not launch forth on the sea. But Gokhale was as the Ganges—it invited one to its bosom." Dr. Pattabhi Sitaramyya gives a masterly comparison of the two in his treatise on the History of the Indian National Congress ; "Tilak and Gokhale were both Maharashtrians ; tney were both Brahmins ; they both belonged to the same chitpavan sect. They were both patriots of the first order. Both had made heavy sacrifice in life. Gokhale was a Moderate and Tilak was an Extremist, if we may use the langauge in vogue at the time. Gokhale's plan was to improve the existing constitution; Tilak's was to reconstruct it. Gokhale had necessarily to work with the bureaucracy. Tilak had necessarily to fight it. Gokhale stood for co-operation wherever possible and oppositon wherever necessary. Tilak inclined towards a policy of obstruction. Gokhale's prime concern was with the administration and its improvement. Tilak' supreme consideration was the Nation and its up building Gokhale's idea was love and sacrifice, Tilak's was service and suffering, Gokhale's methods sought to win the foreigner ; Tilak's to replace him. Gokhale depended upon other's help; Tilak upon self-help. Gokhale looked to the classes and the intelligentsia; Tilak to the masses and the millions, Gokhale's arena was the Council Chamber, Tilak's forum was the village mandap. Gokhale's medium of expression was English ; Tilak's was Marathi. Gokhale's objective was self government for which the people had to fit themselves by answering tests prescribed by the English; Tilak's objective was Swaraj which is the birth-right of every Indian and which he shall have without let or hindrance from the foreigner.

Thus wrote Gokhale in a letter of 1914 to the Congress President, Bhupendranath Basu. Gokhale had doubts when he wrote the above lines, but neither Gokhale nor Tilak who died on August 1, 1920 were there to see that it was Tilak's method which succeeded in wresting swarajya in 1947.

ROLE PLAYED BY MADAN MOHAN MALAVIYA

Pandit Madan Mohan Malaviya joined the Indian National Congress when he was 25 and one year after the Congress was founded, *i.e.*, in 1886 and he remained its member for the rest of his life—a long record of 60 years.

Parliamentarian. He was a great Parliamentarian. He had the distinction of being elected twice the President of the National Congress—one in 1909 and again in 1918. On Malaviyaji's long record of service to the Congress, Dr.Sitaramayya makes a few observations. "The Moderates had manned the Congress in their day, and abandoned it; Mrs. Besant captured it and surrendered it. But through storm and sunshine, through good report and evil, Panditji has stuck to it. Panditji is the one man who has had the courage to be alone in what he considered to be the right. At one time he was one the crest of a wave of popularity, at another he was listened to with indifference on the Congress platform. He never yielded to the current forces, either by sheer inertia or by fear of popular reprobation. When in less than four months the time and occasion demanded it, he resigned in 1930. In 1921 he had opposed the Non-co-operation Movement but in 1932, he found himself a whole-hearted civil resister.

Differences Inside the Congress. Probably because of a noble and sincere life, Pandit Malaviya was elected practically unopposed, even if he was a staunch Hindu, to the Central Legislature for many years, to the Congress as its President twice and to the Hindu Mahasabha as its President thrice. He was a member of the Swaraj Party but being a moderate he left the Party and shared responsibility in forming a political party named the Nationalist Party in order to safeguard the interests of the Hindus. The Congress, he thought, had foregotten the interests of the Hindus in its plank of nationalist policies. It would be a mistake to consider Pandit Malaviya as a communalist, as some writers do, because of his stauch support for the Hindus and Hindus only. He was a nationalist. He found no consistency in the Congress as a national organisation—when it accepted the Muslim Communal demands in the Lucknow Pact of 1916 and again the Communal Award of the British Government. He left the Swaraj Party because in his opinion this party surrendered the Hindu interests to the Muslim Communalists. He opposed the policies of Congress in this regard, but with all his differences with the Congress at times, his advice and opinions were always valued by the Congress and he was invariably offered a seat on the Congress Working Committee. And it is already said that so much universally loved and honoured he was that his seat in the Legislature was seldom contested.

An orthodox like Gandhiji, or more than Gandhiji, Panditji started his politics as a friend of the British Empire but later became bitter against the policy of the British Government in India. A good journalist, he edited the "Hindustan" for two years. He was also for some time editor of the "Indian Union". He started a Hindi Weekly named 'Abhyudaya. He was one of the founders of the "Leader" in Allahabad. He was a good speaker and an effective writer. But the thing for which he would be ever known is the Benaras Hindu University which he founded and developed through years of tireless. In order to give a sound financial backing to the University, he had to travel through the length and breadth of the country for collecting donations. No wonder he was called the Prince of Beggars. It is for his unique personality in the public life of India that Pandit Madan Mohan Malaviya towers above many other leaders in our national struggle for freedom. Unfortunately he could not live a year more to see the independence, though he would have been pained at the partition of his Motherland.

ROLE PLAYED BY SWAMI DAYANAND SARASWATI DURING THE MOVEMENT

Dayanand, as he writes in his autobiography published in "The Theosophist", "was born in a family of Northern Brahmins in a town belonging to the Raja of Morsi in Kathiawar" in 1824. He was "taught to worhsipping the uncouth piece of clay representing Siva known as the Parthiva Linga". In his early days he studied Sanskrit Grammer learnt the Vedas by heart, and accompanied his father in his visits to the Shrines and temples of Siva. Siva was for his father the most divine of all the gods, the Supreme Being. Dayanand lived comfortably with his father who was a banker and Revenue Collector, but the comfortable relations with his father were strained by an incident in the course of the worship of the Parthiva Linga. In this solemn act, he was to keep awake along with his father in order to have the blessings of Lord Shiva. In the late night when his father slept happily. Dayanand true to the rites kept awake but he saw mice going over the idol of Lord Siva. "He roused (his) father, asking him to tell whether this hideous idol was the great god of the scriptures. It was impossible to reconcile the idea of an omnipotent living God with this idol, which allows the mice to run over his body and thus suffers himself to be polluted without the slightest protest". Dayanand writes in his autobiography, "but my faith in the idol was gone, and all I could do was to try to conceal my lack of faith, and devote all my time to study. The death of his sister at the age of 14 followed by the deth of one of his affectionate uncles created in him "a conviction that there was nothing stable, nothing worth living for in this world."

Higher Learning. Dayanand wanted to study Sanskrit at Banaras, but was sent by his father to local Pandit instead. In the meanswhile the preparations for his marriage were on. He was then 21 and he "resolved to place an eternal bar between myself and marriage". He secretly lfet his home and succeeded in escaping from a party of horsemen whom his father had sent after him. He joined the order of Lala Bhagat at Sayla and received the name of Sudha

Chaitanya (pure thought). In a small principality near Ahmedabad he was caught by his father on the information of a Bairagi who knew him, and was handed over to some sepoys there. But he succeeded in escaping once more, and went to Baroda. In the Chetan Math (a temple) he held several discourses with Brahmananda and a number of Sanyasins of the Vedanta Philosophy. He learnt here clearly, "I am Brahma, the Jiva (Soul) and Brahma being one." After traversing through the scholarly atmosphere of Banaras. Dayanand went back to a place on the banks of the Narbada remained under the tuition of Paramanada Paramhansa. On reading books like Vedanta State, Vedanta Paribhasa etc. he became anxious to be a Sanyasin. Here he was given his well-known name Dayanand Saraswati. Then he studied the final secrets of the "Yoga Vidya" and was very much pleased when in 1865 he joined a great meeting of sages and philosophers at Hardwar.

Dayananda got his first serious idea of the evils of Hindu society at Tidee where he was 'horrified at meeting with meat-eating Brahmins, still more at reading some of their sacred books, the Tantras which sanction every kind of immorality." As Dayananda grew older (he wrtes in his letter to Raja Sivaprasad) he rejected all the Hindu sacred books as insipid except the four Vedas and the Isa Upanishad which is foud in the Yayni Veda. Dayanand grew in fame. In 1881 a large convocation of 300 Pandits from Gonda. Navadipa and Kasi was held to discuss with Dayanad his opinions.

His Writings. Besides lecturing, Swami Dayanad devoted some of the later years of his life to the publication of books. Before his death he had completed a translation into Hindi of one-half of the Vedas. The principal points of his teaching are embodies in his "Rig-Vedadi Bhashya Bhumika' (A Prefatory Exposition of the Rig-Veda and others). His 'Satyarath Praskash' (Manifestation of True Meanings) gives his teachings on religious and social customs.

He died at the age of 59 at Ajmer on October 30, 1863. There was a huge funeral procession by the followers of Swami Dayanand. It is said that two maunds of sandal-wood, 8 maunds of common fuel, 4 maunds of ghee, and 2½ seers of camphor were used in the cremation.

Dayanada had a great faith in the Vedas whom, like many Hindus, he considered to be self-evident, requiring no proof. Max Mueller says of him. To him not only was everything contained in the Vedas perfect turth, but he went a step further, and by the most incredible interpretations succeeded in persuading himself and others that everything worth knowing, even the most recent inventions of modern science, were alluded to in the Vedas. Steam engine, railways, and steamboats, all were shown to have been known, at least in their germs, to the poets of the Vedas, for Veda, he argued, means Divine knowledge and how could anything have been hidden from that?" To add to this, Dayanad's ignorance of geography is ridiculous. So too, some say, was his common sense. His doctrine of 'Niyog' appears disgusting to many.

Works. Numerous societies have been formed in North India and the Pubjab called Arya Samaj, professing to follow Dayanand's interpretations of the Vedas and reformatory works, Dayanand himself had established the Arya Samaj in 1875 for these purposes. The Anglo-Vedic Colleges and the English paper called the 'Arya Patrika" are Dayanand's contributions to modern India. The Arya Samaj gave India such great leaders as Lala Lajpat Rai and Swami Shardhananda. The British Government regarded the D.A.V. Colleges and Gurukul Schools as the centres of sedition and breeding grounds of patriots and revolutionaries.

The Arya Samaj did a lot of work in the field of removing untouchability, education of women, weakening of the caste system, remarriage of the widows and the discouragement of early marriage of children. The Arya Samaj made the Hindus militant and agressive and this was a great factor in paving the way for the anti-British struggle of the Indians. The policy of Shuddhi brought many converts to Hinduism.

An Assessment. Swami Dayanand Saraswati, like Raja Ram Mohan Roy, promoted the cause of nationalism in an indirect manner. He inculcated in the people a faith of their future. The Hindu society, purified of its evils was prepared to fight for freedom. He was the first historical figure of India to preach the cult of Swadeshi and India for the Indians. The principle was good government is no substitute for self-government. Through his preaching the people were made aware of India's past and Indians took pride in their heritage and wished to build up a similar future. Thus the ground was prepared for any "mass movement". His followers had learnt a new spirit of discipline. In all these ways he was the fore-runner of Mahatma Gandhi. His life proves to the English-educated Indians that a lack of knowledge of English is no hindrance to self growth into a man of eminence.

Shri Aurobido pays a rich tribute to Sami Dayanand "At the head of the Indian Reniassance, one stands out by himself with the peculiar and solitary distinctness, one unique in his type, as he is unique in his work." He brought back an old Aryan element into the national character. He was "a man with God in his soul, vision in his eyes and power in his hands to show out of life an image according to his vision." His intense faith in the walefare of the fellow Hindus, his belief in the regeneration of India and the Hindus into another golden era of achievements and his organisational legacy through educational institutions and the Samaj, all these make Swami Dayanand Saraswati one of the foremost leaders who shaped modern India.

ROLE OF RAJA RAM MOHAN ROY IN INDIAN NATIONALISM

Raja Ram Mohan Roy was born in a Brahmin family near Calcutta in 1774, the year in which Warren Hastings was appointed the first Governor-General of India. His father was a small zamindar, who had served under the Nawabs of Murshidabad. Persian was still the language of the court and a learning thereof was required for any government employment. At the age of nine, Ram Mohan was sent to Patna, the principal sent of Arabic learning in Bengal. The revolutionary ideas were already visible. In his opposition to idolatory Ram Mohan had a repture with his father and left home. Some say he went once to Tibet in his wanderings. At the age of 20 he was reacalled by his father. Here Ram Mohan learnt English and further knowledge of Sanskrit.

From 1800 to 1813 Ram Mohan was in the employment of the Government but not have any fixed job until he was made a Sheristadar. Either as dewan or head officer of the Collectors and Judges of the district, he spent ten years in Ramgarh. Bhagalpur and Rangpur. He was, therefore, commonly known as the Dewan until he was made a Raja by the Emperor of Delhi.

Ram Mohan Roy returned to Bengal in 1814 but with a zeal to fight out the old superstitions and the manifold evils that had darkened the society in his country. He himself described the state of affairs in Bengal. The worshippers of Sakti and followers of Chaitanya were urging for religious supremacy. But the bigotry of the two sects and "their general immorality and corruption were simply revolting". To this was added the social miseries. The rigid caste system, "the horrible rites of Suttee and Infanticide" were source of much trouble. Women hardly knew anything in the name of education. "Morality was at a very low ebb" and "no man knew when the darkness would be dispelled". It was natural for a man who described this state of affairs to take a keen iterest in reforming his society. The suppression of Sati was a success largely due to his efforts.

His Writings. Soon after his father's death Ram Mohan Roy wrote a Persian book "Against the Idolatory of all Religions". In 1816 his first work in English came out and that was "An Abridgement of the Vedant", though he took much less interest in the Vedas than in the Upanishads. In the Introduction to this book he sought to do away with the excuse that the Europeans offered on the Hindu idolatory—as worship of 'emblematical representations of the Supreme Divinity".

He translated four of the Upanishads according to the commentary of Sankaracharya. He said of them that "they with great consistency inculcate the unity of God, instructing men at the same time, in the pure mode of advising them in spirit". This "unity of God, of the Vedantic philosophy was pantheism—not monotheism. Ekam evadvitigam.

In 1837 Ram Mohan Roy published "A Defence of Hindu Theism" in reply to the attack of the advocates for Idolatory at

Madras, and "A second Defence of the Monotheistical System of the Vedas" in reply to an Apology for the present state of Hindu worship. He strong refuted the common excuse that "Idols were invented for those who are not possessed of sufficient understanding". If it were not so, he said, the common Protestant Christains to idol worship.

He began an intensive study of Christianity and published in 1820 in Bengali and English "The Precepts of Jesus, the Guide to Peace and Happiness" consisting of extracts from the Gospels. This made Ram Mohan hated by the missionaries who contended that Mr. Roy after three or four years of the study of the Bible had misunderstood it and that it did not contain some doctrines which were vital. Ram Mohan published his "Appeals to the Christan Public in Defence" in order to prove that he was correct. Nevertheless "Mr. Roy' did not forget his loyalty to Christianity.

Brahmo Samaj. On his return to Calcutta Ram Mohan Roy had formed an association of a few personal friends, called Almiya Sabha, Spiritual Society, which met in his house periodically for discussion. The opposition of the Brahmins and Pandits ultimately led to the collapse of the society.

In 1821, Mr. W. Adam, a Protestent Missionary friend of Ram Mohan Roy, adopted, unitarianism and sought of preach his opinions by holding meetings and giving lecutres. Ram Mohan Roy, Dwarkanath Tagore, Prosonno Kumar Tagore and others came with assistance and a permanent meeting place was hired on the Chitpore Road. There were services every Staturday evening with four parts, a recitation of Vedic texts, readings from Upanishads ; delivering of a sermon, and singing hymns. It ushered in the dawn of the greatest change that has ever passed over the Hindu mind. It was the first introduction of public worship and united prayer. As Sir Monier Williams writs, a new phase took definite shape which differed essentially from every other that had preached it. For no other reformation has resulted in the same way from the influence of the European education and Christian ideas. The first Hindu Theistic Church was opened in Calcutta in 1830.

Ram Mohan Roy went on a journey to England in April 1931—the first Indian of rank and influence to do so. He was presented to the King and a place was assigned to him at the ceremony of the coronation. He had three special objects of this visit:

(a) To be present at the approaching discussion in the House of Commons on the renewal of the East India Company's Charter, upon which the future Government of India, whether for good or evil, so largely depended.

(b) The orthodox party in Calcutta indignant at being deprived of the privilege of roasting their mother alive when they became widows, sought to appeal to King-in-Council. Ram Mohan Roy wished to oppose this in person. While in England, he was granted all the three special objects of his mission.

(c) To represented the grievances of the Emperor of Delhi, who conferred upon him the title of Raja and sent him as his ambassador to England.

Unhappily Ram Mohan Roy could not bear the stress of the European climate. His health declined after a visit to France in 1833. Upon invitation he took up residence at the house of Miss Castle—a ward of Dr. Carpenter in Bristol. On September 27, he breathed his last in the presence of his son Raja Ram Mohan Roy and his two Hindu servants, by whom he had all along been enabled to preserve his caste. He was buried not in a Christian Cemetery but in a retired spot. Ten years afterwards his remains were removed to a cemetery near Bristol where a tomb was raised over his grave by Dwarkanath Tagore.

His Religious Opinions. The exact nature of Raja Ram Mohan Roy's religious is debatable. Sir Monier Williams characterized the form of theology which the propounded as 'vague' but "undogmatic and comprehensive". He was claimed to be a Vedantist by the Hindus, a Theist by the Unitarians, a Christian by the Christians, and a Muslim by the Mohammandans. He assimilated whatever was good in all these religions.

Mr. Ram Chandra Bose in his "Brahmoism" settles down the opinion that Raja Ram Mohan Roy was decidedy pantheistic. But the later pronouncements of Ram Mohan Roy in England, as Mr. Bose argues, were in favour of the assumption that he was a theist of the Unitarian school. Dr. K.S. MacDonald in a paper argued by numerous quotation that Ram Mohan Roy was a Christian. It is acknowledged however that he denied the doctrine of the Trinity and the Atonement of Christ.

Ram Mohan Roy was in uncompromising reformer like Luther, nor was he prepared to make sacrifices for his faith like many thousands of the early Christians who would rather suffer death than countenance idolatory in any way. He denounced caste as a demoralizing institution, but Ram Mohan Roy sought to remain in the eyes of the law a Brahmin and retained his Brahmanical thread to the last, because until the passing of the Lex Loci Act by Lord William Bentinck, the loss of caste entailed the loss of all property. Ram Mohan Roy nevertheless occupies the highest place among modern Indian theistic reformers.

His Works. Ram Mohan Roy was an "all-round" reformer. He advocated the civil rights of the Hindus and sought to improve their temporal condition. He led the compaign for the abolition of Sati. The religious reformation of India had his chief attention.

In all his activities Raja Ram Mohan Roy was animated by a deep love of his motherland and an intense sympathy for the ignorant and the poor. His means were the means of raising the morale of the people. One of the foremost Orientalists, he nevertheless was convinced that India could progress only through liberal education covering all the branches of Western learning. He was successful in his support for the introduction of the study of English language and Western science in India.

He fought for the freedom of the press—and carried on a vigorous agitation against the Press Resolution of 1823. His Bengali Journal. "The Samvad Kaumudi" was one of the earliest Indian edited newspapers. He submitted a memorial to the Sureme Court in which he dwelt upon the benefits of a free press.

The abolition of Sati put the Raja in the front rank of the world's humanitarian reformers. He was the first Indian to be consulted on Indian affairs by the British Parliament. He suggested reforms in practically all branches of Indian administration. Influenced in his political ideas by European thinkers like Baron, Hume: Bentham, Blackstone and Montesquien he thought of the British rule as a divine dispensation for the good of India. Subsisting on the inter-dependence of religious, social, educational and political progress Ram Mohan Roy held a firm conviction that the Indian society of his times was not fit to assume political responsibility. His thoughts were not confined to the welfare of India, they went, beyond. He advocated the peaceful settlement of international dispute through the mediation of a congress composed of an equal number of members from the Parliaments of the countries concerned. He was an internationalist. We should not be surprised at our (Indian) insistence on strengthening the United Nations, after more than a century of Raja Ram Mohan Roy.

Father of Modern India. Trough various religious, social and educational reforms, Raja Ram Mohan Roy prepared Indians for the political consciousness which followed. The soil which became fit to sprout the seed of nationalism in 1885 was manured properly by Raja Ram Mohan Roy and other socio-religious reformers of the 18th and 19th centuries whose efforts infused a new life into the Indian society trough removal of its evils, corruption and weaknesses. In great sense Raja Ram Mohan Roy is called the Father of Indian Nationalism.

SUBASH CHANDRA BOSE A LEADER OF INDIAN INDEPENDENCE MOVEMENT

Subhas Chandra Bose (1897-1945) was one of the most fearless leaders of the nationalist movement in India. He was twice elected the President of the Indian National Congress in 1938 and 1939. As his election for the second time he was opposed by Mahatma Gandhi and there was strong opposition to him, he resigned from the Congress Presidentship and started a new party known as the Forward Block.

In 1938 when war in Europe was imminent, the view of Subhas Chandra Bose was that "India's immediate requirements were an uncompromising struggle with British Imperialism and methods of struggle more effective than what Mahatma Gandhi had produced." Again, "The Indian people should not be hampered by any philosophical notions like Gandhian non-violence or any sentimentation like Nehru's anti-Axis foreign policy." As President of the Congress he proposed in March 1939 that an ultimatum be given to the Government of India to make Indian free within six months. However, the proposal was truned down by the Congress and he resigned from the Congress Presidentship. When the World War II broke out, he undertook a tour of the country and addressed hundreds of meetings in which he openly criticised the British Government and advised the Indians not to help the British war-effort. On April 6, 1940, he started the civil disobedience campaign. On July 27, 1940, he was imprisoned without trial. While in Jail, he arrived at three conclusions:

(a) First conclusion was that Britain would lose the war and the British Empire would break up.

(b) Second conclusion was that inspite of being in a very weak position, the British would not hand over power to the people of India who would have to fight for their freedom.

(c) Third conclusion was that India would win her independence if she played her part in the war against Britain and collaborated with those powers that were fighting against Britain. He decided to go on hunger strike and on November 26, 1940 addressed a long leter to the Governor of Bengal and its ministers in which he wrote, "The individual must die so that the nation may live. Today I must die so that India may win freedom and glory." He started his indefinite fast on November 29, 1940.

After his release, Subash Chandra Bose remained in his house on Elgin Road, Calcutta, which was under the strict supervision of the police. He was last seen there on January 16, 1941. On January 17, 1941 at about 1.25 a.m. he left his house and reached Gomoh by car. From there he went to Peshawar by train. He passed through

Jamrud and reached Garhi. He crossed the Indian border on foot and reached Kabul. From there he proceeded to Russia with an Italian passport.

Works

He was received well by Ribbentrop, the right-hand man of Hitler. He was given all facilities to broadcast from Berlin to India his denunciation of the British Government. When Germany attacked Russia in June 1941, Subhas proposed to organise an Indian Army which was to follow the German Army to Central Asia from where it was to operate against the British forces on the North-Western Frontier. Subhas wanted the Axis powers to make a declaration regarding the independence of India and although he had a long meeting with Hitler on May 29, 1941 in that connection, he was not successful in his efforts. Out of the Indian prisoners of war caputred in North Africa by the Germans, Subhas was able to from two units in January 1942. He was also able to set up Free India Centres in Rome and Paris. The strength of the legion rose to 3000. However, his further activitis in Germany were suddenly stopped when he heard of the successes of the Japanese against the British and the fall of Singapore on February 15, 1942. Subhas felt that he could do more for India from the Far East than from Germany. Under these circumstances he decided to leave Germany for the Far East.

Formation of Indian National Army

When the war broke out in the East in 1941, there was great enthusiasm among Indians in those regions. A large number of associations were set up to help the liberation of India from the British yoke. Out of these associations was born the idea of an Indian Independence League. Through the efforts of Rash Bihari Bose who had left India and settled in Japan, a Conference was held at Tokyo on March 28-30, 1942. A resolution was passed at that Conference that an Indian National Army should be formed under the direct command of Indian officers who were to conduct the campaign for the liberation of India. An Indian Independence League of overseas Indians was provisionally set up it was decided to have a fully representative conference of the Indians at Bangkok in June 1942.

The Bangkok Conference was held from June 15, to 23, 1942 and was attended by about 100 delegates from Burma, Japan, China, Indo-China, the Philippines, Malaya, etc. The Conference was presided over by Rash Bihari Bose who unfurled the Tricolour Flag of India. The Indian Independence League with a definite constitution was inaugurated. Many resolutions were passed and one of them invited Subhas Chandra Bose to East Asia. The conference was also attended by the representatives of the Indian soldiers who had been captured by the Japanese but had given up their allegiance to the British Government. After the fall of Singapore, 40,000 Indian prisoners of war had fallen into the hands of the Japanese who handed them over the Captain Mohan Singh who was an officer in the British Army and had surrendered to the Japanese but was pursuaded to join Indian Independence movement. Mohan Singh organised an army of volunteers known as the Indian National Army or Azad Hind Fauj. He attended the Tokyo and Bangkok Conferences and was chosen as the Commander-in-Chief of the Indian National Army and also a member of the Council of Action which had been set up by the Bangkok Conference By August 1942, a division of the Indian National Army consisting of more than 16,000 men was raised and approved by the Japanese. Mohan Singh was anxious to extend his forces as more than 40,000 prisoners of war had signed the pledge to join the Indian National Army. His idea was not approved of by the Japanese. Mohan Singh and the Japanese militry oficers disagreed on many other points. There were dissensions within the Council of Action and its members resigned. Rash Bihari Bose and Mohan Singh also quarrelled. The result was that Mohan Singh was dismissed from his post and interned. A deadlock was created.

Subhas in Japan

Subhas had accepted the invitation to lead the Indian Independence Movement in East Asia and had sent a message to the Bangkok Conference where he was hailed as the leader. However, it was not an easy job to reach East Asia from Germany. He had to wait long for the arrangements to be made. On February 8, 1943, he got into a German submarine at Kiel. His submarine avoided the routes controlled by the British ships and ultimately contacted a Japanese submarine 400 miles SSW of Madagascar. On April 28, he was transferred by the rubber dinghy to the Japanese submarine which took him across the Indian Ocean to Sumatra.

Subhas was received by the Japanese Premier Tojo on the day after his arrival. Prime Minister Tojo made the following declaration in the Japenese Diet, "Japan is firmly resolved to extend all means in order to help to expel and elimintate from India the Anglo-Saxon influences which are the enemy of the Indian people and enable India to achieve full independence in the true sense of the term."

Leader of Indian Independence Movement

Subhas spoke over the Tokyo Rajo of his determination to launch an armed fight against the British from India's Eastern borders. He arrived at Singapore on July 2, 1943 and was welcomed by huge crowds. It was felt that the Man of destiny had come to lead them to liberate India. On July 4, 1943, Rash Bihari Bose handed over the leadership of the Indian Independence movement in East Asia to Subhas who took over the Presidentship of the Indian Independence League. On July 5, 1943, the formation of the Azad Hind Fauj was announced to the world. In order to inspire his followers with zeal to fight for freedom of their country, he declared. "We have a grim fight ahead of us for the enemy is powerful unscruplous and ruthless. In this final march to freedom you will have to face hunger, privation, forced marches and death. Only when you pass this test will freedom be yours." On August 25, 1943 Subhas who was now known as Netaji took over the direct command of Indian National Army.

Provisional Government of Free India

On October 21, 1943, the Provisional Government of Free India was inaugurated and Netaji became the Head of the State, Prime Minister and Supreme Commander of the Army. Finance, publicity and Women Organisation were given to A.C. Chatterji, S.A. Ayer and Lakshmi Swaminathan. Netaji took the following oath : "In the name of God, I take this sacred oath to liberate India and the thirty eight crores of my countrymen. I, Subhas Chandra Bose, will continue the secred war of freedom till the last breath of my life". Similr oaths were taken by the other members of the Cabinet and the National Anthem composed by Tagore was sung. The duty of the Provisional Government was described in the following Proclamation : "It will be the task of the Provisional Government to launch and to conduct the struggle that will bring about the expulsion of the British and of their allies from the soil of India. It will then be the task of the Provisional Government to bring about the establishment of a permanent National Government of Azad Hind constituted in accordance with the will of the Indian people and enjoying their confidence. After the British and their allies are overthrown and until a Permanent National Government of Azad Hind is set up on Indian soil, the Provisional Government will administer the affairs of the country in trust for the Indian people." On October 23, 1943, the Provisional Government decided to declare war on Britain and the United States. The declaration was broadcast over Radio by Netaji himself and San Francisco Radio communicated it to the world. On October 28, 1943, Netaji flew to Tokyo where he attended the Greater East Asia Conference in the first week of November and was received by the Japanese Emperor with all the honours due to the Head of a State. Prime Minister Tojo announced on November 6, 1943 at the Greater East Asia Conference that Japan had decided to hand over the Andaman and Nicobar Islands to the Provisional Government of Azad Hind. Netaji left for the Andamans where he reached on December 31, 1943. It was decided to rename the Andaman and Nicobar Islands as Shahid and Swaraj Islands respectively. Netaji transferred the advance Headquarters of the Provisional Government the Indian Independence League and the Indian National Army command to Rangoon.

Subhas Brigade

The first batch of the Subhas Brigade left Taiping on November 9, 1943 and the last batch on November 24, 1943. The main body of the Subhas Brigade arrived in Rangoon early in January 1944. The soldiers had to cover at least 400 miles on foot with about 80 pounds of load carried on their backs. "in their eagerness to reach the front as soon as possible, they generally covered in two days the distance which the Japanese soldiers took five days to travel." Netaji arrived in Rangoon on January 4, 1944. Three days after, he discussed with General Kawabe, the Japanese Commander-in-Chief in Burma, the plan of co-operation between the Japanese Army and the Indian National Army. There were differences about the role of the Indian Army but ultimately it was agreed that no INA formation should be split into smaller formations than a Battalion. The Japanese and INA units were to follow a common strategy agreed to between Netaji and the Japanese Commander-in-Chief. The INA was to be allotted an independent sector of the front. Every inch of Indian territory liberated was to be handed over to INA for administration. The only flag that would fly over Indian territory would be the Indian Tricolour. Afte the general plan was finally settled at a meeting on January 24, 1944 between Netaji and General Katakura, Chief of the Japanese General Staff in Burma, the Subhas Brigade was put under the direct command of the Japanese General Headquarters in Burma for purpose of operations only. Shah Nawaz Khan, Commander of the Subhash Brigade, met the Japanese Commander-in-Chief who apprised him fully of the military situation on the Indo-Burma border.

The Subhas Brigade was divided into three battalions. Battalion Non 1 was to proceed to the Kaladan valley in Arakan. Battalions Nos. 2 and 3 were to proceed to the Chin Hill area of Haka and Falam. On February 3, 1944, Nataji delivered the farewell speech to 3000 soldiers who "in full military kit stood rigidly to attention for an hour and a half and listened to every word he said with rapt attention." He made it clear that they would be put to the severe test by the Japanese authorities and the future of the battle for India's freedom would depend upon them. The was given an assurance by the soldiers that they would sacrifice themselves for their country.

On February 4, 1944, Battalion No. 1 of the Subhas Brigade left Rangoon by train for Prome. From there, they marched on foot and arrived at Kyauktaw (in Akyab) on the Kaladan river, suffering casualties on the way from aerial bombardment by the enemy. They formed the base in the middle of March 1944 and inflicted a defeat upon the Negro troops from West Africa in the British Army. The enemy was driven from the Eastern bank, leaving 250 dead in the field and large quantities of stores. 16 of their boats were sunk. The casualties for the Indian National Army were 14 ded and 22 wounded. Reinforced by Japanese troops, the Indian Battalion advanced along both the banks of the Kaladan for about 50 miles North to Paletwa and captured it after severe fighting. Daletme was also cauptured. From Daletma, the Indian soldiers could see the frontier of India and they were very anxious to reach it. The nearest British post on the Indian side was Mowdok about 50 miles to the East of Cox Bazar. It was captured by a surprise a tack during the night in May 1944 and the enemy fled leaving behind large quantities of arms, ammunitins and rations.

On accound of the difficulty of supply as well as the impending counter-attack by British forces, the Japanese decided to withdraw from Mowdok. The Commander of the INA was also advised to do the some but the INA officers refused to do so. Their reply to their Commander was : "No Sir, the Japanese can retreat because Tokyo lies that way; our goal—the Red Fort, Delhi—lies ahead of us. We have orders to get to Delhi. There is no going back for us."

The INA Commander decided to leave one Company under the command of Captain Suraj Mal at Mowdok to guard the flag and withdrew the rest. The Japanese also left a platoon of their own troops at Mowdok. Those Japanese troops were placed under the direct command of Suraj Mal. The Japanese Commander-in-Chief in Burma was very much impressed by the attitude of the Indian troops and praised them to Netaji in these words. "Your Excellency, we were wrong. We misjudged the soldiers of the INA. We know now that they are no mercenaries, but real patriots." Captain Suraj Mal and the troops under his command remained at Mowdok from May to September 1944. During that period, they were constantly attacked by Britsh troops but the latter were defeated. On one occasion, a small post of 20 men was attacked three times during one day by the enemy about 150 strong with heavy artillery and mortars and the last one was preceded by aerial bombardment. All these attacks were repulsed. When Suraj Mal came with a reinforcement of 50 men, he attacked the British base three miles away at dusk and the result was that the enemy had to run in all directions.

Capture of Kohima

Battalions Nos. 2 and 3 left Rangoon on February 4 and 5 1944 and reached Kalewa via Mandalay. They were asked to take over charge of the Haka-Falam Front and their main work was to defend these sectors against two British Brigades and prevent them from cutting the main supply line of the Japense forces from Kalewa to Tamu and Fort White. They were also to carry out offensive operations on the Haka-Falam Front. The INA men took over charge of Falam and Haka from the Japanese. The Japanese were satisfied with the military skill and efficiency of the INA men and issued instructions "that the main body of the Brigade would proceed to Kohima and would be prepared, on the fall of Imphal, to advance rapidly and cross the Brahmaputra into the heart of Bengal." About 150 and 300 men were left at Haka and Falam respectively and the rest marched towar Kohima where they reached towards the last week of May 1944. Early in March 1944, INA troops of the Bahadur Group and the Azad Hind Dal accompanied the Japanese troops to the Kohima sector and the combined forces took Ukhrul and Kohima. As the new areas were liberated, the Azad Hind Dal took charge of them in the name of the Provisional Government of Azad Hind and did very good work. The Tricolour Flag was hoisted on the mountain tops around Kohima.

LALA LAJPAT RAI A GOOD FIGHTER FOR INDIAN INDEPENDENCE

Lala Lajpat Rai was born in 1865 in Jagraon in the district of Ludhiana (the Punjab). His father Radha Krishan was a teacher of Urdu in a Government School and was a great admirer of Swami Dayanand and Sir Syed Ahmed Khan. His father's influence is discernible inhis interest in the reform of Hinduism and in his enthusiasm for United Indian Nationhood. Mother was a source of his spiritual quality and constructive ideas.

Lala Lajpat Rai was promising youngmen from the very beginning. He qualified himself for the bar and set up his practice at Hissar and later at Lahore. In his student days he was much influenced by Mahatma Hans Raj and Pandit Guru Dutt and now while having an enviable practice as a lawyer he was attracted by the Arya Samaj. He assisted in the establishment of Arya Samajs and educational institutions under their control.

Political Career. In 1888, he entered politics, probably because the Arya Samaj was a small field for his activities. Before it be had written biographies of Mazzini, Garibaldi, Sivaji, Lord Krishna, and Swami Dayanand. They showed the way which Lajpat Rai was to go. Besides being a great political leader, he was also a great servant of the people. In the earthquake in Kangra in 1905, he organised relief for the people there. Within 17 years of his joining the Congress he had been a distinguished leader and in 1907 the National Congress chose him along with Gokhale in a two-man team to be sent abroad to acquaint the public with the conditions in India. Disappointed he returned to homeland. In 1907 he took a leading part in the agitation against the increase in water-rates by the Punjab Government. He was, therefore, deported to Mandalay (Burma). During his stay there he wrote the book "The Story of My deportation". He was growing in popular estimation. When he stood for election to the Lahore Municipal Committee he created so much enthusiasm among the people that even the incapacitated men and women went to vote for him.

In 1914, Lajpat Rai went on a tour abroad. It lasted upto 1920. In America, he gave many lectures on Indian and wrote a number of books—the most important of them being " The Arya Samaj", "England's Debt to India" and "Young India." He created a group of American friends who were to take interest in the Indian cause for freedom. On his return to India in 1920 Lajpat Rai was elected the President of the Special Session of the Indian National Congress held in Calcutta. In this session he had opposed Mahatma Gandhi's programme of non-co-operation. He did not give his hearty support to the non-cooperation movement.

In Swaraj Party. When the Swaraj Party was formed with a programme for council-entry on agenda Lajpat Rai joined it and was elected in 1923 to the Central Legislative Assembly in which he was the Deputy Leader of the Swaraj Party. He was never afraid of advocating national cause. Disgusted with the Congress over its preferential policy towards the Muslims, he joined hands with M.M. Malaviya in organizing the Nationalist Party and the Hindu Sangathan Movement for the protection of Hindu interests. He was not a Hindu communalist. In 1928 while leading a protest procession against the Simon Commission he was severely wounded by a Lathi-Charge on October 20, and he died of it on November 17, 1938. On receiving lathi-charge Lajpat Rai had told the processions, that the lathi blows he received would prove one day nails in the coffin of the British Empire. No doubt, for his undaunted courage and fearlessness, he was nicknamed "Sher-e-Panjab' or the Lion of the Punjab.

Like Tilak, Lajpat Rai was an orator dominating the Punjab as Tilak did Maharashtra. A contemporary described him thus "As a public speaker, I think of Lloyd George and Lajpat Rai together. They had equal capacity for rousing the indignation of the masses. I had heard few speeches which would be placed by the side of Lajpat Rai's speeches in Urdu in the thrilling effect they produced upon the mass mind.

Militant and Constructive Patriot. Lajpat Rai was not a sentimental patriot. He was militant and yet constructive. No one could be more aggressive than Lajpat Rai when a wrong had to be set right or when some injustice had to be redressed. He was at his best when some solid work had to be done for the country. Imprisonment, deportation and exile were his lot. A fierce speaker, he also was a vigorous writer and jouriualist. He founded the Bande Matram' (Urdu daily) and the "People" (English Weekly). He organised the "Servants of People Society' and founded the Tilak School of Politics. It is said of his organizing ability that in 10 days he collected 9 lakhs of ruppes for Tilak Swaraj Fund. The National Congress at Lahore, the Punjab National Bank Ltd. and Lakshmi Insuranea Co. Ltd. bear the impression of his personality. On his death in 1928.

Gandhiji remarked, "Men like Lalaji cannot die so long as the sun shines in the Indian sky."

SERVICES OF MAHATMA GANDHI TO INDIA

Mahatma Gandhi was the greatest leader of modern India. He was born on October 2, 1969, at Porbander in Kathiawar. His father was a Diwan at Porbander and Rajkot. He was married at the early age of 18 and went to England to study law at the age of nineteen. His mother was a religious lady and she made him promise that he would avoid meat, wine and woman. He completed the study of law and became a barrister. Then he returned to India.

Gandhiji started practice at Rajkot and after some time shifted to Bombay. There he came in contact with Rajachandra Ravjibhai and learnt his first lessons in non-violence from him. Then he was engaged by a Muslim firm to plead its case in South Africa and he went there. There he saw how badly the Indians were treated by the South African Government. His conscience revolted against the policy of racial discrimination. The climax of racialism was reached when the Asiatic Registration Act was passed in 1906. It required all Asiatics to register themselves and to give their thumb impressions. It was meant to humiliate the Asiatics. Gandhiji protested against this enactment and led a deputation even to England. This had no effect. The Indians in South Africa under the leadership of Gandhiji refused to get them selves registered and to give their thumb impressions. The Indians were to get themselves registered voluntarily and Gandhiji got himself registered first of all. The Transvaal authorities violated the agreement and to thousand Indians under the leadership of Gandhiji marched into that province. It was a non-violent march for securing justice. A Commission of Inquiry was set up and ultimately Asiatic Registration Act and Pole Tax were repealed.

Mahatma Gandhi returned to India in 1914. First World war started that year. He had faith in the good sense of the British and asked the Indians to co-operate in the war effort. His attitude began to change in 1918 because he felt that the British Government was not going to give anything substantial to the Indians. The Government of India passed Rowlatt Act in opposition to the wishes of the people and Mahatma Gandhi asked the people to observe hartal. The situation became serious in the Punjab and Martial Law was declared. General Dyer enacted Jallianwala Bagh tragedy at Amritsar. This made Mahatma Gandhi feel all the more than justice could not be expected from the British Government. Soon after this, Mahatma Gandhi took up the lead of Khilafat Movement to bring about Hindu-Muslim unity. There was agitation throughout the country and the Hindu co-operated with the Muslims everywhere. He called off Non-Co-operation Movement because of Chauri-Chaura incident in Bihar where a mob attacked a police station and killed 24 policemen including a sub-inspector.

Mahatma Gandhi started Civil Disobedience Movement once more in 1930. It was started with his famous march from Sabarmati Ashram to Dandi Beach to violate Salt Laws. Mahatma Gandhi and thousands of Congress volunteers were thrown in prisons. The Congress did not take part in the deliberations of the First Round Table Conference. Then Gandhi-Irwin Pact was made and Mahatma Gandhi, as the representative of the Congress took part in the deliberations of the Second Round Table Conference. He was arrested on his return for expressing his intention to start Civil Disobedience Movement again. The Congress did not take part in the deliberations of the Third Round Table Conference. The British Government then gave its Communal Award. It was proposed to give separate seats to the Depressed Classes. It was meant to separate them from the Hindus. Mahatma Gandhi protested against this and observed fast unto death. The leaders of Caste Hindus and Depressed Classes met at Poona and made Poona Pact to save the life of Mahatma Gandhi. The Depressed Classes were given some seats out of the general seats.

Mahatma Gandhi was imprisoned again along with other Congress leaders after the passing of Quit India Resolution in 1942. He remained in prison for about three years. It was greatly due to his efforts that India became free on 15th of August, 1947. It was however, a great disappointment to him that he could not keep India united and Pakistan as a separate State came into existence. He was shot dead by Nathuram Godse on the 30th of January, 1948.

Thus it becomes clear that Mahatma Gandhi made immense contribution to the awakening of the feeling of nationalism and the ultimate independence of India. He has rightly been called the Father of the Nation. He was the creator of modern India and it was under his leadership that the Indians achieved indepedence. Even before him, Tilak had advocated the policy of strong action against the British Government but the movement had not generally caught the imagination of the masses. He had tried to make the movement popular with the masses but had succeeded in doing so only partially. Mahatma Gandhi made the movement popular and it now spread to the rank and file of the people. Nagendra Nath Gupta summed up the contribution of Mahatma Gandhi to the National movement in these words : "The movement led by Mahatma Gandhi has brought into prominence some of the greatest men that Indian has known in recent times, men who would be considered great in any country at any time. If Mahatma Gandhi is the Prophet, they are undoubtedly his apostles. The national movement in India may easily be divided into two phases, one before, Mahatma Gandhi had joined the Indian National Conress and the other after he became the most conspicuous figure in it. In the earlier stage, Congressmen confined themselves to agitation and oratory, to over repeated assertation of their birth right to Home Rule and severe criticism of government action, to constitutionalism and reformism. Only the very greatest of them risked and sacrificed everything for a chieving their goal. The rank and file were passive onlookers and onhearers, so to say. This might have gone on for any number of years without any prospect of freedom for India. Then came Mahatma Gandhi with his expreience of the Transvall, his spiritual outlook, his gentle nature, and his inflexible will. There were willing hearts in India waiting for his call and they at once realised the nature of the struggle that lay ahead of them. Since then the struggle for national freedom in India has grown ever wider and today comprehends the entire nation. It has a glorious record which is being added day after day, of sacrifice and suffering of women that vied with men in offering themselves as sacrifices at the altar of liberty. The old caution and timidity have disappeared for ever, the prison has lost its hardships and degradation and there are no signs of hesitation or reluctance to suffer. Men and women are filled with the spirit of martyrdom and the determination to win by suffering what was hitherto accomplished by violence".

Mahatma Gandhi was the greatest advocate of Hindu-Muslim unity. He may rightly be called the apostle of communal harmony and wanted that the people of different communities should live as brothers. There were Hindu-Muslim riots after the failure of Khilafat Movement and Mahatma Gandhi observed a 21-day fast in 1924 as a penance. There were serious Hindu-Muslim riots on the of eve partition of India. These broke out at Calcutta when Muslim League started massacre of the Hindus on the Direct Action Day (16th August, 1946). Thousands of people were killed. Still more bloody riots took place in Noakhali. These had their reprecussions in Bihar and Garhmukteshwar. There were riots at Rowalpindi, Lahore and other places. There were mass massacres in India and Pakistan at the time of Partition. Mahatma Gandhi went to Noakhli and Bihar and succeeded in establishing peace. He visited Calcutta and peace and restored. Thousands of refugees had come to Delhi from West Pakistan and wanted to turn out the Muslims from this city to get accommodation. Mahatma Gandhi at once came to Delhi to prevent the Hindus from turning out the Muslims. He went on fast to achieve this object. Thus the Muslims were able to stay in Delhi.

❒

7

The Montangue Chemsford Reform

THE MINTO-MORLEY REFORMS

The Indian Councils Act of 1892 failed to meet the legitimate wishes of the Congress and Lokamanya Tilak condemned the weak-kneed policy of the Congress in these words : "Political rights will have to be fought for. The Moderates think that these can be won by pesuasion. We think that these can be won by pressure." The continuing economic exploitation by the alien rulers led to the energetic thesis by patriots like R.C. Dutt, Dadabhai Naoroji and others contending that the impoverishment of the country was the direct result of a deliberate and systematic policy of the foreign rulers who naturally wished to encourage "Home" manufacture at the expense of the local industry and trade.

Another factor that caused keen and active discontent was that educated Indians were not given any share, much less their due share in the Government services and the administration. Lord Curzon's imperialist and strong policies and attitudes added fuel to the fire and intensified betterness of the intelligentsia against alien domination. A born bureacreat and effciency-monger, Curzon had no sympathy for the aspirations of the sons of the soil but acted autocratically, brushing aside and ignoring all reactions of the Indians. A similar policy was pursued towards the Indian Universities five years later, which took away the autonomy of these Universities, and in the same year (1904) the Official Secrets Act greatly extended the scope of the term "sedition". But the climax was reached by the infamous Partition of Bengal in 1905 which was considered to be "a subtle attack on the growing solidarity of Bengal nationalism." The Bengalis felt "humiliated, insulted and tricked" and resorted to a vigorous agitation to get the wrong undone.

There were other causes of discontent. Indian overseas and specially in South Africa were being subjected to humiliation and indignities galore simply because they were Indians, or perhaps members of an enslaved race. This fanned national resentment and the people of India began to feel that it was vain and futile to hope for improvement in the conditions and treatment of Indians in the British colonies and overseas possessions unless and until they were free in their own homeland.

The closing years of the nineteenth century witnessed the horrors of famine and bubonic plague, bringing distress and misery to thousands of people. The people blamed the British Government for their plight and they detested even the well-intentioned governmental measures to stay the spread of infection of plague as an intentional violation of their privacy. The press in the country which was free since 1882 took ample notice of all these factors and was extremely critical of the British administration, so much so that Minto had to write to Morley thus : "I am afraid we must consider seriously how to deal with the native press, for in many cases the utterances of newspapers are outrageous." Nor did not platform in this respect lag behind. The famous trio, Bal Gangadhar Tilak, Bipin Chandra Pal and Lala Lajpat Rai, thundered about in the country and electrified the whole atmosphere.

Still another factor which fostered the rise and growth of 'extremism' in the country was the tremendous and shattering blow to the prestige of the White Man in the East by the Oriental dwarf, Japan, defeating in 1904-5 that Occidental giant, Russia—a case of David overthrowing Goliath. All over Asia this led to a new awakening and a new hope that what had been done to the Russian Bear might also be done to the British Lion in India.

Under these circumstances 'extremism' grew apace despite repressive measures by the Government, and the Indian National

Congress was split into camps—the Moderates and the Extremists. The split took place at Surat in 1907. The Moderates still clung to the idea of adopting constitutional means to gain their obejctive. To the Extremists, on the other hand, the end justified all means. They took recourse to boycott to the Swadeshi movement, to educational institutions of the national type and to terrorist methods.

In the meantime another important development had taken place. While the Congress was growing stronger as the exponent of the demand for national freedom, the Muslims generally kept themselves aloof from it. According to Coupland, "the indifference, if not antagonism" of the Muslims towards the nationalist movement was due to their "relative backwardness in education, coupled with the knowledge that they were only about one-quarter of the Indian population as a whole." It radually became something like 'antagonim' when the British bureaucracy, alarmed at the growing influence of the Congress as 'a mighty nationaliser', deliberately adopted a policy of 'divide and rule'. The first official manifestation of this policy may be noticed in Lord Minto's reply to a deputation of Muslim leaders led by the Agha Khan on October 1, 1906. He promised them not only separate communal representation but also representation much in excess of their population on account of "their services to the Empire". If the Indian Councils Act of 1892 was passed to take the wind out of the sails of Congress movment, that of 1909 was taken into hands by the Indian Government to rally to its side the Moderates in the Indian National Congress and the Muslims in order to buttress the authority of British bureaucracy.

The time was now opportune for introducing further reforms for Lord Morley the radical disciple of Gladstone had now become the Secretary of State for India in the Liberal Cabinet. Both Lord, Morley and Lord Minto found themselves in full agreement as to the desirability of some further political advances. Minto had by this time felt that the permanence of the British administration in India "depends upon a sound appreciation of the changing conditions which surround it." While the latter was still framing his proposals, a Committee of the Executive Council of the Viceroy had studied the subject and the

Government of India sent a despatch to England embodying its proposals. Minto now wrote to the Secretary of State : "The time is getting on, and we must arrange a plan of campaign as to our reforms, not only as to the nature of the reforms themselves but as to how and when we are to launch them." Morley sent back the proposals to be referred to the Local Governments in India for public criticism.

Earlier in August 1907 two Indians—K.G. Gupta and Syed Hussain Bilgrami—were made members of the Secretary of State's India Council. In India, on 24 March 1909, Mr Sytendra Sinha was appointed member of the Viceroy's Executive Council.

Central Legislature. The number of 'additional' members here was now raised at the maximum to 60. The Legislature was thus to consist of 69 members of whom 37 were to be officials while the remaining 32 non officials. Of the officials, 9 were to be the *ex-offico* members, namely, the Governor-General, seven ordinary members (Executive Councillors) and one extraordinary member, while the remaining 28 were to be nominated by the Governor-General. Of the 32 non-officials, 5 were to be nominated by the Governor-General while the remaining 27 were to be elected. For the elected members, it was declared that the territorial representation did not suit India and that "representation by classes and interests is the only practicable method of embodying the elective principle in the constitution of the Indian Legislative Councils." Thus, of the 27 elected members, 13 were to come from the General Electorates, consisting of the non-official members of the legislaturs of Bombay, Madras, Bengal and United Provinces, each of which would send two members (=8); and the non-official members of the legislatures of the Central Provinces, Assam, Bihar and Orissa, the Panjab and Burma each of which would send one member (=5). Of the remaining 14, twelve were to come from Class Electorates six of them coming one each from the Landholders' constituencies in the six provinces of Bombay, Madras, Bengal, Bihar and Orissa, United Provinces and the Central Provinces; and six being returned by the separate Muslim constituencies—one each from Madras, Bombay, United Provinces and Bihar and Orissa

(=4) and two from Bengal. The remaining were to be returned from the Special electorates, one each from the Bengal and Bombay chambers of Commerce.

Provincial Legislatures. The membership of the Legislative Councils of the different provinces as enalrged under the Act of 1909 was as follows : Burma, 16 ; Eastern Bengal and Assam, 41, Bengal, 52 ; Madras, Bombay and United Provinces, 47 each; and Punjab 25. However, this did not mean non-official elected majorities, as some of the non-officials were to be nominated by the Governors and through these the official control over the Council was retained. In Madras, for example, the number of the non-officials was 26, while that of the officials 21. Of the non-officials, however, only 21 were to be elected, while the remaining five were to be nominated by the Governor. As these nominated members always sided with the Government, the officials were 'in a manner of speaking in the majority'.

The elected members in the Provincial Legislatures were to be returned by different constituencies. In Bombay for instance, out of the 21 elected members, 6 were to be retunred by the Special electorates consisting of the Bombay Corporation and the Bombay University etc., 8 were to be returned by the General electorates consisting of District Boards and Municipalties etc. and the remaining 7 were to be returned by Class electorates consisting of Muslims (returning 4) and the Landlords (returning 3).

The membership of the Executive Councils of Bengal, Madras and Bombay was raised to 4 and the Government was empowered to constitute similar Councils for the Lieutenant-Governors as well.

Functions of Legislative Councils. The functions of the Legislative Councils, both at the Centre and in the Provinces, were also enlarged. Now the members were given the right of discussion and asking supplementary questions, the Member in-charge for the latter being authorised to demand time, if he could not furnish the information asked for on the spot. Detailed rules were laid down concerning the discussion of budgets in the Central Legislature.

Members, through not empowered to vote, were empowered to move resolutions concerning additional grants to the Local Governments, any alteration in taxation, on a new loan, which might have been proposed in the financial statement or the explanatory memorandum.

Rules were also laid down concerning discussion of matters of general public interest. Members could disucss these matters moving resolutions on them and could also vote, though the President was empowered to disallow the whole or a part of such resolutions, without assigning any reason. Nor was the Government obliged to accept such resolutions, even if passed, whether concerning public interest or concerning financial statements. There were, however, certain subjects which the members could not discuss under the Act. They could not discuss the foreign relations of the Government of India and its relations with the Indian Princes, a matter under adjudication of a court of law, expenditure on state railways, interest on debt etc.

Observations on the Act. The Reform of 1909 afforded no answer and could afford no answer to the Indian political problem. Narrow franchises, indirect elections, limited powers of the Legislative Counciis made a hotch-potch of representative government.

The Reforms created new problems in Indian politics. One such problem was the introduction of separate electorates for Muslims, by which, according to Jawaharlal Nehru, a "political barrier was created round them, isolating them from the rest of India and reversing the unifying and amalgamating process which had been going on for centuries...The barrier was s small one at first, for the electorates were very limited, but with every extension of franchise it grew and affected the whole structure of political and social life like some canker which corrupted the entire system." For the so called pollitical importance of the Muslims, they were accorded not only separate communal representation but also representation much in excess of their population on account of their "services to the Empire."

THE INDIAN COUNCILS ACT, 1892

The growth of the Indian Constitution after the Act of 1861 is largely the story of political disaffection and agitation alternating with Council reform. The reforms grudgingly conceded were always found inadequate, occasioned disaffection and evoked demand for further reforms. It is ture of all subsequent Acts passed by the British Parliament relating to India, namely the Acts of 1892, 1909, 1919 and 1935.

The Legislative Council created by the Act of 1861, Naturally nough, failed to satisfy the aspirations of the people of the land. The element of non-officials, negligible as it was, did not even represent the people. It consisted of either big zamindars, retired officials or Indian princes, none of whom could claim to understand the problems of the people.

During the second half of the nineteenth century nationalism began to grow in India. A number of factors contributed to this growth. The setting up of universities at Calcutta, Madras and Bombay in 1857 spread education bringing nationalism in its wake. The use of English by the educated people brought them closer to one another. The repressive policy pursued by the British Government after quelling the Rebellion of 1857 created feelings of hatred against it. The members of the Indian Civil Service were arrogant and haughty and the gulf between them and the people considerably widened. The twin acts of repression—the Vernacular Press Act and the Indian Arms Act—passed in 1878 greatly exasperated the feelings of the people. The administration of Lytton was accused on emasculting Indian manhood to further British imperialistic aims. The fierce controversy between the Government in England and the Government of India regarding the abolition of 5% cotton duties opened the eyes of Indians. Nothing more had so clearly demonstrated the hollowness and insincerity of the British professions of justice and fairplay than the abolition of cotton duties in which case the interests of the Indian merchants were sacrificed for the sake of Lancashire manufacturers. Then came the Ilbert Bill controversy. All these events highlighted the fact that justice could not be expected from the English rulers where their own interests were involved. The initial objective of the Congress was to mobilise public opinion in India, to ventilate the grievances of the people and to press for reforms in a constitutional but nonetheless in an emphatic manner. In its very first session, the Congress passed the following resolution : " This Congress considers the reform and expansion of the Supreme and existing Local Legislative Councils by the admission of a considerable proportion of elected members and holds that all budgets should be referred to these Councils for consideration, their members being moreover empowered to interpellate the Executive in regard to all branches of administration."

In the beginning the attitude of the British Government was friendly and sympathetic towards the Congress but by 1888 that attitude changed Lord Dufferin in that year made a frontal attack on the Congress by dubbing it as representing only 'a microscopic minority' and Congress demands as 'a big jump into the unknown'.

Though Lord Dufferin thus tried to belittle the importance and representative character of the Congress he was too astute a statesman not to realise the signficance of the movement launched by the Congress and he secretly sent to England proposals for liberalising the Councils. He also appointed a Committee of his Council to prepare a plan for the enlargement of Provincial Councils, for the enhancement of their status, the multiplication of their functions, the partial introduction in them of the elective principle and the liberalisation of their general character as political institutions. At the same time he declared in plain words that it should not be concluded that he was contemplating to set up a parliamentary system after the British model.

The report of the Committee together with Lord Dufferin's own views was sent to the authorities in England proposing changes in the composition and functions of the Councils with the main aim "to give a still wider share in the administration of public affairs to such Indian gentlemen as by their influence, their requirements and the confidence they inspired in their own countrymen, are marked out as fitted to assist with their counsel the responsible rulers of the country." The Conservative Ministry in England at the instance of

Lord Cross, Secretary of State for India, introduced in 1890 a bill in the House of Lords on the basis of these proposals but the measure proceeded at a snail-slow speed and was passed only two years later as the Indian Councils Act.

The Principle of Election Under the Act. The significant feature of the Indian Councils Act of 1892 was the principle of election which it introduced, though the word 'election' was very carefully avoided in it. In addition to the officials, the Central Legislature was to have elected non-officials whose number was to be five and who were to be elected one each by the non-official members of the four Provincial Legislatures of Madras, Bombay, Bengal and the North Western Provinces and one by the Calcatta Chamber of Commerce. In the case of the Provincial Legislatures, the bodies permitted to elect members were Municipalities, District Boards. Universities, and the Chambers of Commerce. The method of election, however, was veiled. The 'elected' members were officially declared as 'nominated' though after taking into consideration the recommendation of the bodies described above. These bodies met to make 'recommendations' to the Governor-General or Head of the Provincial Government. The person favoured by the majority was not described as 'elected' but recommended for nomination.

Provisions of the Act. The Act dealt exclusively with the powers, functions and composition of the Legislative Councils in India. With regards to the Central Legislature, the Act provided that the number of 'additional' members must not be less than ten or more than sixteen (subject to the approval of the Secetary of State in Council, the Governor-General was to make regulations under which the nomination of the additional members was to be made). The increase was described as 'a very paltry and miserable additon'. The Act also provided that two-fifths of the total members of the Council were to be non-officials. These non-officials were partly nominated and party elected.

The principle of election was conceded to a limited extent. In two respects the rights of the members of the Legislatures were increased. They were entitled to express their views upon financial statements which were henceforth to be made on the floor of the Legislatures, although they were not empowered to move resolutions or divide the House in respect of any financial question. Secondly, they were empowered to put questions within certain limits to the Government on matters of public interest after giving a six days' notice.

In regard to the Provincial Legislatures, the Act enlarged the number of 'additional' members to not less than eight or more than twenty in the case of Bombay and Madras. The maximum for Bengal was also fixed at twenty but for the North-Western Province and Oudh the maximum was fixed at fifteen. In their functions the members of the Provincial Legislatures secured the right of interpellation of the executive in the matters of general public interest. They could also discuss the policy of the Government and ask questions, which, however, as in the case of the centre, required a six days' previous notice.

Observations on the Act. The Indian Councils Act of 1892 was undoubtedly an advance on the Act of 1861 and it was as it should have been. The Act of 1892 widened the functions of the legislatures. The members could ask questions and thus obtain information which they desired from the executive. The financial accounts of the current year and the budget for the following year were presented to the legisltures, and the members were permitted to make general observations on the budget and make suggestions for increasing or decreasing revenue or expenditure. Eminent Indian leaders like Gopal Krishna Gokhale, Asutosh Mookerjee, Rash Behari Ghoas and Surendra Nath Benerjee found their way in the Legislatures. Their eloquence and political wisodm amply demostrated the parliamentary capacity and patriotism of the educated Indians. Moreover, the size of the Legislatures both at the Centre and in the Provinces was enlarged. In case of the Centre the maximum and minimum of additional members and the element of non-officials therein were raised by four in each case as compared to the Act of 1861. The Councils in Bombay, Madras and Bengal had a maximum of twenty additional members under the Act of 1892. Of these, nine were officials, four nominated non-officials and seven elected. The electing bodies in the provinces were District Boards and Municipalities, Universities and Chambers of Commerce.

This recognition of the principle of election, veiled though it was in the Act of 1892, was a measure of considerable constitutional signficance. A beginning was made though the goal of the representative government was yet a far cry.

There were, however, certain defects and shortcomings in the Act of 1892 by reason of which the Act failed to satisfy Indian nationalists. The Act was criticised at successive sessions of the Indian National Congress. Critics pointed out that the system of election in the Act was a roundabont one. "The so-called right of election to the Legislatures enjoyed by the local bodies and by other electorates amounted merely to nomination by these bodies, but it was up to the government to accept them or reject them." Then, the functions of the Legislative Councils were strictly circumscribed. The members could not ask supplementary questions. Any question could be disallowed and there was no remedy against it. The rules of election were unsatisfactory. Certain classes were over-represented while others did not get any representation at all. In the case of Bombay, out of six seats two were given to European merchants but none to the Indian mercantile community. Again, two seats were assigned to Sind but none to Poona and Satara. According to Gokhale : "The actual working of the Act manifested its hollowness. Bombay Presidency was given eight seats. The Bombay Government gave two seats to the Euroepan Mercantile Community, one seat to the Sirdars of the Deccan, one to the zamindars of Sind and only two seats to general public." In his Presidential address delivered in 1893 at the Lahore session of the Congress, Dadabhai Naoroji observed : "By the Act of 1892 no member shall have the power to submit or propose any resolution or divide the Council in respect of any such financial discussion, or in answer to any question asked under the authority of this Act or the rules made under this Act. Such is the poor character of the extent of the concession made to discuss finances or to put questions. Rules made under this Act shall not be subject to alterations or amendment at meetings for the purpose of making laws and regualtions."

MAIN EVENTS OF NATIONAL MOVEMENT

The growth of Militant Nationalism or Extremism in the beginning of the 20th century. From almost the beginning of the national movement a school of militant nationalism had existed in the country. This school was represented by leaders like Raj Narain Bose and Ashwani Kumar Dutt in Bengal and Vishnu Shastri Chiplunkar in Maharashtra. The most outstanding representative of this school was Bal Gangadhar Tilak later popularly known as Lokmanya Tilak. From the day of his graduation from Bombay University, he devoted his entire life to the service of his country. He hoped to found during the 1880's the New English School which later became the Ferguson College, and newspapers the Maratha (in English) and the Kesari (in Marathi). From 1889 A.D. he edited the Kesari and preached nationalism in its columns and taught people to become courageous, selfreliant, and selfless fighters in the cause of India's independence. In 1893 A.D., he started using the traditional religious Ganpati festival to propagate nationalist ideas through songs and speeches, and in 1895 A.D. he started the Shivaji festival to stimulate nationalism among young Maharashtrians by holding up the example of Shivaji for emulation. During 1896-97 A.D. he initiated a no-tax campaign in Maharashtra. He asked the famine sticken peasants of Maharashtra to withhold payment of land revenue if their crops had failed. He set a real example of boldness and sacrifice when the authorities arrested him in 1897 A.D. on the charge of spreading hatred and disaffection against the British government. He refused to apologise to the government and was sentences to 18 months rigorous imprisonment.

At the dawn of the 20th century the school of militant nationalism found a favourable political climate and the adherents came forward to lead the second stage of the national movement. The most outstanding leaders of militant nationalism, apart from Balganadhar Tilak, were Bipin Chandra Pal, Lala Lajpat Rai and Aurobindo Ghose. The terrible famines of 1896-97 and 1899-1901 followed by bubonic plague took a very heavy tool of life. The Government relief machinery was inadequate, slow moving and badly organised. Riots broke out in Deccan and the government tried to stifle public opinion and spress lawlessenss. The people attributed the phenomenon of every recurring famines to the anti-national economic policy followed by the British government. In his presidential speech in 1903 A.D., Lal Mohan Ghosh referred to the Darba of 1902 and said, "Nothing could seen more heartless than the spectacle of a great government imposing the heaviest taxation upon the poorest population in the world not then lavishly spending the money so obtained over fire-works and pompous pageants, while millions of the poor were dying of startvation". The militant nationalists believed that Indians themselves must work out their own salvation and make effort to rise from their degraded position. They declared that great sacrifices and sufferings were needed for this taste. Their speeches, writings, and political work were full of boldness and self-confidence and they considered no personal sacrifice too great for the good of their country. They clearly denied that India could progress under the benevolent guidence" and control of the British. They deeply hated foreign rule, and they declared in a clear cut manner that Swaraj or independence was the goal of the national movement. They therefore pressed the congress for political work among the masses and for direct political action by the masses. For example Bal Gangadhar Tilak preached non-cooperation. In 1902 at Poona he said." You (people) must realise that you are a great factor in the power with which the administration of India is conducted. You are yourselves the great lubricants which enable the gigantic machinery to work so smoothly. Though downtrodden and neglected, you must be conscious of your power of making the administration impossible if you but choose to make it." By 1903 Indian possessed a large number of militant leaders who had acquired during the previous period valuable experience in guiding political agitations and leading political struggles.

The Partition of Bengal (1905 A.D.). Thus the conditions for the emergence of militant nationalism had developed when in 1905 A.D. the partition of Bengal was announced and the indian national movement entered its second stage.

At that time Bengal was the largest provinec of British India. It included Bihar and parts of Orissa and a population of over 85 millions people. On 20 July, 1905, Lord Curzon issued an order dividing the province of Bengal into two parts : Eastern Bengal and Assam with a population of 31 millions and the rest of Bengal with a population of 54 millions, of whom 18 millions were Bengalis and 36 millions Biharies and Oriyas. The new province was entitled Eastern Bengal and Assam with its capital Dacca.

The main argument of the British government was that the existing province of Bengal was too big and therefore it was necessary to divide it for administrative convenience. It is also correct that the proposal to divide the province was there since 1891 A.D. But it was not mere administrative convenience which prompted Lord Curzon, the then Viceroy to implement this scheme of partiton. Lord Curzon did not accept India as a nation and was opposed to the consolidation of the people and any region. He was adverse to the proposal of incorporating Berar into the province of Bombay because that might lead of the solidarity of the Maratha community. The same attitude motivated him to partition Bengal because he believed that the intelligentsia of Bengal exercised immense influence over the politics of the whole country. Therefore, he implemented the divison of Bengal to stem the rising tide of nationalism in Bengal by dividing a wedge between the Bangali speaking Hindus and Muslims. For example, Risley, Home Secretary to the Government of India, wrote in an official note on 6 December 1904 : "Bengal united is a power. Bengal divided will pull several ways. That is what the Congress leaders feel. Their apprehensions are perfectly correct and they form one of the great merits of the scheme—in this scheme as in the matter of the amalgamation of Berar to the Central Province one of our main object is to split up and thereby to weaken a solid body of opponents to our rule." Lord Curzon himself wrote in a similar view in February 1905 "Calcutta is the centre from which the Congress Party is manipulated throughout the whole of Bengal and indeed the whole of India—-Any measure in consequence that would divide the Bengali-speaking population; that would permit independent centres of activity and influence to grow up; that would dethrone Calcutta from its place as the centre of successful intrigue—is intensely and hotly resented by them." The Lt. Governor of Bengal, Sir A. Fraser and A.T. Arunder, a member of the Viccroy Council were also of the same opinion. Lord Minto, the successor of Curzon though did not approve of the manner in which Lord Curzon had carried out the partition of Bengal, fully agreed with the partition scheme in principle. Thus, it is quite clear that the whole British official machinery approved of partition of Bengal as it was found a useful measure to break not only the Bengali nationalism but Indian nationalism as a whole.

The Anti-Partition Movement. The Indian National Congress and the nationalists of Bengal firmly opposed the partition. Within Bengal different sections of the population—zamindars, merchants, lawyers, students, the city poor and even women—rose up in spontaneous opposition to the partition of their province. The nationalists saw the act of partition of Bengal as a challenge to Indian nationalism and not merely an adminitrative measure. They saw that it was a deliberate attempt to divide the Bengalis and to disrupt and weaken nationalism in Bengal. It would also be a big blow to the growth of Bengali language and culture. They pointed out that the administrative efficiency could have been better secured by separating the Hindi-speaking Bihar and the Oriya speaking Orissa from the Bengali speaking part of the province.

The Anti-Partition movement was the work of the entire national leadership of Bengal and not of one section of the movement. Its most prominent leaders at the initial stage were moderate leaders like Surendranath Banerjee and Krishan Kumar Mitra; militant and revolutionary nationalists took over in the later stages. In fact, both the moderate and militant nationalists cooperated with one another during the course of Anti-Partition movement.

The Anti-Partition movement was initiated on 7 August 1905 A.D. On the day a massive demonstration against the patrition was organised in the town Hall in Calcutta. From this meeting delegates dispersed to spread the movement to the rest of the province. More than two thousand public meetings were immediatley held in different parts of Bengal to protest against the partition.

The partition took effect on 16 October 1905 A.D. The leaders of the protest movement declared it to be a day of national mourning throughout Bengal. It was observed a day of fasting. There was a strike in Calcutta. People walked barefooted and bathed in the Ganga in the early morning hours. Rabindra Nath Tagore composed a national song for the occasion which was sung by the huge crowds parading the streets. The streets of Calcutta were full of the cries of Bande Mataram (Hail O! Mother) which overnight became the national song of Bengal and which was soon to become the theme song of the national Movement. The ceremony of Raksha Bandhan was utilised in a new way. On the day people of Bengal tied the rakhi on one another's wrists as symbols of the unbreakable unity of the Bengalis and two halves of Bengal. In the afternoon there was a great demonstration when the veteran leader Anandmohan Bose laid the foundation of a Federation Hall to mark the indestructible unity of Bengal. A nation fund was started by him to meet the expenses to carrying on the movement. He addressed a crowed of even 50,000 and the meeting passed a resolution pledging to do their utmost to maintain the unity of Bengal. According to a Government report," Mourning and fasting were more or less successfully carried out in all districts of Bengal, and specially in Calcutta. The Anti-Partition of Bengal movement gave birth to the Boyacott and Swadeshi movement, which was executed on a large scale as a mass movement throughout the country by the extremists. Later on, it was accepted and supported by moderates also.

PASSING THE ACT OF 1919

The Minto-Morley Reforms were passed not with the intention of establishing a partliamentary spstem in India but with the opposite intention of buttressing the authority of the British bureaucracy by rallying to its side the Moderates and the Muslims. This view is clear from the speech made by Lord Morley in the House of Lords on Febrary 23, 1909. He observed : "There are, 1 take it, three classes of people we have to consider in dealing with a scheme of this kind.

There are the Extremists who nurse fantastic dreams that some day they will drive us out of India...The second group nourishes no hopes of this sort, but hopes for autonomy or self-government of the colonial species and pattern, and then the third section of this classification asks for no more than to be admitted to co-operation in our administration, and to find a free and effective voice in expressing the interests and needs of their people. I believe that the effect of the Reforms has been, is being and will be to draw the second class who hope for colonial autonomy into the third class who will be content with being admitted to a fair and full co-operation."

The Indian National Congress, shorn of its left wing, expressed its dissatisfaction at:

(1) the excessive and unfairly preponderant share of representation given to the followers of one particular religion,

(2) the wide, arbitrary and unreasonable disquilifications and restrictions for candidates seeking election to the Councils,

(3) the unjust, invidious and humiliating distinctions made between Muslims and non-Muslims in the matter of electorates, the franchise and the qualifications of the candidates,

(4) the general distrust of the educated classes,

(5) the unsatisfactory composition of the non-official majorities in the Provincial Councils, rendering them ineffective and unreal."

Certain circumstances, both internal and external, led to discontentment among the Muslims also. A proof of it is to be found in the modification of the constitution of the Muslim League. In March 1913 its goal was laid down to be "the promotion among Indians of loyalty to the British Crown, the protection of the rights of the Muslims and, without detriment to the foregoing objects, the attainment of the system of self-government suitable to India." As the

Muslims could not come to a settlement with the British Government in regard to the condition on which a Muslims University was to be founded at Aligarh, the former felt greatly hurt, as also at the annulment of the partition of Bengal in 1911. Certain outside events also led to a detrioration of Anglo-Muslim relations in the country. The hostile attitude of England towards Trukey in the Turco-Italian War (1911-12) was viewed with dismay by the Muslim in India. The Balkan Wars of 1912-13 were considered by them as a great conspiracy of the Christian Powers against Turkey, "the Sword of Islam". These were "represented as a struggle between the Cross and the Crescent". This estrangement of the Muslims with British Government had one salutary effect, namely, that it brought the Hindus and the Muslims closer. The Congress League rapprochement resulted in the Lucknow Pact (1916).

The Extremists who according to Morley "nurse fantastic dreams that some day they will drive us out of India" continued their activities through organisations established both in India and abroad. The Ghadr movement in the Panjab and the Komagatamaru incident in Bengal were only two examples of their terrorist activities. So great was the discontent among the people of India with the Minto-Morley Reforms that the British Government had to resort to repressive measures to suppress the rising tide of discontent. The Indian Press Act of 1910, the Seditious Meetings Act of 1911 and the Criminal Law (Amendment) Act of 1913, were all aimed towards this end. The Defence of India Act of 1915 which provided for the trial of revolutionary offenders by a strong bench without appeal and for the internment of suspects was a particularly obnoxious measure.

Although the outbreak of the war in Europe in August 1914 had no immediate connection with the defence of India yet as a part of the British Empire, the country automatically became involved in it. Once in the war, India made ungrudging contribution to the war effort. Not only did the country furnish the sinews of war—men and munitions—she took up responsibility for one hundred million pounds of the war debt. As the war went on the "the affirmation of the moral values in the war, and the emergence of the doctrine of self-determination, deeply influenced Indian public opinion. If self-determination was to be applied to the politically dormant Arabs in the Turkish Empire, it was asserted, it should be applied to Indians as well."

Under the circumstances, the question of further constitutional reforms did not brook delay. A patent proof of the wide awakening of the Indians at this stages was that they themselves formulated various schemes for reforms for the consideration of the Government. Among those who put forward different schemes for the reforms were the nineteen members of the Central Legislature, including Mr. Jinnah, Srinivasa Shastri and Surendra Nath Banerjee, who in a Memorandum submitted in 1916, observed : "What is wanted is not merely good government or efficient administration, but government that is acceptable to the people because it is responsible to them."

MONTAGUE'S STATEMENT OF 20 AUGUST 1917

Just five weeks after assuming office on August 20, 1917, Montagu, the new Secretary of State, made a statement in the House of Commons regarding the goal of British Government in India He announced:

> "The policy of His Majesty's Government, with which the Government of India are in complete accord, is that of the increasing association of Indians in every branch of the administration and gradual development of self-governing institutions with a view to the progressive realisation of responsible Government in India as an integral part of the British Empire. They have decided that substantial steps in this direction should be taken as soon as possible...I would add that progress in this policy can only be achieved by successive stages. The British Government and the Government of India, on whom the responsibility lies for the welfare and advancement of Indian peoples, must be judges of the time and measure of each advance, and they must be guided by the co-operation received from those upon whom new opportunities of service will thus be

conferred and by the extent to which it is found that confidence can be reposed in their sense of responsibility."

The authors of the Montford Report regarded this declaration as "the most momentous utterance made in India's chequered history" which marked "the end of one epoch and the beginning of a new one". It was based on the idea that 'liberty alone fits men for liberty'. The Declaration eased the tense Indian atmosphere for the time being at least.

There was, however, a section of people in India to whom the declaration failed to satisfy. It was argued that no definite time was prescribed, by which India would reach her goal. Nor was there any standard laid down, by which one could decided whether a certain stage for further reforms had been reached or not. It was indeed insulting to India, it was pointed out, that the British were to be the sole judge to decide whether India was capable of a particular set-up or not.

The Secretary of State came to India in November 1917 and discussed his scheme of reforms with the Viceroy, Lord Chelmsford, and some eminent British civil servants and Indian politicians of all shades of opinion. A committee was appointed consisting of Sir William Duke, Earl of Donoughmore, Bhupendra Nath Basu and Charles Robert (the M.P. who had put the question in the Commons in reply to which the Secretary of State had made the Declaration) which together with the Viceroy, helped Montagu to prepare the draft of a reform scheme which was published in July 1918 and is called the Montagu-Chelmsford (the Montford) Report on the basis of which the Government of India Act 1919 was drafted.

THE GOVERNMENT OF INDIA ACT, 1919

Preamble. The Act laid down in its Preamble the principles on which the reforms were to be progressively carried out in India. These principles were more or less the same as embodied in the Declaration of August 20, 1917. An analysis of the Preamble brings out the following points:

(1) British India is to remain an integral part of the British Empire.

(2) Responsible Government in British India is the objective of the declared policy of Parliament.

(3) In order to achieve Responsible Government, it is necessary to provide for two things : the increasing association of the Indians in every branch of administration and the gradual development of self-governing institutions.

(4) Responsible Government is capable of progressive realisation only.

(5) Concurrently with the development of self-governing institutions in the provinces, it is expedient to give to provinces in provincial matters the highest measure of independence of the Government of India, which is compatible with the due discharge by the latter of its own responsibilities.

The significance of the Preamble was that what was already declared by Montague was now given a definite legal shape. The sovereignty of the British Parliament over India was reasserted and the country was told in clear terms of the basis of the future British action.

Main Provisions of the Act

A. Changes in the 'Home' Government. The Secretary of Stae for India who used to be paid out of the Indian revenues was now to be paid by the British Exchequer, this undoing an injustice dating from 1793. Some of his functions were taken away from him and given to the High Commissioner for India who was to be appointed and paid by the Government of India. This new functionary acted as the agent of the Governor-General-in-Council. The control of the Secretary of State was reduced in the provincial sphere in India in so far as Transferred Subjects were concerned but his control over the Centre remained as complete as before.

The curtailment of the powers and functins of the Secretary of State was done, it appears, in deference to the wishes of the Congress which had passed a resolution at the 1916 session that "India must be governed from Delhi and Simla and not from Whitehall and Downing Street."

B. Changes in the Government of India : On the Executive Side. The Act did not introduce responsible government at the Centre though Indians were to have greater influence there. The number of Indians in the Governor-General's Executive Council was raised to three in a Council of eight. The Indian members were entrusted with departments like that of Law, Education, Labour, Health and Industries.

The now scheme of Government envisaged a division of Subjects into the Central List and the Provincial List. Those subjects which were of national importance or which related to more than one province, such as Foreign Affairs, Defence, Political Relations, Posts and Telegraphs, Public Debt, Communications, Civil and Criminal Law and Procedure, etc, were included in the Central List, while others which were only of provincial importance, such as Public Health, Local Self-Government. Education, Medical Administration, Land Revenue Administration, Water Supply, Famine Relief, Law and Order, Agriculture, etc., were included in the Provincial List.

Comments on the Changes on the Executive Side. The changes introduced in the Executive Council at the Centre left much to be desired. Though a step was taken towards increasing association of Indians by raising their strength to three in a council of eight yet the departments assigned to them were comparatively unimportant.

The division of subjects into two lists left much to be desired, The division was not clear-cut or based upon proper considerations. Critics point out that while subjects like Commerce and law regarding property were placed in the Central List, important subjects like Excise and lows regarding Land Tenure were given to the provinces. Although all subjects in the Provincial List were provincial for purposes of administration, that was not the case for purposes of legislation. Certain portions of them in regard to which uniformity in legislation was considered desirable were made "subject to legislation by the Indian Legislature." These were borrowing and taxing powers of local self-governing bodies, supplies and irrigation, industrial matters including factories, electricity, etc.

The chief executive authority still remained with the Governor-General, who was a representative of the Crown and was constantly in correspondence with the Secretary of State for India. He exercised full control over his Councillors and enjoyed vast powers over the country.

Changes on the Legislative Side. The Act set up a bicameral legislature at the Centre in place of the Imperial Council consisting of one House. The two Houses now were to be the Council of State and the Central Legislative Assembly.

The Council of State which was to be the Upper House was to consist of 60 members, 26 of whom were to be nominated by the Governor-General and 34 were to be elected, introducing thereby an elected majority. The 26 nominated members were to cosist of 20 official and 6 non-officials, while of the 34 elected members, 20 were to be elected by General constituencies, 10 by the Muslims, 3 by the Europeans, and 1 by the Sikh constituencies. The Council of State was renewed partially every year, though a member held his seat for five years. Its President was to be nominated by the Viceroy and its members were called "Honourable". Women were not entitled to become its members.

The Legislative Assembly which was to constitute the Lower House was to consist of 145 members, of whom 41 were to be nominated and 104 elected. Of the 41 nominated members, 26 were officials and 15 non-officials. Of the 104 elected members, 52 were to be returned by the General constituencies, 32 by the Communal constituencies (30 by the Muslims and 2 by the Sikhs), and 20 by the Special constituencies.

The life of the Assembly was to be three years but it could be extended by the Governor-General. It is to be noted that the last Assembly elected in 1936 was dissolved after ten years. The franchise here was much restricted though as compared to Council of State it was not so high. The minimum qualifications were that either a person must be an occupant or an owner of a house of the minimum annual rental value of Rs. 180, or he must be paying the municipal tax of Rs. 15 a year, or must be paying an income tax on an income of not less than Rs. 2,000 a year or he must be paying land revenue of at least Rs. 50 a year. The number of persons who thus became entitled to vote stood at 909,874 in 1920.

The distribution of seats among the different provinces was made on the basis of their so-called importance and not on the basis of their population. For instance, both the Punjab and Bihar and Orissa were granted 12 seats each though the population of the Punjab was only 2/3 of that of Bihar and Orissa. The reason was the Military importance of the Punjab. Bombay and Madras were granted 16 seats each though the population of Bombay was only hall of that of Madras.

Powers of the Central Legislature. The Central Legislature, constituted of the above-mentioned two Houses, was supposed to have been given very wide powers. It could legislate for the whole of British India, for the Indian subjects and servants of the Government, whether inside or outside the country. It could repeal or amend any law already existing in the country. The members were given the right to move resolutions and motions for adjournment of the House, to consider urgent questions of public importance immediately. They had the right to ask questions and supplementaries.

There were, however, certain restrictions imposed on the Legislature. In certain cases, previous sanction of the Governor-General was required for the introduction of a bill such as

(a) Amendment or repeal of an existing law or an ordinance of the Governor-General.

(b) Foreign relations and the relations with the Indian States.

(c) Discipline or maintenance of the military, naval and the air forces.

(d) Public debt and public revenue and

(e) Religion, religious rites and usages of the people. Further, if the Governor-General felt that any bill or a part of it affects of safety or tranquillity of British India or any part thereof, he could prevent its consideration.

If on the the advice of the Governor-General the Legislature refused to pass a law, the Governor-General could pass it himself, subject to the sanction of the Crown. He could make and promulgate ordinances in cases of emergency which could last for six months and which had the same force of law as a law passed by the legislature. His assent was essential for the enactment of law passed by the legislature.

With regard to the budget, it was laid down in the Act that the Government would submit proposals for appropriation in the shape of demands for grant in the Legislative Assembly. Certain items were subject to the vote of the Assembly, others were open for discussion, and some could not even by discussed, much less voted upon.

There is much truth in the statement that the Act of 1919 introduced responsive and not responsible government at the Centre. No vote of no-confidence by the Legislature could turn out the members of the Executive Council of the Governor-General and as such they were irremovable. In fact, they did respond to the wishes of the Legislature and through it to the wishes of the people. Some of the members of the Legislature were put on the standing committees such as that of Public Accounts and Finance and here they got considerable opportunity to influence the governmental policy. Moreover, they could expose the Government by putting it questions, supplementaries and moving motions of adjournment. They could also reject the budget and move and pass resolutions against the Government. The large elected majority in the Assembly, if not heard to, could make things hot for the Government. Even the most irresponsible Executive Councillors could not afford to ride the high horse and domineer over the Legislature.

CONSTITUTION AND POWERS OF THE CENTRAL LEGISLATURE

There was no legislative organ in India before 1833. The Regulating Act of 1773 had created a Council consisting of Governor-General and four other Councillors. Governor-General-in-Council could issue rules and regulations but these had to be registered in the Supreme Court. These could be disallowed by the King-in-Council within two years. Governor-General-in-Council did not constitute a legislature in the real sense. There was no differentiation of personnel in its executive and legislative capacities.

Changes by the Charter Act of 1833. The Charter Act of 1833 added a new member, the Law Member, to Governor-General's Executive Council. He was not to attend or vote in the Council except at the meetings for making laws and regulations. The Act further laid down that Governor-General and three members must be present when it made-laws while Governor-General and only two members could transact executive business.

The Charter Act of 1833 introduced centralisation. The Presidencies were deprived of the power of issuing regulations. The utmost which they could do was to prepare drafts for regulations and send these to the Governor-General-in-Council together with the reasons for proposing these.

There were certain limitations on the powers of Governor-General-in-Council to make regulations. He could not make regulations affecting any past, present or future Acts of Parliament. The previous sanction of the Court of Directors was necessary to empower any non-chartered court to sentence a European British subject to death. All the regulations made by the Governor-General-in-Council were subject to disallowance by the Court of Directors acting under the Board of Control.

Changes made by Charter Act of 1853. The Charter Act of 1853 created a Legislative Council. It was to consist of 12 members, viz., Governor-General and Commander-in-Chief (extra-ordinary members), four members of the Executive Council and six Additional Members or Legislative Councillors. The six Additional members were Chief Justice of Bengal, one judge of Supreme Court and four Civil Servants of ten years' standing to represent Bombay Madras, Bengal and North-West Provinces. These four members were included because they were supposed to possess local knowledge. The judges were included to stregthen the legal element in the Legislative Council. Governor-General was empowered to veto the bills passed by the Legislative Council.

This Act marked the beginning of parliamentary structure of Government of India. The Legislative Council was clearly distinguished from the Executive Council. Discussion in the Legislative Council became oral, bills were now referred to select committees instead of to a single member and legislative business was conducted in public instead of in secret.

Changes by the Indian Councils Act of 1861. The Indian Councils Act of 1861 enlarged Governor-General's Legislative Council by the addition of not less than six and not more than twelve members. At last half of these were to be non-officials. The powers of the Legislative Council were strictly limited to legislation. No motion was to be introduced or entertained unless it was for leave to introduce some mesure or had reference to some measure already introduced in it. These laws could be subsequently disallowed by Her Majesty acting through the Secretary of State for India-in-Council. The previous sanction of the Governor-General was necessary for the introduction of any measure relating to public revenues, debts, religion, army, navy, foreign affairs etc.

Changes Introduced by the Indian Councils Act of 1892. The Indian Councils Act of 1892 increased the number of Additional Members. It was to be between 10 and 16. Two-fifths of these were to be non-officials. Five out of the non-official members were to be persons nominated by Governor-General on the recommendation of certain bodies—one on the recommendation by Calcutta Chamber of Commerce and one each by non-official members of the four Provincial Councils. Thus the word election was avoided.

The budget could be discussed under certain restrictions. It could not be discussed itemwise. The members could ask questions on matters of public interest. Six days' notice was to be given for asking a question. These questions could be asked subject to the restrictions laid down by the Governor-General-in-Council. The president of the Legislative Council could disallow any question without giving reasons.

Changes by Minto-Morley Reforms of 1909. The size of the Imperial Legislative Council was enlarged. It was to have 60 Additional Members. Out of these, 37 were to be officials and 23 non-officials. The Indians could be appointed to the Council. The system of communal electorates was introduced. Elaborate rules were made for the discussion of the budget. The members could move resolutions relating to taxation, new loans or any other proposals in the financial statement. The Council could not discuss interest on debt, ecclesiastical empenditure and expenditure on State Railways.

The members could ask questions and supplementary questions, but the member incharge of the department concerned could refuse to answer supplementary questions put off hand. He could ask for time. The members could move resolutions but these were to be properly expressed and must raise definite issues. Matters of general public interest could be discussed but there could not be any discussion on any matter affecting the relations of Indian Government with a foreign power or a native State or any matter under adjudication by a law court.

Changes by Act of 1919. The Government of India Act 1919 introduced bicameral legislature at the Centre consisting of the Council of States and the Legislative Assembly.

The Council of States was the Upper House and consisted of 60 members. Out of these 60 members, 33 were elected and 27 were nominated. Its life was five years but could be extended by the Governor-General. Its president was nominated by the Governor-General. The Legislative Assembly was the Lower House consisting of 145 members. Out of these, 41 were nominated and 104 were elected. Its life was three years but could be extended by the Governor-General.

The Central Legislature could make laws for the whole of British India. There were, however, some restrictions. The previous sanction of the Secretary of State-in-Council was required to pass any legislation abolishing a High Court. It had no power to amend or repeal any statute of Parliament relating to British India. The previous sanction of Governor-General was required for introducing bills concerning public debt or public revenues of India, religion or religious rites of the British subjects in India, discipline and maintenance of the armed forces, relations of the Government of India with foreign States and Indian States etc. He could give his assent to a bill, send it back for reconsideration or reserve it for His Majesty's approval. The members could ask questions and supplementary questions. It could reduce non-votable items of the budget but the Governor-General could restore any cut if he considered that expenditure essential for the peace and tranquility of India.

Changes Proposed by the Government of India Act of 1935. The Federal part of the Government of India Act of 1935 never came into force. It made provision for a legilature consisting of Council of States and Federal Assembly. The Council of States was to consist of 260 members, out of which 104 were to represent Indian States, 150 were to represent British India and the remaining six were to be nominated by the Governor-General. The members representing the Indian States were to be nominated by their rulers while the members for British India were to be elected. There was to be unequal representation of the units.

The Federal Assembly was to consist of 375 members. Out of these, 125 were to represent Indian States and 250 were to represent British India. The members representing the Indian States were to be nominated by the rulers while the members representing British India were to be elected. The powers of the Federal Legislature were to be limited. It was not to pass laws affecting Royal family and the

Government of India Act of 1935. It was not to pass laws discriminating against British goods. Previous sanction of the Governor-General was needed for introducing certain categories of bills. It was not to have any control over the non-votable items of the budget which were to constitute about 80 per cent of the budget. In case of deadlock between the two chambers over a bill, Governor-General could call a joint session. A bill passed by Federal Legislature could be sent back by the Governor-General for reconsideration. He could veto or reserve it for His Majesty's pleasure. Any Act of federal legislature could be disallowed by the King-in-Council within a year.

❑

8

Wavell Plan

On account of the out break of World War Second, the term of Lord Linlich gow had been extended upto 1944. In 1944 Lord Wavell was appointed the Governor-General and Viceroy of India and continued upto the year 1947. Immediately after taking over his charge, in India he sent relief for the people of famine affected areas in Bengal. He released Mahatma Gandhi and other Congress leaders from the Jail. The following were the important events of his time:

1. **End of Second World War and Simla Conference (1945).** During the Viceroyalty of Lord Wavell the Second World War came to an end. Germany was defeated and Japan was also forced to surrender in 1945. Finding this the most appropriate occasion for solving the constitutional problems Lord Wavell called a conference of the leaders of different parties at Simla. He offered some proposals which are popularly known as Wavell offer to solve the constitutional tangle.

2. **Trial of the Officers of Azad Hind Sena.** During the Second World War. Subash Chandra Bose secretly left India and went to Germany. From Germany, he went to Japan. He had organised an army named Azad Hind Sena for achieving the independence of India After the end of Second World War the main officer's of the said army were arrested and cases were started against them in the Red Fort of Delhi. The prominent leaders of India pleaded on behalf of these officers.

3. **Cabinet Mission Plan (1946).** After the end of the Second World War, the Labour Party came into power in England.

New elections were held for the provincial legislatures in India. In order to solve the constitutional tangle of India a Cabinet Mission consisting of Lord Pathic Lawrence, Sir Stafford Cripps and A.V. Alexander was sent to India. Thus Mission put forward proposals which provided for an inter Government.

The Cabinet Mission reached Delhi on March 24, 1946 and had prolonged discussion with Indian leaders of all parties As the two major parties the Congress and the League could not come to any agreement on the fundamental issue of the unity or partition of India the Mission put forward their own plan for the solution of the constitutional problem. They rejected the Muslim Leagues demand for Pakistan. They gave very Cogent arguments against the partition of the country. The Mission recommended that the constitution of India should the following basic form:

1. There should be a Union of India embracing both British India and the States which should deal with the following subjects. Foreign Affairs, Defence and Communications and should have the powers to raise the finances required for the above subjects.

2. The Union should have an Executive and a Legislative Constituted from British India and the States representatives.

3. The Provinces would enjoy full autonomy for all subjects other than the Union Subjects and all residrary powers should vest in the provinces. Provinces should be free to form groups with Executives ad Legislatures, The six Hindu majority Provinces viz; Madras, Bombay, C.P., U.P., Bihar and Orissa would farm Group A. The Muslim majority provinces in the North West (the Punjab and the N.W.F.P. Sind) would form group B; Bengal, Assam would from group C. of the Chief Commissioner's provinces (Delhi Ajmer Marwara and Coorg would join group A and one Baluchistan join B. The full autonomy of

the Provinces and the provisions for grouping were meant to give Muslim league if not the form, the substance of Pakistan. It was obvious that group B and C would be under absolute control of the Muslims. The constuent Assembly be elected by the Provincial Legislative Assemblies, adult sufferage having be ruled out as if would involve delay in the making of the constitution. The number of representatives allotted to each province and community was to be proportional to its population roughly in the ratio of one to a million. The table of representation is given below:

Group A

Province	General	Muslim	Total
Madras	45	4	49
Bombay	49	2	21
United Provinces	47	8	55
Bihar	31	5	36
Orissa	9	0	9
Central Provinces	16	1	17
	167	20	187

Group B

Province	General	Muslim	Sikh	Total
Punjab	8	16	4	28
N.W.F.P.	0	3	0	3
Sind	1	3	0	4
	9	22	4	35

Group C

Province	General	Muslim	Total	
Bengal	27	33	60	
Assam	7	3	10	
	34	36	70	Grand Total 292

To these 292 members were to be added four members from the four Chief Commissioner's provinces and not more than 93 members from the Indian states whose selection would be determined by consultation.

The constituent Assembly would conclude a treaty with Britain to provide for certain matters arising out of the transfer of power.

The Constituent Assembly. The Cabinet Mission Plan was accepted by the Congress and the Muslim League though with mental reservations.

The Establishment of Interm Government and Communal Riots. After clarifying some doubts the Congress accepted the Plan but the Muslim League rejected it and the communal riots started. The Muslims League declared its 'Jihad' against the Hindus of Noakhali in Bengal. The people of other provinces reacted against the said incident and the communal riots were held in Bihar, Punjab and other places. Mahatma Gandhi himself went to Noakhali to establish peace there. In this background Pt. Jawahar Lal Nehru formed the Interium Government and the constituent Assemly met in December 1946 at New Delhi. On February 20, 1946 the Britsh Prime Minister Attlee declared that the British wanted to leave India before June 1948. The whole world was surprised to hear such a news because no body believed that the British would be prepared to leave India.

CRIPP'S MISSION

The Congress Working Committee passed a resolution on December 30, 1941 offering cooperation provided British created conditions in which India could honourably fight for freedom and democracy. The resolution and confirmed by the All India Congress Committee in January 1942.

On January 2, 1942, Sir Tej Bahadur Sapru with 12 other eminent Indians who did not belong to the Congress Party, sent a cable to Prime Minister Winston Churchill advocating immediate conversion of the Executive Council into a truly national government, the restoration of popular ministries in the provinces, the representation of India at the Imperial War Council through men chosen by the national 'government and the treatment of India on the same footing as the other Dominions. Churchill at that time was in Washington.

On January 21, 1942 Lord Linlithgow sent a despatch to the Secretary of State for India and raised the general issue of constitutional change. He advised the Secretary of State not to bother about pressure from academic theorists or sentimentalists and stand firm. The reaction of Attlee was, "I must confess that the general effect of the despatch does not increase my confidence in the Viceroy's judgement Linlithgow seems to me to be defeatist.... It is worth considering whether some one should not be charged with a mission to try to bring the political leaders together. There is a lot of opinion here which we cannot ignore, which is not satisfied that there is nothing to be done but to sit tight on the declaration of August 1940." On January 28, 1942, L.S. Amery submitted a memorandum to the War Cabinet concerning the Indian issue and expressed his wholehearted approval of the views of the Viceroy. The comment of Attlee was, "I find it quite impossible to accept and act on the crude imperialism of the Viceroy, not only because I think it is wrong, but because I think it is fatally short-sighted and suicidal. I should certainly not be prepared to cover up this ugliness with a cloak of pious sentiment about liberty and democracy."

Chiang Kai-Shek President of the Chinese Republic, was very much perturbed when the Japanese bombers raided Shanghai and Hong Kong and the Japanese army invaded the Philippines, Malaya and Burma. The Japanese inflicted a crippling blow on the British Navy by destroying the Prince of Wales and the Repulse. On February 15, 1942, Singapore was captured by the Japanese.

Visits of Chiang Kai-Shek

Chiang Kai-Shek exchanged his views with the American Government but neither the United States nor the United Kingdom gave them due consideration. The result was that he made up his mind to visit India in order to have a personal exchange of views with the members of the Government of India and prominent men in the public life of India. Besides meeting the officials of the government of India, he also met Jawaharlal Nehru, Maulana Azad Mahatma Gandhi. He appealed to Great Britain in these words : "Without waiting for any demands on the part of the people of India, (she) will as speedily as possible give them real political power so that they may be in a position further to develop their spiritual and material strength and thus realise that their participation in the war is not merely an aid to the anti-aggression nations for securing victory, but also a turning point in their struggle for India's freedom."

Messages to Roosevelt and Churchill

On his return to China, he cabled instructions to his ambassadors in London and Washington on February 24, 1942 in which he conveyed his reactions to Churchill and Roosevelt about his visit to India. The message to Churchill was in these words : "I am personally shocked by the Indian military and political situation which are in such a state that I could never conceive of before I arrived in India I feet strongly that if the Indian political problem is not immediately and urgently solved, the danger will be daily increasing....If the Japanese should know of the real situation and attack India, they would be virtually unopposed." His message to President Roosevelt was : "In a word the danger is extreme. If the British Government does not fundamentally change their policy towards India, it would be like presenting India to the enemy and inviting him to quickly occupy India."

British Decision to Issue Declaration

Although Churchill resisted American pressure, he ultimately had to yield. Inspite of the unwillingness of Churchill and opposition of Amery and Lord Linlithgow, the discussion of the Indian issue in the British Cabinet could not be avoided. Churchill was inclinced to meet the situation by issuing a declaration containing the proposals of the government for the solution of the political problem and the terms of that declaration were discussed between Lord Linlithgow and Amery. The draft declaration was sent to the King with a forwarding note by Amery which contained the following : "I think its (declaration's) bark is really more formidable than its bite. Beyond setting up the procedure for creating the future constitution-making body, It adds very little to what Linlithgow and I were agreed upon in July of 1940." The American Government was also informed about the contents the declaration.

Decision to Send Cripps to India

On March 8, 1942, the Viceroy gave a warning of the harmful consequences of the declaration particularly with regard to the problem of minorities. He wanted to throw the responsibilty on the Indians to settle their own internal problem and not on the British. On March 9, 1942, the Viceroy sent a cable threatening to resign if the declaration was issued in its present form. On the same day, the War Cabinet decided to send Sir Stafford Cripps to visit India with authority to discuss the scheme of the declaration with the leaders of India in order to find out whether it was acceptable to them or not.

Statement in Parliament

Prime Minister Churchill made the following statement in the House of Commons on March 11, 1942, regarding the object of Cripps Mission in India, "He will strive in their name to procure the necessary measure of assent not only from the Hindu majority but also from those great minorities amongst which the Muslims are the most important." It was not clear to Cripps whether he was going to negotiate with the parties in India which implied the authority to modify the terms of the Cabinet proposals or just to persuade the Indian leaders to accept the declaration whose terms were rigid and unalterable. In addition to this, another defect in the proposals was that they did not define the relation of Cripps with the Viceroy and the Government of India. As a matter to fact, the Viceroy complained that he was never consulted though kept informed generally. His Executive Council was never consulted and that was considered to be a discourtesy on the part of Cripps. They worked at cross purposes. One was trying to persuade the Indian leaders to join in the task of preparing the constitution of self govering India, while the other had no faith in a free and united India and was happy when Cripps left India.

Cipps' Proposals

Cripps arrived in Delhi on March 23, 1942, with the following Draft Declaration of the British Government:

(a) Immediately upon cessation of hostilities, steps shall be taken to set up in India, in the manner described hereafter, an elected body charged with the task of framing a new constitution for India.

(b) Provision shall be made, as set out below, for participation of Indian States in the constitutions-making body.

(c) His Majesty's Government undertake to accept and implement forthwith the constitution so framed subject only to:

(i) The right of any province of British India that is not prepared to accept the new constitution to retain its present constitutional position provision being made for its subsequent accession if it so decides. With such non-acceding provinces, should they so desire, His Majesty's Government will be prepared to agree upon a new constitution giving them the same full status as the Indian Union and arrived at by a procedure analogous to that here laid down.

(ii) The signing of a treaty which shall be negotiated between His Majesty's Government and the constitution-making body. This treaty will cover all necessary matters arising out of the complete transfer of responsibility from British to Indian hands; it will make provision, in accordance with undertakings given by His Majesty's Government, for the protection of the racial and religious minorities, but will not impose any restriction on the power of the Indian Union to decide in future its relationship to other member-States of the British Common-wealth.

(d) The constitution making body shall be composed as follows unless the leaders of Indian opinion in the principal communities agree upon some other form before the end of hostilities :

Immediately upon the result being known of provincial elections which will be necessary at the end of hostilities, the entire membership of the Lower Houses of Provincial Legislatures shall as a single electoral college proceed to the election of the constitution-making body by the system of proportional representation.

Indian States shall be invited to appoint representatives in the same proportion to their total population as in the case of representatives of British India as a whole and with the same powers as British Indian members.

(e) During the critical period which now faces India and until the new constitution can be framed. His Majesty's Government must inevitably bear the responsibility for and retain the control and direction of the defence of India as part of their world war effort but the task of organising to the full the military, moral and material resources of India must be the responsibility of the Government of India with the cooperation of the people of India. His Majesty's Government desire and invite the immediate and effective participation of the leaders of the principal sections of the Indian people in the counsels of their country, of the Commonwealth and of the United Nations.

Cripps in India

Soon after his arrival in India, Cripps communicated the constents of the Draft Declaration to the members of the Executive Council on March 23, 1942. The same were communicated to the Indian leaders on March 25, 1942. On March 29, he made public his proposals at a Press Conference. In his broadcast from Delhi on March 30, 1942, Cripps declared that he wanted to make it quite clear "beyond any possibility of doubt or question that the British Government and the British people desire the Indian peoples to have self-government, with a status as free in every respect as our own in Great Britain or as of the great Dominion members of the British Commonwealth of Nations." Regarding the principles on which his proposals were based, he stated that the new Constitution of India was to be framed by the elected representatives of the Indian people themselves. Immediately after the cessation of the hostilities, a constitution-making body was to be set up consisting of elected representatives from British India and the Indian states if the latter wished to become a part of the new Indian Union. He referred to the difficulties arising out of the conflicting interests of the various communities in India. "There are those who claim that India should form a single united country. There are others who say it should be divided up into two, three or more separate countries. These are those who claim that provincial autonomy should be very wide with but few centrally controlled federal services; others stress the need for centralization in view of the growing complexity of economic development. These and many other and various ideas are worthy to be explored and debated, but it is for the Indian peoples and not for outside authority to decide under which of these forms India will in the future govern herself. If the Indian peoples ask our help it will of course, be gladly given, but it is for you, the Indian people to discuss and decide upon your future constitution.

Position of Provinces

Regarding the position of the provinces in the future set-up. Cripps stated that they were to be invited to come for deliberations. "They were to stay in the Indian Union if they decided in its favour or to leave the same. There was to be no compulsion. "Come together to frame a common Constitution—If you find after all your discussions and all the give and take of a constitution making Assembly that you cannot overcome your differences and some provinces are still not satisfied with the constitution, then such provinces can go out and remain out if they wish and just the same degree of self-government and freedom will be available for them as for the Union itself, that is to say, complete self-government. We hope to see the Indian Union strong and united because it is founded upon the free consent of all its peoples, but it is not for us.

Interim Government

Regarding the interim changes to be introduced in the Government of India, Cripps declared that except the responsibility for defence, the rest of the Departments were to be transferred to the hands of the Indian members of the Executive Council of the Governor-General. In the wide-flung war, defence cannot be localised in a single country and its proportion must permeate the activities of every department of the government and must demand from every department the fullest cooperation. If His Majesty's Government are to take full responsibility for the conduct of the naval, military or air defence of India, as it is their duty to do so, then the Defence of India must be dealt with by them as part of the World War effort in which they are now engaged and the direction of that defence must vest in the hands of the Commander-in-Chief under the War Cabinet and their highest staff officers." In order that India might have her full voice in the control of strategy not only in India, but in all the theatres of war, a representative of India was to be appointed to the War Cabinet and the Pacific Council of the United Nations. After the close of the war, India was to appoint her own representatives to the Peace Conference.

Defence

The proposals of the British Government did not include the subject of defence. Cripps declared in his first Press Conference at Delhi that the Department of Defence could not be transferred to the hands of the Indians even if all the parties in the country made a united demand. The result was that the Working Committee of the Congress decided to reject the proposals. When Cripps came to know of it, he asked the Congress President not to publish the decision of the Working Committee. It was at that stage that Col. Johnson, a special representative of the American President, arrived in India on April 3, 1942. Johnson took a prominent part in the discussions on defence for about a week. The centre of gravity shifted from Cripps of Johnson, from London to New York and from Churchill to Roosevelt. Johnson requested Jawaharlal Nehru to see him at his residence on April 7, 1942. As a result of the negotiations, Cripps put forward a new formula on April 7, 1942. According to the new formula, the Commander-in-Chief was to retain his seat in the Executive Council of the Viceroy as a War Member. He was to retain his full control over all the war activities. He was to deal with demobilization, post-war reconstruction, petroleum, representation on the Eastern Group Supply Council, amenities for troops, canteen organisation and certain non-technical educational institutions, stationery, printing of forms for the army, social arrangements for all foreign missions and officers, evacuation of threatened areas, signals of coordination and economic welfare. Even when this offer was rejected by the Congress, Johnson intervened with a letter containing the following proposal:

(a) The Defence Department shall be placed in charge of a representative Indian member with the exception of functions to be exercised by the Commander-in-Chief as War member of the Executive Council.

(b) A War Department will be constituted which will take over such functions of the Defence Department as are not retained by the Defence Member." The new formula was shown to Jawaharlal Nehru who suggested some minor changes but the Viceroy had not seen its final form and he protested that he was ignored. He refused to accept any responsibility for it. Churchill warned Cripps not to commit the government in any way.

Cripps on National Government

When Cripps came to India, he used certain phrases at his meetings with the Press which were taken as promising a wholly Indian National Cabinet. In conversation with political leaders, he said that the relations of the Indian government to the Viceroy were similar to those of the British Cabinet to the King. When questioned on the subject by Abul Kalam Azad and Jawaharlal Nehru, Cripps frankly admitted that there would be no essential difference between the existing Executive Council of the Governor General and the proposed new government.

Differences Between Cripps and Viceroy

There were differences of views between Cripps and the Viceroy who was opposed to the transformation of the Executive Council into a National Government. He telegraphed on April 10, 1942 to the Secretary of State for India to find out the opinion of His Majesty's Government on the point in dispute, viz., "Either the Governor-General must continue to have the right to differ from his colleagues or he must promise that in no circumstances, will he refuse to act upon their advice." The Indian Committee of the War Cabinet met to consider the telegrams of Cripps and Linlithgow under the Chairmanship of Prime Minister Churchill. It appeared to the Committee that the Congress leaders had been informed by Cripps on the formation of a National Government. While there was to be no change in the Constitution, Cripps has assumed that the Governor-General would meet the point by means of a convention. The decision was immediately cabled to the Viceroy and Cripps that "there can be no question of any convention limiting in any way your powers under existing constitution...and no departure from this can be contemplated during the war." Cripps sent an explanatory message and conveyed his annoyance by offering to resign in these words : "I am sorry that my colleagues appear to distrust me over this matter and I am quite prepared to hand the matter over if they would rather someone else carried on the negotiations." The reply of Churchill was that there was no question of want of confidence but the Cabinet definitely rejected the suggestion of a convention to restrict the powers of the Viceroy. The refusal of the Cabinet to support Cripps made him feel humiliated and his conclusion was that his further stay in India would not serve any purpose and he decided to leave India on April 12, 1942.

Reactions of Churchill

The reactions of Churchill to the failure of the Cripps Mission reveal the inner working of his mind. Michael Edwardes writes : "When Churchill received news from India that the Cripps Mission had failed, he is reported to have danced around the Cabinet room. No tea with treason, no truck with American or British Labour sentimentality, but back to the solemn—and exciting—business of war." The same writer says : "Churchill had made his gesture of appeasement to the United States and to Labour members of the War Cabinet. It was a gesture without any meaning." Churchill sent a cable to Cripps on April 11 which shows that he had no regrets for what had happened. It said : "You must not feel unduly discouraged or disappointed by the result. The effect throughout Britain and in the United States has been wholly beneficial.... Even though your hopes have not been fulfilled, you have rendered a very important service to the common cause." H.V. Hodson writes : "When Mr. Churchill learned of the breakdown of the Delhi negotiations, he put on an act of sham tears and sorrow before his guests at Chequers, not troubling to conceal his own pleasure."

One of the closest and most affectionate associates of Churchill told Hopkins : "The President might have known that India was one subject on which Winston would never move a yard." Sherwood wrote thus : "It was indeed one subject on which the normal, broadminded, good-humoured, give-and-take attitude which prevailed between the two statesmen was stopped cold. It may be said that Churchill would see the Empire in ruins and himself buried under them before he would concede the right of any American, however great and illustrious a friend, to make any suggestions as to what he should do about India."

Causes of Failure of Cripps Mission

Many reasons have been given for the failure of the Cripps Mission. Maulana Azad writes, "There has been a great deal of speculation in India and some outside as to why Sir Stafford Cripps changed the position between the first and second interviews. One possible explanation is that Sir Stafford Cripps had hoped to persuade the Congress to accept the proposals, even though there was no change in the basic situation, by his persuasive powers and pleasant manners. When, however, the proposals were examined in detail and he was subjected to cross-examination, he felt that he must be cautious and refrain from raising hopes which he was not in a position to satisfy. An alternatives explanation is that during this interval the inner circle of the Government of India had started to influence him... A third alternative explanation is that during the interval, measages had passed between Delhi and London, and the British War Cabinet had sent him fresh instructions which made him feel that if he went too far he might be repudiated. Cripps was essentially an advocate and as such he was inclined to paint things in a rosier colour than was warranted by the facts."

H.V. Hodson had first hand information about the Cripps Mission and his view is : "The fault clearly lay with Sir Stafford in negotiating on such an issue to a point of vital commitment without the clearest understanding with the Viceroy. But the blame did not rest with him alone; for the War Cabinet, especially the India Committee, made a fundamental mistake, strange in a body so experienced, when they sent an emissary to promote a policy in India which had not been fully agreed with by the Viceroy, though he would have to carry it out."

Professor Laski put the blame on Cripps for his failure. To quote him, "It was psychologically disastrous for Sir Stafford to go to India in a 'take it or leave it' mood, and, on his return, practically announce that he washed his hands off the offer. That was bound to make it iook as though our real thought was less the achievement of Indian freedom than of a coup de main in the propagandist art among our allies."

Cripps himself attributed the failure of his mission to the existence of a number of difficulties. Among them were the involvement of government in the war, the propaganda of the Axis powers producing a defeatist atmosphere, the growth of communal antagonism and the conflicting demands of the parties and communities the objection of the Congress—primarily to the first part of Declaration and to the second part—about the form and character of the Executive Council and the position of the Defence Member in it.

Merits of Cripps' Proposals

It cannot be denied that the Cripps' proposals were an advance on the August offer in many respects. They conceded to the projected Indian Union the liberty to secede from the British Commonwealth if so desired. The framing of the new constitution was to rest not primarily but solely in Indian hands. However, its acceptance was made subject to the fulfilment of British obligations. If the Indians could not become free as a single unit, they could become free as two or more units. Disagreement among the Indians was not to give the British Government an excuse to perpetuate their rule in India. The August offer had invited the Indian leaders to start discussing the principles of the new constitution and the method of framing it. The Cripps' proposals contained a plan for a constitution-making body to be adopted if no Indian plan was agreed upon before the cessation of the hostilities. The offer provided for the inclusion of a certain number of representative Indians in the Executive Council. The Cripps' proposals invited the leaders of the principal sections of the Indian people to participate in the counsels of India, the Commonwealth and the United Nations.

The great merit of the Cripps' proposals was their frankness and precision. There was no hesitancy and generalities as was the case in the declarations of 1939 and 1940. It was declared in unambiguous terms that the new Constitution of India would be framed by the Indians themselves. The device of a bilateral treaty for implementing the new constitution and discharging the British obligations was introduced. The Muslims were also assured that they could have Pakistan if they so desired.

Criticism of Cripps' Proposals

However, the Cripps' proposals were criticised by all the interested parties in India. Each party criticised the proposals from its own point of view. The objection of the Congress was not so much to the long-term arrangement as to the interim arrangement. Cripps had given an understanding to the Congress that with the exception of the Defence Department, other Departments would be completely in the hands of the Indians and the Governor-General would act as a constitutional head. However, at a later stage, he withdrew that offer. That made the Congress suspicious regarding the honesty of the British Government. The Congress wanted the Executive Council of the Governor-General to work as a Cabinet but the British Government was not prepared to make such a concession. It was also opposed to the novel principle of the non-accession of the provinces. It appeared to them that this provision brought in Pakistan by the backdoor. The view of Jawaharlal Nehru was that the Cripps' proposals opened out "a vista of an indefinite number of partitions both of provinces and states." The Congress also opposed it on the ground that 90 millions of people in the Indian States were to have no voice in framing the Constitution and that was a "negation of democracy and self-determination." The Congress wanted a change of kind and not of degree in the composition of the Executive Council of the Viceroy.

The Hindu Maha Sabha opposed the Cripps proposals on two grounds. It was opposed to the freedom given to the provinces to leave the Indian Union and set up separate government of their own. It also objected to the elections on the basis of the Communal Award which was anti-national and undemocratic. The Sikhs also opposed the provisions relating to the non-accession of the provinces.

The firmest stand was taken by the representatives of Depressed Classes who denounced the scheme for its failure to provide the necessary safeguards for their interests. They declared : "The proposals are calculated to do the greatest harm to the Depressed Classes and are sure to place them under an unmitigated system of Hindu rule. Any such result which takes us back to the black days of the recent past will never be tolerated by us and we are all determined to resist any such catastrophe befalling our people with all the means at our command."

Response of Muslim League

The response of the Muslim League was a mixed one. Its members were happy at the prospect of realising their ambition of Pakistan. However, Mr. M.A. Jinnah was a politician and his diplomacy led him to contend that the Pakistan idea as embodied in the Cripps' proposals was nebulous and very serious impediments were placed in the way of its realisation. The Working Committee of the Muslim League passed the following resolution on April 11, 1942 : "The Committee, while expressing their gratification that the possibility of Pakistan is recognised by implication by providing for the establishment of two or more independent Unions in India, regret that the proposals of His Majesty's Government, embodying the fundamentals, are not open to any modification and therefore no alternative proposals are invited." The resolution ended by declaring that the Muslim League would not be satisfied with anything short of what was contained in the Lahore Resolution of March 1940.

Mahatma Gandhi was not at all impressed by the proposals brought by Cripps. He is stated to have told him, "Why did you come if this is what you have to offer? If this is your entire proposal to India, I would advise you to take the next plane home." The reply of Cripps was : "I will consider that."

It is pointed out that there were snags in the proposals brought by Cripps. One was the repetition of the August offer of 1940 and the addition of the explanation that "the present declaration is intended not to supersede, but to close these general declarations with precision and to convince the people of India of the War Cabinet's sincere resolve." This created suspicion in the minds of the people. The second snag was that there was no indication in the proposals that the British Government was prepared to part with power. Another defect in the scheme was that it had either to be accepted as a whole or rejected as a whole. There was no scope for any adjustment. Cripps was placed in a very tight corner by his Conservative associates.

Dr. Pattabhi Sitaramayya writes that the proposals of the British Cabinet were "a cheap but attractive bromide enlargement of the August offer, or to very the simile, they were really the stillborn child of the Cabinet. All that Sir Stafford did in Delhi over a period of twenty days was to restore breathing to the life of its stillborn baby by a process of artificial respiration and by incubation. Strenuous efforts were made in this behalf but they failed, although from time to time there appeared to be a sign of the respiratory muscles acting or the cardiac muscles beating but the child was declared dead by the Working Committee so early as on March 31, 1942, *i.e.*, on the morrow of publication of the proposals....concessions of a halting and limiting character were more an insult added to injury than an honest attempt to repair the wrong.

C. Vijiaraghavachariar was furious on reading the Draft Declaration as it envisaged a possible division of India. He studied the proposals over and over and was convinced that if we accepted the same, the unity of India would be destroyed and chaos would prevail in the country. He declared : "I feel thankful to the British Government for having decided to make British India. Dominion, fully equal to any other part of the British Commonwealth. But I deplore the provision permitting unwilling provinces to separate themselves from the Union and become self-governing entities. This is novel and dangerous is the highest degree, unknown to history or philosophy. The provinces are not yet natural ones resting on linguistic basis. Assuming that they would be soon so or that they are now (and it is immaterial), to let the provinces become independent is fraught with great danger. It will create Pakistan in more places than one—a fantastic and dangerous scheme—and the Dominion of India will consist of parts, if at all, scattered here and there. Neither England nor the British Empire nor India has the right to break up and dismember this ancient country in his way, especially as Mr. Amery has after all recognised the fact that British India was not conquered by England. I am very much dissatisfied with this scheme. I would emphatically state that it would be rather better that we are left as we are, a subject nation, than be dismembered perilously in this way. I pray to God to maintain the unity of India."

MAIN PROPOSALS OF CRIPPS PROPOSAL

Lord Linlithgow was appointed the Governor-General and Viceroy of India in the year 1936. Before his appointment as Governor-General and Viceroy in India, he had been the Chairman of the Royal Commission on Indian Agriculture. He had also served in the Joint Select Committee of the Indian Constitutional Reforms. He had also played an important part in drafting of the Government of India Act 1935. The main events of his reign were :

(1) Government of India Act 1935. The Federal part of the Act was not introduced. Only the Provincial part of the Government of India Act was introduced. Elections was held in the beginning of 1937 and the Congress secured clear majority in six provinces. But the Congress refused to form ministeries unless the Governors gave an assurance that they would not interfere in the day in day affairs of the ministries. The Governor-General Lord Linlithgow directed the Governors to give such an assurance and consequently congress ministries were formed which continued up to 1939 when they resigned after the declaration of Second World War.

(2) August offer 1940. Lord Linlithgow made his famous August offer in order to solve the constitutional deadlook in India. But the offer was rejected by the Congress.

(3) Visit of Chang Kai-Sheik (1941). In 1941 Chang Kai-Sheik the contemporary President of China paid a visit to India. He was given a very warm welcome. His visit strengthened the friendly relations of the Government of India and China.

(4) Split in the Congress. Subash Chandra Bose, the most gallant fighter for India's freedom was elected the Congress President. It was against the wishes of senior Congress leaders including Gandhiji. Subhash Chandra Bose was in favour of following a strong policy. But Gandhiji was not in favour of taking immediate steps against the British. It was on account of these differences that Subhash Chandra Bose Resigned from Congress and formed the Forward Bloc which stood for complete independence of India.

(5) Cripps Mission to India 1942. The British Government realised that it was difficult to remain indifferent to the Indian problem any longer. The War situation was worsening day by day. Invasion by Japan on India was imminent. The Indian National Congress did not want to help the British Government against any body. On March 11,1942, Winston Churchill, the Prime Minister of England sent Sir Stafford Cripps the leader of the House of Commons to India to resolve political deadlock. The following were the causes of appointment of Cripps mission:

(a) Pressure of the President Roosevelt of U.S.A. and Chang Kai Sheik of China.

(b) Growing frustration against the British Government in India.

(c) The public opinion in England was in favour of reconciling India.

(d) Threat of Japanese invasion to India.

(e) Efforts of Sir Tej Bahadur Sapru to bring about a compromise between the British Government and the Congress.

Japan had occupied the whole of South and East Asia by 7th March 1942. Mr. Cripps arrived in India on March 22, 1942. He had a series of interviews with prominent leaders of India. He worked hard to find out a way for negotiations but he failed and had to go disappointed on April 12, 1942.

Text of Cripps Proposals

(1) Immediately upon the cessation of hostilities, steps shall be taken to set up in India in the manner described hereafter an elected body charged with the task of framing a new constitution for India.

(2) Provision shall be made for the participation of Indian States in the constitution making body.

(3) His Majesty's Government undertake to accept and implement forth with the constitution so framed subject to:

(i) The right of any province of British India that is not prepared to accept the new constitution, to retain its present constitutional position, provisions being made for its subsequent accession if it so decides. Such non-acceding provinces will have new constitution.

(ii) The signing of the treaty shall be negotiated between His Majesty's Government and the constitution making body.

(4) The constitution making body shall be composed as follows unless the leaders of the Indian Union in the principal communities agree upon some other form before the end of hostilities. Indian states shall be invited to appoint representatives in the same proportion to their total population as in the case of the representatives of the British India as a whole and with the same powers as British Indian members.

(5) During the critical period which now faces India and until the new constitution can be framed, His Majesty's Government must invitably bear the responsibility for and retain the control and direction of the defence of India as part of their World War effort but the task of organising to the full the military, moral and material resources of India must be the responsibility of the Government of India and with the co-operation of the people of India.

Reactions to Cripps Proposals

Indians could not be satisfied by the proposals put before them by Cripps. There was a lot of frustration in the country against these proposals. The causes of the failure of the Mission were:

(a) ***Inadequacy of the Proposals.*** The Congress party believed in the principles that "one bud in hand is better than two in the bush." Cripps had assured the Congress leaders that with the exception of the Defence Department all other departments would be completely in the hands of the Indians. Later on the withdrew this statement. Gandhiji called it a post dated Cheque on a Bank that was obviously failing.

(b) ***Accessession of Indian States.*** The Congress Party was not prepared to accept the novel principle of the right of non-accession given to five hundred and sixty two Indian princely states.

(c) ***Loose Federation.*** Hindu Mahasabha opposed the proposals put forward by Cripps on the ground that the party was against the freedom given to the Provinces.

(d) ***Opposition of Sikhs.*** Sikhs held the view that they would oppose the separation of Punjab from all India Union by all possible means.

(e) ***Opposition by Depressed Class.*** They opposed the proposals on the ground that there was no provision for safeguarding their interests.

(f) ***Opposition by Muslim League.*** Muslim League opposed the creation of a Single Indian Union.

(6) Quit India Resolution (1942). The famous Quit India Resolution was passed by the Congress in 1942. The Resolution asked the Britishers to leave India. A vigorous movement was launched in pursuance of the Said Resolution. Many prominent leaders were arrested and sent to Jail. They were kept in Jail throughout the war. Despite the arrest of the leaders the movement still continued.

(7) Reforms of Lord Linlithgow. On account of the Second World War and Quit India Movement there prevailed and all round anarchy in India. In the meantime there was a very severe famine in Bengal. In the absence of sufficient relief, lakhs of people died in the famine. However, the Congress worked hard to give relief to the people of the famine stricken areas. The Government started the Control or Rationing system. The prices of essential commodities were also fixed. But this led to an increase in the black marketing and corruption became rampant in the Country.

Lord Linlithgow introduced some reforms in education. In 1938 Gandhiji initiated the Wardha Plan and emphasised the need of basic education. Montessaries Schools opened in 1939. Gurukul Kangri near Hardwar and Tagor's Vishwa Bharti in Shanti Niketan contributed a lot in the field of education. Linlithgow made some amendments in the Sharda Act and in 1938 this Act was made applicable in the native states also. Fines and imprisonment were to be imposed on the persons defying the Act.

EVENTS DURING THE REIGN OF LORD IRWIN

Lord Reading was succeeded by Lord Irwin in 1926 as the Governor-General and Viceroy of India. He had to face many serious problems during his Viceroyalty. He was sympathetic towards the Indians and followed liberel policy. Following were the important events of his reign.

Simon Commission. The Government of India Act 1919 contained a provision for the appointment of a statutory Commission at the expiry of ten years to examine the working of the Indian constitution and to consider the desirability of establishing modifying or restricting the degree of responsible Government which then existed. The members of the commission were:

(a) Lord Burnham.

(b) Lord Stratchona

(c) Mr. Gadogan.

(d) Sir John Simon (Chairman).

(e) Colonel Lane Fox.

(f) Mr. Clement Atlee.

The British government was forced to appoint this Commission due to agitations and movements in India. The terms of reference of the Commission were:

(a) To enquire into the working of the system of the government, the growth of education and the development of the representative institutions in British India and the matters connected with it.

(b) To report as to whether and to what extent it was desirable to establish the principle of the responsible government or to some extent modify or to restrict the degree of the responsible government then existing there in including the question whether the establishment of the second chamber of the Local Legislature was or was not desirable.

The Simon Commission came to India at the beginning of 1928. The Indian political leaders of all parties unanimously decided to boycott the commission because no Indian was considered fit to be its members. The Commission was welcomed in India wherever it went with black flags. Government strictly dealt with the opposition and many leaders were belaboured.

RECOMMENDATIONS OF SIMON COMMISSION

(a) Provincial Government

(i) The Commission recommended that in the provinces dyarchy should be abolished because it was very defective in application. The ministers should be entrusted with full control of the provincial administration and they should be responsible to the legislature. The Governor should be given the right of selecting the ministers from the majority party in the legislature. It should be provided that the central Government should not interfere and exert undue pressure in the legislation and administration of the provinces.

(ii) The governors should be granted special powers to over side the advice of ministers in important, matters and the Central Government should have some control over the provincial Governments.

(iii) The franchise should be extended and the legislature should be enlarged so that the people of the country may become more politically conscious.

(b) Central Government

(i) In the view of the commission it was not possible to establish a federation in the country in the near future.

(ii) Pending the establishment of a federation in the country, the commission proposed that a consultative council of Greater India should be set up in which the representatives of British India and Indian states should be included.

(iii) Sind should be separated from Bombay. Burma should be separated from the British India because it was not a natural party of the sub-continent.

(iv) It was essential to Indianise the army. However, British forces must be retained till the time India was no fully equipped.

(v) The commission recommended that the central legislature should be recommended on the federal pattern.

(vi) The administered areas of the N.W. Frontier province would receive an advance in constitutional status represented by the creation of a local legislature. Both N.W.F.P. and Baluchistan would acquire the right to get represented at the centre.

(1) Criticism. Sir Sira Swami Aiyer, has remarked that the report should be placed on a scrap of heap.' Professor Keith has remarked, "It was probably foolish of Indian opinion to repudiate the report out and out; if it had been accepted, the British Government would bardly have failed to work on it and responsible government in this provinces would have been achieved much earlier than it could be under any other scheme.....

(2) Congress Session and Civil Disobedience Movement. The repressive policies of the Government could not suppress the national Movement. In the Congress Session of December1928 a resolution was passed asking the British Government to grant the dominion status within a year. The Resolution declared to celebrate

26th January 1930 as the Independence day of India. From this day the Civil Disobedience Movement was started under the ledership of Mahatma Gandhi.

(3) First Round Table Conference. When the Simon Commission was submitted, the First Round Table Conference took place in London. But it did not yield any result because the Congress did not participate in it.

(4) Gandhi Irwin Pact. Through the efforts of Tej Bahadur Sapru and Jayokar, the Gandhi Irwin Pact was made in 1911 and Mahatma Gandhi agreed to participate in the Second Round Table Conference as the sole representative of the Congress. Gandhiji called off Civil Disobedience Movement and all political prisoners were released.

(5) Reforms of Lord Irwin. Lord Irwin deserves credit for having introduced a number of reforms:

(i) Lord Irwin increased the rate of Income tax to improve the economic condition of the country.

(ii) Pusa Agricultural Research Institute was expanded to impart agricultural knowledge to the farmers.

(iii) Many new roads were constructed.

(iv) Several new universities were established.

(v) Labour Union were given recognition for the first time by the British Government. The Trade Union Act was passed and the labours got the legal right to go on strike.

(vi) The Sharda Act was passed in 1930 which fixed 18 and 14 years as the minimum marriageable are for boys and girls respectively.

(vii) Indian Navy was organised for the first time and posts were given to Indians in it.

(6) League of Nations. After the end of the First World War league of nations was found and India was also made its member. In 1929 an Indian representative was sent for the first time.

(7) The Problem of the Indians in South Africa. The Government of India made efforts to ensure the security and respect of the Indians living in South Africa. An Indian representative was appointed in South Africa.

VICEROYALTY OF LORD CHELMSFORD

In 1916 Lord Chelmsford succeeded Lord Hardinge as the Viceroy of India. There was acute distress everywhere on account of high price and strikes and other disturbances were frequent. To combatseditions crimes the Government in 1919 passed the Rowlatt Act arming the Executive with special powers to deport individual to control the press and to set up special tribunals for the trial of political leaders without juries. These repressive measures were highly unpopular and there was agitation all over the country for their repeal. Serious riots broke out in several places especially in the Punjab where the Government proclaimed martial Law and adopted a policy of stern repression. It culminated in the massacre of Jallianwalla Bagh at Amritsar where General Dyer disgraced himself by firing upon an unarmed mob which had assembled at a public meeting. About 2000 persons were wounded and killed by this senseless exhibition of military strength. Their brutal tragedy sent a thrill of horror and indignation throughout the country and is one of the immediate causes of the Non Co-operation Movement.

Afghan War. A fanatical party in Afghanistan murdered Amir Habibullah for maintaining neutrality in the Great War. On his death his young son Amunullah Khan became King. Incited by the Bolshavic agents of Russia as well as to please the war party, the new Amir invaded British territory but was beaten back. In the treaty that followed the subsidy to Afghanistan was discontinued and the Amir was given a free hand to regulate his foreign relations.

The Government of India Act 1919. The growing discontent of the people brought home to the British Government the necessity of making some concessions to their roused political consciousness. This was all the more necessary in view of the great services rendered by the Indians to the cause of the Allied Powers in the Great

War. The Government also wanted to really the moderate opinion as the recent repressive measures had driven many moderates to the extremist camp. All these causes led Mr. E.S. Montague, the secretary of state to make a momentous decration of British Policy with regard to India on August 20, 1917. He enunciated two fold principles of increasing association of Indians in every branch of the administration and the gradual development of self governing institutions with a view to the progressive realisation of responsible government in India as an integral part of the British Empire Mr. Montague visited India and in consultation with Lord Chelmsford published a report known as the Montague Chelmsford Report.

Basic Principle of the Act of 1919. The main recommendations of the Montague Chelmsford Report were:

(a) A beginning of responsible Government should be made in the provinces. The provincial Legislative Councils should be enlarged and they should have the largest possible independence from outside control.

(b) The Central Government should remain for the present responsible to be Secretary of State and Parliament. The Legislative Council at the Centre should be enlarged and made more representative and should have a greater opportunities for influencing the Government.

(c) The devolution of powers from the centre should be extended and legalised.

The substance of these recommendations was embodied in the Government of India Act 1919. The Act divided the functions of Government into Central subjects and Provincial subjects and thereby took a significant step in decentralising the authority of the Government. The central subjects was political and external affairs, income tax, Public debt and all India Services. The important provincial subjects were Local Self Government, education, Sanitation, Public health, Public works and irrigation, famine relief, agriculture, maintenance of law and order and administration of justice.

The Central Legislative Assembly was replaced by a bi-cameral system consisting of a Council of State and a Legislative Assembly. The provincial Government was throughly remodelled. The Executive was divided into two halves—The Reserved Department and the transferred Department. The Reserved Subjects were to be administered by the Government and his Executive Council with no responsibility to the legislature, the Governor being responsible only to the Central Government and Parliament. The transferred subjects were placed incharge of the Governor acting with the ministers selected by him from amongst the selected members of the Provincial legislature. Thus dyarchy was introduced in the Provinces.

Khilafat Movement. This movement was organised by the Muslims of India whose aim was to protest against the shabby treatement meted out to Turkey by the Allies inspite of the repeated promises and assurances to the Indian Muslims. The Sultan of Turkey had been defeated by the allies in the First World War. As a consequence of his defeat along with Germany the Turkish territory was greatly reduced. Thus was done in violation of the promises made by the British Government to the Indian Muslims during the War. The aim of the Khilafat movement was to secure the integrity of the Turkish Empire. Besides this the Muslims demanded the establishment of a Muslims State in Palestine.

FRONTIER POLICY OF LORD CURZON

The North West Frontier lying between Afghanistan and the Indus has been a complex problem from early times. Successive imperial powers tried to control this tract in order to reach a scientific frontier towards the North West. The conquest of Sind in 1843 and the annexation of the Punjab in 1849 carried the British boundaries beyond the Indus and brought them into close contact with the territories of the Baluch and Pathan tribes. Most of the tribes were independent though the Amir of Afghanistan claimed a nominal suzerainty over them. This 1200 miles long belt of territory has offered and almost impenetrable barriers to all the invading armies from the North West except when they came by the five passes Kheyber, Khurram, Tochi, Gomal or Bolan.

Sind Frontier. Experience showed that the policy of Sir Charles Naper in suppsessing the Baluchi tribes by ruthless force was not a success. His building of Forts along the Sind frontier and the posting of detachments of the troops at certain Vulnerable points did not prove to be very effective. This policy was reversed by Major John Jacob who succeeded him in Sind. The veiw of Jacob was that the Baluchi tribes could be softened if the benefits of Western Civilization could be extended to them with that object in view he started a vigorous compaign for "pushing back the desart" by providing facilities for wide spread cultivation of land extensive irrigation. He also introduced the system of patrolling of the frontier instead of keeping the troops stationary at certain points. The Baluchi tribes had an aristocratic and oligarchical form of Government and hence the Government of India did not find such difficulty in controlling them though their chiefs. By the treaty of 1954 the Khan of Kalat was given an annual subsidy of 50,000 to control the tribes and maintain law and order. His subsidy was also increased. The main feature of the Sanderman's System was tribal and village responsibility worked through the headman. Sandeman established personal and friendly relation with the Baluchi Chiefs and often visited their mountain retreats.

The Punjab Frontier. As regards the Punjab frontier the Government followed "a policy of non-intervention tempered by punitive expedition." No British officer was allowed to cross the border or meet with the tribes men. The police and military were not allowed to chaise the rarders beyond the foot of the hills. Tribemen entering the Punjab were allowed to trade and provision was made to provide medical and other facilities for them.

Inspite of difficulties this policy of non-intervention was continued. However, certain measures were adopted to protect the frontier. A chain of forts was built along the frontier. Roads were also constructed along with them. A special frontier force consisting of Sikhs, Pathans, Gorkhas and Punjabi Muslims was created to petrol and guard the frontier. The government tried to exercise some control over the tribes through middleman but inspite of that there was tribal raids and the government was forced to hit back.

The Forward Policy. The Government of India followed what is known as the Forward Policy in the time of Lord Lytton that resulted in the Second Afghan War. The failure of the Second Afghan War discredited the Forward Policy for some time but the same was revived during the Viceroyalty of Lord Lansdowne (1888-94). A strategic railway was completed up to the Bolan Pass. A British Officer was sent to Gilgit in 1889. In 1892 the Chief of Chitral died and he was succeeded by his son. The Govt. of India sent Dr. Robertson to Chitral in 1893 as its envoy, Abdur Rehman, the Amir of Afghanistan agreed not to interfere with the Afridis, Waziris and other frontier tribes. Some distries were ceded to Abdul Rehman and he agreed not to interfere in Swat, Bajur, Dir and Chitral. The Govt. of India agreed not to raise any objection to the purchase and import of ammunitions of War by the Amir of Afghanistan. His annual subsidy was raised from 12 lakhs to 18 lakhs.

The Forward Policy of Lord Lansdowne was continued by Lord Elgin (1894-1899). A British agency had been established of Gilgit with an out post in Chitral at Mastry. In January 1895 the ruler of Chitral was assassinated. When Dr. Robertson, the British Agent at Gilgit went to Chitral, he and his small force was besieged by the rebellions Chiefs. A British force was sent from Gilgit to give relief and it succeeded in doing so. Lord Elgin wanted to return Chitral but he was over ruled by the Home Government. However under the Unionist Government of Lord Salisbury, the British Government decided not only to retain Chitral but also ordered the Construction of a military road from Chitral to the frontier with garrisons to protect it. The out break of frontier War of 1897-98 was due to many causes. The tribesmen did not like the intervention of the British Government in Chitral. They also did not like the demarcation of the Durand line and the extension of the British influence over the Sherani Country. The preachings of the Mullahs and the rumoun of the British intention to annex the tribal territory also added to be trouble.

Lord Curzon gave up the forward policy and evolved a new policy of his own. He gradually withdrew a large number of troops from the forward areas such as the Kheyber Pass, The Kurram valley, Waziristan and the tribal Country. Only in exceptional cases isolated post such as Malakand and Dargai were retained and fortified. He replaced regular troops by tribal levies which were trained and Command by British Officers. The 4,000 regular troops stationed at Kheyber Pass were withdrawn and were replaced by the Kheyber Rifles consisting of Afridis and other tribes. The regulars were replaced in the Samana range and the Kurram valley by Samana Rifles and the Kurram Militia. The Gomal Pass was put under the charge of South Waziristan Militia while making these arrangements. Lord Curzon also concentrated a large number of troops at strategic points in British territory so that they could be easily available for crusing and tribal rising, Curzon also started the construction of roads, bridges and rail roads connecting the tribal areas with the settled districts, Railways were built upto Dargai, Jamrud at the entrance of the Kheyber Pass and that the gate of the Kurram Valley. Lord Curzon tried to impress upon the tribesmen that while their independence would be respected their raids into British territory would not to tolerated. It is clear from the fact that with the exception of the blockade of the Mahsud Waziris in 1901, the fierce conflicits of 1897-98 were followed by ten years of peace. Lord Curzon was also responsible for the creation of the new province known as the North West Frontier Province. It is pointed out that the policy of Lord Curzon failed during the Afghan War of 1919. The Tribal Militia failed to check the tribesmen. The Kheyber Militia disappeared. The Waziri Militia either mutinied or deserted Operations were vigourously conducted against the Waziris and Mahsuds. The British forces entered into the heart of Mahsud territory and established a Camp at Ladha.

The new Frontier Policy was tried in Waziristan. The tribal levies were replaced Khassadars and Scouts. They were also required to provided their own rifles. The advantage of the System was that the Khasadars were paid only if they protected the Caravans and performed other police duties and if they deserted they lost their pay but the Government did not lose their or the lives of their officers.

❐

9

Mountbatten Plan

Lord Mountbatten arrived in India on March 22, 1947. On 23 March, the Muslim League observed the Pakistan Day. India is neither a country nor a nation, but is a score of nations. There were serious riots in the Punjab in the month of March. These riots were preceded by a very virulent agitation by the Muslim League in the Punjab, Sind and the North-Western Frontier Province. The Muslim League volunteers were given a free hand to do whatever they pleased. They were allowed to go to the roofs of the Government buildings and hoist the Muslim League flags and there was none to ask them why they were doing so. Whatever the Muslim League did was watched with patience and internal satisfaction by the British bureaucracy. Even when riots broke out in March 1947, there was no Government machinery to stop them. The eye-witness accounts of the havoc brought about by the Muslim rioters at Rawalpindi and its neighbourhood were simply horrific. There was none to care for their dead bodies. In the foundations of present Islamabad, the capital of Pakistan, lies the blood of the innocent Hindus and Sikhs who fell a victim to the fury of mad Muslim mobs. Alan Campbell Johnson, who accompanied Lord Mountbatten on a visit of Kahuta near Rawalpindi, writes : "We arrived to find that the havoc in the small town was very great. Picking our way through the rubble, we could see that the devastation was as thorough as any produced by fire-bomb raids in the war. This particular communal orgy involved the destruction of Sikhs and their livelihood by Moslems who were proving difficult to track down. The Muslims in the area seemed to be quite pleased with themselves, and to be unable to appreciate that the local Sikh traders were one of the principal sources of their own prosperity..." One is really amazed how such a thing could happen in the neighbourhood of Rawalpindi which was one of the biggest Military Headquarters of the Government of India. There was the Chaklala Aerodrome at hand from where the bombers could fly to control the situation and stop the rioters. One cannot help observing that at this critical time, the Englishmen forgot their duty and behaved like partisans. India had a Governor-General in Lord Wavell who was every inch a General but even he failed in his duty to save the innocent populace. His role at the time of the Calcutta killing or Rawalpindi riots belies the traditions which one is apt to attribute to British soldiery.

The fact of the matter is that when Lord Mountbatten reached India, the situation in the country was drifting towards a civil war. In the cities where the Hindus and the Muslims had lived peacefully for centuries, each was determined to destroy the other. A Hindu would not live in the areas where the Muslims predominated and vice versa. There was no security of life or property. People were disposing of properties in areas inhabited by the other community. The whole situation was diabolic. The Government officials were taking sides. Barring noble exceptions, the general trend was that no Muslim was prepared to do anything for a Hindu even though he was formerly his friend or neighbour.

When Lord Mountbatten was faced with such a situation, he came to the inevitable conclusion that the only solution for India was the partitioning of the country. He found that even Congress leaders like Sardar Patel and Jawaharlal Nehru were forced by circumstances to admit that there was no other alternative but to concede partition. The unity of India was very dear to them but it was found that the circumstances were such that the same could not be maintained. Mahatma Gandhi was of the definite opinion that it was better to face a civil war than to have a partition of the country. However, the situation in the country became so intolerable that even he was converted to the point of view that the only solution for the country was its partition. It appears that both Patel and Nehru were impressed by the argument that it was better to have a smaller India where they could be what they pleased than to have a bigger India where the

Muslim League will fetter all their actions. Within two weeks of the arrival of Mountbatten in India, it became clear that India was going to be partitioned. It is pointed out that Lord Mountabatten was not enamoured of the Cabinet Mission Plan as it was not his own child. The circumstances dictated the partitioning of the country. We are told that on 8 April, 1947, Lord Mountbatten was discussing Liaquat Ali Khan's paper on the division of the Armed Forces. On 19 April, Lord Ismay, Chief of the Viceroy's Staff, emphasised the difficulty of East Pakistan and West Pakistan which were separated from each other. On 27 April, the news leaked out in the press that the Government of India was thinking of the partition of the country. The reaction of Lord Mountabatten was : "The more the papers speculate about partition, the more they are preparing public opinion of its arrival". It appears that even before the arrival of Lord Mountbatten, the Cabinet Mission plan had been shelved.

The first plan of Lord Mountbatten was to hand over power to the provinces or to such confederations of provinces as the latter might decide to form. He was also in favour of partitioning the provinces of Bengal and Punjab with a view to separate the predominantly Muslim areas from the predominantly non-Muslim areas. He was also in favour of allowing the Muslim district of Sylhet the option of joining the Muslim Province of Bengal.

There was opposition to his proposals. Sir Even Jenkins, Governor of the Punjab, opposed the partition on the ground that the divided provinces would still be having minorities. The contention of the Governor of Bengal was that the division of Bengal would make East Bengal a rural slum. Mr. Jinnah contended that the division of the Punjab and Bengal would destroy the administrative and economic fabric of the provinces which had been built up during the last century. He contended that ultimately there would be exchange of populations between India and Pakistan and the problem of the minorities would be automatically solved in that manner. Mr. Jinnah's argument was that if the Punjab and Bengal were to be partitioned, then the other provinces where the Muslims lived in large numbers must also be partitioned.

Lord Mountbatten sent his plan to London on 2 May, through Lord Ismay and his secretary, George Abell. He was thinking of putting his plan before a meeting of the party leaders on 17 May, 1947. However, when his plan came back from London, many changes had been made in it. It is said that when he showed the same to Jawaharlal Nehru, he told the Viceroy frankly that the Congress would not accept it. The scheme was likely to result in the Balkanisation of India. When Lord Mountbatten found that Nehru was opposed to the draft he had received from London, he decided to make another attempt. According to that plan, the transfer of power was to take place on the basis of Dominion Status to India and such other areas as wanted to separate from India and form another state. Lord Mountbatten found that Nehru was not opposed to a plan according to which power was to be transferred to two Central governments on the basis of Dominion Status. The provisions with regard to the partitioning of the Punjab, Bengal and Assam were already known. The wishes of the Muslim areas of the Punjab, Bengal, Sind and the North-Western Frontier Province could also be ascertained. The great merit of the scheme of V.P. Menon was that as an able draftsmen, he was able to put together many ideas into one plan. Lord Mountbatten left for London on 18 May, 1947 and came back to India after getting the approval of the British Government.

The 3 June Plan

According to the 3 June Plan, the Provinces of the Punjab and Bengal were to be partitioned into two parts, one part representing the predominantly Muslim areas and the other part representing the predominantly Hindu areas. In order to ascertain the wishes of people of these two provinces, the members of the two parts of each Legislative Assembly were to sit separately and vote whether or not the provinces should be partitioned. If a simple majority of either part decided in favour of partition, partition was to take place and arrangements were to be made accordingly. A Boundary Commission was to settle the details of the boundaries in case partition of the Provinces of Bengal and the Punjab was decided upon. Provision was made for a referendum in the case of North-Western Frontier

Province and the Muslim-majority district of Sylhet in Assam. It is well-Known that the Legislative Assemblies of Bengal and the Punjab decided in favour of partition and a Boundary Commission was appointed to decide which parts of these provinces were to go to Pakistan and which parts to remain in India. The referendum in the case of North-Western Frontier Province went in favour of the Muslim League.

This Plan was broadcast to the people of India by Lord Mountbatten on 3 June, 1947. In his broadcast to the nation, Jawaharlal Nehru, Vice-President of Interim Government, endorsed the Plan and said : "It is with no joy in the heart that I commend these proposals to you, though I have no doubt in my mind that this is the right course. For generations we have dreamt and struggled for a free and independent united India. The proposal to allow certain parts to secede if they so will in painful for any of us to contemplate. Nevertheless, I am convinced that our present decision is the right one even from the larger viewpoint..."

It is obvious that Mr. Jinnah did not say in so many words that he accepted the 3 June Plan on behalf of the Muslim League. He made this vaguely non-committal statement in spite of the fact that Lord Mountbatten had requested him to make a categorical statement with regard to the acceptance of the Plan by the Muslim League. On behalf of the Sikh community, Sardar Baldev Singh who was the Defence Member in the Interim Government, observed thus in his broadcast : "The Plan that has now been announced, is not a compromise. I prefer to call it a settlement. It does not please everybody, not the Sikh community anyway, but it is certainly something worthwhile. Let us take it at that."

On 8 June, 1947, a meeting of the All-India Hindu Mahasabha was held in New Delhi to consider the Plan and it was resolved. "This Committee deeply deplores the fact that the Indian National Congress, after having giving a solemn assurance to the Hindu electorate that it stood by the unity of India and would oppose the disintegration of India, has betrayed the country by agreeing to the partition of India without a reference." On 10 June, 1947, the Council of the All India

Muslim League met in New Delhi and passed a resolution accepting the 3 June Plan. It resolved "to give full authority to the President of the All India Muslim League, Qaide-Azam Jinnah, to accept the fundamental principles of the Plan as a compromise and to leave it to him, with full authority to work out all the details of the plan in an equitable and just manner with regard to carrying out the complete division of India on the basis and fundamental principles embodied in His Majesty's Government's Plan, including Defence, Finance and Communication..." It is to be noted that the resolution of the Muslim League did not say expressly that it accepted the 3 June Plan but rather it authorised Mr. Jinnah "to accept the fundamental principles of Plan." The resolution of the Muslim League was forwarded to the Viceroy. On the same day, the National Executive of the Socialist Party of India met in New Delhi and resolved that it "expresses its disapproval of and grief at the proposed division of the country" as envisaged by the 3 June Plan.

A joint conference of the Sikhs was held at Lahore and it passed a resolution on 12 June in these words : "This joint Conference disapproves of the scheme for the division of India into two sovereign States. In its opinion, the only redeeming feature of the plan is the acceptance of the principle of partition of the Punjab. While the Plan is designed to carve out a sovereign Muslim State to satisfy Muslim demands it falils to provide for the Sikhs any position of power or status or any means for the protection of their interest in the constitution-making machinery..."

The Working Committee of the All-India Majlis-e-Ahrar passed on 13 June, 1947 a resolution in which it declared that the 3 June Plan would result in the "political subjugation of Pakistan in the shape of economics and Defence alliances. An emergency meeting of the All-India Congress Committee was held in New Delhi in the Constitution House to consider the 3 June Plan under the Presidentship of Acharya Kripalani. On 15 June, it passed a resolution by 157 votes to 29 votes. The resolution read : "The All India Congress Committee accept the proposals embodied in the announcement of June 3 which have laid down a procedure for ascertaining the will of the people concerned.

The proposals of June 3, 1947, are likely to lead to the secession of some parts of the country from India.

Speaking on the resolution, Jawaharlal Nehru emphasised the fact that "It must be realised that it is not possible to coerce unwilling parts to remain in the Indian domin." Sardar Patel observed that India had to choose between "partition or complete Balkanisation and anarchy." What Gandhiji said was that although he had previously opposed Pakistan, "sometimes certain decisions however unpalatable they may be, have to be taken."

At the end of the ten-day session, the Central Committee of the Communist Party of India passed the following resolution in New Delhi on 20 June, 1947 : "The Mountbatten Award of June 3 does not give India real independence but is the culmination of a double-faced imperial policy, which while making concessions to the national demand to transfer power, sets in motion disruptive and reactionary forces to obstruct the realisation of real independence. The British policy of divide and rule, exploiting Hindu-Muslim differences, produced an unpreacedented civil war and has now culminated in the final act of partition of the country into two hostile States which they plan to control by entering into new alliances with reactionary forces in the different partitioned areas."

Indian Independence Act (1947)

In order to give effect to the 3 June Plan, the Indian Independence Bill was introduced into the British Parliament on 4 July, 1947 and the same was passed on 18 July, 1947. The Indian Independence Act, 1947 provided for the partition of India and the establishment of the two Dominions of India and Pakistan from the appointed day, *i.e.* 15 August, 1947. The Act also provided for the Legislative supremacy of the two Dominions. The Legislatures of the two Dominions were given full powers to make laws having extra-territorial jurisdiction. The British Government was to have no control over the affairs of the two Dominions after 15 August, 1947. Until a new Constitution was framed for each Dominion, the Indian Independence Act made the existing Constituent Assemblies of India and Pakistan and Dominion Legislatures for the time being. The Dominion Legislatures were to exercise all the powers which were formerly exercised by the Central Legislature in addition to their power with regard to the framing of the Constitution. Pending the framing of a new Constitution, each Dominion was to be governed in accordance with the provisions of the Government of India Act, 1935. Each Dominion was authorised to make modifications in the Government of India Act, 1935 according to its own requirements. The Governor-General was given the power to modify or adapt the Government of India Act, 1935 as might be considered necessary till 31 March, 1948. After that date, the power was to be exercised by the Constituent Assembly of each Dominion. The right of the King to veto laws or to reserve laws for his pleasure was given up. That right was given to the Governor-General of each Dominion. He was given the full authority to assent in the name of His Majesty to any law of the Dominion Legislature made in its ordinary legislative capacity. The office of the Secretary of State for India was abolished.

INDIA ATTAINS INDEPENDENCE

On 15 August, 1947 India became independent. However, just before the midnight of 14-15 August, 1947 when the independence of India was declared, Jawaharlal Nehru addressed the members of the Constituent Assembly in these words :

"Long years ago we made a tryst with destiny, and now the time comes when we shall redeem our pledge, not wholly or in full measure, but very substantially. At the stroke of the midnight hour, when the world sleeps, India will awake to life and freedom. A moment comes, which comes but rarely in history, when we step out from the old to the new, when an age ends, and when the soul of a nation, long suspended, finds utterance.

"At the dawn of history India started on the her unending quest, and trackless centuries are filled with her striving and the grandeur of her success and failures. Through good and ill fortune alike she has never lost sight of the quest of forgotten the ideals which gave her strength. We end today a period of ill fortune and India discovers herself again. The achievement we celebrate today is but a step, an offering of opportunity of the greater triumphs and achievements that await us. That future is not one of ease or resting but of incessant striving so that we may fulfil the pledges we have so often taken and the one we shall take today. The service of India means the service of the millions who suffer....And so we have to labour and to work and work hard to give reality to our dreams. Those dreasm are for India, but they are also for the world....Peace has been said to be indivisible, so is freedom, so is prosperity now, and so also is disaster in this One World that can no longer be split into isolated fragments."

The Assembly resolved that the members should take the following pledge:

"At this solemn moment when the people of India through suffering and sacrifice, have secured freedom, I...., a member of the Constituent Assembly of India, do dedicate myself in all humility to the service of India and her people to the end that this ancient land attain her rightful place in the world and make her full and willing contribution to the promotion of world peace and the welfare of mankind."

Dr. Rajendra Prasad observed: "Let us, on this historic occasion, pay our homage to the maker of our modern history, Mahatma Gandhi, who has inspired us and guided through all those years of trial and travail and who in spite of the weight of years, is still working in his own way to complete what is left yet unaccomplished." Acharya Kripalani, the Congress President, gave the following message to the nation : "This revolution which has ushered in the birth of freedom for this land is a unique one in the history of the world. Never before was so great an event transforming the destiny of many millions of men and women consummated with such little bloodshed and violence. This is a triumph, not of one brute force over another, but of the spirit of freedom and humanity over the blinding greed of imperialism. That this has been possible is due to the inspiring leadership of Mahatma Gandhi, who, if any man may be so called, is Father of our Nation. He has led us in the non-violent battle for freedom and he has shown us the way to make this freedom fruitful in the service of our people. To him we pay our homage."

Why England gave India Independence?

There were many reasons which forced the British Government to grant independence to India and the most important was the strength of the nationalist movement. That movement under the leadership of Mahatma Gandhi had become so strong that the grant of independence could not be postponed for long. The "Quit India" Movement had shown that the people of India could go to any length to bring to an end the British Raj in the country. They made tremendous sacrifices to paralyse the administrative machinery. The slogans : "Do of Die" and "Now of Never" resounded in the ears of the British Government. The organisation of the Indian National Army under Subhas Chandra Bose and the cry of Dilli Chalo made the British government realise the folly of resisting for long the demand of the people of India for independence.

Throughout, Great Britain had relied upon force and military superiority for maintaining its hold over India. Force was always avaiiable to crush any revolt in any part of the country. However, circumstances changed during the Second World War. The loyalty of the Indian troops could not be taken for granted. Lakhs of Indians from all over India joined the armed forces during the War. They not only fought for the victory of the Allied Powers but also hoped that India would achieve indepedence after the War. They were willing to give a helping hand to the nationalist movement in the country.

In January 1946, the British authorities had to face a mutiny among the British. The ground and maintenance units at Dum Dum Airport near Calcutta and at other Royal Air Force stations in India and the Middle East mutinied over delays in repatriation and demobilisation. The great majority of men were civilian conscripts who were anxious to go back home. They did not offer any violence to their officers but in Calcutta the service Chiefs had troops standing by. The mutineers received reassurance from a visiting Labour Member of Parliament about their repatriation and demobilisation and they returned to work. However, the question arose whether an army consisting almost entirely of unwilling conscripts could be kept in India and used on riot and other duties of a like nature. Another question was whether a Labour Prime Minister was prepared to extend the military service of the sons of the Englishmen who were his principal supporters in order to shoot down Indians.

The Royal Indian Air Force also became insubordinate and went to the extent of declaring their sympathy with the members of the Indian National Army. In February 1946, a number of ratings of the Royal Indian Navy at Bombay refused to eat or attend parade. On the next day, 3000 Indian sailors mutinied on board their ships and in barracks ashore. They removed their officers who were all Englishmen and attacked British soldiers in the streets of Bombay and roamed about in the city in lorries covered with slogans and flags of the Congress and the Muslim League. On the next day they tried to break out and the troops guarding them opened fire. Some ratings attacked the Indian soldiers with small arms and grenades. The British Air Force was alerted but was not used. The mutineers who had remained in ships in the harhour trained their guns on the city and threatened to bombard it. A broadhast appeal by the Admiral commanding was received with derision. Congress leaders, particularly Patel who was in Bombay at that time, asked the mutineers to surrender and they did so. However, there were civil riots and disorder for four days in the city of Bombay. There was a very serious mutiny of the navy at Karachi and the military commander turned artillery on the mutineers and there was a lot of loss of life. From these happenings, the British government concluded that it was not possible to hold India with the help of force and hence the decision was taken to give India independence.

After the end of the Second World War, the British authorities decided to try Col. Shah Nawaz, Captain Sehgal and Lt. Dhillon and other members of the Indian National Army for waging war against the King-Emperor before a Court Martial. There was a lot of agitation in the country against the decision of the Government. On 22 September, 1945, the Congress Working Committee appointed a committee to defend the I.N.A. men. the trial started on 5 November, 1945 in the Red Fort of Delhi and lasted upto 31 December. The decision was announced on 3 January, 1946 and Shah Nawaz,

Sehgal and Dhillon were found guilty and sentenced to transportation for life. Many more trials were held and the accused were found guilty. During the trial, the sufferings of the I.N.A. officers and men came to light. The arguments put forward by the defence counsel were published in the newspapers and read by millions of Indians. Shah Nawaz, Sehgal and Dhillon became popular heroes. There were mass demonstrations thoughout the country for their release. On certain occasions, the police resorted to firing and many Indians lost their lives. The result was that Field Marshal Auchinleck, Commander-in-Chief of India, granted clemency to Shah Nawaz, Sehgal and Dhillon. On 2 May, 1946, the Government of India announced its decision not to proceed any further with the trials and consequently cases against the rest of the I.N.A. men were withdrawn. After their release, the I.N.A. officers and men turned all over the country and they were greeted with cries of "Jai Hind". So great was the enthusiasm among the people that the English began to feel that it was not possible for them to keep India in chains.

It had been instilled in the minds of Indian fighters that the British forces were invincible. However, this impression was removed during the Second World War as a result of the military reverses suffered by the British troops at the hands of the Japanese. British troops were forced to avacuate Hong Kong, Singapore, Malaya and Burma. Their best ships "The Repulse" and "Prince of Wales" were sunk. Great Britain was not in a position "to demonstrate in Asia that background of strength and influence which had for so long enabled her to rule a million people with one man on the spot."

Great Britain had to spend so much during the Second World War that she was completely exhausted. She was forced to borrow on an enormous scale. She had to depend upon other countries not only for food-stuffs but also for raw-materials to run her factories. She depended upon American help in every field. It was felt that it was not wise to keep herself involved in India when all her energy was required at home. The American government also put pressure on the British government to grant Indian independence as the Allied Powers had been fighting for freedom and democracy. Even diehards like Churchill began to feel that it was of no avail to keep India under bondage.

Soon after the war, a scheme was prepared to recruit Europeans for service in India but the same had to be given up on account of opposition from Indians. The control of Britain over the Indian army was weakening rapidly as a result of the Indianisation of the Indian army. The British Army troops in India were decreasing at a considerable rate on account of demobilisation after the war. Very soon, most of them had to be discharged. As far as the British Army was concerned, the Labour Government could not extend the service of war-time conscripts. There was also heavy pressure from their parents at home that they must be called back to their country. There were no prospects of Englishmen of Europeans opting for service in India as there was no secure future for them on account of the conditions prevailing in the country. The result of all these factors was that the British Government decided to withdraw from India and give her independence.

Lord Attlee, Prime Minister of England who played an important part in the transfer of power to India had always taken keen interest in the Indian affairs. When he became Prime Minister of England in 1945, he came to the conclusion that even if Great Britain was able to keep India in bondage with the help of force, it was not in her interest to do so as thereby she was bound to lose the goodwill of the people of India. The Indo-British relations were bound to suffer in the long run. His view was that Great Britain would definitely gain if she was able to win the goodwill of the people of India by granting them independence.To begin with, he sent the Cabinet Mission to India but when that failed to deliver the goods, he sent Lord Mountbatten to complete the process of transfer of power in India.

Michael Edwardes writes that Prime Minister Attlee was very conscious as the first Labour Prime Minister with a working majority, that his primary responsibility was to those who had elected him to office. Labour voters were demanding a new deal and the fulfilment of long stated promises. It seemed that Britain could be re-made into a socialist paradise and all pressures for doctrinaire reforms were on the Prime Minister. It is one of the coincidences of history that as a party came to power ready for sacrifice, there appeared to sensible men no alternative but sacrifice and that implied the grant of Independence to India.

Another reason why Great Britain decided to leave India was that she got involved in the cold war after the Second World War. The Russians had an edge over the Americans in the cold war in pointing out the fact that Great Britain was still keeping India in chains. It would raise Great Britain in the eyes of the world if she granted Indian independence.

A large number of persons advocated the cause of India's freedom abroad. Among them were Louis Fischer, Pearl Buck, Lin Yutang, Norman Thomas and J.J. Singh. The Indian view-point was put forward before the Conference at San Francisco which met to finalise the Charter of the united Nations. Great Britain was not only a signatory of the Charter but her delegates played an important part in framing it. This fact was bound to affect the attitude of British Government towards India. Another factor which influenced the British decision to leave India was a change in the concept of the British Commonwealth. In July 1947, the Commonwealth Relations Office was set up. If Great Britain could treat other Dominions in that manner, there was no reason why the same could not be done with regard to India. It was felt that even after India had won her independence, she could be persuaded to be a member of the Commonwealth of Nations and thus be allied to Great Britain on an equal footing. The view of Maulana Azad was that the British Government decided to leave India only after making sure that she would continue to have a foothold on the Indian subcontinent. The British decision to partition India and then to transfer power was the culmination of the policy of "divide and rule". The partition of India in which the Muslim majority provinces formed a separate and independent state would give Britain a foothold in India. We are reliably informed by some respectable Indians who returned to India from England during the year immediately following the end of the Second World War that British soldiers who had first hand knowledge of the poverty of the Indian masses spoke about it feelingly to their friends and relatives. That knowledge filtered down to the people. A feeling was created in England that perhaps with independence, the Indians might be able to improve their economic condition.

The view of Prime Minister Attlee was that the independence of India was the fulfilment of Britain's mission in India. The British were leaving India after fulfilling their mission in the country. They had taught the Indians to govern themselves and they were now leaving the reins of Government in their hands.

As early as 1838 Sir Charles Trevelyn had written about the future of the British Empire in India in these words, "I passed some years in parts of India where, owing to the comparative novelty of our rule and to the absence of any attempt to alter the current of native feelings, the national habit of thinking remained unchanged. There, high and low, rich and poor, had only one idea of improving their political condition. The upper classes live upon the prospect of regaining their former pre-eminence; and the lower, upon that having the avenues to wealth and distinction reopened to them by the re-establishment of a native government. Even sensible and comparatively well-affected natives had not notion that there was no remedy for the existing depressed state of their nation except the sudden and absolute expulsion of the English. After that I resided for some years in Bengal and there I found quite another set of ideas prevalent among the educated natives. Instead of thinking of cutting the throats of the English, they were aspiring to sit with them on the bench of magistrates. The most sanguine dimly look forward in the distant future to the establishment of a national representative assembly as the consummation of their hopes—all of them being fully sensible that these plans of improvement could only be worked out with the aid and protection of the British Government by the gradual improvement of their countrymen in knowledge and morality... No doubt both these schemes of national improvement suppose the termination of the English rule, but while that event is the beginning of one, it is only the conclusion of the other. In one the sudden and violent overthrow of our government is necessary preliminary; in the other a long continuance of our administration and the gradual withdrawl of it as the people become fit to govern themselves, are equally indispensable."

The independence of India was the result of three movements which appeared to run parallel.

(1) First was the Gandhian movement of non-violent non-cooperation which caused such an unprecedented upsurge among the masses that the British Raj could be sustained only at the point of the sword.

(2) The second was the ballot box revolution which contributed to the awakening of political consciousness among the people. The debates in the legislature, being mostly directed against the Government, provided ammunition to the Gandhians who were out to rouse mass enthusiasm for freedom.

(3) The third factor was that the two World Wars made Britain so weak economically that it became impossible for her to defend her far-flung Empire. The increasing pressure from the United States for the liquidations of colonialism made Britain see the wisdom of cutting her losses and withdrawing from her overseas possessions.

LORD MOUNTBATTEN

In March 1947 Lord Wavell was succeeded by Lord Mountbatten. The situation of India was very critical at the time. Communal riots were taking place in almost this whole country. Lord Mountbatten thought that this problem can be effectively solved only by completing the work of transfer of power into the Indian hands with in as short a period as possible. After consulting the Indian leaders he left for London in May, 1947 for consultation with the British Government. He returned to India on June 1, 1947. On June 3, 1947 he published his plan of the Division of India into two independent state through Radio Broadcast.

Provisions of Plan

1. Bengal and Punjab were to be divided into two parts-one consisting of Hindu majority and the other consisting of

Muslim majority, According to the plan the members of the provincial Legislatures of the said Hindu and Muslim areas were to decide whether the devision should take place or not, In case they were of the opinion that the division should not take place they were also to decide whether they would merge with India or Pakistan.

2. It was also decided to take the views of the people Sclbat District in Assam as to whether they would like to live in Eastern or western Bengal.

3. It was also decided to complete the work of transfer of power into the Indian hands immediately instead of doing so in June 1948.

4. It case of division a commission was to be appointed for demarcating the boundary line.

5. Since the congress was in majority in the Fronter Province the people of the province were to be given one more opportunity for deciding whether they wished to live with India or Pakistan.

The plan of Mountbatten for the Division of the country was accepted by the congress as well as the Muslim League, Pt. Jawahar Lal Nehru and Muhammad Ali Jinnah accepted the said plan on behalf of the Congress and Muslim League respectively.

Indian Independence Act of 1947. The British Parliament passed the Indian Independence Act 1947 on June 15th, 1947. In accordance with the Act on 15th August 1947 India was divided into two parts one was named India and the other was named Pakistan. India be came an independent country on 15th August 1947. Thus the whole property of the Government became divided into two parts and on August 15, 1947 the two independent Governments came into existence with there capitals at Delhi and Karachi respectively. Lord Mountbatten was again made the Governor-General of India but the post of viceroy was abolished. The words of Lord Pathic Lawrence former secretary of state for India are worth nothing in connection with the transfer of power to India.

What a wonderful chapter of human history "and how differently it might have turned out but for the courage and wisdom of the principal actors, where so many have given so much it may seem invidous to single cut individual names, yet I feel I must pay special tribute to those Indians who have filled so worthily the principal roles. To Mahatma Gandhi who stood unflinchingly for Indian independence and who to once partition was decided upon threw his life into the seales to 'prevent civil strife; to Shri Raja Gopalachari, the eminent citizen of Madras the first Indian Governor-General who storve with out ceasing to effect a settlement both between the British and India between Muslims and Hindus : to Sardar Vallabhbhai Patel Deputy Primeminister who so brilliantly achieved his ambition to bring into a united whole the provinces and the states of India, Last but not least, to the Prime, Minister Pandit Nehru son of an illustrious father, who by his far-seeing wisdom, has won the respect both of his own country men and the people of the world. So long as India continues to produce men and women of their calibre I have no fear her future."

LORD MOUNTBATTEN FIRST GOVERNOR GENERAL OF FREE INDIA

In accordance with the Indian independence Act of 1947 India was finally divided in to two independent dominions India and Pakistan, Lord Mountbatten was made the first Governor-General of free India. The following were the main events of his time:

1. Communal Riots and the Problems of the Refugees. Inspite of the division of the country, the communal feelings of the Muslim league did not subside. This, lead to the bloodshed which was caused in an unprecedented scale in the areas which it has acquired after the partition. It had its repercussions and reaction in India also. A large number of innocent persons were killed in Punjab and Bengal. The problem of the transfer of the population was very pressing. Likewise many Muslims also left India for Pakistan. Rehabilitation of such a large number of refugees was a gragantic task.

2. Merger of the Native States in to the Union of India. The British had not given any clear decision with regard to the position of the native states. They were left free to merge either with India or Pakistan. The problem of the merger of native states was most skilfully and efficiently solved by Sardar Vallabha Bhai Patel. He made three plans regarding the merger of the Indian States. In accordance with the first plan 219 small states were merged with the neighbouring provinces, According to she second plan 22 states were merged in the territories adminstered by the central Government and according to the third plan 291 states were joined with in Federation. Big Princes or Rajas were made Raj Pramukhs. In each Federation, a Legislative Assembly and an elected cabinet were established. Privy purse was fixed to be given to the native princes.

Hydrabad. After the declaration of the independence the native states were left free to merge either with India or Pakistan or they could maintain their independent status. This created a very difficult situation in case of certain big states like Hyderabad, Junagarh, Kashmir etc. Hyderabad was surrounded from all sides by the provinces of the Indian this on and 20 per cent of its population consisted of Hindus. But the Nizam did not want to merge his state with the union of India also. Hence the Nizam declared that Hyderabed will remain as an independent state. Communal feeling were being formented in the state. Talks for compromise continue for a long time between the two Governments. It was decided that the relations existing between the two Governments before 15th August, 1947 will continue to exist. Both the Governments agreed to send their reprentatives to see whether the terms of agreements were being implemented or not. The Nizam was entitled to send his ambassadors in foreign countries but could not purchase arms and ammunitions from any foreign country and the same will be supplied by the Government of India. In the event of war the Government of India would be entitled to keep its army in the State of Nizam.

Kashmir. Being situated on the border of India and Pakistan the state of Kashmir had great political significance. The state was ruled by a Hindu king but the muslims were in majority in the state. A difficult problem arose at the time of partition with regard to the merger of the state of Kashmir. Both India and Pakistan wanted to merge Kashmir in their respective union. Pakistan started propogating that the Hindu ruler of the state was trealing the Muslim population there most unjuslty. A section of the population of Kashmir which had sympathy for Pakistan wanted Kashmir to merge with Pakistan. This section started revolts in the state being encouraged by the leaders of Pakistan the tribal people attacked Kashmir; This attack was backed, by the Pakistan regular army. The freedom loving Kashmiri's could not tolrate this attack. They sought the help of India. The ruler of Kashmir requested for the merger of his state into the union of India. The Indian army was sent to Kashmir to defend it against the Pakistan intruders. The ruler of Kashmir immediately announced the formation of a Government under the Premiership of Sheikh Abdullah. It was also decided to hold elections in order to know the opinion of the people for merger after the aggressors had been repulsed and peace established in Kashmir.

Pakistan was not prepared to accept that it had any hand in the attack of Kashmir. It said that Azad Kashmir Government which had been established was conducting the War. The Government of India took the dispute of Kashmir before the Security Council of the U.N.O. India charged Pakistan with allowing the way through its territory to the aggressors, allowing them of having their centres in Pakistan, supplying them with petrol and arms and ammunitions, the aggressors being trained by the Pakistani officers and that the citizens of Pakistan were also among the aggressors. After a long debate which lasted for several days it was decided to send a commission which was first to stop war and then to arrange for impartial elections in order to know the opinion of the people with regard to the merger. International situation have became so compilcated that there is no possibility of an early solution of this problem.

3. Death of Mahatma Gandhi and the Departure of Lord Mountbatten. A section of Orthodox Hindus did not like Mahatma Gandhi for his liberal attitude towards the Muslims. On January 30th 1948 in the evening when Gandhiji was going to attend the prayer meeting as usual, a Maratha named Nathu Ram Godse short four bullets at Gandhiji. Gandhiji at once collapsed on the spot and died in

the night. The whole India, hay the whole world was shocked to hear the news of the death of Gandhiji. Prominent leaders of the world paid their homage to the great leader who had lived and died for the good and welfare of the whole mankind. He died when the country was passing through a very critical situation and when his guidence was needed most urgently.

FACTORS RESPONSIBLE FOR INDIA'S PARTITION

It was in the year 1947 that the country was partitioned between India and Pakistan. Different opinions have been advanced regarding the inevitability of partition. Maulana Azad advanced the opinion that Partition was never inescapable, that it was the conscientious choice of the nationalist leaders like Patel and Nehru. Other writers are of the opinion that the events between July 1946 and March 1947 had proved that partition was inevitable. Lord Mountbatten immediately after his arrival in Delhi became convinced that partition was the only solutioin of Indian problem. Mahatma Gandhi was bitterly opposed to the idea of partition. Nehru and Patel accepted it and persuaded even Mahatma Gandhi to reconcile with it. There must be certain factors why both these personalities did accept it. The main factors responsible for partition were as follows:

(1) Uncompromising Attitude of Jinnah. The nationalist leaders mainly directed their energies against the British and they wrongly assumed that communal tangle was a temporary phase. They earnestly desired to find an amicable settlement : with the Muslim League. Some attempts were made in vain in this respect. Rather every effort of theirs made Jinnah the more uncompromising. Jinnah wanted to exploit of the Congress desire for a peaceful settlement of communal problem. He was not ready to accept any settlement which did not promise him Pakistan of his own conception. Cabinet Mission Plan also failed because of his uncompromising attitude. In order to realise his objective Jinnah resorted to baser methods. He talked of British treachery and British-Congress collusion against the Muslims. The differences between League and Congress reached their climax. Every effort at peaceful solution was exhausted and Congress found that Jinnah was too adamant to be set right.

(2) **Communal Riots.** In July 1946 League decided to observe a Direct Action day. The destructive forces were set in motion and communal passions rose high. The observance of 'Direct Action Day' on August 16 led to numerous killings in Calcutta which filled the country with a thrill of horror. The Calcutta riots were followed by the risings in Noakhali where Muslims buthered the Hindus mercilessly. Murders and riots continued for about a year in the whole country and the Congress leaders drew the inference that partition was better than the murder of innocent citizens.

(3) **Failure of Interim Government.** On 15th October, 1946 was formed the interim government. It had five League nominees. Immediately after its formation it became another battle front between the League and the Congress. The chief trouble came from Liaqat Ali who was the Finance Minister of the Interim Government. He rejected or delayed the proposals made by the Congress members. The Congress members soon found out that they could not create the post of a peon without the concurrance of Liaquat Ali. The Government was thus paralysed and the Congress members were now convinced that they could not work with the League. The nationalists now thought that partition was necessary as they could not run any government with the League in future.

(4) **British Attitude on Transfer of Power.** The British gave the threat that they would leave the country by June 1948 whether in peace or in chaos. The nationalists were now to make a choice between the two evils, either to accept a civil war or a partition. They chose the lesser evil, *i.e.* partition of the country. Thus partition became inevitable. In 1956 Mr. Nehru remarked, "The partition of India became inevitable. I think now looking back, that partition

could have been avoided if the British Government Policy had been different."

(5) **Feeling Regarding the Impermanency of the Partition.** In certain political circles it was hoped that partition would prove short-lived. Very soon the area would reunite. Such a hope was expressed by Acharya Kriplani. It is probable that the nationalists might have accepted it as a temporary solution of Indian problem.

(6) **Enforced Unity was Neither Desirable nor Advisable.** It was thought neither desirable nor advisable to keep a section of the Muslims with the union when they were very much desirous to secede. It was also a feeling that the union achieved by force would not be stable and permanent. Secondly it was also against the Democratic procedure. Thirdly it was felt that their inclusion would hamper the progress of India. Nehru told his colleagues frankly, if they (the League) are forced to stay in India, no progress and planning would be possible." The same view was expressed by Sardar Patel in All India Congress Committee Session on June 15, 1947, "If one limb its poisoned it must be removed quickly least the entire organism suffer irreparably." Thus important nationalist leaders accepted that partition was inevitable.

(7) **Influence of Lord and Lady Mountbatten.** Lord Mountbatten, a man of pleasing and powerful personality suceeded in convincing Sarder Patel who accepted partition, Nehru too was convinced. In convincing Nehru to the idea of partition Lady Mountbatten also played an important role. She organised garden parties for this lonely man.

PARTITION OF INDIA

There were many factors which were responsible for the partition of India. The main cause was the isolationist policy followed by the Muslims in India. Under the influence of Sir Syed Ahmed Khan, the Muslims of India began to think and dream separately from the Hindus. They started feeling that their interests were different from those of the Hindus and they had nothing in common with them. They went to the extent of saying that their interests were oppossed to those of the Hindus. If India was given a responsible Government. Hindu majority was bound to dominate the Muslims in India who were in a minority in the country as a whole. The Muslims also felt that they were educationally backward and consequently could not compete with the Hindus. With the passage of time, they drifted more and more away from the Hindus. The Muslims League ideology also estranged the Muslims from the Hindus. Sir Mohammad Iqbal and Mr. M.A. Jinnah put before the Muslims the ideal of setting up a separate state for the Muslims. Particularly after the passing of the Pakistan Resolution in March 1940, the Muslims insisted that they wanted a separate homeland and were not prepared to come to any compromise with the Hindus.

There is no denying the fact that the Muslims were helped immensely by the British Government in India. After the revolt of 1857, the Government of India was in search of allies in the country to stabilize its position against those who were out to drive it away and they found the Indian princes, Zamindars and the Indian Muslims ready to cooperate with them. The Government of India followed the policy of "divide and rule" and kept on favouring the Muslims even at the cost of other communities in India. Bengal was partitioned in 1905 to please the Muslims. The Muslims were given assurances about their future by Lord Minto in 1906 when a deputation of the Muslims waited on him. In 1909, the Muslims were given separate representation. Seats were reserved for them not only in the legislatures but also in the Executive Council of the Governor-Gerneral. Whatever was offered by the Congress to win over the Muslims, the Government of India and the British Government were always ready and willing to offer them more. Under these circumstances the Muslims of India began to look to the British government for everything and were not in a mood to come to any compromise with the Congress or the Hindus. That is what happened on the occasion of the second Round Table Conference and on many other occasions. The British bureaucracy was determined to have its revenge against the Hindus who were fighting for the liberation of their country. The British were determined to crush the nationalist movement in India and if they failed in their efforts, they were determined to divide the country in such a way that it was not worthwhile for the Hindus to have their freedom. It was this attitude which was responsible for the partition of the India. It is well-known that the British bureaucracy in India helped the Muslim League agitation in 1946 and 1947. As a matter of fact, it was this encouragement which helped the Muslim Leagues to hold their demonstrations without any interference or oppression from the side of the British Government. This attitude may be compared with the treatments meted out to the Hindu agitators who were not only beaten mercilessly and put in prison but also actually shot dead on many occasions.

The communal malady grew into unproportioned height and ultimately led to the division of India. the Congress unfortunately never tried to understand the Muslim character of isolation and aggression and, to the end, continued to dally with the false hopes that somehow or other some turn of event would remove communal problem." The same author points out that even in the hour of the division of India, the Congress preferred to indulge in self-deception: "The All India Congress Committee trusted that when present passions subsided, India's problems would be viewed in their proper perspective and the false doctrine of two nations would be discredited and discarded by all." The initial mistake was made by the Indian national Congress in 1916 when it signed the Lucknow Pact. It ought not to have agreed to give the Muslims a fixed percentage of representatives in the legislatures. The Congress attitude towards the Communal Award of 1932 also helped the isolationist policy of the Muslims. Nobody doubts the patriotism of the Congressmen but the fact remains that the Congress policy of appeasement of the Muslims ultimately led to the partitioning of India.

It is true that the Cabinet Mission Scheme ruled out the idea of Pakistan and made provision for a Constitutent Assembly which was to frame a constitution for free India. However, the Muslim League was allowed to join the Interim Government Without committing itself to take part in the deliberations of the Constituent Assembly. Its members in the Interim Government refused to cooperate with the non-Muslim members. They proclaimed their loyalty to the Viceroy whose appointees and nominees they considered themselves to be. They openly talked of carving out a Pakistan. The divison among the members of the Interim Government was reflected in the whole administrative machinery. According to the Report of the General Secretaries of the Indian National Congress, "If the Civil Services, the police and the army became divided in their loyalty and their members functioned on communal lines nothing but mischief and chaos in the administration could result. The Muslim League members of the Interim Government removed the Hindu and Sikh officers from the key posts in their departments and put in their places Muslims who could be depended upon to help the cause of Pakistan.

During the tenure of the Interim Government that communal riots took place on a large scale. "The ever-increasing and ever-deepening chain of communal disturbances involving mass murder, arson or loot accompanied by unthinkable atrocities and horrors obliged the Working Committee of the Indian National Congress to consider the whole communal and political situation afresh." The only way out of the difficulty appeared to be the partitioning of India. Jawaharlal Nehru referred to this fact in these words on June 3, 1947 : "There has been violence shameful, degrading and revolting violence in various parts of this country. This must end." The Congress was not happy about the partitioning of the country as it had consistently fought for the liberation of united India. The following words of Jawaharlal Nehru give an idea of the working of his inner mind : "For generations we have dreamt and struggled for a free and independent, united India."

The announcement of the British Government on February 20, 1947 that it was determined to put power into the hands of the Indians at a very early date worsened the communal situation in the country and helped the cause of Pakistan. While making the declaration, "His Majesty's Government had hoped that it would be possible for the major parties to cooperate in the working out of the

Cabinet Mission's Plan of May 1946 and evolve for India a constitution acceptable to all concerned." However, that hope was not fulfilled as no pressure was put on the Muslim League to take part in the deliberations of the Constituent Assembly. The British Government also accepted the point of view of the Muslim League that the grouping of the provinces under the Cabinet Mission Scheme was compulsory. It appears that it was felt by the Congress leaders in the month of May 1947 that the partition of India was absolutely inevitable. "The Congress had to choose between partition and continuance of a state of affairs which was becoming more and more intolerable. To quote Sarder Patel, "I felt that if we did not accept partition, India would be split into many bits and would be completely ruined. My experience of office for one year convinced me that the way we have been proceeding would lead us to disaster. We would not have had one Pakistan but several. We would have had Pakistan cells in every office." Again, "It was then that I was made fully conscious of the extent to which our interests were being prejudiced everywhere by the machin nations of the Political Department, and came to the conclusion that the best course was to hasten the departure of these foreigners even at the cost of the partition of the country. It was also then that I felt that there was the unification of the rest of India."

Regarding the question of partition of India, Dr. R.C. Majumdar writes that its accptance by Gandhiji and other prominent Congress leaders like Nehru and Patel is generally regarded as inexcusable and inexplicable and many look upon it as a sudden and unexpected decision at the last moment which plunged India into unspeakable misery. Such a view is based on the fact that those leaders were always guided by a false nation of Indian nationality based on Hindu-Muslims unity and persuaded the poeople to ignore the reality and cherished the idea. However, those who carefully review the history of Hindu-Muslim relations, Pakistan can only be regarded as the logical culmination of political developments in India. There were fundamental differences between the Hindus and Muslims of India which stood in the way of fusing them into one nation. This was emphasised by the separate electorates, originally devised by Lord Minto and later on accepted by the Congress. Since then, the Congress had, in practice if not in theory recognised the two-nation theory propounded by Sir Syed Ahmad Khan in the 19th century and Mr. M.A. Jinnah in the 20th century. As far back as 1934, the Congress plegded itself to reject any scheme of solving the communal problem vis-a-vis the Indian constitution which was not agreed to by the Muslims. In 1942, Gandhiji wrote in the Harijan that if the vast majority of the Muslims want to partition India, they must have the partition. In 1945, the Congress Working Committee passed a resolution that it could not think "off compelling the people in any territorial unit to remain in an Indian Union against their declared and established will." Rajagopalachari actually suggested the idea of Pakistan as the only basis for a peaceful settlement of the Hindu-Muslim problem. Even Nehru conceded the possibility of Pakistan in January 1946. Early in March 1947, the Working Committee of the Congress itself suggested the partitioin of the Punjab and Bengal on communal basis.

The Simla talks in 1945 were probably the last chance of getting the League to accept something short of full Pakistan, The Cripps offer of 1942 the last chance for the Congress to smother the League before it became a formidable mass movement. But there is another point to remember before too much regret is felt for the lost unity of India. The federal provisions of the Cripps and later proposals so reduced the powers of the Central Government that it is very doubtful if the great developments of Nehru's India would have been possible under them. It is probable that the centre would have been weak, and political energy spent by the communities in jostling for position instead of re-organising the country. Industrial development would have waited on party tactics, and five-year plans on political polemics. Only a joint directorate of the two parties could have achieved the kind of development which has actually occurred, and of this there was never any sign. However much partition may be regretted in principle, it was perhaps necessary, on this account, in the larger interests of the country." The view of Dr. Lal Bahadur is :

"The partition of India was an event of great importance. It ushered in an era of independence, though the enthusiasm for it was somewhat diminished due to division. Had India remained a united whole, the Mussalmans would surely have dominated and would have shared in the amenities of life more than their due. Right traditions could never have developed as at every step special claims of the Mussalmans would have been advanced. They would have taken roots only if homage was not paid to Muslim appeasement. But seeing the history of the Indian National Congress this would have been impossible... But as it never understood Muslim mind and character, it also never adhered to principles in its dealing with Mussalmans. Expendiency always came in operation in its treatment with the Muslims. The territorial integrity of India could be a benefit to the country only in the event of equal treatment to all and in the absence of Muslim appeasement policy. Since the Congress was incapable of doing if, the division of the country cannot be seriously lamented."

❐

10

Nehru Report

The Secretary of State for India had thrown a challenge that the Indians could not produce a Constitution acceptable to all the parties. In December 1926, the Indian National Congress directed its Working Committee to convene an All India All-Parties Conference for the purpose of drawing up a Constitution for India. Invitations were sent to a number of organisations and the All-Parties Conference met at Delhi in February and March, 1928 to discuss the question of a Constitution for India on the basis of full responsible Government. Many meetings were held, but nothing came out of them on account of the attitude of the members, representing the Hindu Mahasabha and the Muslim League. The Conference met again at Bombay on 19 May 1928. There also it was found that the differences could not be reconciled. In spite of that the Conference appointed a small Committee under the Chairmanship of Motilal Nehru "to determine the principles of the new Constitution for India and draft a report thereon." Sir Imam Ali and Shuaib Qureshi represented the Muslims. M.S. Aney and M.R. Jayakar represented the Hindu Mahasabha, G.R. Pradhan represented the non-Brahmins, Sardar Mangal Singh represented the Sikh League, Sir Tej Bahadur Sapru represented the Liberal Party and N.M. Joshi represented labour. Subhas Chandra Bose and Jawaharlal Nehru were also its members, with Jawaharlal Nehru, who was at that time the General Secretary of the Congress, as the secretary of the Committee. The report submitted by the Committee is known as the Nehru report.

The recommendation of the Nehru Report was that the future Constitution of India should be based on "full responsible Government on the model of the Constitution of the self-governing Dominions."

The grant of Dominion Status should be the next immediate step and not "a remote stage of our evolution." It was declared that "In theory, separate electorates violated the essential principles of responsible government; in practice, they had failed to pave the way to a better understanding between the communities. They should be discarded therefore, and all elections made by joint or mixed electorates." No other safeguard was granted to any other community or group, except to the Non-Muslims in the North-West Frontier Province. No seats were to be reserved for Muslims in provinces where they were in a majority. Seats were to be reserved for them in the provinces where they were in a minority and also at the Centre The North-West-Frontier Province, with a Muslim population of over 90%, was to be given the status of a Province. Sind, with a Muslim majority of over 70% was to be detached from the Bombay Presidency and created a separate Province.

The Constitution of India was to be federal in character and the Indian states were welcomed to join it. However, if they refused to join it, their "claims must not obstruct the advance of the Dominion Status." They must accept the same position in the new Commonwealth of India, as they occupied at present in the Indian Empire." It was stated that all treaties made between the East India Company and the Indian States and all such subsequent treaties, so far as they were in force, would be binding on the Commonwealth of India, which would exercise the same right in relation to and discharge the same obligations towards the Indian States as the Government of India exercised and discharged previously.

Provision was made for a Parliament of two Houses : Senate and House of Representatives. The Senate was to consist of 200 members elected by the Provincial Councils. The House of Representatives was to consist of 500 members who were to be elected on the basis of adult franchise. The life of the Senate was to be seven years and that of the House of Representatives five years. the Parliament of India was empowered to legislate and budget for the Indian Army which was to be put under an Indian Defence Minister.

The Governor-General was to be appointed by the British Government, but he was to be paid out of the Indian revenues. His salary was not to be altered during his continuance in office. He was to act on the advice of the Executive Council. The Prime Minister was to be appointed by the Governor-General and the other Ministers were to be appointed by the Governor-General on the advice of the Prime Minister. The Govenor-General in-Council was to appoint High Commissions and other foreign representatives similar to those appointed by Canada and other Dominions. The Central Executive was to be collectively responsible to Parliament. The Governor-General-in-Council was to appoint a Committee on Defence consisting of Minister of Defence, Minister of Foreign Affairs. Commander-in-Chief of the Air Force, Commander of Naval Forces, Chief of the General Staff and two other experts. The functions of the Committee were to advise the Government and the various Departments concerned on the questions of defence and general policy.

All officers of public services at the time of the establishment of the Commonwealth were to become officers of the Commonwealth. The Governor-General was to appoint a Public Service Commission. All officers of the Army services were to retain all their existing rights regarding the salaries, allowances and pensions.

Provision was made for a Supreme Court of India which was to consist of Lord President and other Justices. The Justices of the Supreme Court were to be appointed by the Governor-General-in-Council and they were not liable to be removed from office except on an address from both Houses of Parliament praying for such removal on the ground of misbehaviour or incapacity.

The Governors of the Provinces were to be appointed by the King of England. Provision was made for a Legislative Council elected on adult franchise. The Legislative Council was to sit for five years, but it could be dissolved earlier by the Governor, who was also given the authority to extend the life of the Legislative Council under special circumstances. Provision was made for a President and a Vice-President of the Legislative Council. The Governor was to act on the advice of the Executive Council whose number was not to exceed five. He was to appoint the Chief Minister, But the other members of the Executive Council were to be appointed by him on the advice of the Chief Minister.

Provision was made in the Report for nineteen fundamental rights which were to be embodied in the statute. No person shall be deprived of his liberty nor shall his dwelling or property be entered, requestered or confiscated, save in accordance with law. Freedom of conscience and free profession and practice of religion shall be guaranteed to all. The right of free expression of opinion and the right of assembling peacefully and without arms and to form associations or unions shall be guaranteed for purposes not opposed to public order or morality. All citizens shall have the right to free elementary education. All citizens shall be equal before law and possess equal civic rights. There shall be no penal law of a discriminatory nature. No person shall be punishable for any act which is not punishable under the law at the time when the offence is committed. No corporal punishment or other punishment involving torture of any kind shall be lawful. Every citizen shall have the right of a writ of Habeas Corpus. There shall be no state religion for the Commonwealth of India or for any Province, nor shall any State endow any religion or give preference to any religion.No person shall, by reason of his religion, caste or creed, be prejudiced in any manner in regard to public employment, office or power or honour and the exercise of any trade or calling. All citizens shall have an equal right of access to and use of public roads, public wells and all other places of public resort. Freedom of combination and association for maintenance and improvement of labour and economic conditions shall be guaranteed to every one. All agreements and measures tending to restrict or obstruct such freedom shall be illegal. No breach of contract of service or abetment shall be made a criminal offence. Parliament shall make suitable laws for the maintenance of health and fitness for work of all citizens, securing of a living wage for every worker, the protection of motherhood, welfare of children and the economic consequences of old age, infirmity and unemployment. Every citizen shall have the right to keep and bear arms in accordance with the regulations made for that purpose.

The Nehru Report was presented to the All-Parties Conference which met at Lucknow from 28 to 30 August 1928. It was declared on behalf of the Conference that it was in favour of Dominion Self-Government. However, it was made clear by Jawaharlal Nehru and Subhash Chandra Bose that although they did not oppose the acceptance of the Nehru Report, they would not vote for it as that would commit them to the acceptance of Dominion States and actually they stood for complete independence. When the All-India Congress Committee met at Delhi on 4 and 5 November 1928, it decided in favour of complete independence as there could be no true freedom till the British connection was cut off. It was declared that the proposals of the Nehru Report were "a great step towards political advance." At its annual session held in December 1928 at Calcutta, the Congress adopted a resolution accepting the recommendations of the Nehru Report on the condition that the Report was "accepted in its entirety by the British Parliament on or before the 31st December 1929." It was made clear by the Congress that in case its demand was not accepted before 31 December 1929, the Congress would not be bound by it and it would organise a campaign of "non-violent non-cooperation by advising the country to refuse taxation and every aid to Government."

Criticism of the Nehru Report

About the Nehru Report, the New Statesmen of London wrote that it was an artificial plan and an abstract and mechanical structure neither Indian nor workable. It was a doctrinaire invention unrelated to the established facts of Indian life and Government an ill-conceived and hasty device, a paper scheme, already disowned by every minority.

It is contended that the weakest feature of the Nehru Report was that it contained all that appeared to satisfy the aspirations of the constitutional-minded and nationalist Hindus, but contained nothing to please the Muslims in the form of complete independence or separate electorates. The majority of the Muslims who joined the Nationalist Movement did so partly because of the Lucknow Pact of 1916 which took cognisance of their demand for separate electorates and party because of the support extended by the National Congress to the Khilafat Movement. Once the Khilafat issue was dead, the only ray of hope for the Muslims to continue in the Nationalist Movement was separate electorates. Most of the Muslims had begun to regard separate electorates as the law of the country and they claimed that they could not be deprived of this right of their without their consent.

The politically conscious Muslims held the British rulers responsible for the collapse of the Khilafat in Turkey and they were bitterly opposed to the Continuation of the British rule in India in any form and consequently, they stood for complete independence. However, the Nehru Report accepted dominion status, which was not acceptable to the Muslims. It is contended that the Nehru Report should have provided for complete independence and thereby won over the Muslims who hated the British connection in any form.

The British could exploit the Muslims by telling them that the Congress wanted to take away their rights. It is contended that while deciding in favour of joint electorates, the Hindu nationalists took into consideration only the views of Muslim leaders like Dr. Ansari, Hakim Ajmal Khan, Maulana Azad and others, but they did not give due weight to the views of the Ali Brothers, who appeared to enjoy the confidence of a large number of their co-religionists. The Ali Brothers enjoyed the same popularity and prestige among the Muslims as Gandhi did among the Hindus. Ignoring these facts, the Congress leaders committed a blunder at the Calcutta Convention held in December 1928. During the course of discussions on the questions of dominion status in the All-Parties Convention on December 23, 1928, Maulana Mohammed Ali got up to speak and opposed the resolution by stating that deviation was the policy of cowards and not that of fighters. Tempers flared up. Mohammed Ali was interrupted and heckled and howled down. Sir C.P. Ramaswamy Iyer came to the platform on behalf of the Liberals and, pointing out to the Maulana said : "I know this talk of killing and get killed a little too much. Let us be realists and face the facts. We may not be heroes, but if we are going to kill and get killed, then your place is not in this Convention, but somewhere else." After him arose Sir C.Y. Chintamani and he also spoke against the proposal of Maulana Mohammed Ali. Maulana Mohammed Ali wanted to refute the allegations by raising a point of order, but he was shouted at to sit down by the audience.

It is said that men like Mahatma Gandhi, Motilal Nehru and Dr. Ansari ought to have interfered but they did not. The result was that the Ali Brothers left the Convention and never came back. They became the bitterest enemies of the Congress. Straight from the Convention, they left for Bihar and Orissa to preside over the Muslim All-Parties Conference. The British restored the hereditary pension which the Ali Brothers used to get from the Nawab of Rampur. The Nizam of Hyderabad and the Nawab of Bhopal also helped the Muslims to carry on a campaign against the Nehru Report.

It is contended that instead of trying to please Liberal leaders like Sir Tej Bahadur Sapru and others the Convention, the Congress leaders should have cared more for the Muslim sentiments as projected by the Ali Brothers. It was a mistake on the part of the Congress leaders not to do so.

Muslim Opposition

The Muslim leaders were to the view that the Muslims alone had made the National Congress a really effective organistion by contributing to it both men and money. Maulana Shaukat Ali had stated on November 4, 1928 at Kanpur at the U.P. Muslim All-Parties Conference : "He was proud of the Muslim sacrifices and sufferings of 1920 and 1921 which emancipated the Congress from a crawling situation and placed it on a glorious and successful career. Muslims contributed about Rs. 6 lakhs towards the National and Khilafat funds and went to jail in untold numbers. Many national papers .... were subsidised out of these funds.

Maulana Mohammed Ali stated at the December 1928 session of the Khilafat Conference that the Congress leaders made compromises in their constitution every day with false doctrines, immoral conceptions and wrong ideas, but they made no compromise with the communalists, with separate electorates and reserved seats. The Muslim population was 25% and yet the Congress leaders were not prepared to give them 33% in the Assembly. Reflecting on the Hindu Congressmen, he observed, "You are a Jew, a Bania ..... Mr. B.C. Pal knows the way to dominion status, but does not know the way of Yarvada Jail." The Muslim distrust of the Congress assumed greater and greater proportions. Mohammed Ali vehemently criticised the Nehru Report. Azad Sobhani observed that the Nehru Report had practically no objective before it. It was unsatisfactory to them as "to live like a slave was not proper and consistent with the religion of the Mussalmans." Hasrat Mohani condemned the Nehru Report as "wrong from start to finish." The constitutional government as embodied in the Nehru Report was very injurious to the Muslims. The real idea of the report was to give "soft moral support" to the Muslims in some of the provinces outwardly and the residuary power had been left under the control of the Central Government.

Maulana Mohammed Ali made the following sarcastic remark about the Nehru Report : "In the days of the East India Company, the beat of drum was accompanied by the cry "Creation of God's, the country is that of the King's and the rule is that of John Company Bahadur.' The Nehru Report in a nutshell meant that the creation was God's the country was the Viceroy's or the Parliament's and the rule was Hindu Mahasabha's."

The Muslim members of the Central Legislature convened a Muslim All-Parties Conference in Delhi on December 31, 1928. Addressing that Conference, Maulana Mohammed Ali advised the Muslims not to be afraid of the Hindu majority as in all their religious battles in the past, one Muslim had overpowered three "Kafirs." By transferring residuary powers to the Central Government. Motilal Nehru was aiming at the destruction of the strength of the Muslims and reducing them to the position of a "fly on his table."

Conference after conference was held by the Muslims to express their indignation. Speaking at the U.P. Muslim All-Parties Conference, Maulana Shaukat Ali stated that he desired that the Hindus should declare in clear terms whether they wanted peace or war. If they wanted war, the Muslims were prepared to take up the challenge at any moment.

To undermine the influence of the Nationalist Muslims—who were supporters of the Nehru Report—among their coreligionists, the latter were forced to secede from the Khilafat Conference. The elections to the Central Committee were forcibly stopped by Ali Brothers and their followers with the help of a few rowdies in Bengal, Bihar and the NWFP. It is worthy of notice that the Muslims in the Provinces where they were in hopeless minority, had been struggling for the supposed rights of the Muslims majorities in the Punjab and Bengal, while the majority of the Muslims in those provinces had already accepted the Calcutta decisions and were neither interested, nor needed their co-religionists in other provinces, to champion their cause.

One of the positive contributions of the Nehru Report was the recognition of the necessity of widening the franchise and thereby accepting the introduction of adult franchise and the principle of majority rule in implementing any future scheme of constitutional reforms. This provided a great impetus to the forces interested in the introduction of a democratic political system. However, Maulana Mohammad Ali began to find fault with this also. He declared on December 9, 1928 at Patna that if the Hindus did not concede the Muslim rights, they would have them by force. On 4 November, 1928, Maulana Shaukat Ali condemned the Hindu community and warned them that the Muslims would not submit to dominations by the Hindus.

Calcutta Convention

On December 28, 1928, Mr. Jinnah put forward his own scheme before the Calcutta Convention. According to him, one-third of the seats in both the Houses of the Central Legislature should be reserved for the Muslims and the excess seats were to be distributed among the Provinces with a Muslim minority. He asked for the reservation of seats for the Muslims in case of adult suffrage in Bengal and the Punjab on population basis for ten years. The residuary powers were to be vested with the Provinces and not with the Central Government. Clause 13-A in the Supplementary Report was to be deleted. Schedules 1 and 2 were to be revised. The Province of Sind was to be immediately separated after the establishment of the new Government. Seats were be reserved for the Muslims in the services. In support of his scheme. Mr. Jinnah made a conciliatory and persuasive statement. "We are sons of this land; we have to live together, We have to work together and whatever our differences may be, let us not arouse bad blood Nothing will make me more happly than to see Hindus and Muslims united." Mr. Jinnah did not ask for separate electorates or weightage for Muslims. Sir Tej Bahadur Sapru pressed the Conference to accept the suggestions of Mr. Jinnah in order to secure a settlement. To quote Sapru, "The simple position is that for the sake of settlement you are invited by Mr. Jinnah, however illogically and unreasonably, to agree to this propositition which I consider not inconsistent with the Nehru Report. Speaking for myself, I would like you to picture Mr. Jinnah, whom I have known intimately for fifteen years, as a spoilt child. If he is a spoilt child, a naughty child, I am prepared to say, give him what he wants and be finished with it. I am not going to ask him to be reasonable but we must, as practical statesmen, try to solve the problem and not be misled by arithmetical figures."

It is pointed out that instead of accepting the advice of Sir Tej Bahadur Sapru, Mr. Jinnah was repeatedly interrupted and his demands were rejected in toto. The Muslim group in the Congress consisting of men like Maulana Azad, Dr. Ansari etc., were not in favour of an agreement between Mr. Jinnah and the Congress because in that case, their own position in the Congress was likely to be weakened. The Hindu Mahasabha gave an ultimatum that if a single word of the Nehru Report in respect of communal settlement was changed, it would immediately withdraw its support. Mr. M.R. Jayakar particularly opposed the demands of Mr. Jinnah. He maintained that by accepting Mr. Jinnah's demands, the Report would be torn to pieces and the whole structure would topple down. He denied the right of Mr. Jinnah to speak on behalf of the Muslims as he represented only a small fraction of them. Kanji Dwarkadas observes that the attack of Mr. Jayakar was "the second and last nail in the coffin of Nehru Report." Mr. Jinnah was reported to have told a friend. "This is the parting of ways." It is pointed out that the organisers of the Calcutta

Convention should have sacrificed the support of Mr. Jayakar and his followers and accepted the demands of Mr. Jinnah and that would have been in the higher interests of the country. The All-Parties Convention of December 1928 marked a turning point in the life of Mr. Jinnah and in the history of India. The Congress lost the support of all sections of the Muslims outside its own ranks.

General Criticism

The view of the Sikhs was that the Nehru Report paved the way for another communal war, as its recommendations were conceived in a spirit of communalism. The Central Sikh League withheld its support and did not participate in the deliberations of the Calcutta Convention. The young intelligentsia dismissed the report as a worthless product of old and aged minds having on relation to the changed times. Political theoreticians picked big loop-holes in it. The non Brahmins and the Depressed Classes were opposed to it. Every one of them approached the report from his own selfish, individual angle. Nobody saw it from the national standpoint. The authors of the Report failed to find and amicable solutions of the communal differences which cast their shadow over all political work. They had no remedy to remove from the minds of all communities a baseless fear of others and in providing a feeling of security to others and thus restoring harmony in human relations in a spirit of nationalism. The report ultimately ended in embittering the communal environment and there ensued open hostility between the Hindus and the Muslims. Public life became unsignified; reticence and restraint were cast to the winds. An attempt to bring unity and present a solid front against British imperialism was not only frustrated, but also the open breach provided to the common enemy an opportunity to get the Muslims out of the National Movement.

❐

11

Leaders of Gandhi Era & Indian Acts

Gandhiji, after returning from Africa in 1915, came before us as a leader of the national movement. He not only appealed to the masses for a national movement but also led the country in its freedom struggle for thirty two years.

Gandhiji first discussed the national movement with leaders of the nation and then toured the country, to learn the exact condition. He was greatly distressed to see poverty,illiteracy, unemployment and back wardness in the country and soon started participating with great enthusiasm in the freedom struggle and serving his country:

(1) The foundation of Sabartmati Ashram (1916). On 1916, Gandhiji founded the Sabarmati Ashrám, which was called Satyagraha Ashram. He made this Ashram the centre of his activities.

(2) Champaran (Bihar) Satyagraha (1917). In 1917 Gandhiji started the first Civil Disobedience Movement against the atrocities committed against the Champaran (Bihar) farmers. When he started investigating the condition of these farmers through European masters, he was ordered by the Champaran District Magistrate to leave the district. Gandhiji openly disobeyed this order. He started satyagraha and was prepared to suffer any punishment. The government was thus compelled not only to take back this order but also formed a committee to look into the condition of farmers. Gandhiji was also a member of this committee. This was Gandhiji's first great victory in India.

(3) **Satyagraha Against the Rowlatt Act (1919).** To put an end to the national movement in the country the British Government passed in 1919, the Rowlatt Act, by which it could put any Indian in jail without any trial. Gandhiji started an agitation against this Act. On his advice, Lakhs of people joined the freedom movement. Hartals and processions were held in large numbers. The air resounded with the cries of "Hindu Muslim Unity Zindabad." The national movement became infact a peoples movement. Gandhiji asked the nationalists workers to go to the villages, that is where India lives, he said.

(4) **Jallianwala Bagh Massacre and Gandhiji's Arrest (April 1919).** Gandhiji called for a hartal on April 6, 1919 against the suppression tactics of the British. The public with all their enthusiasm made the hartal a success, On the other side the government increased their suppression activities. Two national leaders of Punjab, Dr. Satya Pal and Dr. Saifuddin Kitchlu were arrested on 10th April, 1919. When the people in protest against the arrests assembled at Jallinwala Bagh to hold a meeting..., General Dyer arrived there suddenly and without giving any warning to the people ordered his soldiers to fire. To stop the agitation from spreading Gandhiji was arrested, but was soon acquitted as the government was afraid of the mob becoming violent.

(5) **Fast unto Death for Ahmedabad Mill Workers.** Gandhiji supported the Hartal of mill workers for an increase in wages, by going on a fast unto death. The mill owners, seeing his firmness, agreed to the demands of the workers and gave them an increase of 35% in their wages.

(6) **Gandhiji's Role in Khilafat and Non-Cooperation Movement (1919-1922).** In India in 1919 the Khilafat Movement to vindicate Turkey started under the leadership of Muhammad Ali and Shaukat Ali, Abul Kalam Azad, Hakim Ajmal Khan and Hasrat Mohani., Taking this

movement as golden opportunity for Hindu-Muslim unity, Gandhiji announced the Non-cooperation movement. He not only supported the Khilafat Movement but also placed the demand for annulling the 'Rowlatt Act and for granting freedom. He also demanded that the cruelties committed by the British on Punjab and turkey be stopped. When the British Governemnt did not concede to these demands, the Non-Cooperation Movement was started on 31st August 1920. Gandhiji returned the award of Hind Kesri to the government. He asked the people to boycott the government offices and the educational institutions, law courts and legislative sessions. He advised people to adopt khadi, Indian education and home made goods. He did a lot towards promoting Hindu Muslim unity and started Tilak Swariaj Fund to raise money for the movement.

Gandhiji put forward a proposal in the Khilafat committee, asking Muslims to quit the British army. The proposal was reiterated by him in many meetings. On 1st February, 1922 Gandhiji asked people to start to Civil Disobedience Movement and to ignore taxes and British law. He said that if the British Government did not free all political prisoners within seven days and grant freedom peacefully, the Civil Disobedience Movement would begin.

(7) **The First Round Table Conference.** In 1930, the British Government organised a Round Table Conference in London to discuss the report of the Simon Commission. Gandhiji refused to participate in this conference as its aim was not to grant freedom to Indians. As a result the First Round Table Conferene of the British Government was useless.

(8) **The Second Civil Disobedience Movement (1930).** On 26th January, 1930 the first independence day was celebrated all over the country. Side by side Gandhiji made arrangements for Second Civil Disobedience Movement. He opposed the salt tax and marched from Sabarmati

Ashram to Dandi village on 12th March, 1930. His seventy eight followers also joined him in this 200 miles long march. Lakhs of people happily courted arrest. Foreign goods were boycottted and hartals were held every where. Farmers refused to pay land tax. Thousands of women also participated in this Satyagraha. Schools and colleges were also boycottted by the students. Govenrment employees also stopped going to their offices. Khan Abdul Gaffar Khan formed an association of Khudai Khidmatgars (Red Shirts) in Peshawar. It was at this time that a regiment of Garhwal soldiers refused to fire at the demonstrators. Against the repression policy of the Government demonstrations were held all over the country. Gandhiji along with ninety thousand national leaders were arrested. Lathi charge and firing was resorted to every where.

(9) Proposal to Induct the Congress into Constructive Work. On 5th February a violent mob set fire to the Chauri Chaura police station in which 22 policemen died. The votary of Ahimsa, Gandhi was greatly pained. He announced that the National Movement be suspended for some time. The government arrested Gandhiji on 10th March, 1922 and charged him with spreading disaffection against the government. He was given imprisonment for six years. However, he was released with two years. Gandhiji started constructive programms of Charkha and Khadi and combating of untouchability, abolition of casteism, Hindu-Muslim Unity, promotion of national education and village upliftment. On september 1924, Gandhiji resorted Communal harmony by taking fast for three weeks in Delhi. From December 1928, Gandhiji again started taking an active part in the national movement. He took part in Calcutta and Lahore Congress Sessions. Gandhiji organised his Second Civil Disobedience Movement in support of the Congress demand for complete freedom.

(10) Gandhi-Irwin Pact. An agreement was signed between Gandhiji and Lord Irwin, the then Governor-General of India on 5th March, 1931 A.D. which came to be known as Gandhi irwin pact of 1931. Gandhiji agreed to the following terms on behalf of the Congress:

(i) The Civil Disobedience Movement will be suspended.

(ii) Congress will withdraw boycott as a political weapon.

(iii) Indian National Congress will participate in the Second Round Table Conference.

(iv) Congress will drop the demand for enquiring into atrocities committed by the police during the Civil Disobedience Movement.

On the other hand, Lord Irwin agreed:

(a) to release all political prisoners;

(b) to permit people to collect salt on sea shores free of duty;

(c) to withdraw emergency ordinances;

(d) to restore confiscated property and remit fines, and

(e) to permit peaceful picketing of liquor, opium and foreign goods shops.

Gandhi-Irwin Pact resulted in Congress attending the Second Round Table Conference. Mahatma Gandhi was nominated as its sole representative. The Conference failed. The pact raised controversy within the Congress party. It was condemned by radicals as a 'surrender' to British Imperialism. Gandhiji returned home greatly disppointed and talked of resuming Civil Disobedience Movements.

(11) Gandhiji's Fast unto Death Against Communal Decisions. Gandhiji started fast unto death in Jail to protest against to the Medonald's proposal to give Harijans (who were considered distinct from Hindus) separate representation. This was a vicious step towards fanning communalism according to Gandhiji. Government had to changed its decision and Gandhiji was released from Jail in 1933. Gandhiji stopped its agitation and in the next year he ended his Civil Disobedience Movement. Once again Gandhiji retired from active politics.

In 1942, Gandhiji against came before the public as a leader and gave them the famous slogan of 'Quit India' against the British.

(12) The Second Round Table Conference. In 1931, Gandhiji attended Second Round Table Conference in London. The Muslim League placed some unreasonable demands at this Conference. British Government did not accept the proposal of freedom of India. So, Gandhiji returned home and started Civil Disobedience Movement. This Conference a total failure. British Government again imprisoned Gandhiji and other national leaders. It also again put restrictions on the press.

(13) Quit India Movement (1942). At the All India congress Committee meeting in Bombay on August 8, 1942, Gandhiji gave forth the slogan 'Quit India'. In was planned to have Civil Disobedience Movement to force the British to leave India. Gandhiji gave the slogan of "Do or die" He said "Congress is at stake. It will either be victorious or will finish." The Government immediately arrested Gandhiji, Pandit Jawahar Lal Nehru and some other members of Congress in Bombay. Congress was declared illegal. There were demonstrations throughout the country. The Government with the help of the police and army killed thousands of people in a few months. In many places the movement turned into a revolt. Public property was destroyed by the public in anger.

Gandhiji was released from jail in 1944. He tried his best to influence Mohammed Ali Jinnah not to insist on partition of the country, but unfortunately Gandhiji's advice had no effect on Jinnah.

(14) Freedom for the Country. After the Second World War England had a labour Government. In March, 1946, British Government sent the Cabinet Mission to India to hold discussions with Indian leaders. The British prime Minister announced his government's willingness to grant independence to India. Gandhiji's efforts bore fruit and power was transferred to the two states of India and Pakistan. It is regretable that the champion of masses and the lover of non-violence was shot dead by a fanatic on 30th January, 1948. Our country will always remain indebted to this great Soul.

JAWAHAR LAL NEHRU AND HIS HISTORIAL ASSESSMENT

Pandit Nehru was not only a great Indian leader but a great world figure also. His name besides being a houshold word in India is widely known all over the world. He was known as a great political figure, a great socialist, as progressive thinker with an international outlook and man of rare sysmpathies and understanding. He was the political heir of Gandhiji who ones said of him, "He is pure as crystal. He is truthful beyond suspicion."

In India's struggle for freedom, he was second only to Gandhiji His noble idealism, cultured manners and larger heartedness have become proverbial. Tyranny in any form and anywhere moved him deeply. He was a true soldier of freedom and whosever and wherever freedom was in peril he was always already to defend it with all his might. He was really the maker of Modern India.

Pt. Nehru was born on 14th November, 1889 at Allahabad. He was the worthy son of a worthy father, Pt. Moti Lal Nehru, who also played a lading role in India's struggle for independence. Being the only son for almost eleven years of a rich and aristocratic family, he was not sent to any school. He was taught at home by the forign tutors. He was brought up with great care and love in the lap of luxury. In 1905 he went to England for higher studies. He was educated mainly at Harrow and Trinity College Cambridge. He studied law an on his return in 1912 joined the Allahabad High Court as Barrister. But soon he felt restless because he did not like the dull and uneventful life of a lawyer. At the age of 26 he was married to Kamla a young Kashmiri girl of 17 who died of tuberculosis in 1936. He became and member of All India Congress Committee and participated in the Civil Disobedience Movement in 1920. His ardent nationalism was stirred into firm conviction that true freedom of our people can not co-exist with tyranny and oppression of other nations. For his fighting spirit and the deep influence he exercised upon the people of India he became a terror for the British regime and from 1920-1940 he courted imrisonment as many as ten times. In 1929 he was first elected President of the Indian National Congress at Lahore and thereafter also elected President for three more occasions to give a lead to the freedom struggle. He and the entire Nehru Family went to Jail so many times and ultimately the sacrifices bore fruit when India became free on the 15th of August 1947 and he became the first Prime Minister of Free India.

The Jail life offered him an opportunity to examine his thoughts and feelings which he recorded in the shape of books which became world famous. His writings particularly, "My Autography" and "Glimpses of World History", "Discovery of India", give evidence of his wide knowledge, vast experience and facile pen. The books show that he was an artist with words and has a great command over the English language. The book that established him as a writer and which is still his best is 'Autography' published in 1936. It was written to quote the author, "in a mood of self questioning". Nehru was by temperament introspective and his mood of introspection was hightened by long periods of enforced isolation and inactivity in Jail. It had two fold value, if revealed his inner life and secondly his books became signficant commentary on contemporary men and events. In him the East and West had blended, the former showed him the way of life and the latter gave him a wider understanding of the impulses that move the destinies of man. The foreign education gave him Westernised and scientific outlook and yet with his sense of Indian history and his burning patriotism, he truly represented modern India. What he said of India equally applies to him. "Two faced like Janues she looked both back wards into the past and forward in to the future and tried to umpire the two". The dual quality is often reflected in his style of writing. He always wrote-like an intellectual who tried to see the other person's point of view as well as his own. Besides inspiring confidence in the teeming maillions of India and being the idol of the masses, he became the veritable prophet. He became the saviour of the people who looked up to him for succour in all their misfortunes. There is hardly a man in the history who ever enjoyed the intensity and sincerity of devotion which people of India gave to Pt. Nehru. He tried to make India a democratic, secular and, socialistic country. He laid a solid foundation for country's freedom and democracy.

His human sympathies, his wide culture and his internationalism marked him out from rest of the leaders. His reorientation of the politics of his country in terms of world politics was his special contribution. His catholicity of outlook made India a secular republic. His sincerity and love for peace was a force to reckon with in the arena of international politics.

A HISTORICAL ASSESSMENT OF NEHRU

A historical assessment of Jawahar Lal Nehru will undoubtedly give his contribution to the political development of India the first place. In the struggle for India's freedom from foreign domination, the making of a constitution for India, the working of the Parliamentary democracy, the evolution of the economic institution of a socialist society, the removal of the social barriers to the freedom and equality and the evolving and implementing of a foreign neutral policy for the newly independent country, he played the leading part. Since he knew the conditions in India intimately, he was able to select from various political ideals the elements which he thought were suitable under India's social and economic conditions. He felt that democracy with a dose of socialism was best suited to the people of India. In this respect Jawahar Lal Nehru was perhaps unique.

In May 1964 he died. The news of his death spread like wild fire round the country. Gloom enveloped city, town and hamlet. The whole national seemed to be paralysed. The people had lost their beloved leader who for the past seventeen years had become part of their national and personal life. He had led, cajoled, chided and pushed them along the path of progress and development. Never has a national wept so spontaneously and ardently at the death of a leader as the Indians did at Nehru's death. Never in the history of the world has been a leader who ruled his people entirely by love and was held in such deep esteem by them. With his death an epoch in Indian history ended. The long, glorious, eventful Nehru era came to a close. He dreamed great dreams for his country. He was a man in hurry, hustling his people to progress desperately, trying to conquer time by sheer pace.

MAHATMA GANDHIJI'S ROLE

Mahatma Gandhi, the Father of the Indian nation was born on 2nd October 1869 at Porbandar in Kathiawar. At the age of 79 he was shot dead at Delhi. His father was a Dewan at Porbandar and Rajkot. He was married at the age of 12. At the age of 19 he left for Great Britain to qualify for the Bar. Before leaving India he made a promise to his mother that he would avoid three things—meat wine and women.

After qualifying himself for the Bar, Gandhi began to practise at Rajkot and from there he shifted to Bombay. During his stay at Bombay Gandhiji came into intimate contact with Raj Chandra Ramjibhai. The latter exercised a tremendous influence on him.

Gandhiji went to South Africa in connection with a professional work on behalf of a Mohammadan firm. His stay in South Africa was the formative period of his political life. He developed his self confidence and put into practice of weapon of Satygraha in South Africa. He taught his countrymen there to resist evil by truth. The Asiatic Registration Act was passed by the Government of South Africa in 1906. All Asiatic were required to register themselves and give to their thumb impressions. Gandhiji protested against this Act and led a deputation to England. The Indians refused to get themselves registerred and give their thumb impressions. Thousands of Indian including Gandhiji were sent to jail.

Again the Satyagrah movement was started at Transval against the ill treatment of the Indians there. Two thousand men marched into Transvall under the leadership of Gandhiji, The march was a great landmark. It was a march of truth against untruth, of justice against injustice and of non-violence against violence. At last the hated Asiatic Act was cancelled, the Poll Tax was repealed. Gandhiji came to India in 1914. At that time he had faith in the love of justice of the Englishmen. But after 1918 doubts arose in his mind regarding the intentions of Britishers about India. The passing of the Rowlatt Act in the teeth of opposition by the people and the tragedy of Jalianwala Bagh completely shattered his belief in the justice and good faith of England. A special sessions of the Congress was held at Calcutta in september 1920. This session marks the beginning of the Gandhian era. Under Gandhiji the Congress became more and more representative of the people with a distinctive economic, moral, social and political programme and all flowing from the genius of one man. Gandhiji's resolution was carried by a majority of 1865 votes against 884. Gandhiji combined his non-Cooperation Movement with Khilafat movement. He belived in the ideal of Hindu Muslim unity. But differences arose between the Hindus and Muslims. The Moplah revolt in Malabar opend the eyes of the Hindus. Riots took place in Bombay on the day Prince of Wales landed in that city. In February 1922 there took place a serious rioting at Chauri Chaura in Uttar Pradesh. At the place 21 constables and Sub-Inspector of police were shut in a police station and burnt alive by a mob. The result was that Gandhiji withdrew his Non-Cooperation Movement.

There was a split within the Congress on the question of Council entry. Moti Lal Nehru and C.R. Dass founded the Swarajist Party which Congress entering the legislature and fighting the Government from within. Mahatma Gandhi continued to dominate not only the Congress but also the entire politics of the country. His position was absolutely unchallenged. In 1931 he went to London to attend the Second Round Table conference but came back empty handed on account of the attitude of the British Government and Mr. Jinnah. India won her independence on 15th August 1947, under his leadership but he himself was murdered on 30th January 1948 by a fanatical Hindu.

As a father of the nation, Mahatma Gandhi was the creater of modern India. He put great emphasis on communal unity. He was a great social reformer. He took up the cuse of the depressed classes in India and devoted the whole of his life to this noble mission. He regarded untouchability as a curse to the Hindu society and the same was abolished in the Indian Constitution. He stood for Swadeshi. It was one of the weapons in his armoury against the British. The adoption of Swadeshi saved millions of rupees of India and gave employment to a large number of people.

Mahatma Gandhi was known all over the world and rich tributes were paid to the greatness of the saint of Sabarmati. According to Roman Rolland, "Mahatma Gandhi has raised up three hundred millions of his fellow men, shaken the British Empire and inaugurated in human politics the most powerful movement that the whole world has seen for nearly two thousand years". According to Louis Fishcher, "The symbol of India's unanimous wish for freedom is Mahatma Gandhi. He does not represent all of India but he does reflect the will of all India for national liberation. A great man is like good sculpture made of one piece. A great man lives a single tracked life. Lincoln was great he lived for the Union. Lenin was great, he lived in order to make Russia out of the feudal mire Churchill is great because all of his acts have been directed towards the preservation of England as a first class power. And in the same way Gandhi is great because every single act that he performs is calculated to promote the one goal of his life—the liberation of India. He is not the man he has no intention and never had, to rule India or administer India. His function ends when he frees India." According to Sir Stafford Cripps : "There has been no greater spiritual leader in the world in our own time". According to Acharya Kriplani, "The Mahatma is more right when he is wrong than we are when we are right. Many of us are correct in our little correctness and are small in the process. But the Mahatma was incorrect in many things and yet correct in the sum total and big in the very inconsistencies. In the end he seldom or never came out at the wrong place". According to Dr. Rajendra Prasad, "Mahatma Gandhi's contribution of Indian politics has been immense. The Indian National Congress had been in existence for thrity years when he returned to India finally from South Africa in 1915. The Congress has aroused and organised national consciousness to a certain extent; but the awakening was confined largely to the English educated middle classes and had not penetrated the masses. He carried it to the masses and made it a mass movement. Mahatma Gandhi's movement operated both horizontly and vertically. He took up causes which were not entirely political but which touched very intimately the life of large masses of people." Mahatma Gandhi's greatest contribution, however, does not consist in making the masses of India politically self conscious and organising them on a scale they had never before been organised." The message of Gandhiji held a special appeal not only for Indian but for the whole world. His conception of non-violence and on-cooperation for an unarmed nation resulted in independence of India.

GROWTH OF LEFT MOVEMENT IN INDIA

Generally the scholars use the terms left and right in a particular sense. Those who stand for revolutionary changes in the existing social, economic and political systems come within the compass of the left movements and those who stand for status quo are said to belong to the right. Some times they called reactionaries also. While dealing with the left movements in India, the scholar mainly concern themselves with the Communist Party of India, the Congress Socialist Party and Forward Bloc.

There were many circumstances which favoured the rise of the left movements in India. The main were:

(1) The first World War. The result of the World War I (1914-1918 A.D.) was that the prices of essential things rose. There were famine conditions in several parts of the country. The economic situation in the post war years had taken a turn for the worse. There were crippling financial burdens on the people. There was first a rise in prices and then a depression in economic activity. Indian industries, which had prospered during the war because foreign imports of manufactured goods had ceased, no faced losses and closure. The workers facing unemployment and his prices living great poverty, also turned actively towards the left movements.

(2) **Russian Revolution (7th Nov. 1917 A.D.).** A major impetus to labour movements of India was given by the impact of the Russian Revolutions. On 7 November, 1917 A.D. the Bolshevik (Communist) Party by V.I. Lenin overthrew the Czarist regime in Russia and declared formation of the first socialist state, the Soviet Union, in the history of World. About it a historian writes. "The success of the Russian Revoluti in November 1917 fired the imagination of the Indian intellectuals, political leaders, the terrorists and even the workers and made them aware a new ideology (*i.e.* Socialism)".

(3) **The Appearance of Gandhiji on the Platform of Nation Movement.** The slogans of Swaraj, Satyagrah, Non-cooperation and Swadeshi etc. by Mahatma Gandhiji and his efforts to carry the message of National Movement to the people of villages gave a new orientation to the nationalist movement in the country. He took the cause of peasants and labourers. Due to his efforts the workers and peasants were drawn into the mainstream of national life, Definitely these developments helped the growth of the socialist-movement.

(4) **Literary Works of Lala Lajpat Rai and M.N. Roy.** Lala Lajpat Rai was possibly the first Indian writer to write about socialism and Bolshevism (Communists of Russia) but his attitude towards the latter was not sympathetic. He presided over the first All India trade Union Congress

(AITUC) in 1920 A.D. In 1920-1923 M.N. Roy worte two books in which he criticized the bourgeois demination of the Indian National Congress. In short these writings helped up to some extent the growth of the socialist movement in India.

The Foundation of Communist Party of India

Despite repeated allegations of British officials and some later scholars that the whole movement was no more a foreign conspiracy organised from Moscow, Indian Communism really sprang, from roots within the national movement itself, as disillusioned revolutionaries, Non-cooperation Khilafatists, and labour-peasant activists sought new roads to political and social emancipation. Its founder was the famous Yugantar revolutionary, Naren Bhattacherji (alias Manabendra Nath Roy), who came into contact with the Bolshevik Mikhail Borodin in Mexico in 1919, helped to found a Communist Party, there and went to Russia in the summer of 1920 A.D. to attend the Second Congress of the Communist International. Here he embarked on a celebrated and significant controversy with Lenin concerning the strategy of Communists in the colonial world. Lenin urged the necessity of broad support of the predominantly bourageois led national movement in the colonial world; Roy argued that the Indian masses were already disillusioned with bourgeois—nationalist leders like Mahatma Gandhi and were moving towards revolution indpendently of the bourgeois nationalist movement.

In October 1920 A.D., M.N. Roy, Abani Mukherjee and some Khilafatists like Mohammad Ali and Mohammad Shafiq founded a Communist Party of India in Tashkent, together with a political-cum-military school, when hopes of penetrating India through Afghanistan faded away in early 1921, some of the new Indian recruits joined the Communist University of the Toilers of East of Moscow. M.N. Roy himself shifted his headquarters to Berlin (Germany) in 1922 A.D., starting from there the fortnightly Vanguard of Indian Independence and publishing India in Transition, a poineering attempt at a marxist analysis of Indian economy and society. A large number of copies of Vanguard of Indian Independence were sent to individual nationalists, trade unionsts and intellectuals in india. In 1923 S.A. Dange started the publication of an English Weekly entitled "Socialist' from Bombay. At about the same time, Janavani, a Bengali Weekly was started from Calcutta. Other emigre Indian revolutionary groups were meanwhile turning towards Marxism—most notably the old Berlin group headed by Virendranath Chattopadhaya, Bhupendranath Dutt and Barkatullah whose efforts in 1921 to win Soviet backing were blocked by Roy out of essentially factional motives, but who started an Indian Independence Party in Berlin in the following year. By the mid 1920s an important section of the Ghadar movement in exile had also turned Communist under Rattan Singh, Santokh Singh and Teja Singh Swatantra. By the end of 1922 A.D., through emissaries like Nalini Gupta and Shoukat Usmani, Roy had been able to establish some tenuous and often-intecepted secret links with embryonic Communist groups which had emerged from out of the Non-cooperation and Khilafat experience in Bombay (S.A. Dange) Calcutta, Madras and Lahore. In a letter to S.A. Dange on 2 November 1922, Roy outlined a plan for a dual organisation, one legal and another illegal-a secret communist nucleus working within a broad—front workers' and pesants' party. However, most of the Indian histroians accept that the organised Communism came to India when the followers of M.N. Roy came to this country. Nalni Gupta returned to India in 1921 A.D. on behalf of M.N. Roy, Abani Mukherji came to India in 1923 A.D. on behalf of Virendranath Chattopadhyaya, Both of them had been members of the terrorist organisatins in Bengal before they went outside India. In July 1924, the comintern devided to accept the advice of M.N. Roy that the Communist Party of India should be established as a branch of the Communist International Muhajirs trying to re-enter India were tried by the Government in a series of five Peshawar Conspiracy cases between 1922 and 1927, and in May 1924 Muzaffar Ahmed, S.A. Dange, Shaukat Usmani and Nalini Gupta were jailed in the Kanpur Bolshavik Conspiracy Case. The set-back caused by such repressive measure, however, proved only temporary. An open 'Indian communist Conference' was held in Kanpur in December 1925, organised by Satyabhakta—who proved very much a bird of passage—and with Hasrat Mohani as chairman of the Reception Committee and Singaravelu as persident. Though floated by rather diverse groups, which emphasized their indpendence from the Comintern in order to preserve legality, the skeleton organisation set up by this Conference was soon taken over by more determined Communist like S.V. Ghate of Bombay. The Communist organisations in India were directed through the Communist Party of Great Britain and R. Palme Dutt became an important figure in this connection. He was throughout in closer touch with Moscow than most of his colleagues in the Communist Party of Great Britain. But repression of the Government could not check the advance of awakening of working class of India. By 1926-27 A.D., socialist ideas were spreading widely. A new initial form of political working-class and socialist organisation began to appear in the Workers' and peasants' parties, which sprang up and united militant elements in the trade union movement with left elements in the National Congress. The first Workers' and Peasants' party was formed in Bengal in February, 1926; others followed in Bombay, the United Provinces and the Punjab. These were united in 1928 A.D. in the All Indian Workers' and Peasants' Party, which held its first Congress in December, 1928. This political expression, still suffering from many forms of initial confusion, but revealing the growing new forces, accompanied the new wave of working class awakening the first sings of which began to appear in 1927 A.D. Perhaps the greatest success of the Communists during this period was the influence they managed to acquire in trade unions in India. From 1920 to 1928, the influence of the Communists increased immensely.

Soon after the Comintern Resolution of September, 1928 A.D. was passed, the Communist Party of India met at Calcutta on December 1928. It was at this meeting that the swing to the left was applied to India. A new Central Executive was first elected. The main decisions were to make the party active and to do propaganda in the name of the Communist Party of India to affiliate to the Communist International and send Muzaffar Ahmed to Moscow as a delegate to the Executive Committee of the Communist International.

Meerut Conspiracy Caes

The principal government move, however, was the round up on 20 March of 31 labour leaders (most of them but no means all, Communists). They included Dange, Mirajkar, Ghate, Joglekar, Adhikari, Nimbkar, Alve and Kasle from Bombay; Muzaffar Ahmed, Kishorilal Ghosh, Dharnai Goswami, Gopen Chakrabarti, Radharaman Mitra, Gopal Basak, and Sibnath Bannerjee from Calcutta; Sohan Singh Josh from the Pubjab; P.C. Joshi and Viswanath Mukherjee from U.P., as well as three Englishmen, Bradley, Spratt, and Hutchinson. The conpiracy trial was to be staged at Meerut, sicne the British could not...take the chance of submitting the case to a jury, as the Home member. H.G. Haig, admitted on a confidential note on 20th February, 1929. The trial in the end proved somewhat counter-productive, for the Communists in fact made good use of it to propagate their ideals, through defence speeches. But as it lasted for nearly four years, and heavy jail sentences were imposed in January 1933 the most experienced and active labour leaders were kept locked up for much of the early 1930s. The entire national movement condemned the Meerut prosecution. The Communists were able to enlist for their legal advice and defence the services of younger nationalist spokesman. Among them were Pandit Jawaharlal Nehru, Faird-ul-Haq Ansari and Dr. Kailash Nath Katju. The trial lasted for many years and the accused took full advantage of it to make propaganda in favour of communism. However, the removal for the leading communists in March 1929 A.D. dealt a heavy blow to the Communist Party of India. The industrial situation improved considerably. There was Party of India. The industrial situation improved considerably. There was a cessation of strikes in general. Rivalries and petty squabbles grew within the Communist Party. The one cause of it was the new ultra leftist policy laid down for India by the Comintern. The Communist Party was now directed to severe all its relations, with all elements of bourgeoisie and launch an attack on the Congress and its leaders like Gandhi and Jawaharlal Nehru. This policy was pursued by the Communists between the period 1928-34. It brought it discredit in the Indian society and isolated it from other political Parties in India. The party was further weakened by its internal dissensions. There were many, including M.N. Roy, who opposed the ultra-leftist programme of the radicals under the influence of the Comintern and, therefore, broke up from the Party. The Party lost its image further when it tried to sabotage the Civil disobedience Movement led by Gandhi.

The Left leadership, however, which came into control of the trade Union Congress (in 1929) lacked coherence, being composed of very diverse elements and a further split took place (in 1931) mainly on the question of the independent political role of the working class. The Communist section which held this view formed the Red Trade Union Congress.

These splits seriously weakened the trade union movement but the working class fought on through separate strike struggles not only for its economic demands but also against victimisation, that is, the democratic right of association. This can be seen from the increase in the number of strikes from 141 in 1929 to 148 in 1930 A.D. And 166 in 1931 A.D., involving more than 100,000 workers every years. The Communists of the Red Trade Union Congress led these struggles and by the year 1933, the Government had to admit with chagrin that though 'the Meerut leadership was still kept in jail, the Communist "menance, however, remains and had intensified." The Government struck again. An emergency Powers ordinance was brought into-operation and Communists and trade union leaders were detained without trial. The Communist Party was declared illegal. More than a dozen legally registered trade unions were declared illegal, the Young Workers' League was banned, firing was employed to crush the militant and revolutionary organisation of the working class. It was out of this mighty strike struggle that the move began to reunite the working class organisation.

In the political field also new developments took place. The Workers' and Peaṣants; parties which in view of their two-class character could only form a transitional stage of growth, and no permanent basis for political working class organisation, passed out of the picture after Meerut. Though the Communist Party was declared illegal, such measures could not check the growth of

Socialist and Communist influence and of Marxist ideas. New accessions of strength were won after the close of the national civil disobedience struggle of 1930-34, as the younger national elements proceeded to draw the lessons of that struggle.

The Congress Socialist Party

In 1934, a group of younger Left nationalist elements, who had come partially under the influence of Marxist ideas in this period, formed the Congress Socialist Party. The special character of the Congress Socialist Party was that its membership was made conditional on membership of the National Congress, the party thus constituted a wing within the Congress and discouraged mass membership. The objective effect of this programmatice and constitutional basis inevitably represented an attempt to subordinate the independence of the working class movement to the control and discipline of the existing dominant leadership of the National congress, which meant—in practice of the bourgeoisie. This contradiction at the root of the Congress Socialist Party showed itself throughout its history in its role at evey critical stage of the working class struggle. The contradiction showed itself further in the conflict between the Left-wing of the party, which sought co-operation with the Communist Party and the working class forces, and the dominent reactionary right Wing, which was hostile to the Communist Party and to all independent working class activity.

At its first Conference in Bombay in 1934, the Congress Socialist Party adopted a 15-point programme which included:

(a) the repudiation of the public debt of India,

(b) state monopoly of foreign trade,

(c) cooperative and collective farming,

(d) organisation of cooperative for production, distribution and credit,

(e) transfer of all power to producing masses,

(f) planned development of the economic life of the country by the state socialisation of the key industries, and

(g) elimination of princes and landlords without compensation.

The members of the Congress Socialist Party criticised the leadership of the Congress but professed loyalty to the organisation. In the words of Acharya Narendra Deva, their object was "to resuscitate and reinviogorate the Congress" and to draw into it the mass of workers and peasants in order to widen the base of the anti-imperialist front. They criticised Gandhiji and his non-violence, his ethical approach to politics and his theory of trusteeship.

Within the Congress the left-wing tendency found reflection in the election of Jawahar Lal Nehru as president for 1936 and 1937 A.D. and of Subhash Chandra Bose for 1938 and 1939 A.D. In his presidential address to the Lucknow Congress in 1936, Nehru urged the Congress to accept socialism as its goal and to bring itself closer to the peasantry and the working class. This was also, he felt, the best way of weaning away the Muslim masses from the influence of their reactionary communal leaders.

Jawaharlal Nehru included Jayaprakash Narayan, Narendra Deva and Achyut Patwardhan in the congress working Committee. Gandhiji was against the Congress Socialist Party and he made it clear that if the Congress Socialist Party gained ascendancy in the Congress. He did not approve of class war, expropriation and violence. Subhash Chandra Bose asked Nehru to be firm with the Congress establishment but Nehru was not prepared to defy Gandhi or break away from the Congress. Nehru was not prepared to allow Gandhi to give up the leadership of the Congress. The Congress Socialist Party got a lot of support from the youth, the industrial labour and the peasantry, but it was still a minority. It consisted of Marxists J.P. Narayanan and Narendra Deva and Socialist Democrats like Ashok Mehta and M.R. Masani, Gandhians like Patwardhan and populists like Dr. Ram Manohar Lohia.

Subhash Chandra Bose had been elected president of the Congress even though Gandhi had opposed him. But opposition of

Gandhi and his supporters in the Congress Working Committee compelled Bose to resign from the presidentship of the Congress in 1939. He and many of his leftwing followers now founded the forward Bloc.

It is true that the Congress Socialist Party was not able to have its own way on many important issues but it certainly succeeded in giving radical orientation to the Congress policies in certain respects. The World War II and breach with the Government brought the Congress Socialists nearer to Gandhi and the Congress leadership. Both the Congress leadership and Congress Socialists worked against the British Government during the Quit India Movement.

The Forward Bloc was formed by Subhash Chandra Bose after his resignation from the Indian National congress in 1939 A.D. due to differences with Mahatma Gandhi. The party accepted the policy and programmes of the Indian National Congress but it declared that the party had no confidence in the leadership of Mahatma Gandhi. The Party did not hesitate to take help from any power of the world to destroy British imperialism from India. When India got freedom on 15th August 1947, the Forward Bloc described the transfer of power as Bogus one. Its view was that the Bourageois leadership of the Indian National Congress had entered into a partnership with British imperialism to defeat the mass struggle in India.

CIRCUMSTANCE LED TO THE PASSING OF INDIAN COUNCIL ACT OF 1892

following were the circumstances leading to the passing of the Act:

(a) **Spread of Western Education and Political Consciousness.** During the second half of the nineteenth century, the higher education in India made a rapid progress. This spread of added inspiration from the Governments discriminatory measures. The controversy over the Ilbert Bill of 1883 proved a blessing in disguise. It shook Indians' faith in British sense of justice and instilled in them a feeling of racial self-respect. It also advanced the cuase of national unity. Thus, the spread of western education and the consequent political awakening among the Indians created such an atmosphere in the country as could urge the Government to introduce reforms in the existing Indian Councils.

(b) The Native Element in the Councils was not Adequate. Lord Dufferin pointed out that these members were self-constituted, self-nominated and therefore untrustworthy. Hence the expression of Indian opinion through them was not correct as they did not represent true public opinion.

(c) Dissatisfaction with the Act of 1861. There was dissatisfaction with the Indian Coucils Act of 1861. It was felt that nothing substantial had been given by it. Feeling of nationalism began to develop during this period and the Indians began to grow conscious of their rights. They wanted more rights for themselves.

(d) Demand of the European Traders. The European traders in India also wanted to obtain representation in the councils and to secure their trade concessions.

(e) The Indian National Congress. In 1885 the Indian National Congress was formed. The Congress demanded the reforms and the expansion of the Central and Provincial Legislative Councils by the admission of a considerable portion of elected members, the budget should be referred to them and the members should have the right of interpellation. It was party due to the agitation carried on by the Indian National Congress that the Indian Council Act of 1892 was passed.

(f) Role of Lord Dufferin. Fortunately for the demands of the Indians, Lord Dufferin's attitude towards the question of Council reform was quite favourable. He looked upon to desire of the educated Indians to take part in the management of their affairs as a legitimate and reasonable aspirations.' He repeatedly proposed to Lord Cross, the then Secretary of State for India, for the introduction of elective element in legislatures. Lord Dufferin appointed a subcommittee of his council with Sir George Cheshury as its head and sent home his recommendations for reforms. These recommendation proposed the enhancement of the status of the Councils, enlargement of their functions, introduction of elective principal and the liberation of their character as political institutions. Mr. Bradlough, who had presided over the session of the Congress of 1889 introduced a Bill in the House of Commons to amend the Act of 1861 embodying the proposals of the Congress. But it could not be discussed. However the government introduced a Bill in the House of Lords in 1890 based on the recommandations made by Lord Dufferin.

Provisions of the Act. Its main provisions were as under:

(a) Powers. The members of the Councils were given the right of addressing questions to the Government in matters of public interest. A previous notice of 6 days was to be given to the Government for asking a question. The President might disallow any question without giving any reason. Questions on matters of public interest could be asked "subject to such conditions and restrictions as may be prescribed in the rules made by the governor-General for the provincial Governors."

(b) Introduction of Elective Element in the Councils. Though term 'election' was neither mentioned was neither mentioned in the Act nor in the regulations, yet the Act cautiously introduced elective element in the Councils. The rules made by Lord Landsdownes Government provided for the election of *(a)* 8 members for each local council by the Muncipalities, Dstrict Boards, Chamber of Commerce, Universities etc., and *(b)* 4 for the Supreme Council by the non-official members of the Local Council. This was, obviously, indirect election. The Government of India, as a matter of course, accepted the candidates recommended by the representative bodies.

(c) **Expansion of the Legislative Councils.** The Act provided for an increase in the number of the 'Additional Members' both in the Supreme and Provincial Legislative Councils. The Supreme Legislative Council was to have not less than 10 and not more than 16 'Additional Members.' The Maximum number for Bengal was fixed at 20 and N.W.P. and Avadh at 15. There was official majority both in the provincial councils and the Central Council. Out of 16 additional members appointed in the Central Council 10 were non-officials. Thus in the total membership of 25, the official members (15) formed majority as against non-official (10) members.

(d) The Provincial Councils were authorised to frame laws without the approval of the Governor-General. They could also amend and repeal the old laws.

Significance of the Act. Through this Act a beginning was made of the indirect form of voting, the members got the right to freely discuss the government policies and also to put question to the government in matters of public interest. Thus it will have to be admitted that the 1892 Act was more progressive than the Act of1861 and so it had a great constitutional improtance. Sir Surendra Nath Banerjee, a member of the Legislative Council opined that the Act laid down the foundations of the representative government. Formerly, no Indian enjoyed the privilege of sharing counsels at a high level. The Act enabled eminent Indians like G.K. Gokhale, Ashutosh Mukherjee, Rash Behari Gosh and S.N. Banerjee to sit with the Viceroy and his Councilors and give ample proof of their political wisdom and parliamentary capacity. The Act also enlarged the functions of the Legislative Councils in financial matters. Hitherto, the council had no opportunity to discuss the financial policy of the Government.

Although the number of members was icnreased, there was still an official majority in the Governor-General's Council, as well as the Provincial Council. The spread of education developed the political consciousness of the people. The partition of Bengal and several other important political events stirred up political feelings of the people who urgently demanded an extension of the number of non-official members.

CHARACTERSTICS OF THE GOVERNMENT OF INDIA ACT 1909

Following were the Circusmtances, leading to Reforms:

(1) The Council Act of 1892. The reforms of 1892 were inadequate. They were much below the expectations of the Indians. The common people were denied any representation in the Legislative Councils. The electoral procedure was vague and cumbersome. The powers of the councils were strictly limited. It failed to provide a parliamentary structure for which the demand was growing stronger day by day.

(2) Curzon's Despotic Rule. The administration under Curzon was not only despotic and bureaucratic but also had become wooden. It had lost touch with the people. The bureaucracy flouted Indian public opinion and its attitude was insulting to self-respect of Indians. The reduction of popular element in Calcutta Corporation, the officialisation of universities, the insulting remarks by Lord Curzon about the Indians in his Calcutta University Convocation address, his costly Tibetan and Burmese imperialist wars created resentment in the Indian mind.

(3) Indifferent Attitude of the Liberal Party of England. The Liberal Party came to power in England in 1906 and it filled the Indians with hope that something would be done for them. However, they were soon disillusioned. The Liberals did not take the Indian National Movement seriously. Lord Morley, the new Secretary of State for India, believed in "the unchanging East" He believed in a policy of free trade but India needed protection. The Indians felt that even Liberal Government would not do anything for them.

(4) Humiliation of Indian Abroad. The Indians were badly treated in some British colonies. The most humiliating treatment meted out to the people of India in South Africa, Fizi and Canada exercised a continuous influence on the course of the national movement in India. Imposition of a three-pound poll tax on Indian labourers in Natal if they overstayed and prohibition imposed upon the Indians in Transvaal to hold land in their own names fanned the fire of discontent. Expulsion of Indians from the Orange River Colony in 1888 and compelling them to live among during heaps in prescribed localities, outside the town and subjecting them to intolerable discriminations in railway compartments and clubs convinced them that their humiliation abroad was to their degration at home. "The cup of humiliation was filled to the brim when in 1907 A.D. the Transvaal Government passed the Asiatic Registration Act requiring Indians to be registered by means of finger prints." Mahatma Gandhi launched Satyagrah against this most insulting Act. Bal Gangadhar Tilak—the fearless editor of the Kesari and a staunch opponent of British rule began advocating through his paper that a foreign government was less desirable than the worst native government.

(5) Thrilling Developments Outside India. In the early years of the 20th century, there took place some very thrilling development outside India. They not only infused a new spirit among the Indians but also strengthened their movement for self-government. The victory of Japan over Russia, in 1905, was of particular significant. It considerably changed the situation in India as well as Indians' outlook. It also aroused an uncommon enthusiasm among our countrymen. The news of this victory, wrote The Bengallee was discussed not only by the educated classes but also by the masses. It was popularly interpreted as the victory of Asia over Europe, of the East over the West. The defeat of the Italians by the Abyssinians and the new national movements in Egypt, Perisa and China also had a deep impact on the minds of the Indians. Dadabhai Naoroji in his presidential address at the Congress in 1906 pointedly remarked: "Indians cannot continue to remain subject to despotism, when China in the east and Persia in the west of Asia were walking up." He also pleaded for the grant of self-government to the Indians.

(6) The Rise of Extremists within the Indian National Congress. A wing or group of extremists under the leadership of Bal

Gangadhar Tilak had been organised inside the Indian National Congress. He and some other leaders of this ideology vehemently opposed the worng and anti-Indians policy of the British Government. Extremism was becoming more popular in India. It was matter of worry for the moderates. Gopal Krishan Gokhale the leader of the moderates inside the Congress had appealed to the British Government to do something immediately to satisfy the Indian opinion. Gokhale went to England and met Morley the then Secretary of State for India.

(7) All India Muslim League was formed in 1906 A.D.. The Muslims wanted that adequate steps should be taken by the government to secure their interests in the forthcoming reforms. A deputation of Muslims headed by H.H. Aga Khan waited on the Governor-General and requested that separate electorate should be conceded to the Muslims in the coming reforms. Lord Minto, the then Governor-General, agreed to look into their demands with favourable consideration.

(8) Growth of Revolutionary Terrorism. Government repression and frustration caused by the failure of the political struggle (1892-1907 A.D.) ultimately resulted in revolutionary terrorism. The terrorists adopted revolutionary means to over throw the British Government by indulging in political murders and other methods of political terrorism. For example in December 1907 an attempt was made on the life of the Lieutenant Governor of Bengal, and in April 1908 Khudiram Bose and Prafulla Chaki threw a bomb at a carriage which they believd was occupied by Kingsford, the unpopular Judge of Muzzafarpur. The era of revolutionary terrorism had begun. Many secret societies of terrorist youth came into existence. They also established centres of activity abroad. The British Government played the game of 'Divide and Rule' and tried to win over moderate nationalist opinion so that the militant and terrorist nationalists could be isolated and suppressed.

(9) Morley's Letter to Minto. In 1906, Mr. Morley wrote a letter to Lord Minto and emphasised the need of making some political reforms. The correspondence regarding making some reforms continued for three years and ultimately the Parliament passed India council Act of 1909 which is popularly known as Morley-Minto Reforms.

Provisions of the Act. The following were the main provisions of the Indian Councils Act, 1909:

(a) Central or Imperial Legislature. The number of 'additional members here was now raised at the maximum to 60. The Legislative was thus to consist of 69 members of whom 37 were to be officials while the remaining 32 non-officials. Of the officials, 9 were to be ex-officio members, namely, the Governer-General, seven ordinary members (Executive Councilors) and one extraordinary member, while the remain 28 were to be nominated by the Governor-General. Of the 32 non-officials, 5 were to be nominated by the Viceroy while the remaining 27 were to be elected.

(b) Election of the Elected Members. Regarding the elected members it was declared that the territorial representation did not suit India, and that : 'Representation by classes and interests is the only practicable method of embodying the active principle in constitution of the Indian Legislative Councils.' Thus of the 27 elected members, 13 were to come from the General Electorate which consisted of the non-official members of the legislative of Bombay, Madras, Bengal and United Provinces each of which would send two memebrs (=8) and the non-official members of the legislative councils of Central Provinces, Assam, Bihar and Orissa, Punjab and Burma each of which would send one member (=5). Of the remaining 14 twelve were to come from the Class Electorates. Six of them coming one each from the landholders' constituencies in the six provinces of Bombay, Madras, Bengal, Bihar and Orissa, United Provinces and Central Provinces, and six being returned by the separate Muslim constituencies—one each from Madras, Bombay, United Prvinces, Bihar and Orissa (=4), and two from Bengal. The remaining two were to be returned from the Special Electorates. One each from the Bengal and the Bombay Chamber of Commerce.

(c) Provincial Legislative. Membership of the provincial council was also enlarged. The membership of the Legislative Councils of the different provinces as enlarged, was to be as follows:

Burma	16
East Bengal and Assam	41
Bengal	52
Madras	47
Bombay	47
United Provinces	47
Punjab	25

The Act (1909 A.D.) provided for non-official majorities in the provinces. However, this did not mean non-official elected majorities, as some of the non-officials were to be nominated by the Governor and through these the officials control over the council was retained.

(d) Functions of Legislative Councils. The functions of the legislative councils, both Imperial (Central) and Provincial, were also greatly increased. The members were given the right of asking questions and supplementary questions for the purpose of further elucidating any point. But the members in charge of department might refuse to answer the supplementary questions off-hand. He may demand some time for the same.

(e) The membership of Certain Executive Councils of Provinces. The membership of the Executive Councils of Bengal, Madras and Bombay was raised to 4 and the Government was empowered to constitute similar Councils for the Lieutenant—Governor as well.

(f) Nomination of the Indians. Two Indians were already nominated to the Council of the Secretary of State for India in 1907 A.D. In 1909, the Governor-General was also empowered to nominate one Indian member to his Executive Council. Morley the Secretary of State for India, had appointed two Indians, Mr. K.G. Gupta and Sayyid Hussian Bilagrammi to his own council (India Council) in August, 1907 A.D. Under the Morley Minto Scheme Mr. S.P. Sinha, the Advocate-General of Bengal, was appointed as Law Member of the Governor-General's Council. This appointment afforded a great satisfaction to the educated Indians.

(g) Categorical Rejection of Indians' Demand for Responsible Government. The Morley-Minto reforms (or the Councils Act of 1909 A.D.), to the dismay of Indians negatived the grant of responsible government to India. There was, however, nothing surprising in it. This was clearly stated by Lord Morley in his speech in House of Lords in December 1908 A.D.

EVALUATION OF COUNCILS ACT OF 1909

Indian Councils Act of 1909 A.D. or Morley-Minto Reforms of 1909 were not liked by most Indians from the very outset. Even the moderates who welcomed the reforms at first, were soon disillusioned. These reforms have been criticised on the following grounds:

(a) The Councils Act of 1909 A.D. in no way changed the undemocratic and foreign character of British rule or the fact of foreign economic exploitation of the country. They were in fact, not designed to democratise Indian administention. Morley openly declared at the time : "If it could be said that this chapter of reforms led directly or necessarily to the establishment of a parliamentary system in India, I for one would have nothing at all to do with It."

(b) The right of franchise was restrictive and discriminatory. Since the qualifications' required for entitling a person to vote were kept higher, the number of voters were very few. Women were not given the right to vote By introducing a system of commmunal and class electorates, the Act created communal feelings among the people and the unity of the country received a great set-back from this measure. This discriminatory policy of the Government continued to develop in future and had serious repercussions. Separate electorates were constituted for the Sikhs in 1919, and for the Indian Christians, Anglo-Indians, Europeans and Harijans in 1935. This resulted in the division of the India sub-continent into two nations-Indian and Pakistan in 1947.

(c) The Indians wanted responsible government but it was denied to them by the Council's Act of 1909 A.D. Only minor additions were made in the powers of the Legislative Councils. In fact the Act introduced only a change of degree and not of kind.

(d) It also envisaged the future federal structure of the country by doing away with the unitary from of government.

FACTORS LEADING TO THE GOVERNMENT OF INDIA ACT 1919

Following were the circumstances leading to the Act of 1919:

(1) The Policy of Repression. The British policy of placating the Moderates and curshing the Extremists could not be successful. They could neither humour the Moderates nor suppress the Extremists, despite their repressive acts. The repressive laws which were supposed to be temporary measures were to be permanent phase. The Indian Press Act, more stringent than that of 1908, was passed in 1910. The Seditious Meetings Act of 1911, reproduced the similar law passed in 1907. To avenge the attempt on the life of Lord Hardinge in December 1912, the Criminal Law (Amendment) Act was passed. The latter Act made it penal to conspire to commit an offence even though the conspiracy was accompanied by no overt act in persuance of its objects." The enactment of these measures caused great resentment in the country. The non-official in the Legislative Councils Vehemently opposed them but the government did not pay any heed to their protests and warnings.

(2) Reforms of 1909 were not Satisfactory. The Reforms of 1909 could not appease the Indian as they did not get anything out of it. Even the Moderates like Gokhale were disappointed by their hollowness. These did not give enough power to the Indians. The structure of parliamentary form of government was introduced but executive was not made responsible to the legislature. Official majority was restained in case of Imperial Legislative Coucil and non-official majorities were introduced in case of Provincial Legislative Councils. It meant that power was not in the hands of the representatives of the people. It was an inadequate measure and 'only a half way house'. This Act was defective in many respects and was a sad failure.

(3) The Role of Indians Living Outside. The role played by the Indian's abroad was not less significant. These Indians were being subjected to very discriminative and humiliating treatment by the Governments of the countries they inhabited. They realised that the root cause of all this was their slavery at home; and so long as this lasted they could expect no honourable treatment by any country outside Indian. In March 1913 some Indians in the United States of America held a conference at Washington, and founded their Hindi Association when began later to be known as the Lala Har Dayal and Pandit Kanshi Ram of Ambala were among the more important leaders of this movement. In November 1913 the Party started its paper, 'Ghadar', which was published in Hindi, Gurmukhi, Urdu and Marathi. The paper soon began to reach Argentina, Australia New York, Fiji, New Zealand, Zanzibar, East India, Siam, Malaya, Burma, China and Japan, and the branches of the party were like wise established in these countries.

(4) Home Rule Movement. Lockmanya Tilak and Mrs. Annie Besant started the Home-Rule Movement. Tilak gave to the Nation the famous slogan—"Freedom is our birth right and I shall have it." The Muslim League also supported this movement which panicked the British authorities.

(5) The First World War Gave Strength to the Indians Claims and Aspirations. The Solmen declarations of the British statesmen that War was being fought for democracy and freedom did not fall flat on the Indian political leaders. They found in them a new dose of inspiration. Besides, the principle of self-determination for all people, as proclaimed by President Wilson in his 'Fourteen Points'. had a direct bearing on the Indian problem. Self-determination was to be applied to the politically dorment Arabs in the turkish Empire, it was asserted, it should be applied to the Indians as well. In short, influenced by the liberal declarations of the English statesman, the educated Indians, at least, developed a strong feeling that their masters had no moral justification, whatsoever, to deny them the right, for which they were fighting in Europe. Hence, recognition of the right of India to self-government and self-determination became the political objective of the Indian aspirations. The War developed among Indians a new sense of self-esteem'. For as many a field of Europe the Indians troops won distinctions as well as honour. The British statesmen freely referred to their greatness as fighters.

(6) The Dissatisfaction Among the Indian Muslims. The Muslims were at first friendly to the Government because separate Electorates had been granted to them. They also began to feel dissatisfied after a short time. The cancellation of the Partition of Bengal at the time of Delhi Darbar came as a shock to them and they began to lose faith in the British Government. Britain did not help Turkey against Italy during the Turco-Indian War and the Indian Muslims resented this policy of the British Government of leaving Turkey alone. the Balkan Wars of 1912-13 were regarded a Christian—conspiracy against the Muslim Turkey. These factors made the Indian Muslims feel dissatisfied with the British Government.

(7) The Lucknow Pact of 1916. The Lucknow Pact was an important document which struck a compromise between the Hindus and the Muslims. Both the League and the Congress left their original stands and agreed to concede each other's viewpoint as far as possible. In this Pact the Congress accepted the principle of separate Muslim electorates and a weightage to the Muslims in the minority provinces. Several other concessions were made to the League, and he latter agreed with the Congress on a joint scheme which said : India should be "lifted from the position of a Dependency to that of an equal partner in the empire with the self governing Dominions."

Thus the unity was forged between the two parties, and between the two communities. Those indeed were to the days of India's glory when the spirit of nationalism began to dominate once again the patty communal considerations.

Under the circumstances, the question of further constitutional reforms did not brook delay. A pretant proof of the wide awakening of the Indians at this stage was that they themselves formulated various schemes for reforms for the considerations of the Government.

(8) August Declaration. Mr. Montague was a great friend of India. He had sympathised with the aspirations of the people of India and as such can be compared with persons like Lord Pethick Lowrence and Sir Stafford Cripps. He brought a new outlook to his office. Which the fortunes of the Allies were at their lowert ebb, he made the following declaration on 20th August 1917 : "The Policy of His Majesty's Government, with which the Government of India are in complete accord is the increasing association of Indians in every branch of the administration and the gradual development of self-government institutions with a view to the progressive realisation of responsible Government in India as an integral part of the British Empire." They have decided that substantial steps in this direction should be taken as soon as possible, and that it is of the highest importance as a preliminary to considering what these steps should be that there should be a free and informal to exchange of opinion between those in authority at Home and in India.

(9) Montague's Visit to India. With a view to translate his declaration into action and to prepare a reform plan with the help of the Indian leaders and the Indian government after holding consultations with them. Mongtague came to India in November 1917 and remained in the country till the following year. Here in the country he held meetings with the extremists and the moderates in the Congress and with the leaders of the Muslim League.

Main Provisions. The Act brought changes in the Home Government, in the Government of India and the provincial administration as well. Its main, provisions were :

(a) Preamble. According to the Preamble of the Act, British India was to remain an integral part of the British Empire. The objective of the Parliament was to establish a responsible Government in British India. It was necessary to ensure the increasing association of the Indians in every branch of administration and the gradual development self-governing institutions.

(b) The Council of the secretary of State for India. The Act of 1919 introduced the following changes in the composition and powers of the Secretary of State-in-Council:

(i) The strength of the Council was reduced. It was to very between 12 maximum and 8 minimum in place of 14 and 10 respectively.

(ii) Their term of office was reduced to 5 years.

(iii) Their salary was fixed at 1200 a year plus 600 for Indian members.

(iv) The Council was to meet once a month instead of once a week as provided earlier.

(v) One half of them were to have resided or served in India for a period of 10 years and should not have left India for more than 5 years before their appointment.

(vi) The position of Secretary of State was exchanced in his relation to the Council. He was given discretion to consult or not consult the Council in any matter with two expectations : In financial matters and matters relating to Indian services, he was under obligation to consult the Council. So far the salary of the Secretary of State for India was paid out of the Indian revenues. This Act provided that his salary was now to be paid form the treasury of England. His powers and functions were also reduced. He retained control over foreign affairs, military affairs, currency public debts etc.

(c) A new office, the office of High Commissioners for India was created for the first time, and some of the functions of the Secretary of State were transferred to him. The High Commissioner was to be an agent of the Governor-General-in-Council, was to be appointed by the Government of India and paid from the Indian revenues. The functions assigned to the High Commissioner were supposed mainly to be ceremonial, though commercial and certain other functions previously performed by the Secretary of State were now to be performed by him. Thus, he was to handle the function of purchases in England of machinery and stores for India.

(d) In the Executive Council the number of the Indian members was raised to three.

(e) The Central Legislature. The Act of 1919 provided for two Houses *(i)* The Legislative Assembly and *(ii)* The Council of States.

(i) The Legislative Assembly. The Legislative Assembly consisted of 145 members of whom 41 were nominated and 104 were elected. Of the 41 nominated members, 26 used to be official and 15 non-official. The 104 elected members represented various interests, castes, communities and provinces. They were divided as General 52, Muslims 30, Sikhs 2, Europeans 9, Zamindars 7, Chamber of Commarce 4. Its term was for three years unless reduced or extended by the Governor-General. The members were elected by very few selected voters under very strict reglations. Only those person who paid income tax between (Rs. 15-20) or Municipal tax or land Revenue between (Rs. 50-150) or the owners of the properly with rental value of at the least upto Rs. 180/- per year eligible to vote. The qualifications, however, differed a little according to place, religion, caste etc. The Legislative Assembly had its own Chairman who was first-nominated by the Governor-General but subsequently used to be elected by the members themselves.

(ii) ***The Council of State.*** The Council of State was the upper chambers of the Central Legislature. It was to consist of 60 members, one of whom was to be appointed as the President of the Council by the Governor-General. Out of the remaining 59 member, 34 were to be elected and 25 nominated. The 25 nominated members comprised 19 officials and 6 non-officials. The 34 elected members were to be returned in the following manner : 20 by general elactorates, 3 by European Chamber of Commerce and 11 by ammunal electorates (10 by Muslims and 1 by Sikhs). The franchise of the Council of State was extremely restricted. Also, it differed in different provinces.

(f) Powers of the Central Legislature. The central Legislaure as constitued of the above mentioned two Houses, was supposed to have been given very wide powers. It could legislate for the whole of the British India, for the Indian subjects and servants of the Government, whether inside or outside the country. It could repeal or amend any law already exisiting in the country. The members of the Legislature were given the right to instiate a legislation according to rules. They could move a resolution, and a motion for adjournment. The right and freedom of speech was given.

There were, however, certain restrictions imposed on the Legislature. In certain cases, previous sanction of the Governor-General was required for the introduction of a bill such as:

(i) Amendment or repeal of an existing law or an ordinance of the Governor-General.

(ii) Foreign relations and the relations with the Indian state.

(iii) Discipline or maintenance of the military, naval and the air forces.

(iv) Public debt and revenue and.

(v) Religion, religious rites and usages of the people. Further, if the Governor-General felt any bill or a part of it "affects the safety or tranquillity of British India or any part there of, he could prevent its consideration.

(g) Division of Subjects. The Act aimed at introducing partially responsible government in the provinces. This necessitated the division of subjects. The Act contained a list of Central and Provincial subjects. The defence, foreign and political elections, customs, posts and telegraphs, currency, communications etc. were Central subject. The list of the Pronvincail subjects included Local Self-Government, Public health, sanitation, education public works, irrigation, agriculture etc.

(h) Changes Affecting the Provincial Government. In each of the Governor Provinces, the Provincial subjects were further subdivided into two part—'reserved' and 'transferred'. The reserved subejcts were kept under official control where as the transferred subjects were made over to popular controls. Land revenue, and irrigation, famine relief, law and order, industrial matter, control of newspaper, books and printing presses, local fund audit, borrowing money on the sole credit of the Province were known as 'reserved subject'. Local Self-Government, public health, and sanitation, medical administration, edcuation other than European or Anglo-Indian, public works, agriculture and fisheries, excise on alcoholic liquors and drugs, registration of deeds and documents, religions and charitable edowments, development of industries, adulteration of food stuffs and other articles, weights and measure, liberaries, etc. were to be termed as 'transferred subjects'. In case of a conflict, wheather a particular matter related to a 'reserved' or a 'transferred' subject the decision of the Governor was final. This system of dividing the provincial subjects into reserved and transferred subjects and entrusting than to two different authorities appointed in different ways is commonly known as 'Dyarchy'. The reserved subjects were to be administrered by the Governor assisted by an Executive Council, where as the transferred subjects were dealt with by the Governor with the half of his ministers.

Significance of the Act of 1919. There is no doubt that Government of India Act of 1919 was an important instalment of constitutional reform. It was more substantial and comprehensive than any attempted before. It introduced direct election and widened the franchise. The Act undoubtedly made a new departure : for the first time in the history of British rule it provided for transfer of power, even though the transfer was halting and the power extremely limited. As Coupland says, "The Act crossed the line between legislative and executive authority. Previous measures had enabled Indians increasingly to control their legislatures but now their Government......Now Indians were to govern, so to speak, on their own..... as leaders of the elected majorities in their legislatures and responsible to them." The number of the non-official members was increased in the Central Council. The number of members in the Central and Provincial Assemblies was also increased and they were given more powers. The Secretary of State and his staff were to be paid by the British Exchequer which reduced the financial strain on the Indian budget. The powers of the Secretary of State for India were also reduced. The introduction of responsible government to a certain extent, was a important provision of this Act.

The Act of 1919 had Many Defects from the Nationalist Point of View. These were:

(a) It failed to establish even a partial responsible government at the Centre. Nothing substantial was granted to the Cnetral Legislature in vital matters of controlling the executive, formulating legislation and directing the finance. Nearly 60% of the budget was withdrawn from the vote of the Legislative Assembly. And with regard to the remaining 40%, the Governor-General was empowered to restore any demand refused or reduced by the Central Legislature.

(b) The Powers of the Governor-General were very wide in the legislative and financial sphere and he could overside and ignore the Central Legislative in his discretion. Every Bill passed by the Legislature could become law only after it received the absent of the Governor-General. He might refer the Bill for the consideration of the Secretary of State. His veto was absolute.

(c) Division of Subjects between the Centre and the Provinces was defective. According to Punniah, the division was not clear-cut or definite. Overlapping of subjects between the two lists was discernible. For instance 'Comernce' and 'Laws regarding property' were placed in the Central List, Important section like 'excise' and 'Laws regarding land tenure were assigned to the Provinces.

(d) The franchise for both the Houses was extremely restricted. High property qualifications, holding of titles or membership of the University Senate made the Upper House representative and custodian of the vested interests of zamindars and the capitalist classes. The franchise for the Assembly was also very high. Besides the distribution of the seats of the elected members among the Provinces on the basis of their importance and not population, weightage to the minority communities and also to the smaller provinces of India made the Assembly undemocratic in character.

(e) The introduction of dyarchy in the provinces was too complicated to be smoothly worked.

SCHEME OF DYARCHY

The Act of 1919 was passed in pursuance of the Policy Declaration of 1917, which promised 'Responsible Government' to the people of India. The Government wanted to allow the Indians to participate in the administration but felt shy entrusting them with full responsibility. It was probably this feeling that the dyarchial form of Government was established in the provinces. The Dyarchy was introduced in Bengal, Madras, Bombay, Uttar Pradesh, Punjab, Bihar, Orissa, Madhya Pradesh and Assam in 1921 and, much later in 1932, in North-West Frontier Province. With breaks here and there sometimes, the system was continued in the provinces till April 1937.

'Dyarchy' is a derivative of two words—'di' meaning 'twice' and 'archie' meaning 'rule'. Dyarchy was an experiment of 'Double Government' which was imported in India with the advent of

Montford Reforms. Under this system, the Provincial subjects after demarcation from the Central subjects were divided into two parts—the 'reserved' and the 'transferred'. The former comparatively of more importance (*e.g.* Jails, Police, Justice, Finance, Irrigation etc.) were to be governed by the Governor and his Executive Council whereas the latter of less significance (*e.g.* Education, Agriculture, Local Self-Government etc.) were transferred to the Indian ministers and the Governor. These two halves of the Government were to function separately and distinctly, each of them being independent of the other.

Object. The immediate object of the Dyarchieal experiment was to impart training to the Inidans in the art of responsible self-Government preliminary to the progressive realization of responsible government in British India. Moreover, Dyarchy was expected to be bridge between British bureaucracy and the Indians.

Failure of Dyarchy. Dyarchy, no doubt, worked for over a period of sixteen year, yet it worked creakily. According to the Minority Report of the Reforms Enquiry Committee the new system operated in the spirit of reasonablenness during the first three years and there prevailed a spirit of harmony, good will and co-operation between the Legislature and the Executive. But after 1924, the new constitution proved unsatisfactory and unworkable. The constitutional bre?kdowns in Bengal and C.P. clearly demonstrated that the system had fallen short of the expectations of its authros and was also incapable of yielding better results in the future:

(a) The dyarchy divided the provincial administration into two independent parts. It was opposed to political theory and, in practice, it was impossible to work on it. The reserved subjects were administered by the Executive Councillors who were responsible. Only to the Governor while the ministers were responsible not only to the Governor but also to the Legislative Council. The members of these two parts of administration, viz., the Councillors and the Ministers could not work in cooperation by the very nature of the difference in their respective positions. On the contrary, most of the time, they blamed one another for mutual faults.

(b) The divisions in the provinces of the subjects under the two heads of the Reserved and Transferred was neither logicalstat, sensible nor understandable; the result being that neither a Minister could work efficiently without the help of a Councillor, nor could the councillor work without the help of a Minister. Thus, while Agriculture was transferred, irrigation was sought to be separated from it and kept as reserved. Education was similarly transferred, while strangely enough the education of the Anglo-Inidans was kept as reserved. The industries were, again, transferred; while water power, factories, mines, etc. were kept as reserved. Sir K.A. Reddi, a minister of Madras thus remakred : "I was a Minister for development without the Forests, I was the Minster of Agriculture minus irrigation.

(c) At times there was such a confusion that the authorities could not decide whether a particular subject belonged to one department or the other. C.Y. Chinatmani, a Minister of Uttar Pradesh, thus relates an experience. "In 1921, an enquiry was started in the Department of Agriculture on the question of the fragmentation of the holdings. When the report was submitted in the following years, all of a sudden it was discovered that the question should have been handled by the Revenue Department, to which the matter was now referred. But here too, when the question had engaged the attention of the Revenue Department for two years, it was discovered that the subject after all belonged to the Co-operative Department".

(d) The official bloc and the nominated member always voted with the Government. The Joint Committee Report had proposed freedom of voting to the official bloc, but during the working of the reforms they were required to vote with the Government. It was on one or two occasions that the officials were permitted to vote free. If there was a difference opinion between the Governor and the Ministers, the official bloc voted for Governor's policy against that of the minister. This did not promote discipline nor it enhanced the position of ministers.

(e) The relations between the ministers and the services were not always happy or harmonious. The Minister expected the services to be obedient but the latter thought the former to be novices and expected, them to act upon their advice and experience. thus on many occasions, differences between the ministers and the services cropped up. According to the rules, if a ministers differed from the opinion of the Head of the Department, Commissioner of a devision or the Permanent Secretary, the matter was to be referred to the Governor for final decision. Since the Governor, and the Heads of the Departments and the Secretaries belonged to the same class, the former was more akin to them rather, than the ministers. Hence he generally favoured the Heads of the Departments and the Secretaries rather than the ministers. The ministers were not empowered to select their own subordinates when vacancies occurred in their departments, as the more important of these posts were kept reserved for the members of the All-India Services.

(f) Another glaring cause of the failure of Dyarchy was the reservation of the Department of Finance in the hands of an Executive Councillor, though the department was to cater to the needs of both the reserved and the transferred departments. In the words of Mr. Chintamani, "The Finance Member was certainly more anxious to see that his served departments got all the money they required before other Departments got what they wanted." In fact, the Finance Secretary, as a member of the Indian Civil Service, did not sympathise with the popular aspirations represented by ministers.

(g) Joint Responsibility was not encouraged by the Act of 1919. The Governors sometimes consulted the Executive Councillors jointly but they never consulted the ministers jointly. The ministers themselves were several times at variance with each other. The Governors never held joint consultations of the two branches of government *i.e.* Executive Councillors and the Ministers. Hence, in the absence of joint responsibility, every Minister would dance attendance upon the Governor to win his (Governor's) favour. For, this gave him a good chance of his continuing in office.

(h) According to some scholars the time was not in favour of the Act of 1919. The spectre of Jallianwala tragedy still haunted the Indian mind and Gandhiji's Non-Cooperation Movement was swaying through the whole land. The Muslim sentiments had also been injured by the shabby treatment given to Turkish sultan and the 'Khilafat Movement' was at its peak. In short, the Indian mind was full of doubt, suspicion, anger and bitterness against the British policy of repression. Economically too India was passing through hardships. Stringent regulations and repressive measure of the Government made the people still more apprehensive.

(i) The man in the street knew that the reforms of 1919 were in the nature of a half-way house. The Indians knew that they were going to get more in the future. The result was that the people of India were not in a mood to give the reforms a fair trial. Regarding the working of dyarchy, Sir H. Butler says : "In India, it has almost become a term of abuse. I have heard one man shouting to another : 'You are a dyarchy.' 'I will beat you with a dyarchy,' said one Indian boy to another and when questioned as to what dyarchy was, replied, a new kind of tennis racket'. I have been received in Burma village by "a dyarchy band braying against a Home Rule band with all the vigous of village faction, neither having the least idea of what Rule or dyarchy meant."

ENACTMENT OF GOVT. OF INDIA, ACT OF 1935 A.D.

Following were the Circumstances leading to the passing of the Act of 1935:

(a) The Act of 1919 had failed to satisfy the political aspirations of the Indian people. The system of Dyarchy introduced by the Reforms of 1919 was unsound in principle and unworkable in practice. The breaking down of the system of Dyarchy in the Provinces resulted in serious disappointment among nationalist circles. There was, therefore, wide spread dissatisfaction with the reforms an account of their inherent defects.

(b) In order to put an end to agitation launched by the Indian leaders Rowlatt Act was passed. The Act bestowed vast powers on the police which severely dealt with the impending danger. Civil liberty was mercilessly suppressed, self-determination was totally crushed, and those very principles for which the Indians had shed their blood in war were now denied to them. Disturbances broke out in Delhi, Ahmednagar and certain cities of the Punjab. At this moment occurred the Jalianwala Bagh Tragedy. The whole nations now turned against the British. Consequently the Indians felt agitated and Gandhiji decided to launch a 'Satyagraha Movement' against these oppressive laws. Law-yers gave up their practice, Men and women courted arrest in thousands. The English goods were boycotted. In 1922 Chauri Chaura incident happend and Mahatma Gandhi was obliged to suspend the movement. The suspension of bitterly resented by certain leaders. Under the leadership of C.R. Dass and Moti Lal Nehru they organised themselves into 'Swarajist Party.' The Swarajist Party believed in continuous obstruction. They believed in mending or ending the constitution. The general election of 1922 resulted in a thumping success of Swarajists. In 1924 they moved an amendment urging the Governor-General to take early measures for the revision of the Act of 1919.

(c) In 1924 Muddiman Committee was appointed. Its Chairman was Sir Alexander Muddiman. It also included certain important leaders like Sir Tej Bahadur Sapru and Mohammad Ali Jinnah. It submitted a minority report conddeming the Dyarchy as unworkable and unsatisfactory while others recommended that it should be modified. Others held that it was best suited to the transititonal period. The policy of the government remained unchanged.

(d) In 1927 the Simon Commission was appointed to look through the working of the 1919 reforms and submit a report with suggestions there on. It was in 1930, that the commission submitted its report in which the system of dyarchy was flayed and forcefully condemned. The Commissions also pleaded for establishing a representative government in the provinces and abolishing the dyarchy.

(e) The Nehru Report, 1928. While the Simon Commission was carying on its work in isolation from Indian public opinion, the leading Indian political parties were trying to forge a common political programme. An All-Parties Conference, presided over by Dr. M.A. Ansari was convened at Bombay on May 19, 1928 and appointed a committee under Moti Lal Nehru's Chairmanship to consider and determine the principles of a constitution for India. Since the Nehru Report had not been accepted and the Congress had started Satyagraha Movement in 1930, 1931 and 1932 respectively to decide the future of India. Only in the Second Round Table Conference, Mahatama Gandhi participated as a sole representative of the Congress. In August 1932 the British Prime Minister Ramsay Macdonald announced the famous Communal Award and the favours White Paper was published in 1933. The Joint Select Committee submitted its report on 22nd November 1934.

On the basis of its recommendations the government of India Act, 1935 was passed.

Provisions of Government of India Act, 1935

(1) Lengthy Statue. The Government of India Act, 1935, which was a very lengthy statue consisting of 321 sections and 10 Schedules, was in its material drawn from the following sources:

(i) The Simon Commission Reports,

(ii) The Nehru Commission Report,

(iii) The discussions held at the Round Table Conferences,

(iv) The White Paper,

(v) The Joint Select Committee Report.

Besides others, there were two special reasons why the Act was so lengthy : First it had to deal with a very complex type of Government, and second, it tried to provide legal safeguards against the wrong use of power by Legislators and Ministers.

(2) Preamble. An interesting feature of the Act was that it had no preamble of its own. It borrowed the preamble from the Act of 1919. The preamble had envisaged Dominion Status for India by stages, and since the basic principle of this policy was not changed, the authros of the Act while repealing the Act of 1919, retained its preamble which they attached to the Act of 1935.

(3) Supremacy of the British Government. Supremacy of the British Parliament over Indian affairs was maintained. The British Parliament was allowed to retain its power of amending, altering or repealing the Constitutional Law Concerning India. The proposed Federal Legilatures and Provincial Legisaltures were not vested with constitutional powers. They could only recommend changes under certain prescribed conditions and in certain specified matters.

(4) The Indian Council was Abolished. In its place, a few advisers were nominated to help the Secretary of State for India.

Their minimum number was three and the maximum could be six. At least half of them were to be form among those who should have served in India for atleast ten years and should not have remained outside it for more than two years prior to their nomination as advisers. Their tenure was fixed as five years. In certain matters such as the services, their advice was binding on the Secretary of State for India.

(5) According to this Act important changes were made in the powers of the Secretary of State and India Council. The most important of these changes are given below:

(i) The control and authority of the Secretary of State was completely eliminated from those subjects and departments which were administered by the Governors on the advice of their ministers.

(ii) The secretary of State got full powers in the following. Taking loans from the British Government in England, appointing officers for the all India services, deciding their salaries and allowances and to provide security to them.

(iii) The Secretary of State being the adviser of the British Crown could issue instructions and advice to the Governor-General and to the provincial Governors.

(6) The Federal Legislature. There was to be bicameral federal legislature in which the states were given disproportionate weightage. Moreover, the representatives of the states were not to be elected by the people but appointed directly by the rulers. The Council of state or the Upper House was to consist of 260 members and the Federal Assembly or the Lower House 375 members. The Council of State was to be a permanent body one-third of whose members would retire every third year.

(7) Federal Government on Paper. It provided for establishment of an Indian Federation made up of British Indian Provinces and Indian States. The Federation, however, could not come into existence. In the case of states accession to the Federation was voluntary, and the Federation could not be established until the accession of states entitled to fill not less than half the 104 seats of the Council of State and having a population of not less than 29,490,153 persons.

(8) Provincial Autonomy. In the provinces the dyarchial system of Government was abolished and distinction between transferred and Reserved subjects was ended. The Governor was to administer the provinces with the aid and advice of a Council of Ministers. The legislature had now the power to remove the executive from power. The Council of Ministers was collectively responsible to the provincial legislature but the Governor could dismiss them under certain circumstances. They could veto legislative action and legislate on their own. Moreover, they retained full control over the civil services and the police.

(9) Distribution of Powers. Schedule VIII of the Act had three lists. The Central List contained 59 items such as naval, military and airforce, currency and coinage, external affairs, post and telegraph, wireless and telephones, broadcasting, Census and statistics, federal public services, railways, import and export, trade marks, copyrights, insruance etc. The Provincial List contained 54 items such as law and order, justice and courts, prisions, land acquisition, public debts, local self—government, education, taxes on agriculture, professions and stamp duties, public works, water supply, canals and irrigation etc. The Concurrent List contained 36 items such as criminals and civil law and procedure, evidence, and oaths, electricity, industrial and labour disputes, old age pensions, trade unions, newspapers, books and printing press, marriage and divorce, adoption and succession etc.

(10) Federal Court. The Act provided for the establishment of a Federal Court. It was necessitated by the adoption of provincial Autonomy to decided cases of dispute between Provinces and between the Units and the Federation. It could declare laws 'ultra vires' or constitutional. It was also given the ordinary Civil and Criminal jurisdiction. However, it was not Supreme Court. Appeals could go against its decisions to the Judicial Committee of the Privy Council and also against the Judgements of High Courts direct without taking them to the Federal Court. Thus it was the highest Court in India but not the Final Court.

(11) Dyarchy at the Centre. The Federal Executive was to be composed of the Governor-General and a Council of Ministers. In respect of certain specified subjects (*e.g.*, the prevention of any grave menance to the peace and tranquillity of the country or any of its part) the Governor-General had full freedom to accept or to reject the advice of Ministers. In certain other subjects (defence, external affairs etc.) he was empowered to act at his discretion or to manage them through three Councellors appointed by himself. Thus Dyarchy, rejected by the Simon Commission, was deliberately provided for in the Federation by the Act of 1935.

(12) The Head of the State. The Governor-General was to administer. All residual powers were vested in the Governor-General. Defence, external affairs and ecclesiastical affairs in his discretion as reserved subjects. The Governor-General and the Governors were to be appointed by the British Government were to be responsible to it.

(13) Reserve Bank. A Reserve Bank was established with a Governor and fifteen Directors to control currency and keep financial stability in the country.

(14) Separate Communal Electorates. Another important though derogotary feature of the Act was the retention of separate Communal Electorates. If further extended the principle of Communal electorates to Anglo-Indians, Europeans and Harijans. The Muslims were given $33\frac{1}{3}\%$ of the British Indian seats in both the Houses.

(15) Rearrangement of Provinces. Under the Constitution Act of 1935, the provinces of British India was re-arranged. Sind was detached from Bombay and created into a separate province (on purely communal grounds) to increase the number of Muslim majority provinces. Orissa was taken from Bihar to form a new province with portions of Madras and the Central Provinces. Besides, Burma was separted from India and Aden was transferred from the administrative control of the Government of India to that of the Colonial office.

Observations on the Act of 1935. The Government of India Act, 1935 was a great advancement as compared to the Act of 1919. It abolished the system of dyarchy in the provinces and all the provincial subjects were entrusted to the Ministers who were responsible to the Legislature as well as the Governor. The size of the Legislative Councils was enlarged and the franchise was extended. The system of the election was encouraged.

The Act could not satisfy the nationalist aspiration for both political and economic power continued to be concentrated in the hands of the British Government. Foreign rule was to continue as before, only a few popularly elected ministers were to be added to the structure of British administration in India. The Congress condemned the Act as "totaly disappointing." It seems desirable to refer to the important points of criticism levelled against the Act of 1935. According to Pandit Nehru, the new Indian Constitution was a "machine with strong brakes and no engine." According to another critic, "The India Act of 1935 tests to the full Indian capacity for administration and government exactly as a man's capacity with hands and feet tied. Following were the chief defects of this Act:

(1) The federal structure provided in this Act had many inherent and apparent defects. While the provinces of British Indian automatically became the members of the proposed union, the states had the option whether to join it or not. The powers of the legislatures and ministers were limited by the powers of the Governor-General and the Governors. In the provinces though all affairs were handed over to Indian ministers, yet, they had no means to force the Governor to act according to their desires in case their view differed from that of the governor. Thus, the provincial autonomy was only in name. In fact, the Indians were not given independent powers even in a limited field.

(2) No fundamental right was given to citizens and no directive principle for formation of policy was given for the government.

(3) By this Act only 10 per cent of the total population of the country was given the right to vote.

(4) System of communal reservations of seats and communal electorate was still retained which not only injured our national unity but also ended the character of our representative system.

(5) The sovereignity remained vested in the British Parliament, which could make laws, change constitution, enforce new constitution as a whole or a part there of.

(6) Defence and foreign affiars were kept outside the control of ministers.

(7) Dyarchy that had failed in the provinces was introduced at the centre. The Governor-General was to appoint his Councillors other than Ministers to aid and advise him in his Discretionary Functions.

PRINCIPLES OF AUTONOMY

Provincial Autonomy may be defined as the Autonomy of Independence of the Provincial Government in the sphere of legislation, administration and finance, and sufficient freedom from control of the Central Government and the Secretary of State for India. Most of the scholars accept this truth that up to some extent the Indian Councils Act of 1935 A.D. provided Provincial Autonomy or Representative Government in the Provinces.

The Act of 1935 A.D. was said to provide for Provincial Autonomy in India. The basic principles of autonomy (or responsible government) involves three elements. They are:

(1) The provinces (or their government) should be free from the control of the Central Government. In other words the

provincial government should be allowed to act as Independent Units.

(2) The Provincial Legislature must have complete control over the Provincial Executive.

(3) The Provincial Legislature must be national and popular in character *i.e.* it must present the greatest number of the people of the province.

A close examination of the above mentioned three basic principles of provincial autonomy (or responsible government) shows that Provincial Autonomy did not exist in the real sense in the Act of 1935. In fact the Provincial Autonomy was a mere farce and far from being a reality, as will be clear from the following explanation:

(a) Free from the Central or Central Government. The first basic principle of the Provincial Autonomy is that the provincial government should be free from the unnecessarily and frequently interveue of the Central Government. It should be allowed to work and act as independent unit. If we examine the provisions of the Act of 1935, we find that the Central Government could exercise very great control over the Provincial Legislatures. In matters of legislation the Provincial Legislatures were considerably handicapped and were not free to pass what ever laws and regulations they desire. The Governor-General could proclaim a state of emergency and authorise the federal legislature to make laws on provincial subjects. Moreover he could interfere through the Governors. The Governors also were not figureheads. They had special powers. A bill passed by the provincial legislature on the initative of the ministry could vetoed by the Governor. He might not allow a bill to be introduced. He could stop the discussion of a bill at any stage. He could make Governor's Acts and issue ordinances. The ministers did not have a free hand even in the matter of proposing taxes. About 40 per cent of the budget consisted of non-votable items over which provincial legislature and ministry had no control.

(b) The Provincial Legislature should have Complete Control Over the Provincial Executive. The Second pincipal of

Provincial Autonomy is that the Legislature should have full control over the Executive. The Executive in a Province consisted of the Governor and the Councial of Ministers. The Ministers were responsible to the provincial Legislature but the Legislature had no control over the Governor who was the head of the Provincial Executive. The Governor, on the other hand, was clothed with increased powers and the Indian Councils Act of 1935 A.D. had conferred upon him more autocratic powers than before. Besides ordinary powers, he enjoyed several special powers. Special powers of the Governor included:

(i) Issuing of ordinances and the Governor's Acts,

(ii) The power of assume for himself the functions of the Government in the event of a breakdown of the Constitution, or failure of the constituional machinery,

(iii) Stopping the discussion of Bills at any stage,

(iv) Giving or with holding assent to Bills passed by the Legislature or reserving them for the pleasure of His Majesty,

(v) He was also given the power of making regulation for the law and order or for the peace of the province and good government of Exluded or Partially Excluded Areas. He performed most of his functions either in his individual judgement or at his discretion. Many items like the salaries and allowances of Civilans and the expenditure of the Governor's establishment were non-votable, *i.e.*, the Legislature had got no control over them. The special powers of the Governors were not the only hindrances in the free functioning of the Legislature. Prevention of grave menance to the peace and tranquility of the province, safeguardring the legitimate interests of the minorities, looking after the legitimate interests of the services, prevention of discrimination against British subjects and companies protection of the rights of Indian States and the rights and dignities of their rulers, and securing the execution of the orders issued by the Governor-General were some of the important special responsibilities of the Governors. Many occasions proved the truth of the criticism that the special powers of the Governor stood in the way of the development of Cabinet responsibility in the provinces.

(c) The Principle of Representation of the Largest Number of the People. The third principal of Provincial Autonomy is that the legislature must represent the largest number of the people. In practice, we find otherwise or the Provincial Legislatures represented a little more than twelve per cent of the total population of British India, the franchies on the whole was very narrow.

The Congress took the view that the special powers and special reponsibilities of the Governors would make Provincial Autonomy a farce. These would be used by the Governors to interfere in the affairs of the ministers. Pandit Jawahar Lal Nehru remarked, "We are provided with a car-all brakes and no engine." Bitterly opposed the Act though the Congress was, it decided to contest the elections under the new act of 1935, though with the declared aim of showing how unpopular the Act was. The elections concusively demonstrated that a large majority of Indian's supported the Congress which swept the polls in most of the provinces. Congress ministers were formed in July 1937 in seven out of eleven provinces. Later, Congress formed coalition govenrments in two others.

(d) Working of the Provincial Autonomy. This arrangement worked smoothly from 1937 to 1939 as the Governors exercised their 'Special Powers' and Individual judgement carefully and very sparingly. At some stages, some hurdles appeared in some provinces which were satisfactorily cleared. Given below is a brief description of its working in different provinces:

(i) **Khare Controversy in C.P..** Dr. Khare was the Chief Minister of C.P. and he asked his colleagues to resign so that he could reshuffle his Cabinet. Two of the ministers refused to resign unless they get instructions from the Congress High Command. On the Chief Minister's advice, however, the Governor dismissed them. The Congress

High Command did not take it favourably and called it Governor's interference to provoke dissensions among the Congress leaders and replaced Khare by Ravi Shanker Shukla as their Chief Minister.

(ii) **Constitutional Crissis in Orissa.** In 1938 the name of the Chief Secretary to the Government of Orissa was proposed for appointment as the Acting Governor of the province. This elevation of an official subordinate to the ministry to a post above its head was bitterly resented. The ministry of Orissa, there upon, declared its intention to resign if this appointment was not cancelled. The Congress High Command lent full support to the ministerial stand. Before the sitution could take a serious turn, the permanent Governor got his leave cancelled and thus the impending crisis was averted.

(iii) **Question of Political Prisoners in U.P. and Bihar.** In the United Provinces and Bihar again a crisis developed in February 1938 when the Congress Government here took up the question of releasing the political prisoners in order to fulfil their promises. The Governor saw in this a grave menance to peace, and the Governor-General interevened by issiuing orders against this step under Section 126.

(iv) **Allegation of Persecution of the Muslims in U.P..** In U.P. the Muslims League proposed a coalition with the Congress, which the latter did not agree. Congress of persecuting the Muslims in U.P. The Congress offered enquiry into these allegations by the Chief Justice of India, which the League refused to accept and suggested that the enquiry he held by a commission of the Judges headed by the Law Member of the Privy Council. The Congress agreed but the Viceroy dropped the idea of investigation.

In this way the Governors did not interfere in the affairs of the Congress Ministers and Provincial Autonomy was proving a success. The role of the Governors, however, was active in other provinces like Bengal and Sindh where coalition ministers were unstable.

End of the Provincial Autonomy. In 1939 the Second World War broke out and the British Government also declared war on behalf of the Indian Government as well. The National Congress was in full sympathy with the vicitims of Foriest aggression. It was willing to help the forces of democracy in their struggle against fascist. But, the Congress leaders asked, how was it possible for an enslaved nation to aid other in their fight for freedom. They therefore demanded that India must be declared free-or at least effective power put in Indian hands—before it could actively participate in the war.

INDIAN INDEPENDENCE ACT 1947

Power was formally transferred to the Indians hands by the Indian Independence Act 1947, which was passed by the British Parliament in 1947. There were several causes that led to the passing of this act:

(1) They gave undue importance to Jinnah, a great leader of Muslim League.

(2) Opposition of all the policies of Congress by Muslim League was also one of the great reason for passing this act.

(3) Failure of Interim Government was also one of the greatest cause of passing this act.

(4) The communal riots had started by that time in many parts of the country. So it was too difficult to maintain peace and order in the country except to accept the partition of India.

(5) The English had followed the policy of "Divide and Rule".

(6) They never liked the role of Congress, who advocated total freedom of India.

(7) As the political condition of India was first deteriorating, Prime Minister Atlee of Labour Government in England declared that his government would quit India.

(8) Efforts of Lord Mount Batten. In March, 1947 Lord Mountbatten became the Viceroy of India. He presented his proposal of partition of India to the leaders of Congress and Muslim League. They prepared a plan which is known as Mount Batten Plan or June Plan.

According to this plan country was to be divide into two dominions of India and Pakistan. Referrendum was to be held in the Province of N.W.F.P. to know that people wanted to live with India or Pakistan. The provinces of Punjab Bengal and Assam were also to be divided. The states would have the option to join either of two dominions of India or Pakistan. The transfer of Power was to be finalised on 15 August, 1947. As Congress and Muslim League both accepted this plan, British Parliament passed the Indian Independence Act 1947 on July 4, 1947. Following were the provisions of this Act:

(1) Each Dominion was to have a Governor-General, who was to be appointed by the British King on the advice of Cabinet of the concerned dominion.

(2) The Governor-General and Governors of provinces were to act only on the advice of the Ministers.

(3) The British King was to drop the title of Emperor of India.

(4) All the powers of British Government were to be transferred to the Constitutent Assemblies of the two Dominions of India and Pakistan.

(5) This Act put an end to the British Rule in India with effect from 15 August, 1947 and established two Dominions of India and Pakistan.

(6) The office of the Secretary of State was abolished and his functions were transferred to the Secretary of State for Common wealth Affairs.

(7) The Emperor was divested of his power to veto the legislations passed by the Dominion legislatures. This right now vested with the Governor-General.

(8) Agreement with the tribes of N.W.F.P. were to be negotiated by the Dominions concerned.

(9) Till a new Constitution was framed these Dominions were to be administered in accordance with the Government of India Act 1935.

(10) The Suzeranity of Crown over Indian states was to come an end from 15 August, 1947 and they were to be free in their political relations. Thus, India got freedom on 15 August, 1947. New Constitution was prepared by constituent Assembly on 26 November, 1949 but this new constitution came into force on 26 January, 1950.

CIRCUMSTANCES LEADING TO THE PASSING OF THE INDIAN COUNCILS ACT OF 1892

Following were the circumstances leading to the passing of the Act of 1892:

(1) There was dissatisfaction with the Indian Councils Act of 1861. It was felt that nothing substantial had been given by it. Feeling of nationalism began to develop during this period and the Indias began to grow conscious of their rights.

(2) The economic factors also began to cause some dissatisfaction. It was felt that the policy of free trade was adopted in the interests of British Industrialists and it was ruining the cottage industries of India. The destruction of these industries increased pressure on land and caused great poverty. The educated Indians began to feel the pinch of unemployment. They resented Government's policy of keeping well-paid jobs out of the reach of the Indians.

(3) The repressive policy of Lord Lytton's regime intensified the discontent. The lowering of age-limit for admission to Civil Service examination from 21 to 19 years, the abolition of import duties on cotton goods, the discriminatory Vernacular Press Act and the Indian Arms Act caused great dissatisfaction.

(4) The Ilbert Bill controversy made the Indians feel that justice and equal treatment could not be expected from the British bureaucrats

and the Indian National Congress was formed in 1885 by A.O. Hume, a retired British civilian officer. The Congress demanded the reforms and the expansion of the Central and Provincial Legislative Councils by the admission of a considerable portion of elected members, the budget should be referred to them and the members should have the right of interpellation. It was partly due to the agitation carried on by the Indian National Congress that the Indian Councils Act of 1892 was passed.

Provisions of the Act

(1) The number of additional members in the Councils was increased. In case of Central Legislative Council, the number of additional members was to be between 10 and 16. It was to be between 8 and 20 in case of Madras and Bombay. The maximum number for Bengal was fixed at 20 and for North-West Province.

(2) Two-fifths of additional members were to be non-officials.

(3) The rules made under the Act required that a certain proportion of non-official members in each Legislative Council should be nominated by the Head of the Government on the recommendations of certain bodies. The word election was avoided. In case of Provincial Councils, the recommending bodies were Municipal Councils, District Boards, Chambers of Commerce, Universities etc. Out of sixteen members in the Imperial Legislative Council, six were to be officials, five nominative non-officials, and the remaining five elected, one by the Calcutta Chamber of Commerce and one each by non-official members of the four Provincial Councils.

(4) The functions of the Legislative Councils were enlarged. They could discuss the budget under certain restrictions. It could not be discussed item-wise.

(5) The members of the Councils could ask questions no matters of public interest. Six days' notice was to be given to the Government for asking a question. These questions could be asked subject to conditions and restrictions as may be the prescribed by Governor-General or Governors. The president of the Legislative Council could disallow any question without giving any reason.

Significance of the Act

(1) The Act of 1892 was significant as it contributed to the development of representative institutions in India. Sir Surendra Nath Banerjee expressed the view that the foundations of the representative government were well and truly laid by the Act of 1892. The Act brought about reforms.

(2) The Act was an important step towards the participation of Indians in the highest legislative functions. Uptill then the Indians did not enjoy the privilege to sit with the Viceroy and his Councillors. Though they could not override majority, yet they got the opportunity to express their views and opinions in the Councils.

(3) The rules and regulations framed under the Act of 1892 gave the Indians the principle of election though restricted and indirect.

(4) According to this Act the Council got the right of questioning the executive.

(5) The Act also enlarged the functions of the Legislative Councils in financial matters. Hitherto, the Council had no opportunity to dicuss the financial polity of the Government.

(6) The Act was definitely an improvement upon the Act of 1861.

(7) The functions of the Legislative Councils were strictly limited. The members could not ask supplementary questions. The president could refuse any question without assigning any reason. The councils had very little control over the budget and it could not be discussed item-wise.

(8) The system of election was a roundabout one and failed to satisfy the people. The persons who got into the legislatures by this roundabout process did not represent the people in the real sense of the term.

(9) The allocation of seats was also unfair. Some classes were over-represented while others did not get any representation at all. It

case of Bombay, out of six elected seats, two were given to European merchants but none to the Indian merchants. Two seats were given a Sind but no seats were given tȯ Poona and Satara.

(10) The number of elected members was very small. Out of the total strength of twenty-four members of the Imperial Legislative Council, only four were elected members.

(11) Punjab was not given any representation in the Imperial Legislative Council.

Thus the Act of 1892 was highly defective. A critic remarked that the Act of 1892 was "an attempt at compromise between the official view of Councils as pocket legislatures and the educated Indian view of them as embryo parliaments. It made a definite parting of the ways, the first milestone on a road leading eventually to a political deadlock and a strangling of executive government. While no efforts were made to enlarge the boundaries of the educated class to provide them with any training in responsible governments, or to lay the foundations of a future electorate to control them the Act deliberatley attempted to daily with the elective idea."

It may, however, be said in defence of the Act that it was a great advance in the existing state of things. By conceding the principle of election and giving the Legislative Councils some control over the Executive, it prepared the way for future reforms.

Points for Revision Circumstances

There was dissatisfaction with the Indian Councils Act of 1861. It was felt that enough powers had not been given to the Indians.

(1) The economic condition was becoming bad and the people felt that it would improve only when they would get some powers.

(2) The repressive policy of Lord Lytton caused discontent.

(3) Ilbert Bill controversy irritated the Indians and the Indian National Congress was formed in 1885. It carried on

agitation for further reforms. It was partly due to this agitation that the Indian Councils Act of 1892 was passed.

DYARCHY SET UP IN THE PROVINCES

The Declaration of August 20, 1917, and the Preamble to the Government of India Act of 1919 clearly stated that the ultimate aim of His Majesty's Government was to grant Self-government to the Indians by stages. The provinces were considered the fit domain where the beginnings of the responsible system of government were to be made. Even in the provincial sphere, it was considered inadvisable by the authors of the Act to transfer all the departments into the lands of Indians. Only some departments were to be transferred in the beginning. It was introduced in the eight provinces (Bengal, Bihar, Assam, Madras, Bombay, Punjab, U.P. and C.P.), in 1921. It was extended to North-West Frontier Province in 1932. This system remained in operation till 1937.

Under the system of Dyarchy, the Provincial subjects were divided into Reserved and Transferred. The Reserved departments were administered by the Governor with the help of his Executive Council. The number of members ranged from two to four in different provinces. Each member was incharge of one or more departments. The members of the Executive Council were nominated by the Governor and were responsible to him alone. They were not at all responsible to the legislature. Some of the Reserved departments were Finance, Law and Order, Irrigation, Famine Relief. The Transferred department were to be administered with the help of ministers. Their number could differ from province to province and from time to time. Each minister was incharge of one or more departments. The ministers were appointed by the Governor from among the members of the legislature. They had double responsibility. Some of the Transferred departments were Local Self-Government, Public Health, Education (without Anglo-Indian Education), Agriculture, Co-operation, etc. If no minister was incharge of a transferred department at any time, the Governor himself assumed temporary charge of it till minister was appointed. The Governopr-General-in-Council with the previous sanction of the Secretary of

State-in-Council could revoke or suspend the transfer of any or all subjects in the province and in that case these would relapse into the position of Reserved subjects.

FAILURE OF DYARCHY

The system of Dyarchy was in operation from 1921 to 1937 but it did not prove satisfactory. The failure of the system was due to several factors:

(1) Water-Tight Division of Subjects. The Provincial departments were divided into Reserved and Transferred. A water-tight division of departments is never conducive to the smooth working of the governmental system. Government is one organic whole and can not be divided into water-tight compartments.

(2) Joint Responsibility not encouraged. The Governors sometimes consulted the Executive Councillors jointly but they never consulted the ministers jointly. The ministers themselves were several times at variance with each other. The Governors never held joint consultations of the two branches of government *i.e.* Executive Councillors and the Ministers.

(3) Division was not Scientific. The division of the provincial subjects into Reserved and Transferred was not done on any scientific basis. Agriculture was a Transferred subject but Irrigation was a Reserved subject. Education was a Transferred department but Education of the Anglo-Indians fell in the Reserved sphere. This unscientific bifurcation of departments contributed to the failure of the experiment. Sometimes it was very difficult to say to which department a particular matter appertained. An inquiry was started in 1921 in the Department of Agriculture, on the question of the fragmentation of land. A report was submitted in 1922 and then it was felt that the question should have been dealt with by the Revenue Department and the case was transferred to that department. It was decided in 1924 that the case should have been dealt with by the Co-operation Department.

(4) Double Responsibility of Ministers. The position of the ministers under the system of Dyarchy was very precarious. They were appointed by the Governor and were responsible to him. He was not a constitutional head and could dismiss a minister, even if he was liked by the legislature. The ministers were also responsible to the legislature and its adverse vote could lead to their resignation. The ministers had to please two masters whose view-points were always opposed. The ministers very often cared more for the Governor than for the legislature due to two reasons. Firstly, there were several parties in the legislature and the ministers could never be sure of the support of all the elected members. On the other hand they could count upon the support of the official and nominated non-official members because their votes could be available to them en bloc, if they cared for the wishes of the Governor. Thus a minister could not hope to remain in power without pleasing the Governor. Moreover, some ministers aspired to become Executive Councillors after the expiry of their tem of office. Hence the ministers became subservient to the Governors and did not care much for the legislature.

(5) No Ministerial Control Over the Senior Services. The position of the members of All-India Services created difficulties for the ministers. Most of the key positions in the provinces were held by the members of all-India Services. The ministers had no control over their appointment, suspension or dismissal. They were under the Secretary of State-in-Council and tried to put into practice the wishes of the Governors and not of the ministers. They did not care for the ministers.

(6) Non-Co-operation Between the Two Parts. Efficient working of governmental system demands that there should be co-operation between the different departments. This was lacking in case of Dyarchy. The Executive Councillors were generally members of bureaucracy while the ministers were the representatives of the people. There was no co-operation between the members and the ministers and they sometimes publicly criticised each other.

(7) Finance was a Resereved Department. The position of Finance Department created additional diffliculty for the ministers. Finance was a Reserved department and the Honourable Members for Finance was liberal in meeting the demands of other members.

He would give money for the needs of the Transferred departments. only after meeting the demand of the Reserved departments.

(8) Direct Access of Secretaries to the Governors. The differences were bound to arise between the ministers and the departmental secretaries. Such cases were decided by the Governors. The secretaries had direct access to the Governors and poisoned their ears against they stand take by the ministers. The Governors generally belonged to the same services as the secretaries (except in the Presidencies) and generally supported the viewpoint of the secretaries. This stood in the way of proper functioning of Dyarchy.

(9) Introduction of System of Unfavourable Time. The system of Dyarchy was introduced under an unlucky star. The political atmosphere in the country was of suspicion and distrust because of happenings in the Punjab like Jallianwala Bagh tragedy and the attitude of the British Government towards Turkey. There was slump in the market after the First World War and the provincial finances were in a disorganised condition. The provincial government under the scheme of Meston Award, had to make financial contributions to the Centre. Thus the system of Dyarchy was introduced in a politically and economically hamparing atmosphere and this contributed to the failure of Dyarchy.

CHARACTER OF THE INDIAN FEDERATIONS

A Federal form of government is that type of government in which the constitution divides the powers between the Centre and the States. Matters of national importance like defence, external affairs or the subjects requiring uniformity like coinage are given to the federal government while matters of provincial importance are given to the States.

Formation of the Proposed Federation. The Government of India Act of 1935 envisaged the setting up of a federal form of government. The proposed federation was to consist of British Indian provinces and such Indian States as chose to join the federation by executing an Instrument of Accession, whereby certain powers were to be surrendered by the acceding States to the Centre. The federation was to come into existence by a proclamation to be issued by His Majesty if the two Houses of British Parliament presented an address of His Majesty requesting for the formation of the federation. The rulers of Indian States representing at least half the aggregate population of the States and entitled to at least half the seats allotted to the States in the Upper House were also to agree to join the federation.

Character of Proposed Federation. The proposed federation had several features of a federal form of government. Firstly, there were to be two sets of Government, the Federal Government and the State Governments. Secondly, the Act made a division of powers for the proposed federation. Thirdly, the constitution was written. Fourthly, the constitution was rigid in the sense that only the British Parliament could amend the Act. The Indian legislature was not competent to touch it. Fifthly, there was to be a Federal Court to settle the differences among the units, and of the units with the Federal Court to settle the differences among the units, and of the units with the Federal Government.

The proposed federation, however, was unique in many respects. The following were its peculiar features:

(a) There are two methods of forming of a federation. One is the centripetal method whereby independent States surrender a part of their sovereignty to the Federal Government as was done in the case of the U.S.A. The other method is the centrifugal method whereby the unitary State concedes a parts of its sovereignty to the provinces by virtue of a written constitution as had been done in the case of Canada. The proposed federation of India was to be formed by a combination of the two methods. The centripetal method was to be followed more or less in the case of Indian States while the centrifugal method was to be followed in the case of British Indian Provinces.

(b) All States have equal representation in the Upper House of the federal legislature in a true federation. This is the case with U.S.A. In case of the proposed Federation of India, different units were to have differing representations in the Council of States. This was to be a unique feature.

(c) The residuary powers are with the States in true federation like that of the U.S.A. Some federations deviating from this principle, give these powers to the Centre as in Canada. The proposed federation gave residuary powers neither to the States nor to the Centre. These were vested in the Governor-General. This was an innovation.

(d) In a typical federation, the Supreme Court or the Federal Court decides whether a subject in dispute should be with the Centre or with the States. In case of the proposed federation for India, this point was to be decided by the Governor-General.

(e) The federal legislature was not competent to amend the Act. The power of amendment lay with the British Parliament. Even in this respect the proposed federation was unique.

(f) In a typical federation, the federal government exercises equal authority in all the units or states. In case of India, the authority exercisable by the federal government was to differ from State to State in accordance with the terms of the Instruments of Accession.

(g) The accession of British Indian provinces to the proposed federation was to be compulsory but it was to be voluntary in case of Indian States.

(h) The method of sending members to the Upper House (Council of States) of the proposed federation was not to be the same in the case of British Indian provinces and the Indian States. The representatives from the British Indian provinces were to be the representatives of the people but in case of Indian States, these were to be nominated by the autocratic rulers.

CIRCUMSTANCES LEADING TO THE PASSING OF INDIAN INDEPENDENCE ACT OF 1947

The Congress and the Muslim League accepted the Cabinet Mission Plan and the members went back to England. Lord Wavell asked Pandit Nehru to form the Interim Government. The Muslim League decided not to join it. It decided to observe 16th of August 1946 as the Direct Action Day. There were riots in Calcutta on that day and these lasted for four days. Thousands of people were brutally massacred and property worth crores of rupees was burnt. Pandit Nehru formed the Interim Government on September 2, 1946 but the Muslim League refused to join it. Later on it decided to obstruct the Interim Government with the idea of wrecking the administration from within.

The Constituent Assembly met on December 9, 1946 but the Muslim League refused to participate in its deliberations. The Congress blamed Lord Wavell for bringing Muslim League into the Interim Government without getting an assurance that it would participate in the Constituent Assembly sessions. C.R. Attlee, Prime Minister of England, declared on 20th of February, 1947, that the British Government would leave India by June 1948, even if no agreement was reached between the Congress and the Muslim League.

Lord Mountbatten was sent as the Viceroy and Governor-General in March 1947. The new Viceroy held consultations with the Congress and the Muslim League leaders and announced his plan or 3rd of June. It is popularly known as June Third Plan. It announced the following decisions:

(a) Referendum was to be held in North-West Frontier Province to decide whether that province would like to join Pakistan or India.

(b) It was to be decided by referendum whether Sylhet in Assam was to be a part of India or of Pakistan.

(c) India was to be partitioned.

(d) Bengal, Assam and Punjab to be partitioned.

(e) The Native States were to be free to join either of the two Dominions or to remain independent.

(f) Power was to be transferred by 15th of August, 1947.

The plan was accepted by the Congress and the Muslim League. The British Parliament then passed the Indian Independence Act of 1947.

Provision of the Act

(1) The legislative supremacy of the British Parliament for India came to an end. The legislatures of the two countries were to have full powers-of legislation.

(2) Till the framing of the new Constitutions by the Constituent Assemblies of these two Dominions, their Government were to be carried on in accordance with the Government of India Act of 1935 with necessary modifications. The Governor-General in case of each of the two Dominions was authorised to make the necessary changes in the Act till 31st of March, 1948.

(3) India was to be partitioned into the Dominions of India and Pakistan from 15th August, 1947.

(4) The title of Viceroy was to be dropped and henceforth he was to be called only Governor-General.

(5) The paramountcy of the Crown over the Native States came to an end. All treaties and agreements between the Crown and the Native States were to lapse with effect from the date of the transference of power. The existing arrangements between the Government of India and the Indian States were to continue pending the detailed negotiations between the Indian States and the new Dominion concerned.

(6) The Crown was no more to have the right to veto the laws made by a Dominion Legislature. This right was to be

exercised by the Governor-General on the advice of Dominion Cabinet.

(7) The office of the Secretary of State for India was to be abolished and the work was to be taken over by the Secretary of State for Commonwealth Affairs.

(8) The title of Emperor of India was dropped.

(9) Arrangements with the tribes of the North-West Frontier Province of India were to be negotiated by the successor Dominion.

(10) The Indian, Army, Government stores, railways etc., were to be divided between India and Pakistan.

(11) Any Dominion could leave the British Commonwealth if it so liked.

❐

12

Farmer Movement

The condition of workers in modern factories and plantations in the 19th century was miserable. They had to work between 12 and 16 hours a day and there was no weekly day of rest. Women and children worked the same long hours as men. The usages were extremely low, ranging from Rs. 4 to Rs. 20 per month. The factories were over crowded, badly lighted and aired, and completely unhygienic.

The Government of India, which was generally pro-capitalist, took some half-heated and titally inadequate steps to mitigate the sorry state of affairs in the modern factories, many of which were owned by Indians. In this was only in part moved by humanitarian considerations. The manufacturers of Britain put constant pressure as it to pass factory laws. They were afraid that cheap labour would enable India manufacturers to outsell them in the Indian market. The First Indian factory Act was passed in 1881 A.D. The Act dealt primarily with the problem of child labour. It laid down that children below 7 could not work in factories, while children between 7 and 12 would not work for more than 9 hours a day. Children would also get four holdiays in a month. The second Indian Factories Act was passed in 1891 A.D. It provided for a weekly holdiay for all workers. Working hours for women were fixed at 11 per day while daily hours of work for children were reduced to 7 Hours of work for men were still left unregulated.

Neither of the two Acts applied to British owned tea and coffee plantations. On the countrary, the Government gave every help to the forign planters to exploit their workers in a most ruthless manner. Most of the tea plantations were situated in Assam which was very thinkly populated and had an unhealthy climate. Labour to work the plantations had therefore to be brought from outside. The planters would not attract workers from outside by paying high wages. Instead they used coercion and fraud to recruit them and then keep them as virtual slaves on the plantations. The Government of India gave planters full help and passed penal laws in 1863, 1865, 1870, 1873 and 1882 to enable them to do so. Once a labourer had signed a contract to go and work in a plantation he could not refuse to do so. Any breach of contract by a labourer was a criminal offence, the planter also having the power to arrest him. Better labour laws were, however, passed in the 20th century under the pressure of the rising trade union movement.

LABOUR MOVEMENT

(1) Dipesh Chakrabarti has recently used the Calcutta jute mill riots of the mid 1890s as a point of entry into a subject almost entirely unexplored in our country so far the emergences of early labur consciousness, Sizeable proletarian concentrations had developed around the Bombay cotton and Calcutta jute mills by the 1890s, living and working in conditions every bit as appalling, if not worse, as those witnesses in similar phases of early industrial capitlaism in other parts of the world. Even the paltry restrictions on the employment of children and women theoretically imposed by the factory Act of 1881 A.D. and 1891 A.D. were seldom observed, and a working day of 15/16, sometimes even 18 hours remained extremely common. In Bombay, where a predominantly Marathi labour force facilitated some degree of social contact across class lines, middle class philanthrophic efforts to improve labour conditions began fairly carly with N.M. Lokhande starting the weekly Dinabandhu in 1880, organising labour meeting to demand shorter hours in 1884, and even starting a Bombay. Mill hands' Associations in 1890. This, however, was not a trade union, it merely involved Likhande setting up an office to give free advice to mill hands who came to him.

Workers did occasionally fight back in their own way, through assaults on oversees, sporadic riots and spontaneous short-lived strikers. Twenty-five important strikes have been recorded in Bombay and Madras between 1882 and 1890, several big strikes in Bombay in 1892-93 A.D. and 1901, and a new note on militancy was evident among Calcutta jute workers in the mid 1890s, leading the Indian Jute Mills' Association to ask the Bengal Government for additional police supervision to curb riotous combinations's of mill-hands in April 1895. But the important point made by Chakrabarti is the way in which embryonic labour protest could often taken the form of a kind of community-consciousness rather than a clear recognition of class. Muslim workers demanded holidays for Id or Muharram, Hindus for Rathyatra, and at times fought each other bitterly over issues like cow-slaughter of the construction of places of worhship on disputed land, as in the riots in and around Calcutta in 1896-97.

(2) Labour Unrest (1903-1918). An official survey entitled Administration of Bengal under Andrew Fraser (1903-08) described 'industrial unrest' as a marked feature of the quinquennium, and noted the role of 'professional agitators' as quite a novel phenomenon. Strikes in white-controlled enterprises spark off by rising prices and also quite often by racaial insults, now obtained from nationalist quarters considerable newspaper sympathy, occasional financial help, and even aid in setting up trade unions. Four men in particular deserve to be remembered as pioneer labour-leaders: the barristers Ashwinikumar Bannerji, Athanasius Apurbakumar Ghosh, Prabhatkusum Roychandhuri, and Premtosh Bose the proprietor of a small press in north Calcutta. In september 1905 A.D., the entire Swadshi public hailed a walk out of 247 Bengali clekrs of Burn Company in Howrah in protest against a new work regulation felt to be derogatory. The next month saw a tram strike in Calcutta, settled through the efforts of Bennerji and Ghosh, and reports of 16 October convey a bandh like flavour, with most offices closed down, carters off the roads, and strikers in some jute mills and railway workshops. The first real labour union followed soon after, the Printers Union, set up on 21 October in the midst of a bitter strike in government presses. In July 1906, a strike of clerks on the East Indian Railway led to the formation of a Railwaymen's union and efforts to draw in the coolies through meetings at Asansol, Jamalpur and Ranigjum addressed by Swadeshi politial leaders like Bipin Pal, Shyamsunder

Chakrabarti, Liakat Hussian apart from A.C. Banerjee, Premtosh Bose and A.K. Ghose. There was one masive proletatrian intervention at the Jamalpur workshop on 27 August which led to firing, the strike, however, failed, and the union collapsed with it. Jute strike were also frequent between 1905 and 1908 A.D. affecting various times 18 out of 37 mills. There were no really political strikes plantation and mine labour remained unaffected, Swadeshi contacts were devloped in the main only with clerks or at best Bengali jute workers and nationalist interest in labour slumped suddenly and totally after the summer of 1908.

In the pre-1914 period this role of the working class was still in the background; it followed rather than preceeded the national movement; the only outstanding political action was the Bombay general strike against the six years' sentence on tilak. After the war, however, certain circumstances helped in the growth of a genuine class movement and organisation. The econmic depression after the war, the democratic movements of several European countries, the Russian revolution of 1917 and the general dissatisfaction prevailing in the country were primarily responsible for it.

The strike movement which began in 1918 and swept the country in 1919 and 1920 was overwhelming in its intensity. The end of 1918 saw the first great strike affecting an entire industry in a leading centre in the Bombay cotton mills; by January 1919, 1,25,000 workers, covering practically all mills, were out. The response to the hartal against the Rowlatt Act in the spring of 1919 showed the political role of the workers in the forefront of the common national struggle. During 1919 strikes spread over the country. By the end of 1919 and the first half of 1920 the wave reached its height. In the first half of 1920 there were 200 strikes, involying 1-1/2 million workers.

Trade unions were formed by the score during this period. Many were essentially strike committees, springing up in the conditions of an immediate struggle, but without staying power, while the workers were ready for struggle the facilities fort office organisation were inevitably in other hands. Hence acrose the contradiction of the

early Indian labour movement. There was not yet any political movement on the basis of socialism, of the, conceptions of the working class and the class struggle.

(3) Labour Movemnt (1918-1921). The starting point of Indian trade unionism is commonly derived from the Madras Labour Union, formed by B.P. Wadia, an associate of the theosophist Mrs. Besant, in 1918 A.D. This picture is to a certain extent misleading in relations to the living history of the Indian working class. First attempts at trade union organisation were springing up all over India during this period; there is a trace of the Workers in the Ahmedabad cotton mills forming a union in 1917. But the basis of organisation was still very weak, and far behind the level of militancy and activity of the working class. The Madras Labour Union was certainly the first systematic attempt at trade union organisation, with regular membership and dues, of the mass of Indian workers in an industrial centre. For this initiative all credit must be paid to its founders. But the appearance of this initiative in a relatively weak industrial centre reveals its accidental personal character; and it would not be correct to exaggerate its influence in the general development of the Indian labour movement. The limitations of outlook of its founder, B.P. Wadia, were revealed when the Madras workers, having formed their union under his presidency in April, 1918, and having presented their demands to the employers, received no satisfaction and demanded a strike; Wadia opposed any strike on grounds of devotion to the cause of British imperialism. He was successful in preventing any srike; but Messrs. Binny and co. undeterred by Wadia's "patriotic" arguments, then declared a lock-out, and workers, caught unprepared, and having been persuaded to forego the strike weapon, were compelled at the moment to give way to their demands. The main contest in Madras came in 1921 with a lock out followed by a strike; the company used the method of the injuction; the High Court imposed fine of $7,000 on the union, and, as the price of company consenting not to prosecute the judgement.

In other centres many types of helpers, sometimes closely connected with the employers, came forward to take charge of labour ogranisation. In Ahmedabad, Gandhi, in close association with the mill owners, organised a separalist form a labour organisation on a basis of class peace; and to this day the Ahmedabad Labour Organisation remains isolated from the Indian Labour movement.

It was in this period that the Indian Trade Union Congress was founded in 1920 A.D. The inaugral session was held in Bombay in October, 1920 with the national leader, 'Lala Lajpat Rai, as President and Joseph Baptista as vice-President in its early years this body was mainly a "top" organisation, and many of its leaders had very limited connection with the working class movement. The main impetus to its founding was to secure a nominating body for representations at the Inter-national Labour Conference at Geneva. Baptista perhaps spoke for most of these early labour leaders when at the inaugral session of the A.I.T.U.C. in Bombay on 31 October 1920 A.D., he deplored the Via dolorasa of workers but held out to them 'the higher idea of partnership..." They (workers and employers) are partners and co-workers, and not buyers and sellers of labour." Already, however, a few individuals and groups on the fringes of the labour movement were beginning to lean towards marxism—the radical young student. S.A. Dange in Bombay, who talks of his rapid transition from being a chela (disciple) of Bal Gangadhar Tilak to that of Lenin in the course of 1920-21, or the eldery lawyer Singaravelu Chettiar in Madras. It is interesting that though Lajpat Rai presided over the first AITUC sessions and quite a galaxy of leading Indian politicans attended it (Motilal Nehru, Vithal Bhai Patel, Annie Basat, Jinnah), Gandhi kept sternly aloof, not even sending a message and his Ahmedabad Majoor Mahajan never sought affiliation to the AITUC even when it was controlled by entirely moderate groups.

(4) Labour Movement (1922-1927). In the history of the Labour Movements of India, from 1922 A.D. to 1927 A.D. are marked at first sight by a definite decline. The number of strikes as calculatd by the Royal Commission of Labour (1931 A.D.) went down frrom a peak figure of 376 in 1921 A.D. to about 130 annually between 1924 A.D. and 1927 A.D. Though AITUC membership went up, with 183 affiliated unions listed in January 1925, the leadership remained very moderate, being either Liberal or Congress in political tempor, and sessions lacked the elan and rank-and-file participation of the Jharia conference of 1921 A.D. Yet if strikes were less numerous, they also tended to be more prolonged and bitter in face of major employer offensive of these days. The number of working days lost, 70 lakhs in 1921, exceeded that figure every years from 1924 onwars, and 1927 was definitely the beginning of a new labour upsurge, with a 202 lakh loss in working days and the emergence in some centres of a much more radical and increasingly Communist leadership upto 1927, the Trade Union Congress had a very limited practical connection with the working-class struggle. Nevertheless it formed the ground in which the leaders of the newly forming trade union came together and it was therefore only a question of time for the breath of the working-class struggle to reach it.

(5) Political Awakening Among the Indian Labours (1919-1927 A.D.). Despite the character of the early nominal leadership of the Indian labour movement, the British Government of India was under no illusions as to the significance of the emergency of the working class movement in the last two decades. Their concern was shown in the appointment of Bengal Committee on Industrial Unrest in 1921, the Bombay Industrial Dispute Committee of 1922, and Madras Labour Department in 1919-20, followed by the Bombay Labour Department. A Trade Union Bill was prepared in 1921, although it was not passed until 1926 A.D. The main aim of the government was to find the means to direct the labour movement in India into 'safe' channels, or what one of their reports termed the 'right type' of trade unionism. This purpose underly the trade Union Act of 1926, with its special restriction of political activities.

Nevertheless despite all obstacles, through wheatever initial confusions, the beginnings of political working-class awakening of socialist and communist ideas were slowly reaching India in the past war years. From 1920 onwards the literature of the still very weak Communist Party of India had begun to make its way. From 1924 a journal, the Socialist, was appearing in Bombay under the editorship of S.A. Dange, who was to be come Assistant Secretary of the trade Union Congress. The Government lost no time to strike. In 1924 A.D. the Kanpur trail was staged agaisnt four of communist leaders, S.A. Dange, Shaukat Usmani, Muzaffar Ahmed and Das Gupta, all four were sentenced to four years imprisonment. This was the baptism of the political working-class movement in India. Repression could not check the advance of awakening. At the Delhi session of the trade Union Congress in the spring of 1927, and still more markedly at the Kanpur session later in the year, the emergence was revealed of challenging militant voices within the leadership of trade unionism.

(6) Labour Psurge (1928-29). After 1927, a left wing leadership developed within the trade union movement also. Formally the Communist Party of India (CPI) was founded in 1925 in India. The communists believed in class struggle. The socialist did not believe in class-struggle but were, definitely conscious of organising workers and peasants with a view to serve their economic and other interests. The Communists appeared on the scene and their sole objective was to capture the key trade unions with a view to utilizing them for the political ends of their party. From 1926 to 1928 the influence of Communists increased immenssely. Finally it captured the leadership of AITUC. This left wing within the AITUC gradually grew aggressive which resulted in its split in 1929 A.D. Mr. N.M. Joshi had to leave the AITUC. He formed a separate organisation of the workers called the Indian trade Union Federation (ITUF). The All India Trde Union congress (AITUC) now came forward with an extensive and bold programme. "The time has come", declared Shiva Rao, chairman of the executive of the trade Union Congress, already in May, 1928, "When the trade union movement in India should weed out of its organisation mischief makers. In 1929 the Government acted and turned its full offensive to counter the rise of the working class movement. The Public Safety Bill had been introduced in September, 1928, with the object according to the offiical report, "to curb communist activities in India." But had been rejected by the Legislative Assembly, in the spring of 1929 A.D. it was issued as a special

Ordinance by the viceroy. The Whitley Commission on Labour was appointed.

(7) The Meerut Trail (1929-1933). The principal government move, however, was the round-up on 20 March, 1929 of 31 labour leaders (most of them but no means all, communist). They included S.A. Dange, Mirajkar, Ghate, Joglekar, Adhikar, Nimbkar, Alve and Kasle from Bombay; Muzaffar Ahemed, Kshori Lal Ghosh, Dharani Goswami, Gopen Chakrabarti, Radharama Mitra, Gopal Basak etc. from Calcutta; Sohan Singh Josh from Punjab; P.C. Joshi and Viswanath Mukherjee from U.P., as well as three Englishmen, Bradley Spratt, Hutchinson. The Conspiracy trail was to be staged at Meerut, far from any industrial centre. The government dragged out the trail for three and a half years—four critical years of India's history, during which the best leaders of the working class were thus removed.

The trial in the end proved somewhat counter productive, for the Communists in fact made good use of it to propogate their ideals through defence speeches. In January, 1933, savage sentences were awarded transportation for life for Muzaffar Ahmed; twelve years transportation for Dange, Ghate, Joghlkar, Nimbkar and Spratt. ten years trnspotation for Bradley, Mirajkar and Usmani; and so down to the lightest sentence of three years rigorous imprisonment.

(8) Working Class Recovery After Meerut (1929-1938). Labour Militancy was no immediately cowed down by Meerut. When the Fawcett Committee report proved infavourable, and Wadias started largescale dismissals, the Girni Kamgar Union (G.K.U.) Now led by Deshpande and B.T. Ranadive, organised a secod general strike (April-August 1929 A.D.). The mill committee was more militant then ever and an official enquiry condemned the 'choas' brought about by the young inexperienced and illiterate operatives asserting their authority in various ways.

The principal government move however was round up on 20th March of 31 Labour leaders. They included Dange, Mirajkar, Ghate, Joglekar, Nimbkar, Adhikari, Alve and Khasle from Bombay,

Muzzaffar Ahmed, Kishori Lal Ghosh, Dharani Goswami, Gopen Chakrbarti, Radharaman Mitra, Gopal Basak, the trail in the end proved somewhat counter productive for the communists in fact made good use of its to propogate their ideals through defence speeches. The entire national movement condemned the Meerut prosecution, which incidentally involved no less than eight members of the AICC. When the Fowcett Committee report proved unfavourable, and the Wadias started large scale dismissals, the Girni Kamgar now led by Deshpande and B.T. Ranadive organised a second general strike the mill committees were more militant then ever, and an official enquiry condemned the 'chaos' brought about by young, unexperienced, and illiterate operatives asserting their authority in various ways. But the strike was perhaps unwisely prolonged, and its defeat greatly weakened the G.K.U. the first general strike in jute mills took place in July-August 1929 A.D., under the Bengal Jute Workers' Union which was largely controlled by communists; it successfully beat back the employers' bid to extend working hours from 54 to 60 per week. Communist influence over the AITUC seemed greater than ever at the December 1929 A.D. Nagpur session, for the Liberal grop under N.M. Joshi walked out to form the All India trade Union federation, while Nehru remained and presided overthe rump session. The AICC set up a Labour Research Department under Bakar Ali Mirza in 1929, and there were signs that some congress leaders like, Bose in Calcutta and Bhulabhai Desai in Bombay were trying to take advantage of the removal of established communist trade unionsits to extend their own influence over labour. The Congress took a lot of interest, for instance, in the Golmuri tin-plate strike near Jamshedpur—a foriegn owned concern which had benefited incidentaly from Swarajist please for protection, Bose organised a sympathy strike at Budge, and even Rajendra Prasad visited Golmuriy. British officials were considerably alarmed by the possible Congress-labour link up, but found solace in the thought that Congress efforts will meet with every active opposition on the part of those leaders of a Communist complexion who heretofore seem to have exercised by far the most considerable influence over Labour.

The Left ledership, however, which came into control of the trade Union Congress (in 1929) lacked conherence, being composed, of very. Deverse elements and a further split took place (in 1931) mainy on the question of the independent political role of the working class. The Communist section which held this view formed the Red Trade Union Congress.

These splits seriously weaken the Trade Union movements but the working class fought on through separate strike struggles not only for its economic demands but lso against victimisation, that is, for the democratic right of association. This can be seen from the increase in the number of strikes from 141 in 1929 to 148 in 1920 and 166 in 1931, involving more than 100,000 workers every year. The Communists of the Red Trade Union Congress led these struggles and by the year 1933, the Government had to admit with chagrin that though the Meerut leadership was still kept in jail, the Communist "manance, however, remains and has intensified." All these separate strike strugles laid the basis for the big strike wave in 1934 directed against the 'rationalisation' scheme of the mill owners—the system of intensifying labour and greater exploitation. The sweep and intensity of the wave could be seen from this that while in 1933 there were 146 strikes involving 1644,938 workers and resulting in 2,168,961 working days being lost, in the year 1934 there were 159 strikes involving 220,808 workers and covering 4,775,559 working days, that is more than twice the figure for the previous year. The textile general strike in Bombay lasting from April to June and Sholapur from February to May, despite intense repression, was clear proof that the working class had resurrected its scattered forced, reforged its unity and thrown up a crop of militant leadership.

The Government struck again. An emergency Powers Oridnance was brought into operation and Communists and trade union leaders were detained without trial. The Communist Party was declared illegal. More than a dozen legaly registered trade unions were declared illegal, the Young workers' League was banned, firing was employed to crush the militant and revolutionary organisation of the working class. It was out of this mightly strike struggle that the move began to re-unite the working class organisations.

From the platform of this session an appeal was made to the reformist leaders of the National Federation of trade Unions to agree to unite the central leadership of the workers because "nothing but a nation wide offensive of the working class" could fight back the offensive of the owners and the Government. They were assured that, the interests of unity, all their coditions would be met provided they agreed to to basic principles: first, acceptance of class struggle as the basis of the trade union movement; secondly internal trade union democracy. The leaders of the Federation resisted immediate structural unity. So a joint board was set up in 1936 and it was only in 1938 at Nagpur that the National Federation of trade Unions affiliated itself to the All India Trade Union Congress with equal representation to the two sections in the governing body of the Congress.

The All India trade Union Congress (AITUC) now come forward with an extensive and bold economic political programmes. Its decalred objective now included the establishement of a socialist state in India, socialization and nationalization of the means of production, securing of better economic and social conditions, protection of liberties like freedom of speech, association and even strike for the working classes, participation in the national struggle from the point of view of the workers and abolisher of privilages based on caste, sex, creed, race, community or religion. This party of workers succeeded in doing some useful work for them; though its membership did not increse very much. The special character of the Congress Socialist Prty was that in membership was made conditional on membership of the Indian National Congress; the party thus constituted a wing wihtin the Congress and discouraged mass memebrship. The objective effect of this programmetic and constitutional basis inevitably represented an attempt to subordinate the indepenence of the working class movement to the control and discipline of the existing dominant leadership of the National Congress, which meant in practice-of the bourgoisie.

(9) Pre-Second World War Upsurge (1934-1939). Before the beginning of Second World War in India the trade union movement spread leading to the formation of several new unions and powerfully influencing even the workers in seasonal factories and unortganised industries. The number of registered unions which was only 29 in 1928, 75 in 1929 and 191 in 1934 rose to 296 by 1938 with a recorded membership of 261,000, but these trade union were really centres which could mobilise many times that number. The number of strikes, which touched the lowest ever figure since 1921 (396 strikes) in 1932 (118 strikes), began rising again from next year (*i.e.* 1933) there were 146 strikes and in 1934 their number raised to 159). In 1937, the number of strikes reached 379, nearly 676,000 workers participated in these strikes and the total number of working days covered was 8,983,000 or the highest since 1929 A.D. in 45 percent of the strikes, the workers were succeesful in securing concession. A notable feature of the strike wave was its extension to Ahmedabad, the previous stronghold of Gandhist class-peace unionsm; here the Bombay Congress Government brought into operation of the hated Section of 144 of the Penal Code, prohibiting meetings of five or more, a section of 144 of the Penal Code, prohibiting meetings of five or more, a section against which Indian National Congress has consistently protested.

By 30th October 1938, the foundation anniversary day of the Trade Union Congress, it had a membership of 325,000 organised workers. The working class through its powerful political protest actions against imperialist misdeeds, in support of national demands and by its daily battles against imperialist repression, already stood out as s strong, organised section of the anti-imperialist forces.

Alongside these development and because of them the politial role and influence of the labour movement was felt inside the national movement. A wide compaign supported by several trade unions and led by radical conressmen, developed behind the demand from lifting the ban on the Communist Party, Despite the ban, the widened civil liberties under the Congress ministeries made it possible for the Communist Party to bring out the national Front, a weekly in English and Kranti in Marathi, the languge of the majority of the working class in Bombay.

(10) The Working Class in the Second World War (1939-45 A.D.). With the outbreak of the Second World War on 1st September, 1939 A.D., a decisive period opened for the national liberation movement in India and the Indian working class:

(a) While the naitonal leadership temporised it was the labour movement that opened the offensive with a one-day political protest strike on October, 2,1939, when 90,000 workers in Bombay downed tools—the first anti-war strike in the world labour movement.

(b) Against the economic burden of War, the working class opened the offensive with the Dearness Allowance strike of 175,000 textile workers in Bombay on 5th March 1940 A.D. the strike was complete and lasted for 40 days despite wholesale arrest of the strike leaders and terrorisation of workers. The Bombay strike unleased a wave of strikes all over the country, 20,000 textile workers of Kanpur, 20,000 municipal workers in Calcutta, jute workers of Bengal and Bihar, Oil workers of Digboi in Assam, Coal-miners of Dhanbad and Jharia iron and steel workers of Jamshedpur and workers in scored of other industries, struck work demanding dearness allowance. It was clear that working class as whole was on the move. The Government stuck once more. The National Front and Kranti were banned. A country wide round-up of Communists and other radical elements took place. Alongside this on slaught by the authorities against the Communist Party, the Congress Socialist leadership also opened an offensive against the Communists and expelled from its party those suspected of being communists or in sympathy with Communism, on the grounds that they failed to accept the Gandhist theory of non-violence. However, the attacks of the Government and Congress Party did not succeed in breaking the organization or active role of the communist Party.

At the same time the country wide united action of the working class led to the completion of unity in the central trade union orgaisation. The national federation of trade Unions completely merged with the All-India trade Union congress, but not until it had insisted on and secured a clause in the constitution that "all political questions as well as questions of strikes and affiliation with any foreign organisation be decided by a three fourths majority." The period of 1942-45 A.D. was a period of great trial for the working class and the country as a whole. The Government resort to unrestricted inflationary measures to pay for the war, the hoarding and blackmarketing of vital necessarics, the rise in the cost of living by 200 percent; the arrest of the national leaders etc. compelled the working class to go on strike. The Trade Union Congress gave a call to observe September 25, 1942, as Anti-Repression Day. It popularised the ideas of national defence and launched a vigorous compaign for the daily needs of the people such as price control and rationing. This led to a growth in the trade union movement. In brief we can say that the achievement and advance of the working class movement during the Second World War represented a memorable stage of development.

The Peasant Movement in Modern India. In 1765 A.D. (through the treaty of Allahabad, concluded after the War of Buxor, 1964) the East India acquired the Diwani for control over the revenues, of Bengal, Bihar and Orissa. Initially, it made an attempt to continue the old system of revenue collection though it increased the amount to be collected from Rs. 14,290,000 in 1722 A.D. and Rs. 8,180,000 in 1764 A.D. to Rs. 23,400,000 in 1771 A.D. Because from 1765 to 1772 A.D. in Bengal there was Dual system of administration. Under this system of rule as Diwan of the province of East India Company directly collected its revenues, while through the right to nominate the Deputy Subadar, it controlled the Nizamat or the police and judicial powers. The virtual unity of the two branches of the Government under British control was signified by the fact that the same person acted in Bengal as the Deputy Diwan on behalf of the East India India Company and as Deputy Subedar on behalf of the Nawab. The company did not spend any peny for the promotion or progress of agriculture or to solve any problem of the peasants. Under Dual system of the administration the peasants could not complaint about their grievances to any authority—to the Company or to Nawab. The abuses of the Dual Government and the drain of wealth led to the impoverishment and exhaustion of that unluckly province. In 1720, Bengal suffered from a famine which in its effects proved one of the most terrible famine known in human history. People died in lakhs and nearly one-third of Bengal's population fell victim to its ravages. Though the famine was due to failure of rains, its effects were hieghened by the Company's policies. In 1772, Warren Hastings came as a Governor of Bengal. In 1773 he became the first Governor General of British India. In the same year (1773 A.D.) he decided to manage the land revenued directly. He auctioned the right to collect the revenues to the highest bidders. But this experiment did not succeed. Though the amount of land revenue was pushed high by zamindars and speculators bidding against each other, the actual collection varied from year to year and seldom came up to official expectations. This introduced instatbility in the Company's revenues at a time when the Company was hard pressed for money. Moreover, neither the peansants nor the zamindar would do anything to improve cultivation when they did not know what the next year's assessment would be or who would be the next year's revenue collector.

It was at this stage that the idea first emerged of fixing the land revenue at a permanent amount. Finally after prolonged discussion and debate the Permanent Settlement was introuduced in Bengal and Bihar in 1793 by Lord Cornwallis. It had two special features. Firslty, the zamindars and revenue collectors were converted into so many landlords. They were not only to act as agents of the Government in collecting land revenue from the ryot but also to become the owenrs of the entire land in their zamindaris. Their right to ownership was made hereditary and transferable. On the other hand, the cultivators were reduced to the low status of mere tenants and were deprived of long standing rights to the soil and other customary rights. The use of pasture and forest lands irrigation cannals, fisheries, and home-stead plots and protection against enhancement of rent were some of their rights which were secrificed. In fact the tenantry of Bengal was left entirely at the mercy of the zamindars. The attempt of the British officials was to secure the maximum amount rigidly on the due date.

The main burden of providing money for the trade and profits of the Company, the cost of administration, and the wars of British expansion in India had to be borne by the Indian peasant or the ryot. In fact the British could not have conquered such a vast country as India if they had not taxed him, heavily. The Permanent Zamindari Settlement was later extended to Orissa, the Northern districts of Madras, and the Districts of Varanasi. In parts of Central India and Avadh the British introduced a termporary zamindari settlement under which the zamindars were made owners of land but the revenue they had to pay was revised periodically another group of landlords was created all over India when the Government started the practice of giving land to persons who had rendered faithful service to the foreign rulers. They were left to the mercies of the zamindars who raisd rents to unberable limits, compelled them to pay legal dues and to perform forced labour and oppressed them in diverse other ways. Similarly the conditions of the cultivators in the Ryotwari and Mahalwari areas was so no better. Here the Government took palce of the zamindars and levied excessive land revenue. By 1937 the population pressure on agriculture fiad incresed to such an extent that an average size of the holding became very unecomic for smaller farmers. The evil of high revenue demand was made worse the fact that the peasant got little economic return for it. The harmful effects of excessive land revenue were furhter heightened by the rigid manner of its collection. Whenever the peasant failed to pay land revenue the government put up his land on sale to collect the arrears of revenue. But in most cases the peasant himself took this step and sold a part of his land to meet in time the government demand. In either case he lost his land. More often the inability to pay revenue drove the peasant to borrow money at high rate of interst from the money lender.

The Frequency of the Famines and Farmers. The frequency of famines increased during the British rule. For example, in a period of about ninety years of its rule from 1765 to 1808, the country experienced 12 famines and 4 severe scarcities. There was not only increse in the frequency of famines, there was also a change in their nature. The nature of famines in the later half of the 19th century changed from a shortage of food supply as in the past, to a lack of purchasing power which those who suffered from starvation.

In brief, we can say lot of peasant were extremely miserable during the British regime. The various peasant movements and uprisings during the 19th and 20th centuries were in the nature of a protest against the existing condition under which their exploitation knew no limits.

Main Peasants Movements and Uprisings

1. Santhal's Pargans Rebellion (1855-1873). Peasant unrest and peasant uprising can be traced with increasing frequency during the period of British rule in India. In their first primitive and spontaneous forms the anger and unrest of the peasants found expression in violated actions of revenge and violence against individual Baniyas (or local money lenders) and zamindar or land lords.

Outstanding episodes of peasants' uprisings in the second half of the 19th century was the Santhal Rebellion of 1855. Originally, the Santhals belonged to Manbhum, Baraphum, Hazaribagh, Bribhum, Midnapur and Bankura areas. They left their ancestral home on account of the oppressive demands of the zamindars after the Permanent Settlement of Bengal in 1793 and they settled in the plains skirting the Rajmahal hills. When the Santhals cleared the lands and raised crops on them, the zamindars from the adjoining areas claimed those lands and started extorting money from the Santhal peasants. The money lenders also appeared on the scene and oppressed them. The police and revenue and court officials also helped the Zamindars and the money-lenders against the peasants. Sometimes the Government stepped in and handed over their hands on lease to a European. Sometimes a Bengali went to beg at a Santhalee village. The leader of the Santhals *i.e.*, Manjhee, having taken compassion housed him and fed him for sometimes, and then advanced him a small amount to start with as a trader. The Bengali throve so well among those innocent people that he became a Mahajan, lending out small sums at a most usurious rate of interest.

Unfortunately, the position of the Manjhee was rudely shaken by the way the law courts and the revenue department of the Government of India worked some of their grievances may be listed below as given in the Government records:

(1) The Manjhees got short leases, had to pay heavy salaries in order to get them, and at each renewal there was an enhancement.

(2) The leases were not always renewed with the old and time-honoured manjhee-mustajir, but with stranges; in most cases with the hated Bhoojpooria or Bengali money lender who had managed to make a fortune by endless cheating, and established himself in the village.

(3) The new land-jobber at once commenced a new measurement carried on by a dishonest Patwari, who always altered the extent of each holding, and cheated the ryots.

(4) Thus, unsettling the whole village community, and in nine cases of ten forcing the ryots, from utter weariness, to buy peace at any price."

(5) The amlah and peadahs of the zamindars sat dharna at the doors of the ryots, insulted their women until the demands for a higher rate of rent, or some other unjust or disputed claim was not satisfied.

In the year 1861, the ryots collected in their santhal gatherings and threatened disturbances, when the Government of Sir J.P. Grant had to intervence and Mr. Barnes, the landlord who had increased the demand from Rs. 12,000 to 60,000 in 3 or 4 years came down to Rs. 40,000/- In the year 1871 the position worsened and Lord Mayo had to record the following Minute, dated July10,1871:

"There can hardly be found a great instance of keener and more diabolical oppression having been practised, and all this practised on estates leased by our own Court of Words. It is almost too horible to think that we shall be obliged to order our troops to go out and shoot poor ignorant savages who have certainly the balance of right on their side." From 1871 to 1875, there had been manifested various symptoms on uneasiness and restlessness among the Santhals. The Bhagrut Movement was perhaps the most dangerous one. One Bhagrut Manjhee had been arrested in the year 1868 for trying to excite a political disturbance. In September 1874 A.D. This Santhal leader appeared in the sub-division of Godda, and having gained an assendancy over the minds of the people, proceed to turn his power to account by promoting a religious movement in the direction of Hinduism. A large meeting of Santhals was held at Bowse in Bhagalpure district where there was a Hindu temple of note. Subsequently a shrine was established by Bhagrut at his own village. An important feature of the movement was attracted great attention was that all the followers of Bharut were called upon for the purpose of purification. The order was obeyed. The crows of Santhals from parts of the country flocked to Bhagrut Shrine to do worhip. The result of this was panic especially among the Christians. The Government stationed a special police force as a precuationary measure.

Another attempt to revive he Bhagrut movement in Mohespore was made by Dhonaht Manjhee, a well known agitator on the rent question. This was promptly suppressed, Dhonah himself being imprisoned. In December 1874, it suddenly reappeared in the Mohespore with great force. This was now under the leadership of one Gyan, a disciple of Bhagrut. He issued written orders under the authority of the Commissioner to say that no rents or debts were to be paid to the zamindars or money lenders till the Commissioner came himself.

Whatever might be the outward and apparent character of the movement, it was definitely linked up with the question of rent and deep desire of breaking old bonds. Bhagrut himself, and his principal followers, freely talked about starting—"The prosperous time when the Raj and the land should belong to the Santhals, and when the maximum rental should be fixed at 8 annas (a coin) per plough.

Another important feature of the Santhal awakening was its universal character. Even those Santhals who were not concerned or effected by renthencement thought it as their duty to join the upheaval although it meant a sacrifice of their work and wages in hand. For example, the owners of indigo factories at different places often complained that their labourers had given back their advances, saying that they could not work this season, being bound to join in rebellion third important features of the santhal rebellion was that the Santhal peasants defied the unjust order of the British government and they were brutally fired upon and butchered en masse. They displayed exceptional courage and military discipline. They faced successive volleys of British bullets with reckless heroism.

2. The Revolt of 1857 and the Peasants of U.P.. During the great rebellion of 1857 A.D., the peasant of most of Avadh and Western U.P. forget their oppressions by the lozal zamindars and joined hands with the rebellions against the British rule. They played a heroic part, displayed great millitary skill, powers and achieved victorios. However, later on they had to pay very bitterly for their display of patriotism. After the Revolt was crushed the lands of peasants were treated as the property of the zamindars (landlords) and they (the peasants) were reduce from the status of properietors to that the tenenats-at-will-of their own former lands.

3. Strike of Bengal Indigo Cultivators. Another great and notable peasant movement of modern India was the indigo agitation that engulfed Bengal in 1859-60 A.D. The cultivation of indigo was a monopoly of the Europeans. The Europeans planters compelled the peasants to sow indigo on at leas 3/20th of their land and to sell it at prices fixed by the planters. In order to force the peasants to produce indigo at uneconomic rates, the planters resorted to illegal beatings and detentions. The anger of the suppressed peasants burst out in 1859 A.D. Hundreds of thousands of peasant refused to cultivate indigo and resisted the physical brutality and violence of the planters and their armed retainers. They assembled with swards, staffs, bows and arrows and matchlocks to defend their settlements. In Pabhna an army of 2,000 peasants appeared and raised the banner of rebellion against the planters. According to a Bengali author, Lalit Chandra Mitra, who wrote a book in 1903 A.D. about Indigo disturbances. "The story of India Rebellions would not be complete without a reference to the 'Nil Darpan' a novel of Bankim Chandra Chatterjee. According to him," laid the Bengal peasantry udner a debt never to be repaid., The 'Nil Darpan' described how respectable royt, a peasant proprietor, happy with his family in the enjoyment of land, was compelled to take advances; how he was reduced to the condition of a serf; the effect of this on his home, children and relatives; how the magistrates were partial to the planters; and how arbitrary power debased the lord as well as the peasants.

Harishchandra Mukhopadhya, Girish Chandra Basu, Dinabandhu Mitra, Sisir Kumar Ghosh and many other well-known intellectuals supported the cause of the peasants. The Government was forced to appoint the Indigo Commission. The commission asked the peasant about the terms on which they were willing to sow indigo in future. The Government learnt a lesson from the Santhal revolt and took steps to remove the grievances of the peasants by passing a law in 1862 A.D. The Indigo disputes continued even after the report of the Indigo Commission. "In view of the sturdy resistance, the oppression of the planters became occasional. Indigo Cultivation was allowed to be abandoned in many cases. Gradually, the indigo planters of Bengal moved to Bihar and Uttar Pradesh. The indigo peansats of Bihar revolted on a large scale in Darbhanga and Champaran in 1866-68. Likewise, the peasants of Jessore in Bengal revolted in 1883 A.D. and 1889-90 A.D.

4. The Revolt of Maharashtriam Peasants (or Deccan Riots) 1874-1875 A.D.. Deccan or Maharashtra riots were also a clear proof of people's growing aptitude to combine for collective action against their oppression. These riots were against the money-lenders and occured after a period of boom in the cotton trade due to the Civil War in America. May be, that the few years of unwanted prosperity which ended in 1866, had enabled the peasants to borrow freely from village bankers (or local baniyas) on the security of their lands or crops, whereas subsequent unfavourable seasons placed them more fully at the mercy of their creditors.

A major agrarian revolt occured in the Pona and Ahmednagar districts of Maharashtra in 1875 A.D. In Maharashtra, the government had settled the land revenue directly with the peasants. However the Government demand was fixed at such a high level most of the peasant found it impossible to pay without borrowing from the money lenders who charged very high rates of interest. In this regard we can quote the report of the Collector (he reported in 1843 A.D.) of Kaira. He reported that out of 50,000 cultivators of Government land 37,500 were in debt. The result was that more and more land was martaged or sold to the moneylenders. The patience of the peasants was exchausted by the end of 1874 A.D. The trouble began in a village Kardeh in Sirur Taluka in December 1874 A.D. when a Marwari money lender, Kaloo Ram by name, obtained decree of eviction against Baba Saheb Deshmukh, a cultivator in debt to him for Rs. 150. The moneylender pulled down the house of Deshmukh and that led to trouble. The peasants of Poona and Ahmednagar district organised a social boycott of the moneylender which was resulted into a riot on September 9, 1875 due to which 30 people were sent up for trial. In District Poona there was a stronger upheaval. Everywhere the peasants of the district took forcible possession of their debt bonds, decres and their documents dealing with their debt and burnt them in public. The police failed to meet the bury of the peasant resistance. It was suppressed only when the whole military force at Poona, horsefoot and artillery, took the field against them. In connection with these riots nearly 559 people were arrested. The Government appointed the Deccan Riots Commission in 1875 which submitted its report in 1876 A.D. It was reported by the Commission that the real source of the misery of the peasants lay in high land revenue demanded by the Government and its failure to provide credit at low rate of interst to the peasants.

5. Moplah's Peasants. The turbulent history of the Moplahs of Malabar (Kerala State) reveals yet another facet of the complexilies of the Indian situation—the way in which religious fanaticism has served as the outward from for the expression of anti-landlord and anti-foreign discontent, a bitter anti-white temper had developed among sections of the Malabar Muslims ever since the Portuguese had come in 1498 A.D. to capture the spice trade and seck to extend Christianity by fire and sword. British rule with its insistence on landlord rights had reestablished and vastly enhanced the position of the Hindu upper caste Namboodari and Nair Jemmis and correspondingly worsened the condition of the largely Muslim leaseholders and cultivators, locally known as Moplahs. An immdediate consequence was a strengthening of communal solidarity withthe number of mosques in Malabar going up from 637 in 1831 A.D. to 1058 in 1851 A.D., and with the Tangals of manbram near tirurangadi becoming increasing prominent as the religious cum-political heads of Moplah society. There was also large-scale conversion of untouchable Cherunars to a religion which promised a degree of equality and some social ascent. Revolt became practically endenic in the Emad and Walluvanad talukas of South Malabar, with 22 recorded between 1836 and 1854, and more risings in 1882-85 and again in 1896. The number of activities was rather small, 349 in all in the 28 outbreaks recorded between 1836 and 1919, for collective mass resistance was difficult in South Malabar with its poor communication and scattered homesteads. The Moplah outbreaks were thus a peculiar form of rural terrorism which...was probably the most effective means of curbing the enhanced power of the jenmi for the earthly benefit of Moplahs who themselves did not become participants. 62 out of 82 victims of Moplah attacks down to 1919 were high-caste Hindus, while of the 70 whose class background can be traced, 58 were jenmis and/or moneylenders. Most Moplah martyrs were poor peasants or landless labourers, but they usually got the sympathy of the better off kanamdars and petty traders. One hears also of a widespread belief that a ship was coming with arms for the Moplahs—a myth stratingly similarly to the 'cargo-cults' of Malanesia in the Pacific under colonial rule. which have been studied by arthropologists like petter worsley. The roots of Moplah discontent were clearly agrarian—there was a 244% increse in rent suits and a 441% increase in eviction decres between 1862 and 1880 in the talukas of South Malabar, Hindu peasants also suffered, but the form of resistance differed. Large number of Hindu robber bands are reported to have been active in the Malabar villages in the 1860's and

1870s. In the absence of a millenarian ideology such as Islam could offer, Hindu peasant disaffection could not rise above the level of social banditry.

6. Peasant Riots (or No-revenue Movements) in Assam. The British government attempts to hike up land revenue led a series of peasant riots in the plains of Assam during 1893-94 A.D. These riots marked a high degree of unanimity. They were provided leadership by local notables. These riots got support from the intelligentia. In the Kamrup and Darrang district of Assam for instance a new settlement in 1893-94 which enhanced rates by 50 to 70 per cent was met by the organization of raijmels, mass assemblies of vilages led by the rural elite (Brahamas, Gossains and Dolois) which refused to pay the enhanced revenue demand, unitedly resistd official attepts to sieze their fields and fought back the revenue collectors. There was also some looting of market and two case of police firing at Rangiya and Patharught, in January 1894 A.D. The Government mobilised a large numer of soldiers and armed policemen to suppress the peasant movement. A large number of peasants were killed in firings. The demand for revenue deduction was supported by the Jorhat Sarvajanik Sabha, and the issue was raised at Imperial Legislative Council by the Moderate Congress leader of Bengal, Rashbehari Ghosh' eventually some concessions were obtained.

7. (Peasant Movements in Mewar (Rajasthan) (1905-1920 A.D.). Mewar was also the scence of a number of important peasant movements. By a curious coincidence these begain in 1905 A.D. at a time when far-off Bengal patriotic intellectuals like R.C. Dutt, D.L. Roy, Abanidranath Tagore and Rabindranath Tagore were writing novels, plays, stroies and poems extroling the chivalry and heroism of the medieval towards the British with the grossest froms of feudal exploitation of the peasantry. At Bijolia, a big Mewar Jagir held by a Parmer Rajput, there were 86 different types of case on peasants, and in 1905 A.D. and again in 1913 A.D. the latter collectively refused to cultivate lands and tried to emigrate to neighbouring areas. The 1913 protest was led by a Sadhu, sitaram Das, while in 1915 a new element was introduced by the externment in the region of an revolutionary connected with Sachin Sanyal's group named Bhoop Singh, ali a Vijay Singh Pathik. Pathik in exile developed into a peasant leader, and persuaded a State official, Manik Lal Verma, to jointly lead a no-tax movement against the Udaipur Maharaja in 1916 A.D. Peasant refusal to contribute to war-loans was another element in the Bijolia movement, which later developed Gandhian contact, and continued into the 1920s. Both Pathik and Verma later became important Indian National Congress leader in Rajasthan.

8. The Peasants Revolt in Punjab. In the last decade of the nineteenth century, the peasants revolted in many places. The main cause of these agitation was the alicnation of their lands to the urban monylenders for their failure to pay debts. The British Government did not want any revolt in that province due to two reasons. Firstly, it was situated on the boarder, Secondly, it provided a large number of soldiers to the British army in India. Therefore the government passed the Punjab Alienation Act in 1900 to case the situation.

9. Revolt by the Peasants of Champaran (1917-18 A.D.). The European planters of Champaran (a district in Bihar) resorted to illegal and inhuman mothods of indigo cultivation at a cost which was wholly unjust. Under the Tinkathia system in Champaran, the peasants were bound by law to grow indigo on 3/20 part of thier land and to sell it at prices fixed by them (the planters), Having head of Gandhiji's campaigns in South Africa, severla peasants of Champaran invited him to come and help them. Accompanied by Babu Rajendra Prasad, Mazhar-ul-Haq, J.B. Kriplani and Mahadev Desai Gandhi reached Champaran in 1917 and began to conduct a detailed inquiry into the condition of the peasantry. To infuriated district officials ordered him to leave Champaran, but he difled the order and was willing to face trial and imprisonment. This force the government to cancel its earlier order and to appoint a committee of inquiry on which Gandhi served as a member.

10. South India in Ferment. The peasants of the Krishna and Godawari Deltas and those of Karnatka and Rayalageema revolted severai times from the beginning of the 19th century to protest againt the high land revenues, the neglect of irrigation facilities and rigid methods of land-revenue collection. The farmers particiapated in a strong but constitutional agitation against the Madras Tortures Act and got success in getting it repealed.

11. Satyagraha in Kheda (Gujarat). In the Kheda District the crops failed in 1918, but the officers insisted on collection of full land revenue. Mahtma Gandhi organised the peasant to offer Satyagraha. they refused to pay land revenue and were prepared to suffer. Even those who could afford to pay, refused to pay. They suffered imprisonment for defying unjust laws. The Satyagraha lasted till June 1918. The Government was ultimately forced to surrender and a settlement was made with peasants and their just demands were conceded. Thus, prior to 1918, the peasants fought at many places against the injustice done to them but as their efforts were not orgaised they could get only meagre concession from their expthoiters. The Indian National Congress also paid only scanty attention towards the welfare of the peasants. It was only after 1918 that the Indian peasants developed political consciousness, participated in the natoinal movement and gradually formed their own organisations. About the formation of their own orgnisation well-known scholar and historian Mr. R. Palme Dutt writes in this popular book India Today, "But it is in the last two decades since the world war of 1914-1918, and especially in the last decade since the world economic cristis,, that peasant unrest in India has advanced at a speed without previous parallel and rakes on a more and more clearly revolutionary character. The world economic crisis knocked the bottom out the already exhausted agraian economy of India. The resulting process of rack-renting, debt enslavement and expropriation found its reflection in rising movements of the peasants in all parts of India.

The peasants were drawn into the political struggle of the Indian National Congress on the basis of their own grievances; but the political struggle was never directly linked up with the local Kisan Committees (peasant committes). The peasant came to feel the need to develop these and create their own mass organisation.

12. Bardoli Satyagraha. Sardar Ballabh Bhai Patel organised and led the Bardoli peasants against the resettlement enhancements proposed by the Government. The peasants braved all risks, faced with courage the loss of their beloved cattle and ancestrail lands and even risked eviction from their villages. Ultimately, they won. That was in 1929.

13. Khilafat, Non-cooperation Movements and the Peasants. When in 1919 the Khilafat Committe launched Khilafat movement and the Indian National Congress decided to start Non-cooperation Movement under the leadership of Gandhi a call was given for non-payment of land revenue. the peasants from the different parts of the country came forward and participated in these movements. Many peasants felt that the struggle for Swarajaya (Independence) meant struggle against the heavy land revenue and they cooperated with the national leaders. In fact, it was their first participation on a larger scale in an organised movement. The struggle of the peasants however continued even outside the fold of the Indian natioal Congress during this period. For example, they struggled against their landlords in Guntur district and at many places in Karnatka and Avadh. As we have already mentioned the Moplah Rebellion in 1922 was largely revolt of Muslim peasants aggaisnt their landlords, the Namboodri Brahmins of Malabar. Even some historians say that violent incident happened at Chaura Chauri in 1922 was also a result of the active participation of a mob of peasants.

14. Satyagraha between 1930-42. During this period (1930-42) a number of Satyagraha companigns were organised by peasants against unjust land laws, high land revenues high rate of interest etc. We can mention only a few of them. They were : the struggle of the peasants in Karnatka against Karnatka Forest laws in 1931-1934, the rent exactions in Uttar Pradesh and Bihar in 1931-33, the anti-resettlement campaigns of Godawari and Krishna Deltas and a number of peasants struggles against the landlords of Venkatagiri (1931), Tesadumu and Munagala in 1939 were organised in the South. There were also the land Styagraha in Bihar in 1939, the anti-zamindari fight in Bengal and Andhra, Canal duties struggle of the Punjab and Bengal in 1939, the jute prices struggle of 1937-42 and the debut relief agitation of Bengal.

15. Kisan Orgnization and the Government (1927-35). Since the days of withdrawal of non-cooperation movement by Mahatma Gandhi some peasant leaders wanted to have separate and organised unions of farmers so that the attention of the government could be drawn. It gave momentum independent Kisan Movements in the thirties of the 20th century. It resulted in the formation of Bihar Kisan Sabha in 1927, the Provincial Kisan Sabha in Uttar Pradesh in 1935, the Madras Presidency Ryots Association in 1935, the Madras Presidence Agriculturists Association in 1937 and a Kisan school at Nidubrole in 1938 to train the Kisans in organisational work. Some peasants organizations took their birth on communal basis also.

In some cases, the government yielded to their pressure resulting in the passing of a few laws like Debt Relief Acts in U.P. in 1934 A.D., the Regulation of Accounts Act in 1934 A.D. in Punjab, the Moneylenders Act in 1939 A.D. and the Relif of Indebtedness Act in 1935 A.D. in Bengal.

16. The Formation of All-India Kisan Sabha. In 1936 A.D. the first All India Peasant Organisation was formed—the All India Kisan Sabha. The first congress of it was held at faizpur in Decemeber 1936, at the sametime as the Indian National Congress 20,000 peasants took part in the deliberations, many having marched hundreds of miles to attend. Simultaneously at Faizpur the Indian National Congress adopted its agrarian programme and the political solidarity of the two organisations was declared. By its third Congress at Comilla in May 1938 A.D., the membership of the All India Kisan Sabha had reached 550,000. Out of twenty linguistic provinces, nineteen had now provincial Kisan Committees.

The formation of Congress Ministries in 1937 A.D. proved a stimulus to peasant organisation. All through 1938 big peasants' struggles took place in all the provinces of India, and in many cases won partial success against attempted rent increase against evictions, and against forced labour and illegal exactions and for reduction of rents. At the same time gigantic peasant marches and demonstrations, reaching to 30,000 and 40,000 strong, the publication of weekly papers, song-books and leaflets and the initation of peasant schools proved the growing strength and consolidation of the movement.

The fourth All-India Kisan Sabha was held at Gaya in April 1939, and revealed a membership of 800,000. Within a few months of this session at Gaya came the opening of the Second World War (1939-45). Under the Defence of India Act a wave of repression was let loose on the Indians. Country wide mass arrests and detentions without trail of the leaders of the working class and peasant movement took place. But despite all the repression, peasants all over the country continued their determined fight against the imperialist—feudal system. In the Punjab, the Kisans of Lahore and Amritsar organised mass marches and demonstration demanding a reduction in land revenue. More than 5,000 Kisans including hundreds of women were imprisoned; four of them lost their lives in prison before the movement was terminated after six months on partial grant of some of the demands. In Bihar, Bengal, Sind, Andhra Pradesh, C.P., U.P., Malabar and Surma Valley, Kisans struggled valiantly against arbitrary taxations, forcible evictions, etc.

The period 1942-45 was a great trial for the entire kisan movement. In August 1942 A.D., a ruthless attack was launched by imperialism on the entire national movement—the arrest of the Congress leaders was followed by heavy repression. Alongside this developed an extreme breakdown of the country's economy. The landlord trader, hoarders and black marketeers in alliance with the corroupt bureacracy played havoc with the lives of millions. the masses of the peasantry were overtaken by famine and ruin, the poor improvershed Kisans died like flies in Bengal and some other provinces.

IMPACT OF BRITISH POLICIES ON THE INDIAN PEASANTS

India is a land of villages. The main occupation of the people of villages is agriculture. According to scholars nearly 70 per cent of the Indian population is peasantry. The British policies had a pronounced and profound impact on Indian peasantry. A critical study can be done reviewing the different policies of the British Government concerning directly the peasant in the following manner:

(1) The Land Revenue policy of the British Government.

(a) Izaredari System. Since the days of the beginning of the rule of East India Company in the farmers were greatly effected. The main burden of providing money for the trade and profits of the Company, the cost of administration and the wars of British expansion had to be born by the Indian peasant. In 1765 the East India Company acquired the Diwani, or control over the revenues, of Bengal, Bihar and Orissa. Initially, it made an attempt to continue the old system of revenue collection though it increased the amount to be collected from Rs. 14,290,000 in 1722 A.D. and Rs. 8,180,000 in 1764 to Rs. 23,400,000 in 1773 A.D., it decided to manage the land revenue directly. Warren Hastings auctioned the right of collecting revenues to the highest bidders. This system is known as Izaredari System. The system proved helpful neither to the Company as the actual collection never came up to its expectation nor to the preasants who were fleeced by the new zamindars. The zamindars squeezed the peasants for more money to make the demands of the increasing land revenue and to please the greedy and corrupt officials of the East India Company. Under this system the peasants of Bengal, Bihar and the Orissa were crushed upto 1793 A.D. Many peasants were compelled to work as landless labours. One-third land of Bengal, Bihar and Orissa transformed into a jugle of the wild beasts. We can mention as a reference a complaint of Lord cornwallis who came one ear after Warren Hastings. He complained that 1/3 rd of Bengal had been transformed into a jugle inhabited only by wild beasts."

(b) The Permanent Settlement. After prolong discussions and debates permanent Settlement was introduced in Bengal and Bihar in 1793 by Lord Cornwallis. This had two special features. Firstly, the zamindars and revenue collectors were converted into so many landlords. They were not only to act as agents of the Government in collecting land revenue from the Ryot (peasant) but also to became owners of the entire land in their zamindaris. Their right of ownership was made hereditary and transferable. On the other hand, the cultivators were tenants and were deprived of long standing rights to the soil and other customary rights. The use of the pasture and forest lands, irrigation canals, fisheries and homestead plots and protection against enhancement of rent were some of their rights which were sacrificed. Secondly the zamindars were to give 10/11 th of the rental they derived from the peasantry to the state, keeping only 1/11 th for themselves. As the zamindars had to pay his revenue rigidly on the due date even if the crop had failed for some reason therefore, they also adopted a rigid attitude to collect the land revenue from the farmers. In this way we can say in both the permanently and the temporarily Settled Zamindari areas, the lot of Indian peasants remained unenviable. They were left to the mercies of the landlords who raised sents to unbearable limits, compelled them to pay illegal dues and to perform force labour or begar and oppressed them in diverse other ways.

(c) **Ryotwari System.** The Condition of the cultivators in the Ryotwari areas was no better. Here the Government took the place of zamindars and levied excessive land revenue which was in the beginning fixed as high as one-third to one-half of the produce. The system was introduced in parts of Madras and Bombay Presidencies in the begining of the 19th century. The settlement under the Ryotwari system was not made permanent. It was revised periodically after 20 to 30 years when the revenue demand was usually raised. In these areas the peasants had to pay revenue even when his produce was partially or wholly destroyed by drought or floods.

(d) Mahalwari System. A modified version of the zamindari settlement introduced in the gangetic valley, the North—province parts of Central India and the Punjab was known as the Mahalwari System. Revene settlement was to be made village by village or estate (Mahal) by estate with landlords or heads of families who collectively claimed to tbe the landlords of the village of the estate. In Mahalwari areas also, the land revenue was periodically revised. The condition of the peasant in the Mahalwari areas was no better. Gradually the cultivators in these areas sank deeper and deeper into debt and more and more land passed into the hands of taluqdars money-lenders and merchants. In sum, we can say during the British rule either it was the Izaredari or the Permanent Settlement, Ryotwari or Mahalwari System the misery, sorrow and poverty of the peasants increased day by day. Heavy assessment of land was one of the main causes of the growth of poverty of the Indian peasants and the deterioration of agriculture in the days of the British rule. Many contrary writers and officials noted this fact.

Even though the land revenue demand went on increasing year after year it increased from Rs. 15.3 crores in 1857-58 to Rs. 35.8 crores in 1936-37 the proportion of the total produce taken as land revenue lended to decline as the prices rose and production increased. No proportional increase in land revenue was made as the disastrous concequences of demanding exportionate revenue became obvious. But by now the population pressure on agriculture had increased to such an extent that the lesser revenue demand of later years weighted on the peasants as heavily as the higher revenue demand of the earlier years of the Company's administration.

(2) Manner of Revenue Collection. The harmful effects of an excessive land revenue demand were further heightened by the rigid manner of its collection. Land revenue had to be paid promptly on the fixed dates even if the harvest had been below normal or had failed completely due to natural calamities. Whenever the peasant failed to pay the land revenue, the government put up his land on sale on collect of arrears of revenue. But in most cases, the peasant himself took this step and sold part of his land to meet in time the government demand. In either case, he lost his land. More often the inability to pay revenue drovn the peasant to borrow money at high rates of interests from the money lender. He preferred getting into debt by mostgaging his land to a money-lender or to a rich peasant neighbour of loosing it outright. By the end of 19th century the monylender had become a major curse of the countryside and an important cause of the growing poverty of the peasants and other people of the villages. In 1911 the total rural debt was estimated at Rs. 300 crores. By 1937 it amounted to Rs. 1,800 crores. The entire process became a vicious circle. The pressure of taxation and growing poverty pushed the cultivators into debt which in turn increased their poverty. In fact, the cultivators often failed to understand that the money-lender was an inevitable long in the machauism of imperialist exploitation and turned their anger against him as he appeared to be the visible cause of their impoverishment. For instance, during the Revolt of 1857, whenever the peasantry rose in revolt, quite often its first target of attack was the money-lender and his account books.

(3) The Policy of Commercialisation of Agriculture. Commercialisation of agriculture began during the British rule. The British encouraed the production of those agricultural goods which were needed either for feeding their industries or could get them good commercial dividends otherwise. The growing commercialisation of agriculture helped the money-lender-cum-merchant to exploit the cultivator. The poor peasant was forced to sell his produce just after the harvest and at whatever price he could get as he had to meet in time the demands of the government, the landlord, the money-lender and his family members requirements. This placed him at the mercy of the grain merchant, who was in a position to dictate terms and who purchased his produce at much less than the market price. Thus a large share of the benefit of the growing trade in agricultural products was reaped by the merchant, who was very often also the village money-lender.

(4) The Policy to Promote Landlordism. The land revenue policies of the British Government proved very helpful in rise of new landlordism. During British rule more and more land passed into the hands of money-lenders, merchants, and rich peasants who usually got the land cultivated by tenants. One reason why the Indian moneyed classes were keen to buy land and became landlords was the absence of effective outlets for investment of their capital in industry. Many owner-cultivators and occupancy tenants, having a permanent right to hold land, find it more convenient to lease out land to land-hungry tenants at exorbitant rent than to cultivate it themselves. In time, landlordism became the main feature of aggrigarian relations not only in the zamindari areas but also in the 'Ryotwari areas'. A remarkable feature of the spread of landlordism during the British period was the growth of subinfendation or intermadiaries. Since the cultivating tenants to compete with one another to acquire land the rent of land went on increasing. The zaminders and the new landlords found it convenient to sublet their right to collect rent to other eager persons on profitable terms. But as rents increased, subleasers of land in their turn sublet their turn sublet their rights in land. Thus by a chain-process a large number of rent-receiving interme diaries between the actual cultivator and the government sprang up. In some cases in Bengal their number went as high as fifty. The condition of the helpless cultivating tenants who had immediately to bear the unbearable burden of maintaining this horde of superior landlords was precarious beyound imagination. Many of them were little better than slaves. The extrme poverty of the over whelming majority of peasants left them without any resources with which to improve agriculture by using better cattle and seeds, more manures and fertilizers, and improved teachniques of production.

(5) Indifferent Attitude Towards the Farmers and Agriculture. The British Government was a foreign government. It took no interest in solving the problems of Indian farmers and agriculture. Its indifferent attitude proved very harmful for Indian peasantry. The revenue policy of the British, increased pressure of population on agricuture, existence of serveral intermediaries between the peasant and the government, subdivision and fragmentation of land holdings, lack of modern industry, lack of proper provision of banking and other financial agencies to provide long time loans on cheaper rate of interest to the farmers, indifferent attitude of the government to modernize and mechanise the Indian agriculture etc. resulted in the impoverishment of the Indian peasantry and other grave problem of Indian agriculture that is, rural indebtendness. The loss of land and over crowding of land caused by deindustrialisation and lack of modern industry compelled the landless peasants to become either tenats of the money lenders and zamindars by paying rack-rent or agricultural labourers at starvation wages.

After these three had taken their share no such was felt for the cultivator and his family to subsist on. It has been calculated that in 1950-51 land rent and money lenders interest amounted to Rs. 1400 crores or roughly equal to one-third of the total agricultural produce for the year. The result was that the impoverishment of the peasantry continued as also an increase in the incidence of famines. People died in millions whenever droughts or floods caused failure of crops and produced scarcity.

❐

13

Growth of Muslim Separatism

The Muslims organised a separate political association in the year 1906 at Dacca. They christened this association as the Indian Muslim League. The objects of the new organisation were as follows:

(a) to safeguard the political and other rights of the Indian Muslims and to place the demands, for the purpose, before the Government in moderate terms;

(b) to foster among the Indian Muslims a greater loyalty to the British Government in India; and

(c) to establish friendly connections with those Muslims or those other non-Muslim communities which were and opposed to the first and second aim of the League.

Nature of the League

The Muslim League was composed of only the intelligentsia and aristocrats among the Indian Muslims. The masses were not interested in it. So too was the condition of the Indian National Congress in those days. But the League encouraged the Muslims to remain away from the national movement and not to align with the Congress. The session of 1908 was held in Amritsar under the presidentship of Sir Syad Ali Imam. The League resolved here that there should be separate representation of the Muslims and a special emphasis on the Muslims in the Government services.

It should not be forgotten here that it was not because of the establishment of a separate Muslims League that the Indian Muslims drifted away from the Congress. There were still very prominent

Muslim members inside the Congress and some Muslims in the country were even totally opposed to the ideas of the League. Special mention might be made of such illustrious persons like Maulana Abdul Kalam Azad, Maulana Mohammad Ali, Hakim Ajmal Khan and Dr. Ansari. Maulana Mohammad Ali went to the extent of keeping alive inside the League a short of leftist group. On the whole, the League was a creature of British patronage of Muslims and treachery to the solidarity of the Indian nationalism. It was one of the original aims of the Muslim League to controvert the growing influence of the so-called Indian National Congress, which had a tendency to misinterpret and subvert the British Rule in India.

Cordiality with the Congress

Nevertheless, for some years after the formation of the League its relations with the Congress were destined to be cordial. The most important factor was the treatment meted out to Turkey by the European Powers before 1914 and 1919. The Indian Muslims regarded the Calipha and Sultan of Turkey as the spiritual head of Islam. But the symbol of its greatness was put to severe strain by the British policy during the Balkan wars of 1912-13, when Turkey was greatly weakened. Secondly, the Muslims were not consulted by the British Government in its action of terminating the Bengal partition. The leaders of the Muslims who felt offended at such commission and omission of the Government tried to capture and didcapture the power of the Muslim League. Meanwhile in 1913 the constitution of the League was changed to make its purpose more radical. Mr. Mohammed Ali Jinnah had come in. Yet for some years the sessions of the National Congress and Muslim League were held simultaneously in the same city. So it was in Lucknow in 1916. The early cordiality went into collaboration and the result was the Lucknow Pact of 1916.

Provisions of the Lucknow Pact. It is interesting to know that when the eminent Congress leaders like Mahatma Gandhi, Pandit Madan Mohan Malviya, attended the annual sessions of the Muslims League in 1915, 1916 and 1917. They supported Muslims because both considered that interests of the country are paramount.

Communal Provisions. In the Lucknow Pact the National Congress unwittingly went back upon its national character and agreed to the right of separate electorate for the Muslims. More, the minorities were to have weightage—more seats than their numerical strength would warrant. Finally the sinister provisions came to a head with the grant of right of veto to the minority which, if it considered any resolution in the Legislature to be repugnant to its interest, could, decisively oppose it by a three-fourths majority of its own members. The British Parliament recognised the Lucknow Pact as the only agreement between the Hindus and Muslims and it asserted the separate electorate, in the provisions of the Government of India Act of 1919.

Constitutional Provisions. The atmosphere of give-and-take marked itself on the provisions of the Lucknow Pact. The Provinces were to be autonomous in fields of finance and administration, and the control of the Central Government relaxed. The Central and Provincial Legislatures were to be four-fifths elected and one-fifth nominated. The Government at the Centre and in the Provinces were to be carried on under the resolutions passed by the respective legislatures unless they were vetoed by the Governor-General-in Council. The Executive Government, independent of the Central Legistlature was to control execlusively the defence matters, and foreign and political relations of India. The secretary of State for India would behave towards the Indian Government as the Colonial Secretary would towards the Government of the Dominions.

1927 Rift in the League. Mahatma Gandhi had won over the Muslims to the Non-Co-operation Movement of 1920-22 by incorporating Khilafat movement in it. The Khilafat Committee and Jamait-ul-ulema-i-Hind joined the Congress in the movement and the Muslim League was forgotten. But it was a short-lived phenomenon. When Turkey was secularised the Khilafat Movement was no more required for the Un-Islamic State of Turkey, the Muslims required their vigour of non-violence. Mr. Jinnah was now trying to take the leadership of the League into his own hands, but with little success. The Muslim League suffered a split within its ranks on their attitude towards the Simon Commission. Jinnah advocated boycott of the Commission but another section of the League led by Sir Mohammad Shafi wanted co-operation with it. Strangely the two sections of the Muslim League met separately. Jinnah found himself alone. The national leaders of the Muslims, like Hakim Ajmal Khan, Dr. Ansari, Dr. Kitchlew, Maulana Azad. Dr. Syed Mohmud and Asaf Ali went against him. Jinnah was too radical to be in this nationalist group, yet too distasteful of the programme of direct action to join the Congress.

General Elections. On the basis of the Government of India Act of 1935, general elections were held in the provinces in the year 1937, two years after the passage of the Act. It these elections, the Muslims League did not fare well even in the Muslim majority provinces. Mr. Jinnah said, probably because he was in search for power, "there is really no subsiantial difference now at any rate, between the League and the Congress". He conducted negotiations in favour of coalition government, but the conditions for such governments as put forward by the Congress were not acceptable to him. One example of such terms as the Congress wanted was in the United Provinces, where the coalition government, if any, was made conditional upon non-functioning of the League as a functional group, and upon becoming part of the Congress organisation. The Muslim League naturally got "a direct rebuff" as Jinnah saw it. The League became convinced that, "the Muslims can expect neither justice nor fair play under Congress Government. The ranks of the League were swelled by the Muslim landlords who feared the Congress agrarian policy of "land to the tillers". The middle class of the Muslim community was inefficient and unable to complete with the middle class of the Hindu society in industry, professions and public services. They joined the League with the hope that in case a separate State for Muslims were to be set up.

Hindu Muslims Rift. The League found its principles diametrically opposed to these of the Congress. The educational policy of the Congress was professedly based on handicrafts—an essentially Hindu Policy. The Muslims thought it an attack on the very existence of their community. Brailsford in his book "Subject

India" gives an account of a Muslim leader within the Congress, who deserted Congress but returned to the victorious Congress for some post in the 1937 government only to be refused bluntly and he argues that events like this swelled the number of anti-Congress Muslim adherents of the League. The principle of the Congress on masscontract was also directed at winning the poor, rustic Mussalmans. Jinnah found it a means to death of Muslims from their professed leaders and cried 'Islam is in danger'. The League fell upon the expedient of arousing religious sentiments of the Muslims to swell its ranks and capture power.

Report of Raja of Pirpur. The Muslim League could not tolerate the sight of the Congress in power and charged it with tyranny over the Muslim minority. In March, 1938 the League appointed a committee of investigation under the Raja of Pirpur. True to its spirit the Pirpur Report gave an exaggerated list of sufferings of the Muslims under the Congress regimes, though Coupland testifies that the Congress Ministries did not pursue a policy of communal injustice, still less of deliberate persecution. Yet the Muslim League did never agree to the Congress proposals of referring the charges to an impartial tribunal. When the Congress ministries resigned in 1939 as a protest against the British war policy on India, the League was very much pleased to observe the "Deliverance day". Between 1937 and 1942 the League could capture 47 out of 61 Muslim seats in bye-elections whereas the Congress won only four.

Birth of Two nation Theory. It was not until the Allahabad Session of 1930 that the Muslim League knew of a probability of Pakistan. Sir Mohammad Iqbal nursed the idea when he said, first ever so in hitory, that a North West Indian Muslim State was desirable for the final destiny of the Indian Muslims. Coupland argues that Iqbal stood for a loose federation of all Indian provinces, not a separate Pakistan. But the idea once generated worked miraculously. Some Muslim students at Cambridge caught the infection, with Iqbal's suggestion. In 1933 their leader Rahmat-Ali described the Indian Muslims as a separate nation, and advocated a separate Pakistan of the Punjab, Kashmir, Sindh, Baluchistan and N.W.F.

Province including an Osmanistan of Hyderabad and another Bang-i-Islam of Bengal and Assam. This idea which Sir Zafarulla Khan described in 1933 as 'chimerical did not improve upto 1938 when Jinnah came forward with a demand for the division of India.

The Lahor session of the Muslim League of 1940 was presided over by Jinnah. In his presidential speech on March 22, Mr. Jinnah declared in an advisory way that the British Government, for the happiness of the Indians, should allow the major nations separate homelands by dividing India into two autonomous national states. In this division he saw the vision of friendliness between the Muslims and the Hindus. A single nation of India would, therefore, mean tyranny of the majority Hindus over minority Muslims. Though this thesis was rejected by Dr. Rajendra Prasad in his book "India Undivided" yet his contradiction could not bring the Muslims round.

League Resolution on Pakistan. The Lahore Session of the Muslim League, after the presidential speech and propaganda, passed the Pakistan Resolution on March 23, 1940. This Resolution demanded the creation of a Muslim State out of geographically contiguous regions—both in the "North Western and the Eastern Zones of India." Pakistan thus formed was to be an independent State under the rule of the Muslims themselves. The Resolution authorised the Working Committee of the League to frame a constitution for Pakistan. The Pakistan Resolution, as we have seen, was a great personal triumph of Mohammad Ali Jinnah.

The Viceroy who had encouraged the Muslim factionalism now discovered that the League had grown up to be a power to rockon with. As Mr. Jinnah designed it, the Muslim League henceforward challenged the sole authority of the Congress to speak on behalf of India. Before the Second World War was declared, the greatest danger to the Muslims was the possible inauguration of the federal scheme in the Central Government—that had remained so far inoperative under the 1935 Act.

Cause for the Pakistan Demand. The causes that encouraged the Muslims to formulate a demand for a separate State of Pakistan were numerous, among which the following were the important ones:

(a) The mass-contact movement that was started by the Indian National Congress to win the village people also led the Muslim League to press the demand for a separate Muslim State. This was because the Muslim League objected to the contact of Muslim masses by the Congress.

(b) The Muslim middle classes found themselves unable to compete with the Hindu middle classes. If India was divided and Pakistan was created these middle class Muslims would be able to procure high jobs for themselves—a state of affairs which would be impossible otherwise.

(c) Refusal of the Congress to form coalition Ministries with the Muslim League after 1937 elections. Hence the League began to accuse the ministries of oppressing the Muslims, particularly the members of the Muslim League.

(d) The Wardha Scheme of education followed by the Congress also led the League to champion the cause of Pakistan.

(e) Religious hatred of the Hindus was another factor which gave a fillip to the demand for Pakistan. The Hindus did not like to mix up with the Muslims as they thought the Muslims to be mlechhas.

(f) The Hindu Mahasabha was preaching the gospel of Hindu-Rashtra. Muslims felt insulted. Besides, the utterances of Hindu Mahasabha leaders also irritated the Muslims. Vinayak Damodar Savarkar openly advocated that the Hindus and the Muslims were fundamentally different and branded the Congress as an anti-Hindu and pro-Muslim organisation.

(g) The members of the Muslim League were convinced that in case Pakistan was created their idea of Pan-Islamism would be accomplished.

(h) The influence of Sudetan Germans is Czechoslovakia for their self-determination, also encouraged the Muslims to demand Pakistan. The Sudetan Movement had succeeded and the Muslims thought they would also succeed.

(i) Encouragement of British officials to the Muslim leaders was also, responsible for emboldening the Muslims. The British bureaucracy had encouraged the Muslims to demand Pakistan. The Cripps Proposals of 1942 indirectly recognised the League's claim for Pakistan.

Proposals of Sir Stafford Cripps. In a way the Cripps Proposals of March, 1942 recognised the claim of the Muslim League for Pakistan. The "right of any province of British India that is not prepared to accept the new constitution to retain its present position, provision being made for its accession if it so decides" was a right intended for the recalcitrant Muslim majority provinces. "With such non-accepting provinces should they so desire. His Majesty's Government would be prepared to agree upon a new constitution, giving them the same full status as the Indian Union." To accept the right of non-accession of a province, prior to the framing of a constitution would be to provide a veritable "apple of discord likely to generate trouble in the provinces which may well lead to further difficulties in the way of the Indian States merging themselves in the Indian Union." However, Mohammad Ali Jinnah could not be satisfied with a mere hint at the idea of Pakistan, and he charged the proposals of Cripps as being nebulous.

Nevertheless the Muslim League showed some satisfaction at its working committee and resolved on April 11, 1942. The Cripps Proposals whetted the appetite of the Muslim League for an ever increasing demand for Pakistan. The League took the vow that "any scheme which seeks to torpedo the Pakistan demand for Muslim India will be resisted by the Muslim League and as such any political party which stands for the establishment of a democratic State in India can have no agreement with the Muslim League." The Cripps Proposals, as Dr. Shyama Prasad Mukherji saw it, would make India a field of warring provinces.

Results of Cripps Proposals. The effect of Cripps Proposals on the Indian political scene is beautifully summed up by Sir Bijoy Prasad Singh Roy.

At least for the time being the Cripps Proposals so encouraged the League as to form the strongest opposition to the Congress. In Cripps Proposals, therefore, lay the germs of strained relations between the two communities of India. The year that followed saw a number of schemes in favour of the formation of Pakistan; mainly they were four, namely, *(a)* Dr. Latif's Scheme, *(b)* The Aligarh Scheme, *(c)* The C.R. Formula and *(d)* The Mountbatten Plan, which ultimately partitioned India in 1947. Now we shall consider them one by one.

(a) **Dr. Latif's Scheme.** The essence of Dr. Latif's Scheme was the assumption that India was a mosaic of different cultures and it was possible to divide India into cultural units. Dr. Latif devised his plan of a confederation of all the cultural zones of India federating together. He advocated transfer of populations on a large scale in order to foster homegeneity in the designated cultural zones. The Muslims of U.P. and Bihar were to resettle in 'a block extending in a line from the estern border of Patiala to Lunknow, rouding up Rampur on the way"—the block to be named "Delhi-Lucknow State" There were he said, twelve million Muslims 'below the Vindhyas and Satpuras." He gave vent to the idea of "the communal school of thought among the Muslims" who preferred to get a corridor to the Western Coast—that is, through Bijapur. Dr. Latif did not forget to have calcutta port for the Muslims, but he seemed to lack logical sense, when he included Madras port in the Muslim zone.

(b) **The Aligarh Scheme.** Profossor Zafrul Hassan of Aligarh University and Mohammed Afzal Hassan Quadri gave out a scheme in which Berar and Carnatic were to be restored to Hyderabad, and every Indian town with over fifty thousand population would have the status of a borough with large antonomy. In case there was a partititon of India, the Muslims would be recognised as a separate nation with consequent right to have a separate political organisation. Thus the two-nation theory had laid its roots deep in the minds of the Muslim leaders. When Edward Thompson is reported to have remarked "That is a very terrible solution, Mr. Jinnah", he got the reply, "But it is the only one."

(c) **Towards Mounbatten Plan. Cabinet Mission.** The general elections were held following the end of hostilities of the World War II and in the provincial legislatures the League caputred 446 out of a total 495 Muslim seats. Under Attlee's announcement the Cabinet Mission was sent to India in March 1946. The three-members Commission produced a report on March, 16, 1946, but the Plan that they gave for the solution of Indian political deadlock embodied a plea for the rejection of the demand for Pakistan. Pakistan, they argued, would not solve even the communal problem. The Cabinet Mission Plan proposed a Federal Union of India with a scheme for grouping of Indian provinces into three Groups, the Groups B and C consisting of Muslim-majority provinces of the North West and North East India respectively. The National Congress wanted the grouping to be a voluntary affair for every province, but the Muslim League demanded it to be compulsorilly imposed on the relevant provinces, so that there would be no scope for the Nationalist Muslim leaders to play into the hands of the National Congress.

(d) **C.R. Formula.** In the background of such fanatical demands of the Muslim League Mr. Chakravarty Rajgogalachariar devised a formula for partition of India with the consent of Mahatma Gandhi. This scheme of 1944 conceded the demand of Pakistan. But the Muslim League was to support the Congress demand for independence. During the transitional period the League would co-operate with the Congress in forming an interim Government. After the war, an indepdence commussion was to be set up for demarcating the boundaries in the disputed North West and North East India to separate the Muslim majority areas from those of Hindus. The League and the Congress were to agree on common defence, communications etc. prior to partition. In any case the C.R. Formula was to be implemented in the event the British left India. His Pakistan was to consist of six provinces of Sind, the Punjab, the North West Frontier Province, Baluchiastan, Bengal and Assam with necessary adjustments in the territories, but also with exclusion of non-Muslim inhabitans from the Muslim majority areas.

Interim Government. The formation of the Interim Government was also a veritable tangle which the Cabinet Mission could not foresee. Lord Wavell had invited on June 16, 1946 the political parties of India to form the provisional government in the ratio of six representatives for the Congress, five to the Muslim League and three to the minorities. The Muslim League even demanded its right to form the provisional government with non-Congress elements but Mr. Jinnah could not succeed. Disillusioned, he attacked the British Government for its bad faith on the Muslims and the League rejected the Cabinet Mission Plan on July 29, 1946, but resolved that the Muslims would resort to Direct Action "to achieve Pakistan and to get rid of (both) the present slavery under the British and the contemplated future of Hindu domination."

On August 6, 1946, Lord Wavell could not but invite the Congress to form the Interim Government. Ten days later the Muslim League was to start Direct Action, the day being declared a public holiday by the Muslim League Ministry of Bengal. The 16th August was a day of bloodshed in Calcutta and Sylhet. Noakhali and Tipperah bore testimony to the Muslim creed of violence and butchery and compulsory conversion to Islam. But the Muslim League could not give up the idea of having loaves and fished and moreover to wreck the Congress "Caretaker" Government. The anxious League was allowed to participate in the Provisional Government in which they were allowed five representatives.

Constituent Assembly. The plan of the Cabinet Mission on constitution-making was going to materialise. The Constituent Assembly held its first meeting on December 9, 1946: The League denounced it as "ultra vires, invalid and illegal". Communal riots became the order of the day and the Muslim fanatics took the initiative in the butchery.

Attlee's Declaration on Independence. Mr Clement Attle found it intolerable to have a British Raj in India and he declared on February 20, 1947 to transfer the power to the Indians by "a date not later than June 1948." But the declaration added a sister note. The British Government "would have to consider to whom the powers of the Central Government in British India should be handed over on the due date, whether as a whole to some form, of Central Government for British India or in some areas to the existing Provincial Government or in some such other way as may seem most reasonable and in the best interest of the Indian people."

June 3, Plan. And Lord Mountbatten, who became the new Governor-General only for the task of transferring power to the Indians gave out his plan of June 3, 1947. Besidese, the full share of the Muslim majority provinces, Pakistan would have a partition of Bengal and the Punjab. The Indian Independence Act was passed by the British Parliament and the British Government was to withdrraw from the Indian soil on August 15, 1947. On August 14, Mr. M.A. Jinnah was declared to have been appointed the Governor-General of Pakistan and the world added one more new State to its list of States.

DIFFERENCES BETWEEN MODERATES AND EXTREMISTS

There were fundamental differences between the Moderates and the Extremists on the question of loyalty to the English throne and the continuance of the British rule in India. The Moderates believed in loyalty to the English throne. They also believed that the continuance of the British rule was in the interests of the people of India. The view of Bhupendra Nath Basu was: "To the British nation, British rule in India may be a source of glory of prestige of rank in the scale of nations; to us, it is our very life and what is dearer than life." Pandit Madan Mohan Malviya expressed himself in these words: "The foundation of the Congress rests on loyalty to the British Government. I do believed that British rule is meant for the goods of India. Our duty to our country itself demands that we should loyally accept that rule..." The view of the Extremists was that the British rule in India was a curse and the question of lovalty to the English throne was beside the point. To quote B.C. Pal : "The time has come when all lies must be conscientiously eschewed from our political platform. We are not loyal in any sense, except in original or radical sense of mere obedience to law...But when we prclaim our so-called loyalty to the British Government here or to the BritishtThrone in England—we utter a lie, though only a white lie. These loud professions of loyalty throw doubts on the truth of our grievances, and the reality of our wrath Intelligent people do not understand how loyalty can exist in the face of injustice and misgovernment with which we persistently charge the rulers."

Another difference between the two was regarding the emphasis on the ultimate goal as well as the actual from of ultimate goal. The Moderates believed in a policy of conciliation and compromise. They were satisfied with the small concessions given by the British Government from time to time. A little representation here and a few jobs there were enough to satisfy them. Moreover, they stood for self-government for India in the same way as the position of the British Dominions like Canada and Austrialia, etc. was. The Extremists did not bother about the petty concessions given by the British Government from time to time. They did not care for the petty reforms which they considerd to be merely palliatives and not the final remedy. According to the Extremists, Swaraj alone was the final remedy. They considered intalments of constitutional reforms as mere local application. The Extremists also feared that the acceptance of petty reforms from time to time might ultimately prove "more effectual to stem the rising tide of nationality. Therein probably lies a greater danger to the rapid growth of the idea of nationality in the country than in a system of repression." The Extremists did not believe that the Indians could expect anything good from the Englishmen in India.

The Extremists were convinced that the Englishmen will not treat the Indians in the same way as they were treating the people of Canada or Austrilia. In support of their contention, they pointed out that Australia and Canada were white and that made all the difference. England sent her surplus population to those colonies, but India was already over-populated. There existed a perpetual conflict of interests, economic, intellectual and moral, between England and India which did not exist in the case of the colonies.

The Moderates believed in adoting strictly constitutional methods for agitation and that also of the feeblest type, so that there was not the slightest chance of any violence. They believed in reasoned and emotional appeals, lucid presentation of the case, irresistible statements of facts, irrefutable arguments and presenting petitions. A.C. Mazumdar considered that right of petition to be the highest privilege of a nation. The Moderates were not prepared to resort to a policy of non-cooperation or passive resistance. They did not accept even the programme of Swadeshi whole heartedly. They considered boycott as a vindictive act which was liable to create feelings of ill will. On the other hand, the Extremists were convinced that constitutional agitation will lead them nowhere. They believed that constitutional methods would not cut ice against the autocratic rule of a foreign nation. To quote Tilak: "The Government of India is irresponsible and non-constitutional and we have to take our rights from them." The view of B.C. Pal was that as the Government of India itself was not a constitutional Government, the question of constitutional agitation did not arise. He also belived that the Government of India would not allow even peaceful propaganda to go on and would intervene at every step to hinder and stop the progress of the nationalist movement. They believed that the national problems could not be solved by resorting to arguments, ethics and peity. Only a vigorous agitation could meet the needs of the situation. They believed in a policy of passive resistance which could make the Government of India impossible.

Again, "We shall not give them assistance in fighting beyond the frontiers or outside India with Indian blood and money. We shall not assist in carrying on the administration of justice. We shall have our own courts and when time comes, we shall not pay taxes." B.C. Pal expressed his viewpoint in these words: "Our programme is that we shall so work in the country, so combine the resources of the people, so organise the forces of the nation, so develop the instinct of freedom in the community, that we shall—in the imperative—compel the submission to our will of any power that may set itself against us." Again, "We hope to develop the spirit of self-sacrifice, the spirit of self-reliance, the spirit of self-combination, the spirit of self-determination in the people and by these means we hope some day to attain the ideal of Swaraj."

Another point of difference between the Moderate and the Extremists was with regard to their approach and strategy. Under the Moderates, the Congress movement was not a popular movement. It had not touch with the masses. As a matter of fact, the Moderates dependend for their success on the goodwill and sympathy of the Englishmen. The Moderates worked on the hypothesis that if the grievances of the people of India were brought to the notice of the Englishmen, the same would be redressed. The Extremists rejected such an approach. They believed that the people of India were the masters of their own destiney and not any foreign power. To quote Aurobindo Ghose: "The fate of the country is in ourselves, it is not in any outward force, it is in...our hearts, in our courage." Tilak rightly pointed out that although Dadabhai Naoroji had spent twentyfive years in England to convince the people of England that injustice was being done to India, nothing had come out of it. Again, "The New Party (Extremist) perceives that it is futile to convert the whole electorate of England to your opinion and then to get indirect presssure to bear upon the Members of the Parliament, they in their turn to return a Cabinet favourable to India and the whole Parliament, the Liberal Party and the Cabinet to bring pressure on the bureacracy to yield—we say this is hopeless." After a visit to England, Lala Lajpatrai observed thus in 1905: "The British democracy was too busy with their own affairs to do anyting for them, that the British press was not willing to champion Indian aspiration, that it was hard to get a hearing in England and that the influence and the credit of the Anglo-Indians was too strong to be met successfully by the necessarily inadequate agitation which the Congress could set up in England." On his return to India the message he brought for his people was that if they really cared for their country, they would have to strike the blow for freedom themselves.

Another point of difference between the Moderates and the Extremists was regarding the fitness of the Indians to rule themselves without depending upon the British Government. The Moderates believed that the people of India were still not fit for self-government. To quote Rash Behari Ghose : "If you really want self-government, you must show that you are fit for such a responsibility." The view of the Extremists was that the people of India were fit to rule themselves and self-Government could not be denied to them on the ground of their unfitness. To quote B.C. Pal. "It recognises no other teacher in the art of self-Government except self-Government itself. It values freedom for its own sake, and desires autonomy, immediate and unconditional, regardless of any considerations of fitness or unfitness of the people for it, because it does not believe in serfdom, in any shape or form, to be a school for real freedom in any country and under any condition whatever. It holds that the struggle for freedom itself is the highest tutor of freedom."

Another point of difference between the Moderates and the Extremists was that while the Moderates believed that they would get what they asked for without any suffering, the Extremists were of the definite view that the salvation of India was not possible without sufferings and self-sacrifice. B.C. Pal observed thus in 1902 : "Agitation is not, in any sense, a test of true patriotism. That test is self-help and self-sacrifice; and the time perhaps is coming, faster than we thought, when Indian patriotism will be put to this test." A similar view was held by Tilak and Aurobindo Ghose. To quote

Aurobindo : "No man should lightly undertake the profession of Nationalism, as the tests before him are severer than those from which the place-hunter, the title hunter, the popularity-hunter, the politician of mixed motives and crooked ways, the trimmers, the light speakers and ready swarers, of the old politics have paled and recoiled so early and so easily."

The real difference between the Moderates and the Extremists lay primarily in the political goal to be achieved and the method to be adopted for achieving it. As regards the goal, the ideal set up by the Cogress was defined in 1905 as "colonial form of self-Government" but the ideal of the Extremists was that of absolute autonomy free from foreign control. Dadabhai Naoroji, in his presidential address in 1906, detined the political goal of the Congress as "self-Government or Swaraj like that of the United Kingdom or the colonies." As this goal was not clearly spelt out, each party out its own iterpretation on it. The Congress had already accepted a resolution at its Banaras Session in 1905 demanding the colonial form of self-Government. The Extemists were at first of the same opinion but later on they interpreted Swaraj to mean complete autonomy without any dependence on the British rule. As regards the method, the Extremist party concentratd its whole attention upon the attainment of Swaraj or self-Government. To quote Aurobindo, "Political freedom is the life-breath of a nation; to attempt social reform, educational reform, industrial expansion, the moral improvement of the race without aiming first and foremost at political freedom is the very hight of ignorance and futility." The Extremists rejected petitioning as mad and fantastic. They prescribed organised passive resistane as the only effective means by which the nation could wrest the control of national life from the grip of an alien bureaucracy. The Moderates correctly understood that the doctrine of passive resistance was the basic method of the Extremists.

The Moderate party criticised both the ultimate goal set up by the Extremists as well as the method suggested and pursued by them. They were of the opinion that the future progress of the country was possible under the aegis of British rule alone and the causes of this were to be found in the incapacity and disunion of the Indians. C.Y. Chintamani wrote. "The two weakest links in the chain are our incapacity and our disunion : with patriotism unknown to, and unrecognised as a virtue by, perhaps 99,999 people out a lakh; with education so little spread; with the idea and ideals of the people so time-worn and anachronistic; with so many racial and provincial differences still luxuriantly thriving; with the almost entire womanhood of the country living in a world apart as it were, and knowing so little of, and caring so much less for, country and nation; with six crores of low castes not recognised as a part of the body-politic; with the myriad of castes and sub-caste and sub-sections of sub-castes into which the Hindus are divided and with the complicated and almost hope killing Hindu-Muhammadan problem clogging the wheels of progress at every step..." Some have gone so far as to talk of independence as an object of practical pursuit. We owe it to the best interests of the country to resist the propagada with all our resources. It means the sure destruction, or at any rate, the indefinite postponement of all these opportunities for slow but peaceful progress which are at present within our reach. There is no alternative of British rule, not only now but for a long time to come, and any attempts made to dusturb it, directly or indirectly, are bound to recoil on our own heads. But the attainment of a democratic form of Government is bound to be slow and weary affair—it must depend upon the average strength in the character and capactiy of our people taken as a whole—and our average today is far below the English average.

The Modertes did their best to defend the methods adopted by them in dealing with the Government. Dadabhai Naoroji observed that "petitioning is not begging for any favours any more than the conventional 'your obedient servant' in letters makes a man an obedient servant. It is the conventional way of approaching higher authorities. The petitions are claims for rights or for justice or for reforms, to influence and put pressure on Parliament by showing how the public regard any particular matter. The fact that we have more or less failed hitherto is not because we have petitioned too much but that we have petitioned too little." It was pointed out that the petitioning method had not been altogether a failure as the Reforms Act of 1892 showed.

Many Moderates pointed out that all the items of passive resistance were more or less impracticable in the shape in which they were put before the people by the Extremists. The greatest opposition was to the boycott of English goods. Boycott means a complete and sudden cessation of commercial intercourse with the country the use of whose products is forbidden; it is in effect declaration of commercial war.

"After eighteen months of boycott agitation, with patristism at fever-heat, we import a larger quantity of cotton goods and a sugar, the two articles against which the boycott is principally directed, than we did at the commencement of the agitation. In the birth-place of the boycott agitation, I mean the province of Bengal, they have not succeeded in keeping out even an article of luxury, which is further productive of harm, foreign cigarettes, in spite of patriotic vows innumerable, and self-denying ordinances many.

As regards the boycott of paid and honorary offices under the Government, it was pointed out that those who knew Indian character and Indian conditions would regard it as the most impracticable. The boycott of Government offices by those who hold them now would be of no avail as others would fill their places. The same argument applied to the honorary offices. If one Indian resigned his place, hundreds would apply to the post within 24 hours. As regard the boycott of Indian universities and educational institutions affiliated to them, it was pointed out that it would be a suicidal folly to deprive the people even of those meagre facilities in the absence of better alterantive facilities. As regards strikes and trade unions, it was contended that the country was not yet ripe as was amply proved by the Railway Union and the Printers' Union and a few such other organisations brought into existence in Bengal. There was no good reason to lose faith in the justice and good sense of the British. Though not much result had been achieved by the Congress, we should not forget that 21 years, though a long time in the life of an individual, was a very short period in the life of a nation. We should not lose faith in our efforts to obtain our ends. Although the people of Ireland had far closer association with the English, their long agitation for Home Rule had not yet borne fruit. If Ireland had failed to achieve indpendence after a struggle for nearly a century, there was no cause for despair or criticism of the Congress because it had failed to achieve its end within 21 years.

The Moderates were not satisfied merely by criticising the views of the Extremists. They also attributed some deliberate evil designs to them. To quote Bhal Chandra Krishna. "They (Moderates) are sensible that extreme demands will never be granted and will only retard our progress. They see that the present temper of the British Government in England and India is favourable to our advancement, and they are therefore anxious that the cause of the country should not be spoilt by any unworkable or disagreeable claims. The so-called progressives, on the other hand, would rather not have any concessions granted, and would of set purpose pitch their demands to the utomost extent, so as to make their refusal certain. Their professed object is to embarras the Government and to heighten its unpopularity by making it appear that it refuses to make popular concessions.

As the Swadeshi Movement gained in momentum, the Moderates in Bengal were unable to keep pace with the Extremists and the two gradually drifted apart. While the Moderates expressed sympathy with the establishment of the National Council of Education, they were definitely opposed to the idea of boycotting schools and colleges under the Calcutta University. Surendranath Banerjee became unpopular for opposing boycott.

The main points at issue between the Extremists and the Moderates were that the followers of Tilak smarted under the autocratic rule "of some Liberal leaders." They felt that the Liberals did not want to allow the Extremist element to come into the Congress. By tact and power, they always had a President of their own choice. In 1907, the Extremists were determined to have a President of their party, perferably Tilak himself. The Extremists were not prepared for any change in the four resolutions passed at Calcutta. In the former formula could be included not only the boycott of foreign goods but of everything foreign—appointments, agitation, authority, taxation and government itself. Here was no half-way house, no common ground for a compromise. The Moderates wanted to do a think but considered it to be imprudent to make a fuss of it. Tilak put it bluntly like this : "We do what is right", whereas the Moderates said, "Do but don't displease the Government." The advent of Morley to the India Office and his policy of 'rallying the Moderates" made a compromise between the two difficult.

On account of these differences, there were clashes between the Moderates and Extremists even during the 19th century. There is no denying the fact that the Moderates were as much vehement in their denuciation of the partition of Bengal as the Extremists. Gokhale is said to have observed in 1905 that Lord Curzon did not believe in the principle of liberty and he showed utter contempt for public opinion. To the end of his administration, he did not really understand the people of India. On another occasion, he observed that for a parallel to the administration of Lord Curzon, we must go back to the times of Aurangezeb. Certain Moderate leaders also began to express their dissatisfaction with the response of the British Government towards the aspirations of the Indians. To quote Gokhale, "Twenty years have since elapsed and during that time, much has happened to chill that hope and dim that faith."

However, the Moderates had their own limitations and they could not go beyond them. The Congress passed resolutions on boycott, Swadeshi and national education in 1906 but there was opposition from the Moderates. The result was that some of them were shouted down by the audience. When Madan Mohan Malaviya got up to speak the audience shouted : "Sit down, sit down, you today."

SURAT SESSION

The Moderates did not approve all that happend at the Calcutta Session in 1906 and they tried to undo the same at the next session of the Congress in 1907 at Surat. Under the circumstances, an open clash between the Moderates and the Extremists was inevitable.

When the Congress met on 27 December 1907, the atmosphere was surcharged and there were all kinds of rumours. The name of Dr. Rash Behari Ghose was proposed for the Presidentship. When Surendra Nath Banerjee got up to second the proposal, attempts were made to shout him down and pandemonium prevailed in the Pandal. The meeting had to be adjourned. On the next day, Dr. Ghose was elected the President, but when he got up to deliver his Presidential address, Tilak ascended the platform, stood in front of the President and demanded that he be allowed to address the audience. He refused to submit to the ruling of the Chair that he could not be allowed to address at that stage. While this tussle was going on, the rank and file of the Extremists created trouble and there were clashes. All efforts to persuade Tilak failed. He stood with folded hands and refused to go to his seat unless he was bodily removed.

On 28 December 1907, a Convention of the Moderates was held in the Congress Pandal from which the Extremists were excluded although some of them were willing to sign the necessary declaration. Those who did not wish to go back from the position taken at the Calcutta Congress met at a separate place to consider what steps were to be taken to continue the work of the Congress. It was in this way that the Surat Session of the Congress ended. After the Surat fiasco, it was clear that the Moderates were not prepared to yield to the Extremists. They were not prepared for any compromise. Tilak was ridiculed, abused and called a traitor. In spite of the attcks from the Moderates, Tilak was prepared to accommodate them. He wrote thus in the Kesari : "It is a mistake to suppose that a difference of opinion as to ultimate ideals should prevent Indians from cooperating with one another, for gaining a common end. We see that Radicals, Socialists, Democrats and others, though labouring for widely different ideals, are able to cooperate with one another in Parliament for advancing the interests of their country as a whole. With this example before our eyes, does it not betake a lack of liberality to insist that the representatives of a certain school of Indian politicians should alone be admitted to the National Congress. The duty that lies before our politicians is not to seek to eradicate all differences of opinion but to secure the cooperation of men holding divergent views for the accomplishment of common ends. Whatever our difference may be about the ideals, we Moderates.

RISE OF EXTREMISM

The years between 1892 and 1905 saw the gradual rise of Extremism and terrorism in Indian politics. This was due to many factors:

1. **Dissatisfaction with the Indian Councils Act of 1892.** Indian Councils Act of 1892 failed to satisfy the aspirations of the Indians. It did not give anything substantial to the Indians and even the Moderates were not pleased with it. Many people felt that the policy of appeals and prayers had yielded nothing and the Government regarded this policy as a sign of weakness.

2. **Bad Economic Condition.** The economic condition of the people was becoming bad. There was a constant drain on the economic resources of the country due to foriegn rule. Dadabhai Naoroji, R.C. Dutt and others proved by their writings that the policy of the Government was impovershing the people. It cared only for the interests of the British manufacturers. Many educated Indians were unemloyed and it was felt that only the freedom of the country would solve the economic difficulties of the people.

3. **Ill-Treatment of the Indians Abroad.** The Indians were not well-treated in other countries. The treatment meted out to them in South Africa was very bad. Restrictions were impopsed on their free movement without any reason. They could not walk on footpaths or travel in first class railway compartments. They could not travel without passes or go out after 9.00 p.m. The Indians felt that the cause of such humiliations abroad was their slavery and India must become free to end this.

4. **Famine and Plageu.** Famine caused great discontent amongst the people. Between 1876 and 1900 eighteen

famines broke out in the country. The famine of 1897 affected about twenty million people. While the people were starving, the Government celebrated the Jubilee of Queen Victoria. The Indians felt that this money should have been spent to give relief to the starving people. The Jubilee celebrations at such a time were considered an act of callousness on the part of the Government.

The outbreak of plague added further to the discontent of the people. The Government adopted some measures to check this fatal disease, but these were adopted without regard to the sentiments of the people. Mr. Rand, the Plague Commissioner of Poona, and his men freely entered even places of worship and apartments of women. Infectious houses were demolished without making alternative arrangements for the staying of their occupants. The result was that Mr. Rand with one of his juniors was shot dead while returning from Bombay after the Jubilee celebrations.

5. **Defeats of Italy and Russia.** Italy attacked Abyssinia but the Italian forces were defeated at Adowa in 1896. There was war between Japan and Russia in 1904-5 in which the Russians were very badly defeated. These defeats of Italy and Russia broke the spell of the invinciability of European arms. It gave hope to the Indian that they could become free. There was a feeling that England was declining. In the field of commerce, Germany and the U.S.A. were supposed to have gained the upper hand.

6. **Reactionary Regime of Curzon.** The reactionary regime of Curzon also embittered the Indians. They were not given good jobs. He declared that Englishmen alone by birth and training were fit to rule India, and not the Indians. God had selected Englishmen to rule over Indian and to give them freedom was going against the will of God. He passed many reactionary Acts. The Calcutta Corporation Act of 1899 reduced the number of elected members of

Calcutta Corporation from 75 to 50. This reduction of 25 members was only in case of elected members. Thus the elected members lost majority in the Calcutta Corporation and non-elected members came to have majority. The Indian Universities Act of 1904 increased Government control over the Universities. In other words, it officialised the universities. These were left with practically no autonomy. The Official Secrets Act of 1904 increased the powers of the Government. The Official Secrets Acts of 1889 and 1898 related to the disclosure of only military secrets. The Official Secrets Act of 1904 covered also the official secrets relating to information about civil affairs.

7. **Partition of Bengal.** The partition of Bengal by Lord Curzon in 1904 was resented the most by Indians. The idea of Lord Curzon probably was to create a Muslim majority province, though he declared that Bengal was too big a province and the partition of Bengal had been done to increase administrative efficiency. The Indians felt that it had been done to weaken the solidarity of Bengal because it was a politically advanced province. There was vigorous agitation for its repeal.

8. **Influence of Revolutionary Doctrines.** Extremism also drew its inspiration from the revolutionary doctrines of the west. The struggles for Independence waged by America, France, Italy and Germany had revealed to the Indians that freedom could be achieved not by constitutional agitations but by revolutionary methods. The Indians thus lost faith in legislation and constitutional means and they resorted to violence.

9. **Leadership of Bal, Pal, and Lal.** The leadership of Bal, Pal and Lal gave a great impetus to extremism. Bal Ganga Dhar Tilak was the first to call upon the nation. It was he who preached the ideas of Boycott, Swadeshi, non-cooperation etc. He said, "You must realise that you are a

great factor in the power with which the administration in India is conducted. You are youself the useful lubricants which enable the gigantic machinery to run smoothly. Though down-trodden and neglected, you must be conscious of your power of making the administration impossible if you but choose to make it so. It is you who manage the railroad and the telegraph, it is you who make settlements and collect revenues. It is in fact your who do everything for the administration."

B.C. Paul and Lala Lajpat Rai also worked for the spread of extremist ideas. He also published a series of articles in which he strongly criticised the policies of the British Government. Tilak even said, 'Swarajya is my birth right and I shall have it".

METHODS OF EXTREMISTS AND MODERATES

Extremism had become a strong force by 1905 and it continued to be so for about a decade. The methods of extremists were boycott of foreign goods, use of Swadeshi goods and national education. Boycott was directed not only against foreign goods but also against Government services, honours and titles.

The most important leader of the Extremists was B.G. Tilak. The extremists differed from the Moderates in the following respects:

1. The Moderates wanted to co-operate with the Government, wherever possible; the extemists stood for opposing it at every step.
2. The Moderates tried to win over the British; the Etremists wanted to turn them out by all means.
3. The Moderates wanted to improve the existing constitution; the Extremists wanted to reconstruct it.
4. The Moderates wanted to work with the existing bureaucracy; the Extremists were out to obstruct it.

There occurred a split between the Moderates and the Extremists in 1907 at the Surat session. The Extremists, however, failed to capture the Congress.

Government Measures Against Extremists. The Government took a serious view of the rise Extremism in the country and did its best to suppress it. the Extremists were arrested and imprisoned. Section 124A and 153-A were added to the Indian Penal Code to deal with the situation. The Government was authorised to ban political organisations suspected of subvervise tendencies and to conduct summary trials of political offenders. The right to hold public meetings was curtailed.

Founding of Muslim League. Another development took place in the meantime. The All-India Muslim League was founded in 1906 by H.H. the Aga Khan. It was an association of loyalist Muslims and was meant to act as a counterpoise to the Indian National Congress. It was to look to the interests of Indian Muslims. A deputation of the Muslims under the leadership of H.H. Agha Khan waited on the Governor-General, Lord Minto, and requested him for separate communal representation for the Muslims in the forthcoming reforms. Lord Minto agreed to concede their viewpoint.

Co-operation between the Congress and the Government (1909-16). The Extremists felt dissatisfied with the Minto-Morley Reforms of 1909 but the Moderates wanted to give a trial to these. There was co-operation between the Congress and the Government between 1909 and 1916 due to several factors. Firstly, the Moderates were incharge of the Congress. Secondly, Lord Hardings followed a sysmpathetic policy towards the Congress. Thirdly, the Partition of Bengal was cancelled in 1911. Fourthly, the most important leader of the Extremists.

Drawing Closer of Congress and Muslim League. The Moderates found the Reforms of 1909 unsatisfactory after some time. Then the Moderates and the Extremists began to draw closer. A change came in the attitude of edcuated Muslims due to three factors. Firstly, the Turco-Italian War of 1911 annoyed them. Britain had helped Turkey in the past but now she did not do so. Secondly, they lost faith in the promises of the Government due to the cancellation of the Partition of Bengal. Thirdly, the Balkan Wars of 1912 were regarded by them as a Christian conspiracy to turn Turkey out of Europe.

The Congress also began to feel that War was drawing on but the British Governement was not prepared to declare that self-government for the Indians was its aim. ln 1916. the Congress and the Muslim League at their Lucknow Session formulated a joint scheme of reforms which is popularly known as Lucknow Pact. This scheme was never put into practice.

Home Rule Movement. The Indians began to feel by 1916 that the British Government was not going to make a declaration of granting home rule to the Indians. Hence Mrs. Annie Besant and B.G. Tilak started Home Rule Movement in 1916. It was not a revolutionary movement. She wanted to awaken the people of India to demand their rights. She delcared that Home Rule was the birth right of the Indians. They were not to have it as a reward for their war services to the British. The movement reached its climax in 1917. The Government took strong action. Mrs. Annie Basant was interned, Tiiak threatened to start passive resistance. Then came the August Declartion of the Secretary of State for India in 1917 promising Self-Government by gradual stages.

The Terrorist Movement. While the Indian National Movement was progressing by stages, some persons turned terrorists to achieve independence. Terrorism may be called the militant pahse of Indian Nationalism. The terrorists believed that it would not be possible to end foriegn rule without the use of force. They were exasperated by the reactionary and repressive policy of the Government. They believed in violent action to demoralise the British administration in India and its Indian collaborators. They smuggled arms and manufactured them for using these against the British. Funds were collected even by dacoities. The earliest storm centre of terrorist movement was Maharashtra. Shyamji Krishan Verma, V.D. Savarkar and Ganesh Savarkar were its important leaders. The revolutionary movement became strong in Bengal after its partition in 1905. Its leaders were B.K. Ghose and B.N. Dutt Pondicherry was another centre.

The revolutionary movement greatly weakned after 1916 due to several factors. Firstly, the movement was confined to a small circle of youngmen ; it did not have the backing of the general public. Secondly, the terrorist movement had no central ogranisation to direct its activities. Thirdly, the emergence of Mahatma Gandhi as a leader of the National Movement greatly weakned revolutionary movement. The Gandhian method of non-co-operation, civil disobedience and non-violence appealed more to the people than the methods of the terrorists.

❐

14

Constitution of Indian Republic

The Gonstitution of lndia was finalised by the Constituent Assembly on November 26, 1949 and came into force on January, 26, 1950.

The Indian Constitution is a very loing and elaborate document. It originally contained 395 Articles arranged in twenty-two parts and ten Schedules. Siuce then additions have been made by numerous amendments and some provisions have been repealed.

The Preamble. The Preamble to the Constitution reads:

We, the people of India, having solemnly resolved to constitute India into a Sovereign Socialist Secular Democration Republic and to secure all its citizens:

JUSTICE, social, economic and political;

LIBERTY of thought, expression belief, faith and worship;

EQUALITY of status and of opportunity; and to promote among them all

FRATERNITY assuring the dignity of the individual and the unity of the Nation;

In our Constituent Assembly this twenty-sixth day of November, 1949, do hereby adopt, enact and give to ourselves this Constitution.

Thus the sovereign authority in India is vested in the people. The four essentials of democracy—Justice, Liberty, Equality and Fraternity—are the principal objectives of the Constitution.

The chapters on Fundamental Rights and Direotive Principles of State Policy contain elaborate provisions for giving practical shape to these basic principles.

Fundamental Rights. The rights which a constitution guarantees to the citizens are usually known as Natural Rights or Fundamental Rights. Democraoy means the government of the majority party. Fundamental Rights aim at preventmg the government in power and the legislature from becoming totalitarian; in so doing Fundamental Rights afford the individual an opportunity for fuller selt-development. Fundamental Rights are justiciable and any citizen can move the Supreme Court for their enforcement. The Supreme Court can deolare all laws incosistent with or in derogation of the Fundamental Rights 'as void. However, the Fundamental Rights are not absolute and the state is allowed to impose limitations on them in case of necessity.' The 42nd Constitution Amendment Bill (1976) has upheld the power of the Parliament to amend the Fundamental Rights.

Part II of the Constitution provides for six broad categories of Fundamentall Rights *viz.*:

(i) *Right to Equality* including equality before the law, prohibition of discrimination on grounds of re!igion, race caste, sex, or place of birth and equality of opportunity in matters of employment;

(ii) *Right to Freedom* of speach and expresion, assembly, association or union, movement, residence, and the right to practise any profession or occupation subject to the security of the State, friendly relations with foreign countries, public order, decency and morality;

(iii) *Right against Exploitation*, prohibiting all forms of forced labour child labour and traffic in human beings;

(iv) *Right to Freedom of Religion* and free profession, practice and propagation of religion;

(v) *Cultural and Educational* Rights to minorities to conserve their culture, language and script and to receive education and establish. and administer educational institutions of their choice;

(vi) *Right to Constitutional Remedies* for the enforcement of Fundamental Rights.

Directive Principle of State Policy. While the Fundamental Rights are enforceable through law courts, the Directive Principles of State Policy are not enforceable by any court of law. These principles are in the nature of extra. legal instructions issued to the Legislature and the Executive for their guidance. The principles have been described as "fundamental in the governance of the country and it shall be the duty of the State to apply these principles in making laws" (Article 37).

The Constitution declares India to be a democratic republic, but mere political democracy is not of much value unless it is accompanied by sooial and economic democracy. These principles lay down that the State shall strive "to promote the welfare of the people by securing and protecting as effectively as it may a social order in which justice, social, economic and political, shall inform all the institutions of the national life". The principles further require the State to direct its policy in such a manner as to secure the right of all men and women to an adequate means of livelihood, equal pay for equal work, and within the limits of its economic capacity and development to make effective provision for securing the right to work, education and public assistanoe in the event of unemployment, old age, sickness, disablement, etc. The State shall also secure for the workers humane conditions of work, a decent standard of life and full enjoyment of leisure and social and cultural opportunities.

In the economic sphere, the State is required to direct its policy in a manner as to secure the distribution of ownership and control of the material resources of the community to subserve the common good and to ensure that the operation of the economic system does not result in the concentration of wealth and means of produotion to common detriment.

Some Directive Principles are meant to promote and realise the Gandhian principles like organisation of village panohayats, promotion of cottage industries, enforcement of prohibition, betterment of educational and economic interests of Scheduled Castes and Scheduled Tribes, etc.

Another—group of Directive Principles emphasizes provision of free and compulsory education for children below 14 years of age, separation of the judiciary from the executive and the promotion of international peace and security and honourable relations between nations, respect for international law, and treaty obligations and settlement of international disputes by arbitration.

Fundamental Duties. The 42nd Amendment (1976) has enumerated a set of ten Fundamental Duties for citizens, namely, *(i)* to abide by the Constitution and respect its ideals and the institutions, the National Flag and the National Anthem, *(ii)* to cherish and follow the noble ideals of the national struggle for freedom, *(iii)* to uphold and protect the sovereignty, unity and integrity of India, *(iv)* to defend the country and render national service, when called upon to do so, *(v)* to promote harmony and the spirit of common brotherhood among all the people of India, *(vi)* to preserve the rich heritage of our composite culture, *(vii)* to protect and improve the natural environment, *(viii)* to develop the scientific temper, humanism and spirit of enquiry and reform, *(ix)* to safeguard public property and abjure violence and *(x)* to strive towards excellence in all spheres of individual and collective activity.

The Union Executive. The Union Executive consists of the Precident, the Vice. President and the Council of Ministers with the Prime Minister at its head.

The President is elected by all electoral college consisting of the elected members of both Houses of Parliament and the elected members of the legislative assemblies of the States in accordance with the system of proportional representation by means of the single transferable vote. The term of the office of the President is five years and he is eligible for re-election. The President must be citizen of India, not less than 35 years of age and eligible for election as member of the House of the People. He is entitled to a rent-free official residence and a monthly salary of Rs. 15,000 besides prescribed allowances. The President can be impeached for any violation of the Constitution and can be removed from office in accordance with the procedure laid down in Article 61.

The President, in his capacity as head of State, is empowered to make appointments, summon, prorogue, address, send messages to Parliament and dissolve the House of the People; issue ordinances when the Parliament is in recess, make recommendations for introducing or moving money bills and give assent to bills; 'grant pardons, reprieves, respites or remissions of punishment and suspend, remit or commute sentences in certain cases. The executive power of the Union vested in the. President is exercised by him either directly or through officers of the Government in accordance with the Constitution.

The Vice-President. The Vice-President elected by the members of both Houses of Parliament in accordanoe with the system of proportional representation by means of the single transferable vote. He must be a citizen of India, not lees than 35 years of age and eligible for election as a member of the Council of State. His term of office is five years. The Vice-President is the *ex-officio* Chairman of the vouncil of States and acts as President when the latter is unable to discharge his functions due to illness, absence or any other cause, or till the election of a new President in case of a vacancy. The Vice-President can be removed from office by a resolution of the Council of States by a majority of the members of the Council of States (*i.e.* total members of the House, vacant seats excepting) and approved by the Lok Sabha (*i.e.* of the members present and voting).

Council of Ministers. The Council of Ministers with the Prime Minister at the head aids and advises the President in the exercise of his functions. The Prime Minister is appointed by the President who also appoints other Ministers on the advice of the Prime Minister. The Council of Ministers is collectively responsible to the House of the People. It is the duty of the Prime Minister to communicate to the President all decisions of the Council of Ministers relating to the administration and legislation and to furnish such other information as the President may call for.

The Union Parliament. The legislature of the Union also called Parliament, consists of the President and the two Houses known as Rajya Sabha (Council of States) and Lok Sabha (House of the People).

The Rajya Sabha. The Council of States consists of not more than 250 members, 12 of whom are nominated by the President and the rest are elected. It is a permanent body not subject to dissolution, but one-third of the members retire at the expiration of every second year. The elections to the Council are indirect, . the quota of seats allotted to each State is provided in the Fourth Schedule to the Constitution. The elected members of the Legislative Assemblies of the States elect members for the Council of States in accordance with the system of proportional representation by means of the single transferable vote. The representatives of the Union Territories are chosen in such manner as Parliament by law prescribes. The nominated members are persons having special or practical experience in literature, science, art and social service.

The Lok Sabha. As per Act 18 of 1987 the House of the people consists of not more than 530 members directly elected from territorial constituencies in the States and not more than 20 members to represent the Union Territories. The number of seats for each State is so allocated that the ratio between the number and the population of the State is, so far as practicable the same for all States. Up to 2000 'the President may nominate two Anglo-Indian members to the House of the People. Unless dissolved earlier, the term of the House is five years from the date of its first meeting.

Functions and Powers of Parliament. The main functions of Parliamen are to make laws for the country and to find finances for the running of the Government. All legislation requires to be passed by both Houses of Parliament. Delegated leglslation is also subject to review and control by Parliament. A Money Bill can only be introduced in the House of the People on the recommendation of the President.

The Council of members is collectively responsible to the House of the People which also votes the salaries and allowances of Ministers low onces of isters and can force the resignation of the council of Ministers by refusing to pass the budget or any other major legislative measures or by adopting a vote of no-confidence.

The power to amend the Constitution including the Fundamental Rights rests solely in Parliament. The Parliament can impeach the President, ask for removal of Judges of the Supreme Court and High Courts, the Election Commissioner and the Comptroller and Auditor-General in accordance with the procedure laid down in the Constitution.

Parliament can appoint Parliamentary Committees to assist in its deliberations. The committees fall under three groups: those concerned with the organisation and power of the Houses, those assisting the Houses in their legislative functions and those dealing with financial functions.

The Supreme Court of India. The highest court of the land is the Supreme Court. It consists of a Chief Justice and not more than twenty six Judges appointed by the President. The judges hold office till the age of 65. The salaries of he judges of the Supreme Court are fixed by the Constitution itself. A Judge.of.the Supreme Court cannot be removed from office except by an order of the President passed after an address by each. House of Parliament supported by a majority of the total membership of the House and by authority of not less than two. thirds of the members of that House present and voting has been presented to the President in the same session asking for his removal on the ground of proved misbehaviour or incapacity.

The Supreme Court has both original and appellate jurisdiction. It has exclusive jurisdiction in all disputes between the Union and one or more States or between two or more States inter Se. It also has extensive original jurisdiction in regard to enforcement of Fundamental Rights. Its appellate jurisdiction extends in all cases from every High Court involving question of law as to the interpretation of the Constitution. In civil cases, the right to appeal to the Supreme Court has been provided where the amount or value of the subject matter of the dispute is not less than Rs. 20,000 or of property of like amount (this value test was abolished in 1972) or where the High Court certifies that the case is a fit one for appeal to the Supreme Court. In criminal cases, an appeal is possible to the Supreme Court if the High Court *(a)* has, on appeal, reversed an order of acquital of an accused person and sentenced him to death *(b)* has withdrawn for trial before itself any case from any court subordinate to its authority and has in such trial convicted the accused person and sentenced him to death; or *(c)* certifies that the case is a fit one for appeal to the Supreme Court.

Government of the States. The system of government in the States closely resembles that of the Union. The Governor assisted by a Council Minister with the Chief Minister at its head constitutes the executive. The Governor is appointed by the President of India for a term of five years and holds office during his pleasure. The Chief Minister advises the Governor in the exercise of his functions except in so far as he is required by and under the Constitution to exercise his functions in his discretion The Chief Minister and the Council of Ministers are collectively responsible to the Legislative Assembly of the State. In the case of the breakdown of the constitutional machinery in a State the Governor takes the administration into his own hands in the name of the President.

Each State has a Legislature which consists of the Governor and two Houses, or only one House called the Legislative Assembly. Parliament can, by law, provide for the abolition of an existing Legislative Council or for the creation of one where one does not exist if the proposal is supported by a resolution of the Legislative Assembly concerned.

The Legislative Council of a State comprises not more than one third of the total number of members of the Legislative Assembly of the State and in no case less than 40 members. The Legislative Assembly of a State should consist of not more than 500 and not less than 60 members chosen by direct election from territorial constituencies in the State. The State Legislature has exclusive powers over subjects enumerated in List II of the Seventh Schedule to the Constitution and concurrent powers over those enumerated in List III. All money bills originate in the Legislative Assembly.

An Overview of the New Constitution. (1) It is said that the Indian Constitution is an assemblage of the pofitical systems of Great Britain, the U.S.A., Canada, Ireland, etc. Again, a good part of the Government of India Act 1935 has been reproduced in the new Constitution. Some have accused the constitution-makers of large-scale plagiarism. True, the makers of the Indian Constitution have borrowed freely from the working. constitutions of the world. The idea all long was not to evolve an original or purely indigenous system of government but to adopt a good and workable system suited to the needs of the country. And the constitution-makers have succeeded admirably in that objective.

(2) The Indian Constitution is federal, but the term federation has not been used anywhere in the constitutional document unstead the word Union has been employed all through. The word Union has been used deliberately; it emphasizes unity and integrity of the country more than the word 'federation'. Some Indian jurists have described the Indian Constitution as a 'co-operative federation', Dr. Ambedkar explained why the Drafting Committee preferred the word Union to Federation. He said. "We wanted to make it clear that though India was to be a Federation, the Federation was not the result of an agreement. by the States to join in a federation and that the Federation not being the result of an agreement no State has the right to secede from it. The Federation is a Union because it is indestructible".

(3) It'is maintained that the Fundamental Rights as listed in the Constitution are illusory and not real. The Parliament has the right to amend any part of the Constitution including fundamentel Rights. True, the Supreme Court has the right to sit in judgement over the validity of the laws passed by the Parliament and to declare as void any law or part of it whicn infringes Fundamental Rights. However, the Parliament has the right to abridge Fundametal Rights through amendments to the Constitution. And it is not for the Supreme Court to go into the merits of such amendments. The 42nd amendment to the Constitution (1976) has upheld the right of the Parliament to

amend all parts of the Constitution of put such amendments above judicial review. President Roosevelt's remarks on the role of Judicial Review in the U.S.A. have relevance to Democratic India. The President said: "The Court...has improperly set itself up as a third House of Congress—a super legislature... reading into the constitution words and implications which were never intended to be there...We have therefore reached the point as a Nation where we must take action to save the Constitution from the court and the court from itself. We want a Supreme Court which will do justice under the Constitution—not over it".

(4) Critics maintain that the Directive Principles of State Policy as enshrined in the Constitution are pious platitudes, since these are not enforceable in any court of law. Dr. Ambedkar justified the Directive Principles by comparing them to the Instrument of Instructions issued to the Governor-General under the Government of India Act. No Government in power, he maintained, coan ignore them. The Government may not have to answer for their breach in a court of law, but will certainly have to answer for them before the electorate at election time.

It is held that Fundamental Rights are meaningless today to millions who have no economic means to enjoy thom and it is the Directive Principles that are meant to set this right in the long run. Thus there is an unmistakable relationship between Fundamental Rights and Directive Priciples. Chief Justice Bhagwati explains that the Directive Principles impose an obligation on the State to take steps to create an egalitarian social order which can .ensure socio-economic justice and individual liberty to all. Thus the Fundamental Rights are intended to operate in the larger socio-economic framework, envisaged in the Directive Principles. It is obvious therefore that if anything has to give way, it will be the so-called Fundamental Rights and not the Directive Principles.

(5) The appointment of Mr. A.N. Ray as the new Chief Justice of India in April 1973 in disregard of the recommedations of the retiring Chief Justice, Mr. S.M. Sikri, and in supersession of the claims of Justice J.M. Shelat, Justice K.S. Hegde and Justice A.N.

Grover has evoked Comments from many quarters. While the Government has described this appointment in accordance with the recommendations of the Law Commission of 1958, the Opposition has described the appointment as "politically motivated". However, there is much weight in the comments of Shri Jayaprakash Narayan that "if the appointment of the Chief Justice of India remained entirely in the hands of the Prime Minister...then the hightest judicial institution of this country cannot but become a creature of the Government of the day".

(6) Critics maintain that the Emergency powers given to the President, particularly those urder Article 359 giving him the right to susptend the right to enforce Fundamental Rights, was that "grand finale and crowning glory of the most reactionary chapter of the Constitution" and "arch of autocratic reaction".In this context it is relevant to quote the pronouncement of the U.S. Supreme Court in ex-parte Miligan case, "No doctrine involving pernicious consequences was ever invented by the wit of man, than that any of its (Bill of Rights) provisions can be suspended during any of the great exigencies of the Government."

(7) It is also maintained that the powers given to the President (actually to the Prime Minister) to supersede the government of a State in case of failure of constitutional machinery in the State are very wide and open to .misuse. At the time of adoption of this Article, Pt. Hriday Nath Kunzru had warned, "The electors (of the State) must be made to feel that the power to apply proper remedy, if any mismanagement occurred, rested with them. It depended upon them to choose their representatives who would be capable of working in accordance with their best interest. If the Central Government or Parliament were given power to interfere, there was a danger that whenever there was a dissatisfaction in a State, appeals would be made to the Central Government to come to their rescue. The State electors would throw their responsibility on the shoulders of the Central Government. It was not right to encourage this tendency", The events in Kerala, U.P., West Bengal, etc., have proved how correct Prof. Kunzru was!

(8) Eminent Indian jurists believe that Parliament is only a creature of the Constitution and as such does not have the power to destroy the basic structure of the Constitution. A.N. Palkhivala contends that Parliament cannot overthrow the supremacy of the Constitution to make itself supreme, However, there is no consensus among legal luminaries as to what constitutes the 'basic structure' of the Constitution. All the same, Palkhivala asserts that the supremacy of the Constitution and the limited amending powers of Parliament constitute the basic structure and fundamental features of the Constitution. These ensure the identity of the Constitution, The debate seems unending.

FEDERAL FEATURES OF INDIAN CONSTITUTION

There is a great controversy among the writers on Indian Constitution as regards its nature. Some call it federal whereas others regard it as 'quasi-federal' or 'unitary with subsidiary federal features' or 'federal with strong centralising tendency. As a matter of fact this controversy has developed because the Indian Constitution has sought to blend the American federal system with the British Parliamentary system in the light of the peculiar conditions prevailing in India. These conditions peculiar to India led the constitution makers to give to the country a constitution most fitted in the circumstances without however caring for any strict theory of constitution making. Their approach was practical and they sought to have a constitution appropriate for the conditions in which India was put in.

Its Federal Features. Let us study A.V. Dicey as to what is a federal constitution. According to him, there are four, essential marks of a federation. *(i)* A written constitution. *(ii)* Distribution of powers *(iii)* A Supreme Court with a power to interpret the constitution and *(iv)* two sets of Government. About the first essential mark Dicey wrote. "To base an arrangement of this kind (federation) upon understanding of conventions would be certain to generate misunderstandings and disagreements." Writing about the second mark he writes. "Federation means the distribution of force of the state among a number of co-ordinate bodies each organising in and controlled by the constitution."

All these three marks are present in Indian constitution. Ours is a written constitution no doubt. There is a clear demarcation of the central and state spheres, each authority being supreme within its own sphere. Enactments in excess of the powers of Union or the State Legislatures are invalid. The Supreme Court is there to decide the disputes arising between the Union and the States. Thus though the word 'federation' is nowhere used in the constitution, yet the constitution has all the marks of a federation.

Its Unitary Features. But there are certain features of the constitution which have led the critics to deny its federal character. On account of these features the constitution has been called a 'quasi-federal', 'a unitary with subsidiary federal features', 'a federation with strong centralising tendency'. The following are those features which give to our constitution a unitary character:

(1) Under Article 249 the Parliament of India can make a law on any matter in the State List, if the Council of States passes a resolution by two-thirds majority declaring that it is necessary or expedient in the national interest to make a law on a particular subject.

(2) If the President declares an Emergency in the country, the Union Parliament can make law in relation to the matters in the state list and give directions to the states as to how they should exercise their executive authority in matters which are within their purview. During the proclamation of Emergency the Union Government may empower the union officials to execute matters mentioned in the state list and suspend the financial provisions of the constitution.

(3) If the President is satisfied that the Government cannot be carried in accordance with the constitution, he can under Article 356 issue a proclamation to the effect and can thereby assume all the powers of the State Government.

(4) In case the President declares financial emergency in the country, he can issue necessary directions, including orders

for reduction of salaries and allowances of public servants. He may also direct that all the money bills passed by the State Legislatures during the period of emergency will be subject to the control of the Union.

(5) Under Articles 256 and 257 the Union Government may issue administrative directions to the states in relation to certain matters and it shall be the duty of the states to carry out such directions.

(6) Under Article 371 the President has been empowered to provide, by order, for the constitution and functions of the Regional Committees for the states of Andhra, Maharashtra and Gujarat.

(7) Certain bills under Articles 31(3), 286(3) and 288(2) are to be reserved for the assent of the President and the same will not come into effect unless the President assents to them. Certain Bills passed by the State legislature necessitate final approval of the President.

In addition to the above provision the following ones are worthy of note:

(1) The Governors of the States are appointed by the President and in the exercise of their powers are answerable to him.

(2) The states cannot initiate amendments to the constitution. This power belongs to the centre alone.

(3) The powers have been so divided as to make the centre strong. The Central Government has power to make laws on 97 subjects enumerated in the Union List, 47 matters in the Concurrent List and on residuary matters. In case of concurrent matters, the central law prevails over the state law even if the former is a later in time and repugnant to the state law. In matters of State List, the Union can legislate under certain conditions and moreover it has full power to legislate on such subjects under Article 253 if a law is needed to implement any treaty, agreement or convention with another country.

(4) There is one constitution. The states unlike the states of the United States cannot have their separate constitution.

(5) There is only one citizenship recognised by the constitution. There is no citizenship of the states as it is in the United States.

(6) There is a single judiciary. There is no system of separate federal courts for the interpretation of federal laws. The High Courts and district courts take cognizance of central laws and the Supreme Court supervises the work of High Courts and hears appeals from them.

(7) The Council of States is not exclusively representative of the states. It has 12 members nominated by the President. The States are not equally represented in the Council. Unlike USA where senate accords equal representation to each state big or small.

(8) Though there are two sets of services—All India Services and State Services but there is no clear-cut demarcation of state laws and union laws. The state services administer the central as well as the state laws.

(9) The Election Commission is a centralised electoral machinery which superintends, directs and controls elections not only to the Parliament but also to the State Legislatures. The Commission is appointed by the President.

(10) The Comptroller and Auditor-General is appointed by the President who keeps vigilance not only over the union finances but also on the finances of the states.

There are other provisions which the critics point out in support of their contention and say that the Indian Constitution is more unitary than federal in nature. They not only look to the theory of the constitution but also point out to the practice adopted so far by the federal Government. The Chief Ministers of the States receive directions from the centre as to whom to include in their cabinets. The composition of the Ministry in the States is really the choice of the Government at the Centre. The Governors are party choices. On more than one occassion the Governors. Chief Ministers, Food Ministers, Education Ministers and others are called at Delhi to confer with the central bosses and receive instructions. The dominance of a single party both at the centre and in the states further adds to the centralised structure. The Central Government treats State Governments as subordinate Governor heading the states as their boy-errands and this habit has sufficiently entrenched itself. The Planning Commission has become a part of the Government.

These facts of the constitution and the realities of its working led Dr. K.C. Wheare to remark that "the new constitution establishes, almost devolutionary in character: a unitary state with subsidiary federal features". Our constitution has only the form of federation, but a mere form does not make it a federation, whatever may be the reasons for the constitution-makers to make the centre so strong and powerful as to make the states appear subordinate, the fact cannot be denied that to vest the centre with such vast powers as the Constitution of India has done, is a negation of the accepted theory of federation. D.D. Basu stressing the uniqueness of the Indian federal small system said, "The Constitution of India is neither purely federal nor purely unitary but is a combination of both. It is a union or composite state of a novel type".

SALIENT FEATURES OF CONSTITUTIONS

The Constitution of India is a native gift to the Indian people. It is the result of the deliberations of the Constituent Assembly—a representative body of the Indian citizens established in 1946 under the Cabinet Mission Plan. The Members were elected indirectly by Provincial Legislatures by the System of Proportional Representation by means of single transferable vote. The constitution-makers have given us a constitution unique in several respects. Its main features are the as follows:

(1) A Written and Comprehensive Document. The first feature which strikes a student of the Indian Constitution is its written and bulky nature. It contains 395 articles divided into twenty two parts and nine schedules. It is the bulkiest constitution in the world. There is hardly any constitution of the world which is so lengthy and so comprehensive as the Indian Constitution. Our Constitution is five times lengthier than the American Constitution. There are a number of reasons which explain the comprehensiveness of our constitution. Among these are:

(a) The Constitution of India includes provisions relating tot he governmental machinery of the States. In this respect it differs from the Constitution of United States and follows the example of Canada.

(b) The vastness of the country and the peculiar problems—social, linguistic, communal and geographical, led the founding Fathers to provide special provisions to meet these problems.

(c) The constitution carries a full chapter on the Directive principles of State Policy. This is novel. Besides it incorporate a detailed chapter on Fundamental Rights. Later through an amendment (42nd) fundamental duties were also added.

(d) Many provisions are of transitional nature. Part XXI only carries such provisions.

(e) The constitution makers have provided not only the structure of the government but also have provided matters of administrative detail.

(f) The provisions relating to the distribution of powers are more detailed than those of the Canadian and American Constitutions.

(2) Sovereign Democratic Republic. The Constitution of India establishes a Sovereign Democratic Republic in the country. It means that the country is sovereign in its internal and external matters. Internally, it is supreme, and externally, it is independent. Our membership of the Commonwealth of Nations and the United Nations is purely voluntary. The emphasis on Democracy is noteworthy, Ours is a democracy where the voice of the people is supreme. Our constitution is for the people, their welfare and prosperity. The word "Republic" also is significant in as much as it lays emphasis on the fact that the head of our state cannot be a king. He alone can be the President who is elected by the people in an indirect way. Justice, Liberty, Equality and Fraternity are the four pillars of Indian Democracy. The Preamble to the Constitution clearly emphasizes the fact that India is a democracy in form as well as in substance. Democracy, Socialism and Secularism are our ideals.

(3) Fundamental Rights. Another main feature of the Constitution of India is the incorporation of fundamental rights in it. A full chapter-Part III-including twenty-four Articles have been incorporated defining the rights of Indian citizens and those living in India. The main rights included under this chapter are:

(a) Right to Equality.

(b) Right to Freedom.

(c) Right against Exploitation.

(d) Right to Freedom of Religion.

(e) Cultural and Educational Rights

(f) Right to Property, and

(g) Right to Constitutional Remedies.

These rights are not only on paper but they are inviolable and justiciable. The Constitution by Article 32 has recognised the right of every person to move the Supreme Court for the enforcement of any of these rights. No law, ordinance, custom or usage or administrative order can abridge or take away any of these rights. A law which violates any of the fundamental rights is repugnant. It may, however, be mentioned that our rights are not absolute. The State may impose reasonable restrictions upon the enjoyment of these rights and may suspend their enforcement under conditions of grave emergency. It may also be important to note that during the British regime in India no Parliamentary Act had ever contained a list of fundamental rights. It is for the first time that the rights of the Indian citizens have been given a constitutional recognition. At a later stage according to 44th amendment Right to Property ceased to be a Fundamental Right; (See chapter on amendments). So these are six fundamental rights.

(4) Directive Principles of State Policy. A new and an important feature of the Indian Constitution is the incorporation of what have been called the Directive Principles of State Policy in Part IV of the Constitution. Dr. Ambedkar described it as a "novel feature" of the Constitution of India. These principles are those which seek to make economic and social democracy in India real. Some of these principles are; adequate means of livelihood, equal pay for equal work, fair distribution of wealth, employment for all, free and compulsory primary education, social security, adequate wages for all, organisation of village panchayats, introduction of prohibition and separation of Judiciary from Executive.

(5) Independent Judiciary. The constitution establishes the Supreme Court which is independent of the influence of the executive. The High Courts also may be said to be independent. The constitution includes a number of provisions like Articles 124, 221, 360, 112, 211, which guarantee the independence of Indian judiciary. The Supreme Court has the power of judicial review. In other words, it can determine the validity of any law passed by the State and declare it unconstitutional in case it violates any of the provisions of the constitution.

(6) Parliamentary Government. The constitution establishes a parliamentary form of Government for India. Under a parliamentary government, the head of the state is nominal. The real authority is vested in the cabinet which is collectively responsible to Parliament and remains in office so long as it enjoys the confidence of the latter. All the requisites of the parliamentary government exist in the Indian Constitution. The head of the state, *i.e.*, the President is the nominal head. The real power is exercised by the cabinet. The provision of a President does not make India a Presidential Government. The position of the Indian President is analogous to the position of the British King or Queen.

(7) Partly Rigid and Partly Flexible. The constitution of India may be said to be neither rigid nor flexible. It is partly rigid and partly flexible. It is less flexible than the British Constitution and less rigid than the American one. There are certain provisions like Articles 4, 169, 240 which can be amended by a simple majority in Parliament. Some provisions, for example, 73(2); 75(6); 97; 125(2); 148(3) are of a transitional nature which shall remain in force only so long as Parliament otherwise provides. No article of the constitution is unamendable. However, there are certain provisions of a federal nature whose amendment requires not only a special majority in Parliament but also ratification by not less than half of the legislatures of the States.

(8) Single Citizenship. The Constitution of India recognises only one citizenship, i.e., Indian citizenship. In the U.S. and Switzerland there is double citizenship, citizenship of the Union and the citizenship of the state to which the citizen belongs. In India we are the citizens of the Union of India. This is unlike of true federation.

(9) A Secular State. The constitution of India establishes a secular state, although the world secular never occurred in the constitution in the original constitution. At a later stage it was added in the Preamble. The state is not to be guided by any particular religion in the discharge of its functions. There is no official or state religion. All religions are of equal significance and the people are free to profess and practise any faith. The state is wholly detached from religious dogmas and activities and is neutral in religious matters. No religion is to be given priority or preference over the other. All citizens enjoy equal rights without any distinction of religion, caste or creed. As a step towards secularism the constitution has abolished communal electorates and rights since the inception of the constitution introduced joint electorates.

(10) Other Features. In addition to the above main features there are some other features which may be discerned in the Indian Constitution. The constitution provides for Universal Adult Suffrage and abolishes communal electorates. The Introduction of adult suffrage", writes Prof. Srinivasan, "without any qualifications of any kin is the boldest step taken by the Constituent Assembly and is an act of faith". Hindi is devnagri script has been prescribed as the national language of India. It shall be the duty of the union to promote the spread of the Hindi language.

FUNDAMENTAL RIGHTS

It has always been a baffling problem for the constitution-makers as how to reconcile law with liberty, authority with freedom. If power is necessary for the maintenance of order in society, the abuse of power by those in authority is also likely. This likelihood of misuse of power has been sought to be minimised in modern constitution-making by incorporating certain rights as fundamental in the constitution of a country. The Indian constitution also carries as elaborate and comprehensive statement of fundamental rights. It covers an entire Part (Part III) of the constitution containing twenty-four (12-35) Articles. The provisions are detailed. They not only define the different rights but also minutely add to each right an elaborate set of limitations and reservations. The 42nd amendment of the constitution added a new part to chapter IV as IV A. It incorporates the fundamental rights of every citizen under article 51-A.

The fundamental rights as contained in our constitution are grouped under seven categories, they are:

1. Right to Equality. Articles 14-18 of the constitution deal with the right to equality. Article 14 guarantees to all persons equality before the law and equal protection of laws within the territory of India. In other words this Article assert the supremacy of the same law or Rule of Law. Every man irrespective of his status is subject to the same law and is amenable the same courts. No law will be held constitutional if it is discriminatory in its character. Article 15 provides that the state shall not discriminate against any citizen on grounds only of religion, race, caste, sex or place of birth; nor will any citizen be subject to any disability on any one of the above grounds in regard to access to shops, hotels, places of public entertainment or the use of wells, tanks ghats, roads and other public places wholly or partly maintained out of state funds. Article 16 guarantees equality of opportunity in matters relating to employment or appointment to public services to all citizens irrespective of religion, race, sex, descent, place of birth or residence. Under Article 17 untouchability in any form has been declared unconstitutional. Article 18 lays down that "no titles, not being military or academic distinction shall be conferred by the State."

2. Right to Freedom. Articles 19 to 22 cover the right to freedom. Of these Articles, Article 19 is the most significant. This Article guarantees seven fundamental freedoms. These are:

(a) freedom of speech and expression;

(b) freedom to assemble peaceably and without arms;

(c) freedom to form associations or unions:

(d) freedom to move freely throughout the territory of India;

(e) freedom to reside and settle in any part of India;

(f) freedom to acquire, hold and dispose of property; and

(g) freedom to practise any profession, or to carry on any occupation, trade or business.

However, the enjoyment of these freedoms is subject to certain conditions. Limitations may be imposed in the interest of security of state, friendly relations with foreign states, public order, decency or morality or to prevent contempt of courts, defamation, incitement to an offence. The right to assemble peaceably is subject to the conditions that the assembly must be peaceable and unarmed. The state may always impose reasonable restrictions in the interests of public order. It may be worthy of note that the seven freedoms guaranteed by the constitution are not absolute. The state has power to impose reasonable restrictions on their enjoyment.

Article 20-22 protect the individual's life and personal liberty,. Under Article 20 "no person shall be convicted of any offence except for violation of law in force at the time of the commission of the act charged as an offence, nor be subject to a penalty greater than that which might have been inflected under the law in force at the time of the commission of the offence. "The constitution prohibits the enactment of ex-post facto laws. Article 21 secures the most cherished of all fundamental rights. Under the said Article "no person shall be deprived of his life or personal liberty except according to the procedure established by law." The phrase 'procedure established by law' is a technical one and it is not the place to examine the phrase at length here. One thing, however, may be noted that the phrase 'procedure established by law' carries a meaning different from 'due process of law' - a phrase used in the American Constitution. By adopting the phrase 'procedure established by law' the Constitution makers have limited the authority of the courts in the matter of judicial review and placed supreme authority in the hands of legislature to lay down any procedure subject of course to the limitations in Articles 14, 20 and 22. Preventive Detection Act is sometimes considered an encroachment on personal liberty but in fact it is just like a loaded gun which can kill the people and also safeguard them. The gun must therefore be used safely.

3. Right to Freedom of Religion. This right is dealt under Article 25 to 28. Article 25 gives freedom of conscience and freedom to profess, practise and propagate any religion subject, of course, to public order, morality and health. The freedom of religion guaranteed by this Article has two aspects. in its positive aspect this Article safeguards the free exercise of religion by all persons. Negatively it prohibits the state to compel by law the person to accept any particular creed or religion. Article 26 allows everyone the right to establish and maintain institutions for religious and charitable purposes, to manage its own affairs in matters of religion, to own and acquire movable and immovable property and to administer such property in accordance with law. Under Article 27 "no person shall be compelled to pay any taxes, the proceeds of which are specifically appropriated in payment of expenses for the promotion or maintenance of any particular religion or religious denomination." Under Article 28 "no religious instructions shall be imparted in any educational institution wholly maintained out of state funds.

4. Right against Exploitation. Articles 23 and 24 deal with this right. Article 23 prohibits traffic in human beings including traffic in women for immoral purposes, begging and other similar forms of forced labour, Article 24 provides that "no child below the age of fourteen years shall be employed to work in any factory or mine or engaged in any other hazardous employment." However, the state may impose compulsory service for public purposes, but in doing so "the state shall not make any discrimination or grounds only of religion, race, caste or class or any one of them." it may be remarked that in prohibiting the employment of children below the age of fourteen years our constitution has gone in advance of that of the United States where there is no constitutional prohibition against employment of children in any industry.

5. Cultural and Educational Rights. Article 29 and 30 ensure to every section of citizens the protection of their language, script or culture. Article 29 also provides that "no citizen shall be denied admission into any educational institution maintained by the state or receiving aid out of state funds on grounds only of religion, race, caste, language or any of them." Article 30 "guarantees to all minorities whether based on religion or language the right to establish and administer educational institutions of their choice and declared that in granting aid to educational institutions, the state shall not discriminate against any educational institution on the ground that it is managed by a religious and linguistic minority." It is a matter to be considered if these provisions guaranteeing protection to linguistic minorities are not likely to hinder the growth of national unity, a national language and national culture in India.

6. Right to Property. Article 31 states that no person shall be deprived of his property except by authority of law and on payment of compensation. This right, however, will not prevent a state from making a law for the purpose of imposing or levying any tax or penalty for the promotion of public health or the prevention of danger to life or property or for fulfilling objections in regard to what is Declared to be evacuee property.

Article 31 was amended for the first time in 1951 and two additional Articles 31A and 31B were inserted. Article 31A was further amended in 1955 by the Fourth Amendment Act which added four new categories of legislation which shall not be open to challenge on the ground that they are inconsistent with or take away or abridge any of the rights conferred by Article 14, 19 or 31. The said Amendment also added a new clause (2A) to Article 31 to make away the jurisdiction of the Supreme Court in respect of the determination of compensation.

7. Right to Constitutional Remedies. Article 32 of the constitution confers upon every person the right to move the Supreme Court by appropriate proceedings for the enforcement of his fundamental rights. The appropriate proceedings or remedies are applications for the issue of directions or orders or writs including writs in the nature of Habeas Corpus, Mandamus, Prohibition, Quo-Warranto and Certiorari. These writs can be issued by the High Courts for protecting fundamental rights. Thus the jurisdictions of the Supreme Court and High Court is concurrent.

The provision relating to constitutional remedies was aptly described by Dr. Ambedkar as "the heart and soul of the constitution". And in fact it is so because it gives the assurance that the fundamental rights given by the constitution of India are not merely rights on paper but on the contrary are justiciable and that the Supreme Court cannot refuse to entertain applications seeking protection against violation of fundamental rights.

Before this discussion of fundamental rights is concluded it may be remarked that the fundamental rights to move the Supreme Court may be suspended by the President during the proclamation of an emergency by him. Secondly, it may also be noted that our fundamental rights are not absolute. They are subject to certain restrictions and we can enjoy them only within certain bounds. The critics have pointed out that so many limitations of such a wide import have been placed on enjoyment of fundamental rights that nothing substantial is left in them. The phrase like 'decency', 'morality', 'public order', 'health', 'security of state' etc. are so general and of so wise import that it would be simple to invoke them to curtail the rights guaranteed by the constitution.

However, it may be said that the limitations imposed upon the enjoyment of fundamental rights make a sense and are in a way necessary to ensure the security of state and equal enjoyment of rights by all. Absolute or unrestricted rights are not possible in a civilised society. In every country the rights of individuals are restricted directly or indirectly. In spite of the several limitations on our rights the fact remains that these rights are fundamental as they have been incorporated in the fundamental law of the land and are justiciable.

Significance of Fundamental Rights. Although the fundamental rights can be suspended in times of national emergency, the very fact that they have been incorporated in the constitution and backed with judicial safeguards gives them a unique importance for the people of our country. Their enjoyment has been assured to all under the normal circumstances. In Motilal Vs. Uttar Pradesh Government. Mr. Justice Sapru observed, "the object of these Fundamental Rights as far as I can gather from a reading of the Constitution itself, was not merely to provide security to and equality of citizenship of the people living in this land and thereby helping the process of nation building, but also, and not less important, to provide certain standards of conduct, citizenship, justice and fair play. In the background of the Indian Constitution, they were intended to make all citizens and persons appreciate that the paramount law of the land has swept away privileges and has laid down that there is to be perfect equality between one section of the community and another in the matter of all those rights which are essential for the material and moral perfection of man."

Fundamental Duties. The 42nd amendment of the constitution added fundamental duties in the Chapter on Fundamental Rights. It is a sort of code of conduct which every citizen is required to follow in his action and conduct. Following are the Fundamental Duties:

(i) to abide by the constitution and respect the ideals and institutions, the National flag and the national anthem;

(ii) to cherish and follow the noble in deals which inspired our national struggle for freedom;

(iii) to uphold and protect the sovereignty, unity and integrity of India;

(iv) to defend the country and render national service when called upon to do so;

(v) to promote harmony and the spirit of common brotherhood amongst all peoples of India transcending religious linguistic and regional or sectional diversities, to renounce practices derogatory to the dignity of women;

(vi) to value and pressure the rich heritage of our composite culture;

(vii) to protect and improve the natural environment including forests, lakes, rivers and wildlife and to have compassion for living creatures;

(viii) to develop a scientific temper humanism and the spirit of inquiry and reform;

(ix) to safeguard public property and abjure violence; and

(x) to strive towards excellence in all sphere of individual and collective activity so that the nation constantly rises to higher levels of endeavour and achievement.

The critics point out futility of mere enumeration of duties, in the absence of effective provisions for enforcing them.

❐